Transitional Justice and the Arab Spring

This book presents a varied and critical picture of how the Arab Spring demands a re-examination and re-conceptualization of issues of transitional justice. It demonstrates how unique features of this wave of revolutions and popular protests that have swept the Arab world since December 2010 give rise to distinctive concerns and problems relative to transitional justice. The contributors also explore how these issues in turn add fresh perspective and nuance to the field more generally. In so doing, it explores fundamental questions of social justice, reconstruction and healing in the context of the Arab Spring.

Including the perspectives of academics and practitioners, *Transitional Justice and the Arab Spring* will be of considerable interest to those working on the politics of the Middle East, normative political theory, transitional justice, international law, international relations and human rights.

Kirsten J. Fisher is a researcher at the Human Rights Research and Education Centre, University of Ottawa and an affiliated research fellow at the Erik Castrén Institute of International Law and Human Rights, University of Helsinki. She is the author of *Moral Accountability and International Criminal Law* and *Transitional Justice for Child Soldiers.*

Robert Stewart is a researcher at McGill University's Interuniversity Consortium for Arab and Middle Eastern Studies, and has recently returned to his doctoral studies at the University of Exeter. His work focuses on Islamist groups and Islamist political parties, as well as on transitional justice in the Arab world.

Transitional Justice

Series Editor: Kieran McEvoy

Queen's University Belfast

The study of justice in transition has emerged as one of the most diverse and intellectually exciting developments in the social sciences. From its origins in human rights activism and comparative political science, the field is increasingly characterised by its geographic and disciplinary breadth. This series aims to publish the most innovative scholarship from a range of disciplines working on transitional justice related topics, including law, sociology, criminology, psychology, anthropology, political science, development studies and international relations.

Titles in this series:

Transitional Justice, Judicial Accountability and the Rule of Law
Hakeem O. Yusuf (2010)

The Era of Transitional Justice: The Aftermath of the Truth and Reconciliation Commission in South Africa and Beyond
Paul Gready (2010)

The Dynamics of Transitional Justice
Lia Kent (2012)

Gender Politics in Transitional Justice
Catherine O'Rourke (2013)

Identity, Reconciliation and Transitional Justice
Nevin T. Aiken (2013)

Corporate Accountability in the Context of Transitional Justice
Sabine Michalowski (2013)

Families of the Missing
Simon Robins (2013)

Transitional Justice Theories
Edited by Susanne Buckley Zistel, Teresa Koloma Beck, Christian Braun, Friederike Mieth (2014)

Truth, Denial and Transition: The Contested Past in Northern Ireland
Cheryl Lawther (2014)

Transitional Justice and the Arab Spring
Edited by Kirsten Fisher and Robert Stewart (2014)

Forthcoming titles in the series:

The Concept of the Civilian
Claire Garbett

The Judiciary and the Politics of Transition: Saviours, Scoundrels, Scapegoats
Marny Requa

The Art of Post-Dictatorship: Ethics and Aesthetics in Transitional Argentina
Vikki Bell

International Trials and Reconciliation
Janine Clark

The Trouble with Truth: Dealing with the Past in Northern Ireland
Kieran McEvoy

Transitional Justice, Peace and Democracy: Conflict Resolution in Context
Elin Skaar, Camila Gianella and Trine Eide

Transitional Justice and the Arab Spring

Edited by
Kirsten J. Fisher
and Robert Stewart

Routledge
Taylor & Francis Group
LONDON AND NEW YORK

First published 2014
by Routledge
2 Park Square, Milton Park, Abingdon, Oxfordshire OX14 4RN

and by Routledge
711 Third Avenue, New York, NY 10017

a GlassHouse Book

Routledge is an imprint of the Taylor and Francis Group, an informa business

First issued in paperback 2015

British Library Cataloguing in Publication Data
A catalogue record for this book is available from the British Library

Library of Congress Cataloging-in-Publication Data
Transitional justice and the Arab spring / edited by Kirsten J. Fisher, Robert Stewart.
pages cm. – (Transitional justice)
Includes bibliographical references and index.
ISBN 978-0-415-82636-5 (hardback) – ISBN 978-0-203-43114-6 (ebk) 1. Law–Political aspects–Arab countries. 2. Transitional justice–Arab countries. 3. Arab Spring, 2010- I. Fisher, Kirsten, editor of compilation. II. Stewart, Robert, editor of compilation.
KMC70.T73 2014
340'.115–dc23
2013043458

ISBN 978-0-415-82636-5 (hbk)
ISBN 978-1-138-64480-9 (pbk)
ISBN 978-0-203-43114-6 (ebk)

Typeset in Baskerville by
Servis Filmsetting Ltd, Stockport, Cheshire

Contents

Notes on Contributors

Klaus Bachmann is a Professor of Political Science at the University of Social Sciences and Humanities in Warsaw, Poland. Previous assignments include The American Institute for Contemporary German Studies at Johns Hopkins University in Washington, DC, the Center for European Studies at Renmin University, Beijing and the Universities of Stellenbosch, South Africa, Vienna and Bordeaux. He specialises in European integration and transitional justice and is the author (together with Thomas Sparrow-Botero and Peter Lambertz) of *When Justice Meets Politics: Independence and Autonomy of Ad Hoc International Criminal Tribunals* (Peter Lang International, 2013).

Kirsten J. Fisher is a researcher at the University of Ottawa's Human Rights Research and Education Centre, an adjunct Professor in the School of Political Studies and an affiliated research fellow at the Erik Castrén Institute of International Law and Human Rights at the University of Helsinki. She is the author of *Moral Accountability and International Criminal Law* (Routledge, 2012) and *Transitional Justice for Child Soldiers* (Palgrave Macmillan, 2013). She writes on issues of transitional justice, specifically post-atrocity accountability, and is an associate editor of the *Finnish Yearbook of International Law*.

Michael Wahid Hanna is a senior fellow at The Century Foundation. He works on issues of international security, international law and US foreign policy in the Middle East and South Asia. He has published widely on US foreign policy, arab politics and international law, including articles in the *New York Times*, *Los Angeles Times*, *Boston Globe*, *New Republic*, *Democracy*, *Middle East Report* and *World Policy Journal*, and contributes frequently to *Foreign Policy*. He served as a consultant for Human Rights Watch in Baghdad in 2008. Prior to joining Century, Hanna was a senior fellow at the International Human Rights Law Institute. He received a JD from NYU School of Law. Hanna is a term-member of the Council on Foreign Relations.

Mark Kersten is a PhD student in international relations at the London School of Economics where his research focuses on the effects of the International Criminal Court's investigations and arrest warrants on peace processes in

Libya and northern Uganda. Kersten is also the creator and co-author of *Justice in Conflict*, a blog that examines the challenges and dilemmas of pursuing justice in the context of ongoing and recently concluded conflicts. In addition to his studies, Kersten has worked as a researcher for Lawyers for Justice in Libya, Justice Africa and the Refugee Law Project.

Line Khatib is a senior fellow at the Interuniversity Consortium for Arab and Middle Eastern Studies (ICAMES), McGill University (Canada), and an Assistant Professor at the American University of Sharjah (United Arab Emirates) where she teaches political science. She is the author of a number of works including *Islamic Revivalism in Syria: the Rise and Fall of Ba'thist Secularism* (Routledge, 2011) and 'Islamic Revival and the Promotion of Moderate Islam from Above' (2013). Her research interests lie within the fields of comparative politics, religion and politics, and authoritarianism and democratisation in the Arab region, with a particular focus on Islamic groups as political movements.

Anthony F. Lang, Jr. is Professor in the School of International Relations at the University of St Andrews, holds a Chair in International Political Theory, and also directs the Centre for Global Constitutionalism. He has taught at the American University in Cairo and served as a programme officer at the Carnegie Council for Ethics in International Affairs. His research and teaching focus on international political theory, global constitutionalism, the just war tradition and Middle East politics.

Elham Manea is an Associate Professor (Privatdozentin) of Political Science at the University of Zurich specialising in the Middle East. She is also a writer, a human rights activist and is of dual nationalities, Yemeni and Swiss. She has published academic and non-fiction books in English, German and Arabic in addition to two novels in Arabic. Her latest academic book is entitled *The Arab State and Women's Rights: The Trap of Authoritarian Governance* (Routledge, 2011). She works at the Political Science Institute, University of Zurich and is a consultant for Swiss government agencies and international human rights organisations. She is a Member of the Federal Commission for Women Affairs.

Anne Massagee is an expert in human rights and transitional justice in the Middle East and North Africa, with over 20 years of experience across the region. From 2006 to 2013, she worked for the International Center for Transitional Justice, and previously with such NGOs as al-Haq: Law in the Service of Man and Amnesty International. She has authored numerous publications on human rights and humanitarian law, including, most recently, 'Beyond Compensation: Reparations, Transitional Justice and the Palestinian Refugee Question', in *Compensation to Palestinian Refugees and the Search for Palestinian/Israeli Peace* (available online at www.peacepalacelibrary.nl/plinklet/index.php?ppn=357965604). She has an LLM in International Human Rights Law from the University of Essex (UK) and a BA in History from Emory University (US).

Habib Nassar has 15 years of experience working on human rights and transitional justice in the Arab region. He is currently the Director for the Middle East and North Africa at PILnet. Before joining PILnet, he advised the UN Office of the High Commisioner for Human Rrights on transitional justice in North Africa, worked at the International Center for Transitional Justice where his positions included Director of the MENA Program, and worked for several grassroots and international human rights groups. He teaches transitional justice and human rights at Hunter College in New York. He has an LLM from New York University, an MA in International Law from Université Paris II and a law degree from Université Saint-Joseph in Beirut.

Andrew G. Reiter (PhD, University of Wisconsin-Madison) is an Assistant Professor of Politics at Mount Holyoke College, where his teaching and research focus on political violence, conflict-resolution, and transitional justice. He is co-author of *Transitional Justice in Balance: Comparing Processes, Weighing Efficacy* (United States Institute of Peace Press, 2010) and has published widely on global transitional justice processes. Reiter is co-founder of the Transitional Justice Data Base, a project that has developed a global dataset of transitional justice mechanisms, and he is also a collaborator on two ongoing transitional justice data collection projects funded by the National Science Foundation.

Bassel F. Salloukh is Associate Dean of the School of Arts and Sciences and Associate Professor of Political Science at the Lebanese American University (LAU) in Beirut. He is author, co-author and co-editor of a number of books, chapters and journal articles on Arab politics, the domestic and foreign politics of Lebanon and Syria and Middle East international relations, including *Beyond the Arab Spring: Authoritarianism and Democratization in the Arab World* (Lynne Rienner Publishers, 2012), *Mapping the Political Landscape: An Introduction to Political Science*, 2nd edn (Nelson Publishers, 2007) and *Persistent Permeability: Regionalism, Localism, and Globalization in the Middle East* (Ashgate Publishing Limited, 2004).

Robert Stewart is a research fellow at McGill University's ICAMES, has worked as a researcher at the Montreal Institute for Genocide and Human Rights Studies run by Lieutenant-General (retired) Roméo Dallaire and Professor Frank Chalk, and has recently returned to his doctoral studies at the University of Exeter. His work focuses on Islamist groups and Islamist political parties, as well as on transitional justice in the Arab world. His most recent publication is a co-authored chapter on Syria entitled 'The Secular Uprising and the Possible Resurgence of Post-Islamism', in *Popular Protest, Politics and Post-Islamism in the New Middle East* (IB Tauris).

Ora Szekely is an Assistant Professor in the Department of Political Science at Clark University in Worcester, MA, where she teaches classes on civil war, comparative politics and the politics of the Middle East. Her research examines the consequences of the domestic and foreign policy decisions made by non-state military actors in the Middle East. Her current book project explores the use of 'resistance' as a message to mobilise political and military resources by militant organisations in the Lebanese and Palestinian contexts. Her research is based on fieldwork (and several years spent living and working) in Jordan, Syria, Lebanon, Israel, Egypt and the West Bank.

Hugo van der Merwe is the Head of Research at the Centre for the Study of Violence and Reconciliation in South Africa where he manages transitional justice and violence prevention projects. He is the Co-Editor in Chief of the *International Journal of Transitional Justice*. He is the co-editor of *Assessing the Impact of Transitional Justice* (USIP Press, 2009), *Truth and Reconciliation in South Africa: Did the TRC Deliver?* (University of Pennsylvania Press, 2008) and *Conflict Resolution Theory and Practice* (Manchester University Press, 1993). He received his doctorate in Conflict Analysis and Resolution from George Mason University (1999). He teaches transitional justice at the University of Cape Town.

Foreword

In his book, *The Political Language of Islam*, Bernard Lewis sets out to explore how linguistic valences in Arabic can help us to understand crucial elements of the Islamic and Arab world (Lewis 1988). While the aim of such an endeavour is laudable, it has been used by some (perhaps including Lewis himself) to make Orientalist claims about the exceptional nature of Middle East countries. The idea that Arabic words are so foreign to European languages and that, as a result, their political practices are foreign suggests that there is no possibility to employ terms developed in Europe or North America when discussing the region.

The Arabic word for justice suggests that the assumption of radical linguistic and conceptual differences is problematic. The root word for justice, *adl*, has all the same valences as the English-language justice – balance, fairness, and equality. The basic idea underlying both concepts is the same. Of course, as Ludwig Wittgenstein taught us meaning comes through use, but even here we are on safe grounds. The concept of justice is a powerful organizing principle in Arabic political discourse, one that is often employed to criticize the unfairness of Western policies toward the region. As such, there is very little disconnect between what justice means in the region and what it means in Washington, London, Brussels, or Paris.

The efforts of authors in this book to explore the idea of transitional justice in the context of the 'Arab Spring' demonstrates how a concept that has emerged in multiple contexts around the world can be usefully deployed to understand the dynamics of this region. Transitional justice, as the chapters suggest, provides an overarching term by which to explore a number of different elements of the process by which communities move from one political order to the next. Additionally, in the current global political climate, transitional justice does not take place in a purely domestic space, but must, inevitably, occur in the context of international organizations, great powers, and regional actors all playing roles in how communities seek to orient their politics.

Indeed, participants in the region have also found the idea of transitional justice to be a useful one. Egypt appointed a Minister for Transitional Justice and National Reconciliation when Mohamed Morsi was elected president. The office was created with much fanfare and hope, yet it remains problematic, failing to have a permanent office and often appearing as a rhetorical gesture by the authorities to avoid difficult decisions about the fate of individuals in the military (Howeidy 2013). Egypt's experience reveals the promise and pitfalls of transitional justice. The promise can be seen in the care and attention paid to the constitution, both in the original stages of the protest movements and even into the rocky shift from Morsi to the new regime (Lang 2013). Yet the twists and turns surrounding the fate of Hosni Mubarak have inspired both hope and frustration.

The chapters in this book are an important contribution to our understanding of such dynamics. They reach across a range of regions and topics. The great benefit of this book is that it puts these events in a comparative context with regions that have undergone such changes, and in the context of different theoretical frameworks such as political Islam and feminism. As such, this much needed text will provide insights into not only the events of recent years, but longer term ideas about transitional justice in any context.

The events described here will undoubtedly change over the months and years to come, but this is in fact the nature of transitional justice. Its very unpredictability is what defines the political: continuing efforts to create anew structures and institutions that can provide justice and peace in a complex world (Arendt 1958).

Professor Anthony F. Lang, Jr.
University of St Andrews

References

Arendt, Hannah. 1958. *The Human Condition*. Chicago: University of Chicago Press.

Howeidy, Amira. 2013. Impunity Rules. *Al Ahram Weekly*. 25 October, available online at: http://weekly.ahram.org.eg/News/4475/17/Impunity-rules.aspx.

Lang, Jr., Anthony. 2013. From Revolutions to Constitutions: The Case of Egypt. *International Affairs* 89, 2 (March): 345–364.

Lewis, Bernard. 1988. *The Political Language of Islam*. Chicago: University of Chicago Press.

After the Arab Spring: a new wave of transitional justice?

Kirsten J. Fisher and Robert Stewart

The Arab Spring, and the political changes and transitions to which it has given rise, have altered the political landscape of the Middle East and North Africa in a way that seemed almost impossible to imagine only half a decade ago. Authoritarian rulers have been forced from power in Tunisia, Egypt, Libya and Yemen; Syria has degenerated into a bloody civil war; and, to a greater or lesser extent, political reforms have taken place in countries from Bahrain to Morocco. Some Arab Spring countries have begun to address long histories of oppression and mass human rights violations, including violations committed during the Arab Spring itself. How best to address these histories, offer justice to the victims and heal as societies are questions with which each state and its citizens must grapple. Enter the field of transitional justice, the name given to the study and practice of trying to establish principled justice after atrocity by employing a range of approaches, including both judicial and non-judicial measures, to help address a legacy of mass human rights abuses.

Transitional justice is a term that came into use in the mid-1980s, not to refer to any particular approach to justice, but rather to refer to a strategy, a way of thinking about justice after atrocity. It is 'a convenient way of describing the search for a just society in the wake of undemocratic, often oppressive and even violent systems' that offers 'a deeper, richer and broader vision of justice which seeks to confront perpetrators, address the needs of victims and assist in the start of a process of reconciliation and transformation' (Boraine 2006: 18). In his 2011 report, the United Nations Secretary General claims that, 'Transitional justice initiatives promote accountability, reinforce respect for human rights and are critical to fostering the strong levels of civic trust required to bolster rule of law reform, economic development and democratic governance. Transitional justice initiatives may encompass both judicial and non-judicial mechanisms, including individual prosecutions, reparations, truth-seeking, institutional reform, vetting and dismissals' (UN 2011: Section IV, 17).

Transitional justice has followed the waves of political change and democratic transition that have occurred in Latin America, Central and Eastern Europe and Africa, beginning in the 1980s. Moreover, it is possible to discern certain shared and distinctive characteristics in the transitional justice experiences of countries within each regional wave, in terms of the questions that have been debated, the forms of justice that have been pursued, the needs that have been prioritized and the methods and mechanisms that have been used to meet those needs. Each wave has in turn influenced the broader field of transitional justice, contributing to its continuing evolution as a result of adapting to the contextual particularities that have existed. Each has caused academics, policy makers and practitioners to think about the goals of transitional justice in new ways and to consider different options in pursuing them, cognizant of evolving understandings of the opportunities and challenges that it faces.

The roots of transitional justice are notable for the manner in which there was creative engagement with particular contexts, with approaches determined based upon an assessment of the harms suffered and the present and future needs of the affected societies. Reflections of this approach can be seen in the trials – which are generally acknowledged as being the precursor to what we now know as transitional justice – at Nuremberg and Tokyo after the Second World War. These trials saw criminal justice being applied in a way that had never been done before, based partly on ideas about principled justice after atrocity and practical concerns such as a reluctance to apply collective responsibility, which might have risked hampering post-war rebuilding (especially in Europe). Thus, the leaders who were considered most responsible for the systemic atrocities committed during the war were prosecuted for war crimes. Since that time, there have been other transitions that have relied heavily on international criminal justice, including those of the former Yugoslavia and Rwanda – for which the United Nations created international tribunals – as well as those in Cambodia, East Timor, Liberia and Sierra Leone. Overall, criminal prosecutions are generally regarded as the main mechanism of transitional justice, influenced, no doubt, by domestic practice.

Yet, while prosecutions and criminal justice processes have been a key component of nearly all transitions, other approaches, such as truth telling mechanisms or memorials, have also been pursued. Thus, when Latin America sought to come to terms with its past gross human rights violations following the democratic transitions of the 1980s, it employed national prosecutions but also advanced truth commissions. Indeed, the main new element in Latin American transitional justice was experiments in various forms of truth commissions, as well as the debates that surrounded their use as a way of satisfying the need of communities and individuals to know and to publicly acknowledge the wrongdoing they suffered and thus to deny impunity to the perpetrators.

After authoritarian Central and Eastern European communist regimes fell in the early 1990s, transitional justice primarily took the form of lustration (also known as vetting). Lustration is a policy of institutional reform whose measures include identifying and publicly exposing collaborators with or officials of the old regime, and barring such individuals from employment in positions of public influence. It is traditionally seen as a system of purification, employed to restore and ensure, as much as possible, public order and safety, as well as to re-establish trust in public institutions and, more generally, to counteract the secrecy that surrounded the old regime. Lustration policies were carried out in Poland, Czechoslovakia (and later in the Czech Republic), East Germany and Hungary. Of course, as with criminal prosecutions and truth commissions, lustration schemes have not been limited to the Central and Eastern European context in which they were first popularized; but the concerted focus on these policies in the region was certainly the defining feature of the transitions there, and played a key role in propelling forward new discussions about institutional reform in transitional contexts.

When transitional justice began to be pursued in various African countries in the 1990s and early twenty-first century as part of an effort to put legacies of war, civil strife and authoritarianism behind them, criminal justice was again at the forefront of discussions and the measures undertaken, with the international community playing a lead role. The UN Security Council created an international tribunal for Rwanda and a hybrid court for Sierra Leone, and the International Criminal Court (ICC) issued arrest warrants in connection to numerous conflicts, such as the wars in northern Uganda and the Democratic Republic of Congo (DRC). There were also truth and reconciliation commissions, for example, in South Africa, Liberia and Sierra Leone. Yet the unique feature of African transitional justice was the debate regarding the inconsistency of criminal justice with some cultures. In particular, South Africa's transition was marked by arguments that individual prosecutions would not produce the desired results and were inimical to local conceptions of justice. Instead, those leading the transitional process, Archbishop Desmond Tutu and Nelson Mandela, argued for the pursuit of a uniquely African conception of justice based on *ubuntu* (a philosophy grounded in notions of unity and forgiveness). Similar arguments arose in Uganda, when civil society members promoted traditional processes over international or national prosecutions. Whereas Rwanda adapted traditional practices to judge lower level perpetrators in community-based forums, Uganda argued that traditional practices of reconciliation would be more effective and consistent with local culture. Thus, African transitional justice gave rise to debates about the possible imperialism of international justice in a way that was not evident in other regional transitions, and in response put forward locally legitimate, culturally particular alternatives.

Today, after over three decades of being studied, debated and put into practice in very different contexts, transitional justice has come to encompass a range of measures, most prominently criminal prosecutions, truth commissions, reparations programmes, programmes of institutional reform and, to a lesser extent, traditional mechanisms of accountability and healing. Contemporary transitional justice debates usually revolve around which measures on the list should be implemented and to what degree, to best support truth, accountability and post-atrocity positive peace. Questions asked include: how best to pursue accountability for those individuals most responsible, whether prosecutions are appropriate or useful for bringing about the cessation of violence and preventing further violence, how to go about discovering and promulgating the truth regarding what happened in the past, and how to compensate for harms endured. Significantly, then, the original creative and relatively open-minded engagement with particular contexts to determine what transitional justice measures would be most appropriate to pursue has increasingly given way to a more definitive set of strategies that a transitioning society should pursue, what Margaret Urban Walker calls 'the standard menu of transitional justice devices' (Walker 2012: 11).[1]

All of this raises the question: will the transitional justice discussions and processes underway in Arab Spring countries bring to the table unique problems, perspectives and approaches that they will, to some extent, share and that will be distinct from previous transitional justice waves? And, will they, as a result, nudge the field of transitional justice forward on a different path, demanding new ways of thinking about the field and the options that it puts forward? It is probably too early to make any definitive claims about the broad effects that Arab Spring transitions will have on the field of transitional justice. However, it is not too early to identify some of the unique features and challenges of this regional transition, and perhaps even to speculate about what some of the broader implications might be. Nor is it too early to suggest that the Arab Spring transitions come at a time in the evolution of the field of transitional justice when there is a growing sense that questions need to be asked about whether it is most appropriate to adopt ready-made and tested approaches or rather to push for more creativity and advancement of locally generated solutions that draw upon other experiences, thereby taking the field back to its roots of inventive and resourceful approaches to finding justice for past abuses and advancing positive peace for the future.

So far, transitional justice in Arab Spring countries is following the well-trod path by adopting tools from the established toolbox of prosecutions, truth commissions, vetting and memorials. The primary focus has been on prosecutions. Although there is talk about the possibility of truth commissions in some Arab Spring countries, transitional justice debates have mainly revolved around how best to promote retributive justice rather than the options of restorative, retributive or restitutive justice. The questions being asked are not 'what processes should be employed?', but principally 'who should be prosecuted?' and 'in what forum?'. This, in itself, is an interesting development and invites its own questions, such as: Are prosecutions the best approach in the Arab Spring context? Why has this focus emerged – is it a result of the nature of the previous regimes (overwhelmingly authoritarian) or is it due to other factors, perhaps political, social or economic? And, is this focus a result of reasons particular to the regional/national contexts, or might it be reflective of more fundamental current perceptions of the aims of transitional justice and obligations under international law?

Criminal justice has always had the lion's share of support as the paramount form of justice and the best means of holding wrongdoers accountable, while the employment of non-retributive measures usually demanded an explanation for why it was necessary to sidestep trial justice. Other regional transitions, however, have grappled more readily with alternative approaches to securing peace and attempting to account for the past. Arguably, despite the continued use of amnesty laws and restorative measures that do not promote or satisfy retributive pursuits, international law is moving towards a prohibition on the use of amnesty in transitional justice. This may account for part of the retributive focus in Arab Spring countries – an attempt to satisfy international obligations. It seems likely, however, that there is more to this focus than simply international obligations promoted primarily by advocates of the ICC, of which no Arab Spring country besides Tunisia is a member state.

One possibility relates to the issue of political culture.[2] If we consider what occurred in Central and Eastern European countries, an ideology failed – communism – and was replaced by a relative agreement within society about the way forward, based upon the Washington consensus: essentially, 'they could either share in the economic and social decay of the shrinking Soviet empire or "go West"'.[3] To a greater or lesser extent, this relative consensus also existed in many Latin American countries, where liberal democracy was seen as the clear route forward. It is conceivable that it was this relative consensus and the degree of social cohesion that it implies that made possible creative solutions regarding transitional justice, since there was a certain level of trust that enabled discussions and, moreover, these discussions were taking place within parameters that were largely agreed upon.

In the Arab Spring countries, by contrast, such consensus is notably lacking. That is, while authoritarianism has failed – or has at least been deeply challenged, a caveat that reflects the apparent authoritarian resurgence in, for instance, Egypt, where a democratically elected Islamist government was forcibly removed by a military council which had apparently never really given up power, with the support of large parts of society – it has not been replaced by any sort of consensus about the way forward and, more fundamentally, the shared basis of society. This is due to the rise of political Islam, a long-suppressed ideology which boasts a significant number of supporters and simultaneously inspires strong antipathy among large swathes of the populace, who frequently deeply distrust the Islamists.[4] In the absence of relative societal consensus about the way forward and trust among citizens, it seems likely that creative engagement regarding transitional justice measures will not occur, hence the falling back on the tried and true tools of retributive justice. Simultaneously, it is possible to imagine a uniquely Arab Spring set of transitional justice measures based on local customs or traditions similar to the African *ubuntu*. For example, in Arab Spring countries it may be based upon Islamic law. Yet it seems clear that such measures would not be supported by significant parts of the population in those countries, nor are there clear leaders who could galvanize a population behind a particular plan, as arguably happened in South Africa; thus, such measures would be hard pressed to achieve the fundamental transitional justice goal of bringing society together in a process of healing.[5] Transitional justice in the Arab Spring countries seems, then, to be hamstrung to a certain extent by the lack of societal consensus on the way forward and a lack of fundamental trust.

The rise of political Islam also has important implications for Arab Spring transitional justice as a result of the actual content of its beliefs. This is because transitional justice has come to be associated with addressing legacies of past human rights abuses and ushering in liberal democracy, based upon a strong faith in a Kantian liberal peace theory (Kant 1795). Yet, notwithstanding a few marginal liberal interpretations of political Islam (see Kurzman 1998), the ideology has some relatively illiberal elements, for example in terms of the rights of religious minorities.[6] More fundamentally, rather than imagining a neutral public space where every citizen is equal, to some degree it privileges Muslims and their mores. Thus, there is a strong current in Arab Spring societies that supports an ideology which is at odds with transitional justice's aim of moving toward liberal democracy. Perhaps more significant is that Islamist political parties have become very prominent political actors, even winning the presidency in Tunisia and Egypt. They therefore have inordinate influence over governmental policy and constitution writing, which of course has significant longer-term implications because it makes it possible to enshrine certain precepts that will play a role in dictating the direction of society.

A challenge, then, for transitional justice arising out of the particular Arab Spring context is to see whether a fundamentally liberal process can successfully incorporate actors whose belief system has important illiberal elements (since excluding them would seem to undermine the goal of an inclusive process of societal healing). More broadly, it will be interesting to see whether, in doing so, transitional justice moves away from its liberal roots and, if it were to do so, whether it would be able to foster societal healing on another basis. Complicating this latter process of course is the fact that Arab Spring countries are frequently the focus of pressures and direct interventions by external, international actors who have an interest in promoting liberal norms, which could undermine any sort of organic move away from *liberal* democracy as a goal of transitional justice.

Another unique feature of the Arab Spring transitions is the spotlight on the role of women, and more particularly the appropriate place of women in just societies.[7] This can particularly be seen in debates about the degree and manner in which women should be incorporated into transitional justice processes in these countries, and the extent to which those processes can be legitimate if they exclude or marginalize approximately half of the populace. Similarly, debates are arising about making women's rights, and violations of these rights, an explicit focus of transitional justice, something that has not been nearly as prominent in other transitional justice waves. These debates are locally driven – and reflect many of the divisions about the place of women and women's rights that exist in the region – but they also have an international dimension. More particularly, the Chief Prosecutor of the ICC, Fatou Bensouda, has suggested a new focus on gender crimes, including additional charges or requests for new arrest warrants by the ICC's Office of the Prosecutor (OTP) on gender crimes in the context of Libya (Kersten 2012; Papenfuss 2012). The ICC has, however, faced significant challenges in regards to its first indictments in the Middle East, as is discussed in Mark Kersten's and Kirsten Fisher's chapters, and the controversy may act as an obstacle to international actors putting gender issues onto the Arab Spring transitional justice agenda immediately.

A final element that can be seen as particular to Arab Spring transitional justice is the fundamental importance of, and the attention being given to, economic issues.[8] That is, while there has tended to be a focus on demands for political rights and political change within the Arab Spring (particularly by international observers), it could be argued that widespread poverty, unemployment and general lack of economic opportunities in all Arab Spring countries are just as important explanatory factors for the uprisings, and just as important priorities for protestors (see, for example, Malik and Awadallah 2011; see also Brynen et al. 2013: Ch 2).[9] While profound economic challenges are certainly not unique to the Arab Spring transitions, what is unique is the manner in which there is increasing debate about the need to expand the scope of transitional justice to incorporate economic elements. At its root, this debate reflects an understanding that profound economic inequalities and economic problems represent huge challenges to transitional justice's aim of societal healing, and that artificially separating out economic factors from other socio-political challenges can fatally undermine the efficacy of measures aimed at treating those challenges. The debates about including economic factors within transitional justice are at present nascent and, similarly, the concrete measures through which they might be effectively incorporated remain to be clearly worked out. Notwithstanding the complexity of this latter task and the vested interests militating against changing the economic status quo, it seems clear at this point that the Arab Spring is highlighting the need for economic elements to be incorporated into transitional justice in a way that has not been seen in other regional transitions.

The following chapters of this book explore the various themes touched on in this introduction from multiple perspectives and in multiple national contexts. Organizationally, the book is divided into two sections. The first section, 'The context and getting Arab Spring transitional justice right', examines the history and significance of the Arab Spring to the region's politics and outlines transitional justice experiences in Arab Spring countries so far, while also offering a series of 'lessons learned' from other waves of regional transitional justice. In adopting a lessons-learned approach, it is important to underline that the book is not suggesting that these lessons can be directly transposed into the Arab Spring context. Rather, the aim is to extract insights about why particular things were done or not done and what the results were, as a means of informing our understanding of what is going on in Arab Spring transitional justice and what the repercussions of this may be. Used carefully, such lessons can help us to develop insights and a more informed perspective on what is still a very embryonic set of transitions.

In Chapter 1, Bassel Salloukh describes the context within which regional transitional justice is taking place by outlining the events of the Arab Spring itself as well as the recent history from which it emerged. Through its overview and analysis of authoritarian regime breakdown and (nascent) democratization, as well as its discussion of socio-political struggle and debate about the social and moral basis of society, particularly as a result of the emergence of Islamist groups, we are able to understand just how profound the changes sweeping the region are, and, as a result, just how much is at stake in regional transitional justice.

Following Salloukh, Anne Massagee, in Chapter 2, offers an overview of Arab Spring transitional justice to date, giving a country-by-country summary that incorporates analysis of progress made and challenges being faced. Massagee then highlights common factors that can be seen across the region, from demands for truth seeking and criminal justice to institutional and constitutional reforms and calls for reparations. She also points to an interesting regional trend of attempts to incorporate a variety of transitional justice approaches into a single law. In conclusion, Massagee looks to the future by warning of the need to take local context carefully into consideration when determining transitional justice measures, of the importance of ensuring adequate buy-in to transitional justice processes and of the need to give those processes the time to succeed by taking a long-term view of transitional justice.

While the focus of this book is on Arab Spring transitional justice, it is important to recognize that transitional justice has taken place in the MENA region before. In Chapter 3, Habib Nassar looks at regional transitional justice precedents in Algeria, Morocco and Iraq. He notes that Algeria's prioritizing of national reconciliation over pursuing justice and accountability has handicapped the country's ability to move on from its past, and links this to developments in Egypt; that Morocco's top-down, controlled and gradualist approach has brought limited progress on transitional justice though no political transition, a model that may be drawn upon by other monarchical regimes such as in Jordan; and that Iraq's limited transitional justice process has been greatly handicapped by too little public consultation and by perceptions that it constitutes victors' justice and has been dictated by outside actors. Nassar also outlines some key factors to keep in mind regarding Arab Spring transitional justice: the present ambiguity of nearly all the transitions; the importance of socio-economic inequalities and the fundamental entangling of economic and political power in Arab Spring countries (with which transitional justice may very well have to engage if it is to succeed in the region); the important legacies of division and exclusion sowed by the former regimes; and the decades-long history of human rights violations. He ends by cautioning about the dangers of what he calls the international transitional justice industry, whose tendency to prescribe standardized, ready-made measures risks minimizing contextual issues as well as steamrollering local agency in determining needs and priorities and thus compromising legitimacy.

In Chapter 4, Andrew Reiter focuses on the Latin American transitions, and extracts four relevant lessons. The first is that the particularities of local context are very important for understanding the course of transitional justice. While countries in which past abuses were high, relatively one-sided and perpetrated by individuals who have lost power tended to push for more accountability for past human rights violations, in countries where the opposite conditions existed, transitional justice tended to involve less-contentious measures such as amnesties.

Reiter also argues that engaging and re-engaging with the past is a long-term process that can fruitfully continue for decades, and he underlines that transitional justice is greatly influenced by international actors and not just domestic priorities. Finally, Reiter makes clear that transitional justice is not an easy process, that it can involve contentious debates and even violence as well as set-backs; yet, based on the Latin American experience, transitional justice is ultimately worth all the challenges experienced along the way.

Reiter's point of view on the long-term worth of transitional justice is in many ways supported in Chapter 5 by Ora Szekely's largely cautionary examination of Lebanon's decision following its civil war to avoid transitional justice, which she says has greatly contributed to the ongoing instability and communal tensions within the state. Szekely notes that fundamental institutional reform aimed at addressing structural weaknesses is important if a country is to achieve long-term socio-political stability. She further states that foreign aid and sponsorship risk undermining trust and social cohesion and thus compromising transitional justice. Counter-intuitively, she shows that it can be possible to effectively integrate militias into the post-war political order. While blanket amnesties may be appealing in that they seem to help avoid the painful process of dealing with the past, they come with a high price in terms of longer-term national reconciliation. Similarly, developing a shared memory and memorializing the painful past, while difficult, is ultimately preferable to collective amnesia given the aim of promoting political stability and democratization.

The final chapter in Part One elaborates lessons for Arab Spring countries by examining the Central and Eastern European experiences of transitional justice. Chapter 6, by Klaus Bachmann in collaboration with the editors, emphasizes that having an agreed-upon way forward for a society in terms of what path to pursue, coupled with the presence of stabilizing external actors and legal frameworks, can help to facilitate a transition (and that the lack of these can compromise it). Another observation is that which transitional justice measures are prioritized is greatly influenced by what trends are popular within the field at that time, as well as the strength of the old regime after transition and the effects of external hegemons. The chapter's examination of prosecutions, security sector reform and vetting, as well as victim compensation, warns that while these transitional justice measures can have great benefits, they are also a potential minefield in that they can risk undermining societal harmony and political stability; when employed, steps should be taken to mitigate the negative aspects.

Part Two of the book focuses on particular themes that are relevant in the Arab Spring context and are important in terms of attempts to secure post-Arab Spring justice. In Chapter 7, Line Khatib engages with one of the most salient issues – the rise of political Islam in many Arab Spring countries. She argues that there are important tensions between transitional justice and political Islamists because the former's liberal assumptions clash with the latter's illiberal political agenda. This argument is elaborated through case studies that focus on women's rights, freedom of expression and factionalism in Tunisia, Egypt and Syria. Ultimately,

Khatib concludes that the tensions remain unresolved despite declarations to the contrary by mainstream Islamists, and that this risks strongly impacting upon transitions toward democracy and a culture founded on human rights, as well as more fundamentally on societal healing and cohesion.

In Chapter 8, Elham Manea explores issues of gender in Arab Spring transitions, adopting an approach that focuses on the consequences of not applying international human rights norms to women's rights. Manea outlines the important role played by women in the Arab Spring uprisings and the manner in which they were often the targets of violence, and draws on examples of other, earlier regional uprisings to show that such participation rarely translates into inclusion in political processes or indeed concrete gender gains afterwards. With the possible exception of Tunisia, this pattern seems to be playing out again in the Arab Spring context. Manea concludes that the parameters of transitional justice must be widened to incorporate restoration of gender justice and equality, and that the challenge of the rise of illiberal socio-political actors – the Islamists – must be met by emphasizing the universality of human rights in a way that guarantees women's dignity and rights.

Egypt is by far the most populous and prominent Arab Spring country, and its dramatic and at times turbulent uprising and transition highlight almost all of the most important themes and trends that have come to characterize the Arab Spring: the rise of Islamism, the exposure of deep societal cleavages on many fundamental issues, the salience of gender and economic issues and the ongoing role of the military. In Chapter 9, Michael Wahid Hanna touches on these themes in delineating the state of the various transitional justice measures in Egypt, from a generally weak record on prosecutions – other than for a few key figures – to very little effective security sector reform, significant attention given to vetting through a non-systematic approach, only very nascent and relatively incoherent efforts at preservation of historical memory and truth telling, and clear though limited initial moves made towards victims' compensation. Hanna argues that progress on transitional justice in general reflects the existing political situation in a particular country – since transitional justice is inherently a political process – and that we can use one to help understand the state of the other. He thus explains Egypt's so-far poor record on transitional justice by referring to the confused and often tangled politics of the country's transition period. Hanna concludes by observing that there is still very strong support for transitional justice measures in Egypt and that such measures must be advanced at the same time as the political context is made more stable and democratic if each is to prove successful.

In Chapter 10, Mark Kersten looks specifically at Libya and the disagreement over whether to try senior members of the past regime at the ICC in the Hague or in Libya with Libyan judges, as well as the implications of this decision. Supporters of the Libyan option argue that it is essential for establishing the country's sovereignty, and are concerned that holding the proceedings outside the country risks undermining the revolution and potentially destabilizing Libya. Proponents of the international option are concerned about the strong possibility of victor's justice if the suspects are tried in Libya. This latter concern highlights a challenging question that arises in regards to the ICC's principle of complementarity: can any state emerging from decades of authoritarian rule be judged able to satisfactorily carry out such investigations and prosecutions? Finally, the illegal arrest and detention of ICC staff in Libya and the weak and divided reaction of the organization to it has, Kersten argues, potentially weakened the legitimacy of the ICC to operate in fragile settings and undermined perceptions of its impartiality and independence.

In Chapter 11, Kirsten Fisher looks more broadly at international criminal justice and explores how the situation in Libya and the decisions to intervene there and not – at the time of writing – in Syria affect its global legitimacy. She argues that the role played by international criminal law (ICL) in post-Arab Spring transitional justice could have important implications for future international interventions for the purposes of criminal prosecutions, at a time when such interventions are arguably already decreasing in perceived moral standing. This is especially because of questions about selectivity and bias in the application of ICL. Such questions could cause the ICC and ICL to be viewed as instruments wielded by the world's powerful actors against the international community's outsiders, which could in turn undermine their legitimacy and therefore their effectiveness. Significantly, the impact of these developments would be magnified by virtue of the high profile nature of Arab Spring transitional justice.

Finally, in Chapter 12 Hugo van der Merwe shows that the Arab Spring transitions are giving rise to debates about transitional justice's fundamental assumptions, methods and goals, as well as who does and who should define these. He develops his analysis by elucidating themes and issues that are emerging as particularly relevant within those particular transitions: the role and legitimacy of international actors, the opportunities and dangers in drawing upon other transitional justice experiences, the challenge of broadening transitional justice to focus upon social and economic inequalities, the importance of addressing gender justice and the fundamental need to deepen democracy. Ultimately, van der Merwe concludes that we are at a pivotal moment in the continuing development of transitional justice, where the accretion of measures and of goals, as well as the multiplying number of actors – both national and international – that are pushing them, has arguably brought the field to a crossroads where a new consensus about what it is trying to do and how it is trying to do it may have to be forged.

As we survey the landscape of the Arab Spring some three years after the uprisings first broke out, we can see a region that is undergoing huge transformations, with all the turmoil and challenges that that brings. Uncertainty, disagreements and debates, violence and failures, but also some successes and real progress can be seen in almost all countries. The same is true of the still relatively nascent transitional justice processes, something that should not surprise us in light of Andrew Reiter's argument that engaging with the past is a process that can and should continue for a long time. Neither pessimism nor enthusiasm is yet merited, particularly when we consider the complexity and depth of the challenges that these countries are facing. Yet while it is much too early to form any sort of judgment about the success or failure of regional transitional justice, it is clear from the richness of the debates and the concrete measures either called for, planned or underway, that there is a strong appetite for transitional justice in the Arab Spring countries, and simultaneously that it remains highly relevant there. The challenge for us is to try to make sense of the various facets of Arab Spring transitional justice, both to understand the particular issues at play and the ongoing developments in each country as well as to grasp the actual and potential impacts of these on the larger field.[10]

Notes

1 See Habib Nassar in Ch 3 of this volume. Nassar refers to the burgeoning 'international transitional justice industry' as a key reason for this.

2 In asking this question, we remain cognizant of the dangers inherent in using political culture as an analytical tool in a manner that essentializes and reifies. Yet in reference to the argument made by Rex Brynen (Brynen et al. 2013, Ch 5), we believe that it is still possible to use political culture carefully and thoughtfully to help understand what is going on, by remaining cognizant that culture is only one factor among many, and that it is dynamic rather than eternal and unchanging.

3 See Klaus Bachmann, Robert Stewart and Kirsten Fisher in Ch 6 of this volume.

4 This distrust is especially based on the belief that political Islamists are not good democratic actors and cannot share power, as well as on the particular positions they take on such issues as human rights.

5 Moreover, there does not seem to be another shared basis upon which the societies could come together and generate such ideas (more inclusive ideologies that might have offered such a basis, such as pan-Arabism or a more civic nationalism, are not ascendant at the present time).

6 See Line Khatib in Ch 7 of this volume for more on this.

7 See Elham Manea in Ch 8 of this volume for a detailed consideration of these issues.

8 A point that emerges in Habib Nassar's chapter, as well as in Hugo van der Merwe's conclusion in this volume.

9 Indeed, the self-immolation of Tunisian street vendor Mohamed Bouazizi, who was protesting police harassment and the lack of economic opportunities, set off protests that ultimately gathered momentum and became the Arab Spring.

10 The editors of this book would like to thank all the contributors, as well as Kieran McEvoy and the editorial staff at Routledge.

Bibliography

Boraine, Alexander L. (2006) 'Transitional Justice: A Holistic Interpretation', 60(1) *Journal of International Affairs* 17.

Brynen, Rex, Moore, Peter W., Salloukh, Bassel F. and Zahar, Marie-Joelle (2013) *Beyond the Arab Spring: Authoritarianism and Democratization in the Arab World* (Lynne Rienner Publishers) 95–117.

Kant, Immanuel (1795) *Perpetual Peace: a Philosophical Sketch*, available online at www.mtholyoke.edu/acad/intrel/kant/kant1.htm.

Kersten, Mark (2012) 'Changing of the Guard: Besouda In, Ocampo Out', London School of Economics and Political Science: Africa at LSE (20 June), available online at http://blogs.lse.ac.uk/africaatlse/2012/06/20/changing-of-the-guard-bensouda-in-ocampo-out/.

Kurzman, Charles (ed.) (1998) *Liberal Islam* (Oxford University Press).

Malik, Adeel and Awadallah, Bassem (2011) 'The Economics of the Arab Spring', Middle East Insight No 46, 23 November.

Papenfuss, Till (2012) 'Interview with Fatou Bensouda, Chief Prosecutor, International Criminal Court', *The Global Observatory* (15 November), available online at http://theglobalobservatory.org/interviews/384-interview-with-fatou-bensouda-chief-prosecutor-international-criminal-court.html.

United Nations (2011) *The rule of law and transitional justice in conflict and post-conflict societies*, Report of the Secretary-General to the United Nations Security Council, 12 October, S/2011/634.

Walker, Margaret Urban (2012) 'Post-Conflict Truth Telling', in Larry May and Andrew Forcehimes (eds), *Morality, Jus Post Bellum, and International Law* (Cambridge University Press) 11.

Part One

The context and getting Arab Spring transitional justice right

Chapter 1

The Arab world after the popular uprisings: a spirit restored?

Bassel F. Salloukh

In his magisterial *A History of the Arab Peoples*, Albert Hourani (1992: ch 26 and p 442) labeled the years following the 1967 crisis 'a disturbance of spirits', a period laden with 'that sense of a world gone wrong'. The Arab nationalist promise of a progressive and independent post-colonial order had given way first to corporatist authoritarian regimes of the conservative and populist types, and then in 1967 to military defeat at the hands of Israel and a concomitant existential crisis.[1] Democracy and individual liberties, these so-called 'revolutionary' regimes argued, had to be shelved as Arab states industrialized their economies, expanded socioeconomic benefits, modernized their armies, and liberated Palestine from Israeli occupation. Decades later, however, none of these promises had materialized. Instead, authoritarian regimes across the Arab world appeared durable as they militarized society and manufactured a political culture of fear and subservience, deployed a complex set of strategies to defuse pressures generated by the fiscal crisis of the Arab state, deflected post 9/11 democracy promotion pressures from the international community into meaningless elections and civil society promotional organizations that failed to disturb the balance of power between regime and society, and, finally, manipulated international and regional geopolitical interests in favor of regime survival.[2]

While acknowledging their ostensible stability, Hourani (1992: 452) nevertheless underscored 'the fragility of [these] regimes'. He noted that they contained within them the sources of their own unmaking, suggesting that 'Even the most stable and the longest-lasting regimes … might prove to be fragile' (Hourani 1992: 455). Some two decades after Hourani offered that analysis, the popular uprisings triggered by Mohamed Bouazizi's self-immolation on 17 December 2010 in Tunisia wreaked havoc in what once looked like a durable authoritarian Arab order. Largely non-violent popular uprisings in Tunisia and Egypt toppled the authoritarian regimes of Zine al-Abidine Ben Ali and Hosni Mubarak, respectively, but genuine progress in democratization has been derailed by a bloody contest over the new political order. In Bahrain, another non-violent nationalist uprising against the al-Khalifa monarchy was swiftly sectarianized and violently crushed by regime forces, with the help of military forces from neighboring Saudi Arabia. In Yemen a negotiated transition was arranged to advance the geopolitical interests of Washington and Riyadh, but not the democratic aspirations of those Yemenis who braved Ali Abdullah Saleh's tanks and bullets. Authoritarian regime change in Libya unleashed powerful centrifugal forces that threaten to tear the country apart. The promise of political reforms in Jordan remains elusive, while Morocco's constitutional changes failed to undermine the monarchy's power. A peaceful popular protest movement in Syria avalanched into a full-scale military confrontation between, on the one hand, the regime and its regional and international allies, and, on the other, armed rebels, army deserters and local and foreign Salafi-jihadi fighters supported by an alliance of regional and international actors. Here, again, the Syrian peoples' democratic aspirations were sacrificed at the altar of a crude geopolitical contest. Just when the Arab peoples celebrated the dawn of what looked like a new era, a set of old challenges resurfaced to scuttle their democratic aspirations.

It is within this context of transition and uncertainty, of old regimes teetering and falling and of new ones rising up, and of societies beginning the difficult process of interrogating their recent past while exploring their way into the future, that many are turning to transitional justice processes. As with all such processes, those now transpiring in the Middle East must be contextualized by their particular circumstances to be properly understood, in this case of a region in the throes of complex transformations. This chapter offers a multi-level overview of the dynamics opened up by the recent Arab uprisings. It unpacks the challenges and opportunities that emerge from current processes unfolding in the Arab world – of authoritarian regime breakdown, of democratic transitions, of domestic upheavals and of societies reconstituting and reimagining themselves. The chapter also examines the impact of the Arab uprisings on the states and societies of the Arab world, the new role of very different Islamist groups in Arab politics, and the concomitant struggles over alternative visions of the political, moral and social orders. In so doing the chapter sets the stage for the book's subsequent exploration of transitional justice in the context of the Arab Spring.

A new Arab order in the making

One of the most salient effects of the Arab uprisings is the end of a political and ideological order built on the ruins of the 1948 Arab–Israeli war and the loss of Palestine. That order had itself brought to an end the earlier era of the post-independence liberal oligarchies, which had been characterized by a measure of elite competition but very low levels of mass inclusion (Hinnebusch 2010: 201). The post-1948 Arab order privileged pan-national (*qawmi*) causes – but mainly the Palestinian one – over domestic concerns, namely democracy. Indeed, the era's populist but non-competitive 'revolutionary' Arab republics constructed a binary but false choice between pan-national solidarity with the Palestinian cause and democracy at home. Support for the Palestinian cause soon became a pretext for state-building strategies and authoritarian regime consolidation, however (Brynen 1991: 595; Gause 1992: 441). A complex ideological and institutional edifice was organized to justify the authoritarian political order that lasted for almost six decades.

The popular uprisings that began in 2010 ushered in a nascent Arab order, one built on a novel counterpoint between democracy and Arab solidarity that is bound to give rise to a new contract between state and society in many countries. Gone are the days when Arab leaders could justify authoritarian rule by invoking the fig leaf of stability or the specter of external threats and foreign conspiracies. Those who did, such as Yemen's Saleh, Libya's Muammar Gaddafi and Syria's Bashar Assad, swiftly realized that the strategy was futile. The people who peacefully challenged authoritarian rule in the squares of many Arab capitals effectively debunked the old, regime-constructed arguments to justify authoritarian rule. Their non-violent popular uprisings expressed a commitment to democracy and democratic procedures that, alongside social justice and freedom, are the new litmus test of Arab solidarity at the mass level (al-Zayn 2011). As James Tully reminds us, these non-violent uprisings are:

> the *demand* of a diverse people, the demos, not to be governed in the *way* they have been governed. This is, first and foremost, a demand to remove and prosecute their governors and to set up new ones. However, for many participants, it is more than this. It is a demand to call into question, subject to public discussion, negotiate, modify, and perhaps even transform their form of government and law (2012: 2).

The way these non-violent uprisings unfolded, with people organizing collectively but democratically, and proceeding steadily in their quest to hold office holders accountable for past deeds, manifested a new democratic ethos reflected in 'the activities of a self-governing people changing the way they are governed' (Tully 2012: 2). The cathartic celebrations of peoples reclaiming their streets, cities, capitals and voices registered the return of the Demos as the agent of Arab political life and history after they had long been sidelined by the coercive and ideological instruments of the authoritarian state. This return of the Demos to the forefront of Arab politics – an accomplishment best expressed in the deafening popular cry '*Al-sha'byuridisqat al-nizam*' ('people want to overthrow the regime') – will henceforth be difficult to reverse or contain. In turn it has profound implications for how transitional justice plays out in the region, as a process in which new groups and individuals feel their way into socio-political participation and ultimately work toward the rehabilitation of their societies.

The fact that a number of regimes – namely in Bahrain, Libya and Yemen – militarized, sectarianized or tribalized the popular uprisings, or that in Syria's case the uprising escalated into a full-scale civil war, does not detract from the importance of the original non-violent ethos that triggered these uprisings. Rather, it underscores the challenges facing Arab societies as they either continue to battle against stubborn authoritarian regimes or try to complete their democratic transitions and commence the difficult process of democratic consolidation.[3] Nor do these challenges emanate from the Arab peoples' cultural aversion to democracy, a lingering Orientalist thesis finally torpedoed by the popular uprisings. They are instead rooted in the institutional legacy of decades of authoritarian rule, as well as of frequent international intervention and meddling in the region due to its centrality to the global capitalist economy and its geostrategic location. How Arab societies manage the multiple challenges they face after the popular uprisings will shape the new Arab order in the making.

The perils of interrogating the past

The popular uprisings and their aftermath have underscored the fragility of the political societies built following the collapse of the Ottoman Empire and during the subsequent colonial and decolonization periods. Lebanon is a constant reminder of the weakness of the new states' political identities and of the dangers of being perpetually vulnerable to international and regional pressures.[4] The result in Lebanon was a confessional-*cum*-sectarian power-sharing pact that hinged on an overlapping domestic and external balance of power. This overlap between domestic and external dynamics shaped Lebanon's politics, was responsible – alongside other domestic factors – for a protracted civil war and exposed the country to the permanent vulnerabilities of geopolitical contests. With time it became difficult to untangle Lebanon's domestic politics from its regional and international environments (Salloukh 2008: 282). However, Sudan's partition into two states along ethnic and regional lines, unification followed by civil war in Yemen (and the risk of a new descent into civil war today), centrifugal pressures in Iraq and Libya, the sectarian fissures that have (re)surfaced in Bahrain and Saudi Arabia and particularly in Syria, and the ideological struggles over the new political orders in all the other Arab states visited by the popular uprisings suggests that the Lebanese case may not be that anomalous. Rather, the sectarian, tribal, regional and ethnic Pandora's Box opened up by the uprisings has complicated any attempt to interrogate the authoritarian past as a precondition for constructing a just and democratic future.

This is in large measure a direct consequence of the policies pursued by the authoritarian regimes that dominated the post-1948 Arab order. Privileging the political model of a homogenizing authoritarian centralized unitary state, and concentrating political and coercive power in the hands of a family, sect, tribe, class, region or a combination thereof, these regimes alienated and excluded substantial ethnic, sectarian, socio-economic or regional groups (Traboulsi 2012a: 53). For example, authoritarian Arab regimes systematically discriminated against the Shi'a and Kurds in Iraq, the southerners in Sudan and Yemen, the Berber communities in Algeria, the rural Sunnis and the Kurds in Syria, the eastern Barqa province and the Amazigh, Tuareg and Tabu minorities in Libya, the Bedoon (stateless) in Kuwait, and the Shi'a in Bahrain and Saudi Arabia. Even in Egypt, where the 'imagined community' was assumed to be far stronger and denser than in other Arab states, Mubarak's regime manipulated Muslim-Coptic tensions to deflect attention away from far more pressing socio-economic and foreign policy challenges.

Iraq provides an early example of the long-term legacy of regime-imposed 'ethno-religious chauvinism' in Arab states and societies (Hamad 2010: 155). The sectarianization of politics in Iraq was a decades-long, ruthless process that entailed inordinate violence against the Shi'a and Kurdish communities, and the elimination of even the memory of the pre-Ba'ath pluralistic, democratic nationalist movement (Davis 2005: 229). As the regime grew narrower at the top after the 1990–91 Gulf War, it became composed of close family friends and tribal allies of Saddam Hussein, and retrenched toward the Baghdad-Ramadi-Tikrit Sunni triangle. Iraqi Kurdistan enjoyed autonomy following the first Gulf War as a result of protection by US-demarcated no-fly zones, while the southern Shi'a regions bore the brunt of the UN sanctions regime. Not surprisingly, then, regime change following the 2003 US invasion of Iraq, the disastrous de-Ba'athification policy, the disbanding of the Iraqi army and the concomitant geopolitical struggle over post-Saddam Hussein Iraq brought about total state collapse and a sectarian civil war. Moreover, Washington's embrace of 'the primordialism of the Iraqi exiles' in administering post-Saddam Iraq led to the institutionalization of a sectarian power-sharing pact in the context of a loose federal state structure (Dodge 2005: 715). The result is the hardening of ethnic and sectarian identities in a country whose constitutive communities live largely separate from one another.

The collapse of the Iraqi state after regime change and the subsequent institutionalization of an ethno-sectarian power-sharing pact has not gone unnoticed by those regimes and societies that experienced popular uprisings. This is especially the case in states with deep ethnic, sectarian, tribal or regional divisions. In Yemen, Libya, Bahrain and Syria, popular uprisings have threatened national unity and the very fabric of society. Regional divisions are especially prominent in Yemen and Libya.

In Yemen, former president Saleh's neopatrimonial rule discriminated systematically against some northern tribes but more so against the southern region, refusing to recognize the latter's share of power after the 1990 unification and the 1994 war. The uprising against his regime was led mainly by Yemen's youth, and ultimately forced his regional and international allies – Riyadh and Washington respectively – to forsake him to retain control over this strategic stretch of territory. South Yemen's separatist groups, gathered loosely in the Southern Peaceful Movement (*al-Hirak al-Silmi al-Janubi*, or Hirak), view the Saudi-US brokered transition agreement as an attempt to preserve northern Yemen's control over a marginalized south. Yemen's new president, Abed Rabbo Mansour Hadi, inflamed southern grievances by appointing a governor in Aden of the northern-oriented Islamist Islah party (*al-Tajamo' al-Yamani lil-Islah*), one viewed as antithetical to southern aspirations (Alley 2012; Arrabvee 2012). The Islamist Islah party raced to control state institutions in the post-Saleh transitional phase. It consequently penetrated the ministries of finance, electricity, planning and international cooperation, interior and education. Moreover, the post-Saleh government has yet to engage the south with meaningful confidence-building measures geared toward assuaging their fears of northern domination; nor has it commenced a reconciliation process to reverse the injustices committed toward the south after Yemen's unification. In fact, Islah is bent on dominating the post-Saleh order and excluding all the other groups that helped engineer the uprising. The result is a creeping sectarianism overtaking the country. Southerners continue to feel politically and economically marginalized. They reject proposals that aim to perpetuate northern control, championing instead an array of options ranging from federalism, broad autonomy to the complete independence of the south.

Similarly, Libya's Gaddafi ruled by dispensing patronage on the basis of tribe and city, concentrating his efforts on his hometown of Sirte and other western cities from which he drew his support, while under-developing and subjugating the eastern region, especially Benghazi. Such practices fueled regional resentment and separatist sentiments following regime change. Six months after Gaddafi's ouster following a peaceful uprising that escalated into heavy fighting involving domestic groups and an external military intervention led by Qatari and NATO forces, a confederacy of tribal leaders and militia commanders declared the oil-rich eastern region of Libya semi-autonomous. In so doing, they signaled their rejection of both the central government's authority and the unitary state model, and their preference for a federal or confederal arrangement (Hauslohner 2012). A natural reaction to decades of central rule by fiat, this is also a demand by communities that suffered the most as a result of Gaddafi's brutal practices for the renegotiation of a fairer socio-economic and political power-sharing pact between Libya's various tribal and regional groups. In both Yemen and Libya, then, transitional justice is not only a call for accountability and democracy; it is also a demand to reconstitute the country and its national unity on the basis of a new pluralism denied by past homogenizing authoritarian regimes, with all the attendant complications that such a renegotiation implies in terms of trust-building.

Despite the regime's concerted effort to derail and sectarianize opposition protests, Bahrain's popular uprising is also the demand of the Demos to hold the authoritarian regime accountable for past injustices, as well as a peaceful attempt to transform Bahrain's form of government and law. The al-Khalifas ruled this small kingdom by politically and socio-economically disenfranchising the majority Shi'a population. Wealth, executive power and state institutions remained the preserve of the Sunni minority and the royal family's close protégés. The regime resorted to gerrymandering electoral districts to under-represent the Shi'a community in parliament, and naturalized non-Bahraini Sunnis – Yemenis, Syrians and Pakistanis – in an attempt to alter the demographic balance of power (Caryl 2012). When it erupted on 14 February 2011, Bahrain's popular uprising was a veritable trans-sectarian movement gathering Shi'as and Sunnis against the authoritarian al-Khalifa regime. The protestors demanded the establishment of a constitutional monarchy anchored on a popularly elected parliament, a more representative – read proportional representation – electoral law and a reform of discriminatory citizenship laws and the state's coercive and judicial institutions to ensure fairer representation of the hitherto marginalized Shi'a community (Fadel 2012).

However, Bahrain's geostrategic significance to both Riyadh and Washington – it borders on Saudi Arabia's Shi'a populated oil-rich Eastern Province and is home to US Naval Forces Central Command and the US Fifth Fleet – provided the regime political cover to crush an otherwise peaceful uprising and convert it into a sectarian conflict (Aslan 2013). Subsequently, the regime launched a powerful media campaign demonizing the peaceful protestors as foreign 'Iranian agents' bent on destabilizing the kingdom to serve Tehran's geopolitical interests in the ongoing Saudi-Iranian geopolitical contest. But the Bahraini protestors refused to militarize their popular uprising, and continued peacefully to demand the creation of a democratic constitutional monarchy for all Bahrainis, one that reverses past injustices without creating new ones against the Sunni minority. This ethos of democracy and reconciliation is Bahrain's best safeguard against a post-authoritarian sectarian backlash.

It is in Syria, however, where the legacy of past injustices has returned with a vengeance. The Syrian Ba'ath regime was built on a trans-sectarian coalition gathering together the peasants and minorities of the rural areas and the urban lower-middle classes (Hinnebusch 1991: 29). Hafez Assad's consolidation of power after 1970, and the bloody conflict with the Muslim Brotherhood in 1978–84, entailed the addition of the urban Damascene commercial Sunni bourgeoisie to this coalition. Bashar inherited this coalition when he assumed power in June 2000, and expanded it to include the industrial bourgeoisie of Aleppo. In the following decade, and as the regime engaged in 'authoritarian upgrading' through a mix of neoliberal economic reforms and by diversifying its international linkages (Heydemann 2007), it lost its populist base, narrowing its political coalition to an alliance of ethnic and religious minorities and its socio-economic coalition to a crony capitalist elite, thus creating the reservoir of resentment that later exploded in its face (Marzouq 2011). A number of factors combined to create the underpinnings of Syria's popular uprising and its footsoldiers – the urban youth and the impoverished peasants (Seale 2012a). These include 'the ravages of youth unemployment; the brutality of Syria's security services; the domination of key centres of economic, military and political life by the minority Alawi community; and the blatant consumerism of a privileged class, grown rich on state patronage, in sharp contrast with the hardship suffered by the mass population, including in particular the inhabitants of the "poverty belt" around Damascus, Aleppo and other cities' (Seale 2012b). Moreover, as Patrick Seale observes, these 'deprived suburbs are largely the result of inward migration from the long-neglected countryside, which in the past decade has suffered catastrophic losses from a drought of unprecedented severity' (Seale 2012b).

The Syrian uprising, which commenced as a trans-sectarian call by most Syrians for democracy, social justice, accountability and an end to the crony capitalism of the regime and its socio-economic allies, evolved into an overlapping class, sectarian and geopolitical conflict. At one level it is the revolt of the urban youth, the underprivileged peasants and rural communities against a one-time populist regime that gradually disowned them, failed to address their economic needs and concentrated economic growth in the big urban cities, such as Damascus and Aleppo, or the strategic Latakia coastal area and its Alawi hinterland. At another level, it is a 'death-feud' between the Sunni Muslim Brotherhood and the secular Ba'ath Party and the regime's 'Alawi core' (Seale 2012b). For the former, it is their chance to finally settle a long overdue score with the regime's Alawi security and political leadership, one that goes back to the 1982 Hama massacres and beyond. Finally, the Syrian uprising is an extension of an overlapping regional-international geopolitical contest between Saudi Arabia – supported by the United States, France, Turkey and Qatar – and Iran – supported by Russia and China, one that extends to other theaters, namely Iraq, Lebanon, Yemen and Afghanistan. Tehran's material and political support of Bashar's regime is a defensive realist strategy to protect its own regional geopolitical interests. Riyadh's strategy, on the other hand, is to undermine Iran's regional influence by destabilizing and besieging Tehran's allies and clients, Iraq and Hezbollah respectively, or, as is the case in Syria, by toppling the Alawi regime and replacing it with a Sunni protégé. It has consequently provided the rebel Free Syrian Army and local Salafi groups with material and financial support, and has turned a blind eye to Salafi mobilization of transnational Salafi-jihadi fighters into the battlefield to expedite regime collapse, which, according to its own geopolitical calculations, compensates for the loss of Sunni-ruled Iraq with control over a post-Ba'ath, Sunni-dominated Syria (Luttwak 2011). Riyadh's decision to deploy sectarianism to achieve these otherwise strictly realist geostrategic objectives has inflamed sectarian animosity in the region and rendered the Syrian uprising, in part, a bloody sectarian conflict. Sectarian massacres, reprisal killings and mass executions, on both sides of the divide, shattered Syria's national unity. As in Iraq, demands for justice and accountability in the post-authoritarian phase may assume violent sectarian and centrifugal overtones. De-Ba'athification and the disbanding of the army are not viable options following Iraq's disastrous experience. Nothing short of a power-sharing pact redistributing political, economic and military/security power between the country's different ethnic, religious and sectarian groups, and rectifying past socio-economic and political injustices will end Syria's destruction and restore its national unity.

The antinomies of the present

The states and societies of the Arab world face Herculean challenges as they rebuild or reconstitute themselves democratically after decades of authoritarian rule. How to prosecute members or supporters of former authoritarian regimes – whether locally, by a reconstituted national judicial authority or internationally, at the International Criminal Court (ICC) – is one such challenge. In Libya, for example, the new authorities engaged in a debate over retributive justice with the ICC over the prosecution of Saif al-Islam Gaddafi and former spy chief, Abdullah al-Senussi, extradited on 5 September 2012 from Mauritania. While Libyan authorities demanded that the accused stand trial in a Libyan court – where serious questions have been raised about their ability to receive a fair trial – the ICC favors that they be tried in its courts for crimes committed against humanity (Black 2012).[5] But hundreds of other former regime supporters await trial, and whether or not these trials will be fair remains an open question. Moreover, some tribes and militias have targeted Gaddafi sympathizers and sanctuaries with brutal retribution in the name of retributive justice. Misrata militias committed war crimes against Gaddafi's escape convoy and invaded the western city of Bani Walid, a refuge for Gaddafi followers after regime change (Fahim 2012). These retributive acts threaten to ignite a tribal civil war in post-Gaddafi Libya, and are a bad omen of what may await some minorities in a post-Assad Syria.

By contrast, in Yemen the transition agreement guaranteed Saleh domestic immunity from prosecution in exchange for his resignation (Alley 2012). This has had adverse effects on the democratic transition and the prospects for transitional justice, however. With his sophisticated tribal system of allegiances and substantial neo-patrimonial networks, Saleh emerged as a principal spoiler of the transition agreement and of any prospects for national reconciliation. This latter objective is also threatened by fears of whole scale 'de-Salehfication' in the military and the bureaucracy (Alley 2012). Purges of Saleh loyalists at both the upper echelons and the lower levels of the bureaucracy and the military-security services, at a time when the new president flavors his own civilian and military appointments with family, tribal and regional biases, have aggravated multiple insecurities between the different political players, and undermined the cause of transitional justice and national reconciliation.

In societies free from the kind of deep cleavages found in Iraq, Libya, Yemen and Syria, and where power was not monopolized by a family, sect, tribe or ethnic group, the challenges facing retributive justice in the post-authoritarian order tend to be different. There, demands for justice and accountability first focused on prosecuting members of the old regime and banning them from participating in politics. In Tunisia, President Ben Ali's swift escape from the country and his flight to Saudi Arabia rendered his prosecution untenable. Nevertheless, and in preparation for Tunisia's first democratic elections, a new electoral law drafted by the High Commission for the Fulfillment of Revolutionary Goals, Political Reform and Democratic Transition banned a number of former government officials, who were also members of the ruling Constitutional Democratic Rally (Rassemblement constitutionnel démocratique or RCD), from running for office (International Foundation for Electoral Systems 2011). While a similar electoral ban was struck down by Egypt's Supreme Constitutional Court, prosecution of the Mubarak family and its neo-patrimonial clients remained an unshakable popular demand that the Supreme Council of the Armed Forces (SCAF), then the country's transitional authority, succumbed to quickly. Indeed, the image of a resigned Mubarak hauled on a hospital bed into court underscored the Egyptian peoples' determination to hold their authoritarian ruler accountable for the corruption and criminality of his family and regime.

Yet once the euphoria of authoritarian regime breakdown passed, and Islamist parties achieved stunning electoral victories and assumed power, the Demos in Tunisia and Egypt fractured over how best to rebuild their new forms of government and law. Tunisia's Ennahda and Egypt's Freedom and Justice Party (FJP), the Muslim Brotherhood's political arm, became preoccupied with consolidating their control over state institutions and the public sphere, with special care given to controlling the agents of cultural production, but especially the media.

Tunisia's ruling troika failed to replicate the all-inclusive process that defined the democratic transition phase. The transitional period bridging the democratic transition phase with that of democratic consolidation was consequently marred by crises. The drafting of a new constitution emerged as a battleground between, on the one hand, the proponents of the sanctity of personal liberties and freedoms and, on the other hand, Islamist parties and Salafi groups who sought to include in its text a set of basic religious stipulations that could pave the way for future censorship and discrimination. The former group insists on enshrining the constitution's prelude with clauses underscoring the universality of human rights, while the latter demands clear references to the role of Islamic law (sharia) as the principal source of legislation in the country (Beltaveb 2013). Other constitutional provisions open the way for the creation of paramilitary militias outside the purview of the army and the security forces, thus risking the militarization of political conflict. All this has cast doubt on the legitimacy of the National Constituent Assembly (NCA), the body responsible for completing the new constitution, and alienated the opposition.

Ennahda also sought to pack state institutions with its own cadres throughout the transitional phase. No less than 1,300 hardline Ennahda supporters were appointed to state institutions only months after the party assumed the premiership in December 2011 in a purportedly transitional political arrangement. In fact, Ennahda seems to have brokered an agreement with some former RCD bureaucrats whereby the latter would enable it to entrench itself in the bureaucracy in return for a promise of immunity from future prosecution (al-Marzouki 2012). Consequently, and rather than altering the way government was practiced in the past, Ennahda has replicated in certain respects the RCD's hegemonic institutional and clientelistic practices. It also preserved the former regime's neoliberal economic policies and its regional bias in favor of the coastal areas at the expense of the underdeveloped and impoverished rural hinterland.

Appointing itself judge, jury and witness, Ennahda-affiliated militias led campaigns to expel what they call RCD sympathizers from state institutions, the political sphere and the media, a process that should otherwise be led by the reconstituted state institutions. All this has transpired amid fears by secular groups and opposition parties that Ennahda's call for a purge of state institutions and the media is but a first step in a calculated incremental strategy to assume full control of the country. A leaked tape of a 2012 meeting between Rashid Ghannouchi, Ennahda's spiritual leader, and a Salafi delegation, shows the former describing an intricate but incremental plan to assume control of Tunisia. Ghannouchi is heard advising his Salafi interlocutors to bide their time and fight a war of ideas with their secular opponents, who are accused of controlling the media, the state administration, the economy, the police forces and the military institution (ProlaiquesTunisies 2012). These exclusionist practices have deeply divided the polity over the form of their future government and law. Political tensions finally exploded into street clashes after the assassination of the secularist opposition leader, Chokri Belaid, in February 2013, a crime blamed in part on the atmosphere of vigilante justice sanctioned by Ennahda. Over the subsequent year, the country has continued to see many changes, with the Ennahda-led government stepping down and a new constitution being written and ratified; but the fundamental fact of deep societal divisions continues to challenge the emerging social and political order.

A similar situation transpired in Egypt after authoritarian regime breakdown, albeit there the democratic transition remains incomplete given the army's considerable weight in the post-authoritarian order. The winner in both the 28 November 2011 to 11 January 2012 parliamentary and June 2012 presidential elections, the FJP soon discarded its campaign slogans and embraced the former regime's foreign policy and neoliberal economic choices. It reversed its promise to form a coalition government gathering Egypt's different ideological currents, launched a conquest of state institutions from which the Muslim Brotherhood had hitherto been barred, and replaced the former regime's appointees with its own in the army, the Presidential Guard, the Military Police, the intelligence services, the state media and the different governorates. Far from contributing toward establishing a genuine democratic form of government and law, the FJP preoccupied itself with arranging a loose partnership with the army at the expense of the groups that triggered the uprising, sacrificing life and limb to topple Mubarak's regime, and persist in demanding the establishment of a far more just, socio-economic order as well as a more tolerant political order.

As in Tunisia, this unilateral approach to a transitional period that most believed should involve the Demos collectively and democratically negotiating and agreeing on their new form of government and law alienated substantial sectors of Egyptian society, particularly those for whom justice in the post-authoritarian phase is organically connected to the objectives that galvanized Egypt's popular uprising. These include an inclusive democratic state, the redistribution of national wealth in a manner that achieves greater social and economic equality after decades of crony capitalism, guaranteeing public and personal freedoms and ending the country's dependence on external powers and institutions. Acting like a latter-day Mubarak, and in total disregard of the ethos of the popular uprising, President Mohamed Morsi promulgated on 22 November 2012 a Constitutional Declaration that granted him sweeping powers under the pretext of protecting the revolution. The draft Constitution was ratified hastily by the Constituent Assembly despite the boycott of liberal and Christian members and the objections of an array of civil groups and political parties; it was later passed unconvincingly in a popular referendum. Liberal and leftist groups returned to the streets demanding a rectification of the process by which their new form of government and law is produced. Whole cities, such as Port Said, rebelled against Morsi's authority.

The crescendo of popular opposition climaxed when Tamarrod (Rebellion) – a grassroots youth opposition movement that had spent the past months collecting some 22 million signatures from citizens all over Egypt in support of Morsi's resignation – staged the biggest demonstration in Egypt's history on 30 June 2013, the first anniversary of Morsi's presidential inauguration. The demonstrators demanded Morsi's ouster and insisted on holding early presidential elections. With the country on the brink of civil war between the pro-Morsi Muslim Brotherhood supporters and the opposition, General Abdel Fatah al-Sisi, commander of the SCAF, supported by leaders of the opposition, the Salafi al-Nour party and the heads of al-Azhar and the Coptic Church, removed Morsi from the presidency on 3 July; concurrently, the army rounded up a number of Muslim Brotherhood leaders and cadres accused of instigating violence against the opposition. The SCAF subsequently appointed Adly Mansour, head of the Supreme Constitutional Court, interim president tasked with overseeing the promulgation of a new Constitution and arranging for fresh parliamentary elections to be followed by a new round of presidential elections (Kirkpatrick and El Sheikh 2013). Tellingly, the justice portfolio in a new cabinet composed of liberal technocrats was renamed the Transitional Justice and National Reconciliation Ministry, and was awarded to a career judge. Albeit the return of the army to central stage and the bloody clashes accompanying the president's ouster complicated Egypt's democratic transition, nevertheless the explosion of popular anger in Morsi and the Muslim Brotherhood's face underscored the Demos' unwavering determination to resist the use of the transitional phase to institutionalize an Islamist form of despotism in Egypt.

Islam in the post-authoritarian order

The antinomies of the post-authoritarian order are most acute in the debate pertaining to Islam's role in state legislation and public life, however. At the heart of this debate is a struggle between two camps over the juridical and moral foundations of the post-authoritarian order (Traboulsi 2012a 33-51; Traboulsi 2012b). The first, a hybrid Islamist camp, is bent on consecrating its interpretation of Islamic law as the primary source of state legislation and public morality in a self-declared civil state (*dawla madaniya*). Proponents of this perspective contend that the laws of the sharia contain within them the necessary and sufficient guidelines to regulate both public and personal matters for Muslims and non-Muslims alike. On this view, then, a particular, purportedly 'authentic' interpretation of Islamic law – be it that of the Muslim Brotherhood, Ennahda or the Salafis – determines the role of the state in society and citizens' relations with the state and with each other rather than universal principles of equality, human rights and democracy. The FJP's leader, Saad al-Katatni, did not even mince his words when he declared that 'the Moslem Brotherhood created this party to express its own political program as it seeks to achieve the virtuous rule whose terminal stage is the implementation of Islamic Shari'a' in Egypt (Al-Havat 2012b).[6]

The second camp is liberal and secular but not anti-religious. It protests that the civil state propounded by Islamist parties is a hodgepodge of conservative populism and neoliberal economics that serves the socio-economic interests of an alliance of the religiously conservative bourgeoisie and professional middle classes (Traboulsi 2012b). On this view, then, the civil state promised by Islamists is bound to be devoid of any sense of political and legal equality, or religious and cultural pluralism. Instead of treating religious minorities as equal citizens before a religiously neutral law, it will place them at the mercy of a religious majority. Its legislation will not be based on universal human rights charters, nor the popular will of equal citizens bound together by republican contracts, but rather on all-too-human interpretations of the religious texts. Anchored in exclusionist religious dogma, this state will use politics to eliminate political competition, and will 'use democracy … to proscribe it' (Abdul-Fattah 2012). The civil state adumbrated by Egypt's FJP, Tunisia's Ennahda or Morocco's Justice and Development Party (JDP) is thus a far cry from the one dreamed up by those who took to the streets and squares of Arab capitals in pursuit of a democratic and more just Arab order.

This struggle by the Demos to shape their post-authoritarian forms of government and law is more than a case of two incommensurate visions of state and society or of the role of religion in politics. Nor is it just about finding a way by both camps to respect what Alfred Stepan labels the principle of the 'twin tolerations' governing the relationship between religious citizens and the state: namely, for citizens to 'accord democratically elected officials the freedom to legislate and govern without having to confront denials of their authority based on religious claims', and, the second toleration, 'that laws and officials must permit religious citizens, as a matter of right, to freely take part in politics, as long as religious activists and organizations respect other citizens' constitutional rights and the law' (Stepahn 2012: 89). At stake in the agonic struggles now underway in the Arab world are the rules of the game 'of being a free people', which in turn permit the participation and deliberation of individuals as citizens – rather than subjects – in shaping their formal legal institutions that govern relations between the state and its diverse citizens, citizens with each other, and religious, ethnic or sectarian minorities with the majority.[7]

These struggles have often turned violent, however. To be sure, the Islamist groups that exploded into the political arena after the popular uprisings are not monolithic. They may be divided into at least three broad categories: the Muslim Brotherhood-affiliated parties such as the FJP, Ennahda and the JDP; the apolitical and non-violent Salafis preoccupied with doctrinal and behavioral matters; and the violent Salafi-jihadi groups (see Bin Khalifa 2012). Nevertheless, they have all used different levels of violence to intimidate their opponents in the debate over the nature of post-authoritarian governments and laws. In Egypt, supporters of the FJP attacked demonstrators and the Army after Morsi's ouster, and used violence to restore the status quo ante. Some religious clerics had even tried to use religious edicts to ban anti-Muslim Brotherhood demonstrations and sanction the use of violence against them (Al-Havat 2012a). The Grand Mufti of al-Azhar, Ahmad al-Tayyeb, intervened to block a constitutional amendment requested by Salafi parties to make the specific rules of the sharia, rather than its principles, the main source of legislation in Egypt, a proviso that potentially could have reinforced medieval forms of corporeal punishment and relegated religious minorities to the status of *dhimmis* – protected but nevertheless unequal subjects (Al-Safir 2012a). Similar sentiments were voiced in Libya's constitutional-making process. Libyans are divided on whether the sharia should be the sole or the main source for the country's constitution, or simply a source of inspiration for it (Feha and Doumit 2012).

Salafi groups in Tunisia declared war on the defenders of Tunisia's secular legacy, clashing with intellectuals, artists and civil society activists who refused to abide by a new code of religious ethics that, for example, allows veiled women to sit for university exams or bans cultural products or artworks that may be considered an offense against religion or God (*al-dhat al-ilahiya*) (Bin Khalifa 2012). Often financed by Saudi Arabia, these groups are unabashedly anti-Shi'a, and have instigated Sunni-Shi'a sectarian animosity in a country hitherto free from sectarian troubles. This has prompted some Ennahda ideologues to warn Tunisians of the pernicious impact of Saudi-financed Wahhabi Salafi preaching on Tunisia's otherwise moderate legal tradition of Islamic jurisprudence.[8] Intolerant of cultural, religious or sectarian diversity, Salafi groups represent a not insignificant challenge to the emergence of democratic and plural post-authoritarian political and social orders.

Unlike the FJP, Ennahda or the non-violent Salafi groups, local Salafi-jihadi groups follow an altogether different agenda. Militant, battle-hardened and deeply uncompromising, they target Western interests, sectarian minorities, Sufi shrines and cultural sites, and demand a return to an imagined pristine Islamic way of life. They raise equal objections to both liberal-secular groups and the Muslim Brotherhood, who they view as too moderate and in cahoots with Western countries. Blamed for the notorious 2012 attack on the American consulate in Benghazi that resulted in the death of the US ambassador in Libya, the 2012 Sinai massacre of members of the Egyptian army and other assaults after Morsi's ouster, and the assassination of some 60 military-security figures in Yemen in 2012 (Wehrey 2012), they are often courted by al-Qaeda as the latter seeks to export its transnational army of irregular fighters into new sites for armed struggle (*sahat jihad*).

Nowhere is this post-uprisings trend more troubling than in Syria, where Salafi-jihadi groups, assisted logistically by Turkish intelligence and supported financially by various private sources in the Gulf region, have penetrated and derailed what was otherwise a non-violent popular uprising (International Crisis Group 2012). Jabhat al-Nusra li-Ahl al-Sham (Support Front for the Peoples of Greater Syria) soon emerged as the strongest and most ruthless of all such groups. Like other Salafi-jihadi groups operating in Syria, it refuses to coordinate its military efforts with the Free Syrian Army, and proscribes cooperation with both the liberal-secular and Muslim Brotherhood wings of the Syrian opposition on the grounds that the former are ideological enemies, while the latter are corrupt and tend to cooperate with non-Muslim actors and states (al-'Abad 2012). The result is an all-out war against the regime and Syria's civilians and cultural heritage. The war has assumed overt sectarian undertones, with Salafi-jihadi groups labeling it an Alawi massacre of Sunnis. It has attracted transnational Salafi-jihadi fighters from across the globe, turning Syria into a latter-day Iraq that has also destabilized neighboring Lebanon, helped shift the opinion of large swathes of the public against the popular uprising and furnished the regime with a fig leaf for the wholescale destruction of opposition areas and cities. This wanton, systematic and deliberate destruction of Syria will deprive the country of its pivotal geopolitical role for decades to come, to say nothing of the profound and likely long-term domestic consequences for Syrians in terms of post-war reconstruction and reconciliation.

Conclusion

The states and societies of the Arab world face multiple and overlapping challenges after the popular uprisings. Negotiating new forms of government and law and rectifying the injustices of the past will be neither uncomplicated nor unilinear processes. The legacy of the authoritarian years, the antinomies of the emerging new order and the geopolitics of the region have complicated, and in some cases derailed, the non-violent and democratic ethos of the popular uprisings. Demands for justice raised by the Demos of the popular uprisings span a broad spectrum. They consist of removing and prosecuting former regime members and their cronies, negotiating new forms of democratic governments and laws and, in some cases, reimagining the nation and reconstituting the state's political geography anew.

While some states have navigated their way through authoritarian regime breakdown, others have collapsed completely, opening up a future laden with fears and trepidation. This latter threat is especially acute in deeply divided societies, where the violence of regime breakdown, combined with the accumulated injustices of the authoritarian era, have created centrifugal forces that threaten the state's national unity and territorial integrity. And even where popular uprisings were muted or absent, such as in some of the oil-rich Gulf countries, the use of the Salafi card to insulate society from these upheavals or from the danger of an alternative Muslim Brotherhood Islamist ideology may backfire. The current balance of power between the Saudi royal family and the Wahhabi Salafi religious hierarchy may one day tip in the latter's favor, and instead of being content with theorizing for the Al Saud family, they might seek to replace them (Ibrahim 2012). Alternatively, Salafi-jihadi ideology and fighters exported to new battle zones may wreak havoc in their own homelands, as Belaid's assassination attests (Barakat 2013).

Of all the challenges facing Arab states after the popular uprisings, the explosion of Islamist groups onto the political scene has created special cause for concern. This is rooted in a number of factors. Violating the democratic and non-violent ethos that characterized the uprisings, some Islamist groups have tended to act in exclusionist and violent ways once they assumed power. They also opted to perpetuate or recognize policies and values that large parts of the Demos had rallied against during the popular uprisings: neoliberal economic programs, financial and geostrategic dependence on the West and a set of core US interests, especially regional stability, Israel, oil and the so-called 'war on terror' (Agha and Malley 2012: 72). However, it is their flirtations with putting in place the sharia as a privileged source of legislation and public morality that most unnerves religious minorities, secular Arabs and many Muslims. Not that the sharia is immune from a creative interpretation, one that applies a modernist hermeneutic to the problems of contemporary Muslim societies (Hallaw 1997). Rather, the problem lies with the actors making these demands, since, as Wael Hallaq insists, they seem oblivious to the homogenizing and codified impact that colonialism, and the concomitant imposition of modern states and legal systems, had on an otherwise malleable and juristically relative pre-modern sharia, thus rendering present calls for its restoration both ahistorical and moot (Hallaq 2007: 151). Tully is optimistic that the agonic struggles of the non-violent popular uprisings may democratize these calls, thus helping to transcend the religious-secular demarcation dividing Arab societies as they negotiate their new forms of laws and governments (Tully 2012: 36-8). In this he seems to be echoing Hourani's own sentiments, voiced at the end of his great oeuvre referred to at the outset of this chapter: 'It might happen', Hourani concludes, 'that, at a certain stage of national development, the appeal of religious ideas – at least of ideas sanctified by the cumulative tradition – would cease to have the same force as another system of ideas: a blend of social morality and law which were basically secular, but might have some relationship to general principles of social justice inherent in the Qur'an' (Hourani 1992: 458).

There is much at stake for Arab states and societies before this long-term vision is attained. To be sure, it is the restored spirit of the popular uprisings that shall determine whether the governments and laws of post-authoritarian Arab political orders will be truly liberal, democratic and pluralistic, where religious, ethnic, sectarian, tribal and ideological differences are reconciled peacefully or, alternatively, be hijacked by actors bent on taking Arab societies back to a homogenized and illiberal future under the mantle of democracy. Transitional justice can help in reinventing societal stability predicated on trust and justice, even in the face of fundamental disagreements about the bases of justice in many countries. That being said, it is by no means a foregone conclusion that Arab states and societies will choose to pursue transitional justice mechanisms in a manner that will produce the desired outcome, or indeed that they will pursue them at all. It is with these challenges in mind that the next chapters turn to a detailed consideration of the actual transitional justice measures that are being carried out and planned in the Arab countries.[9]

Notes

1 Israel's stunning military victory in the June 1967 War – when the combined armies of Egypt, Jordan and Syria suffered a crippling military defeat and lost significant territory

including the Sinai Peninsula, the Golan Heights, the West Bank and Gaza Strip, and the symbolically important old city of Jerusalem – underlined the relative weakness of the revolutionary authoritarian Arab regimes in these countries. The defeat prompted extensive introspection and self-criticism about the best way forward in the post-colonial period across a broader swathe of the Arab world. See Fouad Ajami, *The Arab Predicament: Arab Political Thought and Practice Since 1967* (Cambridge University Press, 1992).

2 For a comprehensive analysis of these themes, see Rex Brynen, Pete W. Moore, Bassel F. Salloukh and Marie-Joëlle Zahar, *Beyond the Arab Spring: Authoritarianism and Democratization in the Arab World* (Lynne Rienner Publishers, 2012).

3 For a discussion of the difference between the two stages, see Juan J. Linz and Alfred Stepan, *Problems of Democratic Transition and Consolidation: Southern Europe, South America, and Post-Communist Europe* (The Johns Hopkins University Press, 1996).

4 See Ch 5 for more discussion of this issue.

5 See also Ch 10 for discussion of this issue.

6 al-Katatni made these comments upon his election as leader of the FJP.

7 For a discussion of this kind of Foucauldian agonism, see Tully 2008: 135-59, and 146 for quote.

8 See Ennahdada's Abdelfattah Mourou's comments in *al-Safir* 2012b.

9 I am grateful to James Tully, Wadood Hamad and Robert Stewart for their invaluable comments.

Bibliography

Abdul-Fattah, W. (2012) 'Dawlat al-Dhat al-Ilahiya' ['The State of the Sacred'], *al-Akhbar*, 6 September.

Agha, H. and Malley, R. (2012) 'This Is Not a Revolution', *New York Review of Books*, 8 November.

Al Jazeera English (2012) *Bahrain: Shouting in the Dark*, 19 June, available online at http://www.aljazeera.com/programmes/2011/08/201184144547798162.html

Al-'Abed, T. (2012) 'Al-Salafiyun fi Suriya…Khilaf ma' al-Jami' bayna al-Silah wa-l-Takfir' ['Salafis in Syria: Disagreement with all between Weapons and Excommunication'], *al-Safir*, 2 November.

Al-Hayat (2012a) 17 August.

Al-Hayat (2012b) 20 October.

Al-Safir (2012a) 17 August.

Al-Safir (2012b) 22 August.

Al-Zayn, J. (2011) 'Muqarana Bayna Shari'ayn 'Arabiyayn' ['Comparing Two Arab Streets'] *al-Nahar*, 23 March.

Alley, A. L. (2012) 'Triage for a Fracturing Yemen', *The Middle East Channel*, 31 October, available online at http://mideast.foreignpolicy.com/posts/2012/10/31/triage_for_a_fracturing_yemen.

Ajami, F. (1992) *The Arab Predicament: Arab Political Thought and Practice Since 1967* (Cambridge University Press).

Arrabyee, N. (2012) 'National Dialogue in Yemen', Carnegie Endowment for International Peace, 1 November, available online at http://carnegieendowment.org/2012/11/01/national-dialogue-in-yemen/eb4g.

Aslan, R. (2013) 'Bahrain's Fake Sectarian War', *Foreign Affairs*, 30 June, available online at www.foreignaffairs.com/features/letters-from/bahrains-fake-sectarian-war.

Barakat, R. (2013) 'Ightiyal Bel'eed wa Tasdeer al-'onf al-Suri' ['Belaid's Assassination and the Export of Syria's Violence'], *al-Safir*, 13 February.

Beltayeb, N. (2013) 'Miswadat al-Dustour Bawabat Diktatoriyat al-Nahda' ['The Draft Constitution as a Prelude to Ennahda's Dictatorship'], *al-Akhbar*, 22 January.

Bin Khalifa, G. (2012) 'Al-Salafiyun fi Tunis: Al-La'eb al-Sa'ed fi-l-Kharita al-Siyasiya' ['The Salafis in Tunisia: The Rising Player in the Political Map'], *al-Safir al-'Arabi*, 13 September.

Black, I. (2012) 'Gaddafi Spy Chief Should Be Tried by ICC Not Libya, Says Family', *Guardian*, 19 October, available online at www.guardian.co.uk/world/2012/oct/19/gaddafi-spy-chief-icc-libya.

Brynen, R. (1991) 'Palestine and the Arab State System: Permeability, State Consolidation and the *Intifada*', *Canadian Journal of Political Science* 24(3) (September).

Brynen, R. et al. (2012) *Beyond the Arab Spring: Authoritarianism and Democratization in the Arab World* (Lynne Rienner Publishers).

Caryl, C. (2012) 'The Strange Revolution in Bahrain, One Year On', *Foreign Policy*, 14 February, available online at www.foreignpolicy.com/articles/2012/02/14/the_strange_revolution_in_bahrain_one_year_on.

Davis, E. (2005) 'History Matters: Past as Prologue in Building Democracy in Iraq', *Orbis* 49(2) (Spring).

Dodge, T. (2005) 'Iraqi Transitions: From Regime Change to State Collapse', *Third World Quarterly* 26(4) & (5) (June).

Fahim, K. (2012) 'Libyan Town under Siege is a Center of Resistance to the New Government', *New York Times*, 21 October, available online at www.nytimes.com/2012/10/22/world/africa/libyan-town-under-siege-is-a-center-of-resistance.html?_r=0.

Fadel, M. A. (2012) 'Intifadat al-Bahrain Ba'ada 'Am' ['One Year after Bahrain's Uprising'] *al-Safir al-'Arabi*, 5 July.

Gause, F. G. III (1992) 'Sovereignty, Statecraft and Stability in the Middle East', *Journal of International Affairs* 45(2) (Winter).

Geha, C. and Doumit, G. (2012) 'Libya's Constitutional Twilight', Carnegie Endowment for International Peace, 25 October, available online at http://carnegieendowment.org/2012/10/25/libya-s-constitutional-twilight/e5zw.

Hallaq, W. B. (2007) 'What is Shari'a', *Yearbook of Islamic and Middle Eastern Law 2005–2006* 12.

Hallaq, W. B. (1997) *A History of Islamic Legal Theories: An Introduction to Sunni usul al-fiqh* (Cambridge University Press).

Hamad, W. (2010) 'A Socio-Political Critique of Ethno-Religious Chauvinism in Contemporary Arab Societies', in Benjamin J. Pauli (ed.), *Radical Religion: Contemporary Perspectives on Religion and the Left* (Lexington Books).

Hauslohner, A. (2012) 'Benghazi Breakaway Highlights Libya's Uncertain Future', *Time*, 7 March, available online at www.time.com/time/world/article/0,8599,2108425,00.html.

Heydemann, S. (2007) *Upgrading Authoritarianism in the Arab World*, Analysis Paper No 13, (Brookings Institution, October).

Hinnebusch, R. (2010) 'Toward a Historical Sociology of State Formation in the Middle East', *Middle East Critique* 19(3) (Fall).

Hinnebusch, R. (1991) 'Class and State in Ba'athist Syria', in Richard T. Antoun and Donald Quataert (eds), *Syria: Society, Culture, and Polity* (State University of New York Press).

Hourani, A. (1992) *A History of the Arab Peoples* (Warner Books).

Ibrahim, F. (2012) 'Al-'Ikhwan wa-l-Salafiyun … wa-l-Sa'odiya Baynahuma' ['The Brotherhood and the Salafis … and Saudi Arabia in between'], *al-Safir*, 30 October.

International Crisis Group (2012), *Tentative Jihad: Syria's Fundamentalist Opposition*, Middle East Report No 131, 12 October, available online at www.crisisgroup.org/en/regions/middle-east-north-africa/egypt-syria-lebanon/syria/131-tentative-jihad-syrias-fundamentalist-opposition.aspx.

International Foundation for Electoral Systems (2011), *Elections in Tunisia: The 2011 Constituent Assembly*, available online at www.ifes.org/~/media/Files/Publications/White%20PaperReport/2011/Tunisia_FAQs_072011.pdf.

Kirkpatrick, D. and El Sheikh, M. (2013) 'Morsi Spurned Deals, Seeing Military as Tamed', *New York Times*, 6 July, available online at www.nytimes.com/2013/07/07/world/middleeast/morsi-spurned-deals-to-the-end-seeing-the-military-as-tamed.html?pagewanted=all&_r=0.

Linz, J. and Stepan, A. (1996) *Problems of Democratic Transition and Consolidation: Southern Europe, South America, and Post-Communist Europe* (The Johns Hopkins University Press).

Luttwak, E. (2011) 'Revenge of the Sunnis: What the Arab Spring is really about', *Foreign Policy*, 7 December, available online at www.foreignpolicy.com/articles/2011/12/07/revenge_of_the_sunnis.

Marzouq, N. (2011) 'Awamel Iqtisadiya lil-Intifada al-Suriya' ['The Syrian Uprising's Economic Causes'], *al-Akhbar*, 17 August.

Muqni, N. (2012) 'Sahwat al-Marzouki' ['Marzouki's Awakening'], *al-Akhbar*, 27 July.

ProlaiquesTunisie (2012) *Leaked Video Ghannouchi with Salafis*, 9 October, available online at www.youtube.com/watch?feature=player_embedded&v=m5vqhT8TxRw#!.

Salloukh, B. F. (2008) 'The Art of the Impossible: The Foreign Policy of Lebanon', in Korany, B. and Dessouki, A. (eds), *The Foreign Policies of Arab States: The Challenge of Globalization* (American University in Cairo Press).

Seale, P. (2012a) 'The Destruction of Syria', Agence Global, 24 July, available online at www.agenceglobal.com/index.php?show=article&Tid=2840.

Seale, P. (2012b) 'Syria's Long War', Agence Global, 28 September, available online at www.agenceglobal.com/index.php?show=article&Tid=2883.

Shatz, A. (2013) 'Short Cuts', *London Review of Books*, 8 August, available online at www.lrb.co.uk/v35/n15/adam-shatz/short-cuts.

Stepan, A. (2012) 'Tunisia's Transition and the Twin Tolerations', *Journal of Democracy* 23(2) (April).

Traboulsi, F. (2012a) *Al-Dimoqratiya Thawra* [*Democracy is a Revolution*] (Riyad al-Rayyes lil-Kutub wa-l-Nasher).

Traboulsi, F. (2012b) 'Al-Ra'smaliya al-Mou'mina wa-l-Dawla al-Madaniya' ['Pious Capitalism and the Civil State'], *al-Safir*, 18 July.

Tully, J. (2012) 'Middle East Legal and Governmental Pluralism: A View of the Field from the Demos', *Middle East Law and Governance* 4.

Tully, J. (2008) *Public Philosophy in a New Key Volume 1: Democracy and Civic Freedom* (Cambridge University Press).

Wehrey, F. (2012) 'The Wrath of Libya's Salafis', Carnegie Endowment for International Peace, 12 September, available online at http://carnegieendowment.org/2012/09/12/wrath-of-libya-s-salafis/dtaz.

Chapter 2

Building a future, exhuming the past: the struggle for accountability in the wake of regional uprisings

Anne Massagee[1]

The unprecedented changes in the Middle East and North Africa (MENA) which began in December 2010 riveted the world's attention on the region, as youth and other protesters called not merely for reform but for outright revolution. Over the course of the next two years, multitudes across the region demanded accountability for the legacies of past abuse and corruption. This chapter explores the first steps, opportunities, challenges and lessons of the early engagements with transitional justice in the wake of the MENA uprisings.

Demands for accountability included, *inter alia*, bringing officials to trial; investigating corruption and returning its profits to the state; investigating what happened during or prior to the uprisings; providing compensation and other remedy to those harmed; and reforming state structures which were involved in abuse. Demonstrators sought to draft new constitutions, establish democratic parliaments, implement economic reforms and rebuild trust within society as well as between citizens and officials. For those on the ground, justice plainly has many meanings. This more comprehensive view of justice undertaken in the wake of such upheavals is often called 'transitional justice', a term which came into use in the late 1980s as human rights activists, jurists, policy makers and others began exploring the specific contexts of countries in transition to democracy (Arthur 2009a: 324).

The challenges of processes of transitional justice are considerable: they are implemented at times when national rule of law systems are often incomplete or broken, and at a point when countries are seeking to address violence which is longstanding and of a scale beyond the capacity of existing structures. Moreover, they need to recognise the variance of justice priorities among the victims, who will not speak as one voice in their demands. It is also complicated when mechanisms to deal with the past are implemented in politically divided contexts where there is debate on broader societal vision or on transitional justice priorities. Even stakeholders who agree on transitional justice priorities may get entangled in arguments over their implementation.

Dealing with the past in the MENA uprisings

Prior to the uprisings, regional experience with transitional justice was limited. Until 2011, Morocco and Iraq – and to some extent Algeria – were the only MENA countries that had attempted to deal with the past in this way. While the Moroccan experience was groundbreaking for the MENA region – not least in jettisoning traditional religious guidelines and applying the principle of non-discrimination in allocating compensation to descendants – little has been done to address questions of criminal accountability for past abuses. More significantly, it raises questions as to how much merely implementing transitional justice mechanisms reflects change. At the other end of the spectrum, the Iraqi experience is often one that highlights pitfalls to avoid rather than examples to follow, not least in its sweeping approach to de-Ba'athification. Regardless of the success of these contexts, they provide an important background that informs the current transitional justice landscape in countries across the region. Undoubtedly, the flagship revolution to date has been Tunisia.

Tunisia: the first revolution

The self-immolation of Mohamed Bouazizi – a street vendor who set himself alight in protest of humiliation by local police – impassioned people across the country, and his funeral became a protest not just about employment and economics, but the broader oppressive policies of President Zine al-Abidine Ben Ali's regime. By the time Ben Ali fled the country on 14 January 2011, it was clear that a new Tunisia had been born. Three days later, the Prime Minister's office announced the establishment of three investigative bodies – one to focus on political reform,[2] the second to probe violations that had taken place since 17 December 2010,[3] and the third to investigate corruption.[4] A number of legal reforms soon followed, with the passage of decrees on such subjects as access to administrative documents from public authorities (Decree 41 2011; Decree 54 2011), and amending the Code of Military Justice and the Penal Code (Decree 69 2011; Decree 106 2011). In March 2011, a Tunisian court dissolved Ben Ali's political party, the Constitutional Democratic Rally (RCD: *Rassemblement constitutionel démocratique*).

A number of trials were launched in the wake of the Tunisian revolution. Initial prosecution efforts were conducted speedily, with the Court of First Instance of Tunis convicting Ben Ali on charges including embezzlement, money laundering, drug trafficking and unlawful possession of money and jewellery. The Permanent Military Court of Tunis found him guilty of torture related to a 1991 coup attempt. Most notable was the military trial known as Le Kef, in which Ben Ali and a number of other senior officials were charged with murder and attempted murder of protesters during the revolution. While a handful of Le Kef defendants were acquitted, the majority were convicted, with sentences ranging from 10 years' imprisonment to life. Given his departure from the country in January, Ben

Ali was prosecuted *in absentia* in all of these trials.[5] In June 2011, five months after Ben Ali's flight, Tunisia moved beyond domestic prosecution efforts and became the second State Party in the MENA region to join the International Criminal Court (Jordan being the first), signaling renewed support for the struggle against impunity.

Considering the social and economic marginalisation which enflamed the Tunisian revolution, it was no surprise that reparation was swiftly identified as a key priority. Initial steps in this area included the provision of lump sum compensation for those from particular governorates who were killed (TND 20,000) or injured (TND 3,000) during the uprising. This approach was clearly limited, however, and it became evident that more rigorous documentation and criteria were needed. Over the coming months, the government passed several reparation-related decrees, including those providing compensation for physical injury caused during demonstrations (Decree 40 2011), and empowering military tribunals considering uprising-related cases to determine material claims of victims (Decree 69 2011). Subsequent decrees provided for broader material remedies such as education and health care services, as well as more symbolic measures such as establishing monuments and renaming public spaces.[6] These various approaches have caused some confusion due to conflicting definitions and practices as well as lack of clarity of how the individual decrees – and the victims identified therein – relate to each other. These issues may be more clearly resolved now that the Organic Law on Establishing and Organising Transitional Justice has been promulgated and begins to be implemented (see *infra*), as it outlines a reparations policy.

The dissolution of the RCD in March 2011 brought to an end what had been a virtual one-party-rule for decades. In late 2012, a draft Law on Political Isolation of the Revolution was proposed, banning former RCD politicians and other supporters from political life for a period of ten years (later reduced to seven) from when the law comes into force. Human rights organisations objected that without amendments such as the inclusion of due process provisions, the law would effectively ban thousands of Tunisian citizens from their right under international law to take part in the conduct of public affairs.

Tunisians underwent an extensive consultation process, discussing what a transitional justice law can and should look like in order to set the country on a more democratic path. Through this process, undertaken at the behest of the fact-finding commission, a core team, the Technical Commission Supervising the National Dialogue on Transitional Justice, travelled across the country, speaking to men, women and youths in all areas about how they would like to see the abuses of the past addressed.

The fruit of this consultation was born in late 2013, when the Organic Law on Establishing and Organising Transitional Justice was promulgated by the National Constituent Assembly (NCA). The law provides for the establishment of a 15-member Truth and Dignity Commission that would be responsible for addressing the period from 1 July 1955 to the date of the law's issuance. Now that the law has passed, the Commission will need to further develop a comprehensive individual and collective reparations programme, including criteria for compensation and a Fund for the Dignity and Restitution for Victims of Tyranny.

Egypt: a staggered transition?

Given Egypt's place as the largest and most powerful country in the MENA, the image of Egyptian protestors forcing President Hosni Mubarak to step down on 11 February 2011 sent shockwaves across the region. Two months later, his National Democratic Party (NDP) was dissolved by the Higher Administrative Court, which ordered the party's assets to be transferred to the state. Although Mubarak and the NDP left the political scene, the Supreme Council of the Armed Forces (SCAF) remained in power until June 2012, bringing into question how much things had actually changed. More than two years after Mubarak's fall, hopes for real change were fading. The situation in the country deteriorated substantially, and some would argue that the political space became more limited than it had been under Mubarak.

In terms of transitional justice measures, an official investigation was launched in February 2011 to investigate violations committed between 25 January and 11 February of that year.[7] The commission issued its report in April, finding *inter alia* that more than 800 Egyptians were killed during the uprising. Beyond this clarification of the scale of violence, the investigation had several shortcomings, as none of the dead were identified and the commission undertook no investigations into their deaths.[8] Soon after he came to power in 2012, President Morsi established a commission to investigate abuses during the revolution period as well as during the period in which the SCAF ruled the country. While commission members submitted their report – said to be 700 pages long – to the president in December 2012, as of the time of writing it has yet to be made public, despite sustained demands by civil society and multiple commissioners for its release.

Since Mubarak remained in the country, Egypt had an opportunity that Tunisia did not: to prosecute a head of state accused of serious violations of international law. Mubarak was charged with complicity in the murder of demonstrators during the revolution, as well as with other charges related to bribery and corruption. Former Interior Minister Habib al-Adly and four of his aides were brought before the court on charges relating to the killing of demonstrators (Adly and several aides also faced charges relating to damages caused to property during the revolution and failure to adequately maintain public order). The former president's sons Gamal and Ala'a were charged with bribery and corruption.[9]

The trial of Hosni Mubarak began in August 2011, galvanising attention around the globe. As it was the first time a head of state was in the dock in the wake of the revolutions, the event was deeply symbolic and the image of Mubarak in the mesh cage appeared in both national and international media. Although the court found him guilty of complicity in the murder of the demonstrators, no determinations were made about direct responsibility, and several lower-level officials were acquitted entirely. A decision by the Court of Cassation in January 2013 to overturn the verdict (on the ground of procedural lapses in the original trial) resulted in a retrial for the former president and the other defendants charged with the killing of demonstrators. Following delays in the wake of the presiding judge's referral of the matter to another court, the first session of the retrial was held in May 2013.

In October 2011, officials announced that the SCAF was considering reviving the Law on Political Treachery, originally passed in the 1950s to repress Nasser's opposition, in order to address the problem of political corruption. Popular demand for systemic change of abusive and corrupt institutions remained high, and the renamed Political Corruption Law was soon adopted in response. However, like the law that it recycled, the Political Corruption Law had a sweeping effect that could easily facilitate abuse, not only permitting the imprisonment of those convicted of what is broadly defined as political corruption, but also prohibiting them from running for office or even voting. It contained no adequate due process guarantees for those accused of the offence.

Reforms in other key areas – constitutional and legislative – were problematic. In late 2012, amid a welter of criticism of legal shortcomings in the text, members of parliament voted on a draft constitution that placed no limits on military trials of civilians, failed to provide for equality of and non-discrimination against women, did not ensure adequate protections for freedom of expression and allowed for discrimination against members of several religious minorities. The assembly approved the draft soon thereafter, enabling the text to be brought before a referendum. About a week prior to the vote, Morsi issued a declaration that exempted his decrees from judicial review. The declaration had a built-in expiry date – the national adoption of the new constitution and the election of a new parliament. The constitutional draft approved by the parliament passed the national referendum by 64 per cent in December 2012.

In June 2013, sweeping discontent with the actions and policies of Morsi and his government saw millions of Egyptians come out in protest again, in numbers that compared with – and exceeded – those calling for Mubarak's ouster in early 2011. After threatening to intervene if the government did not respond to popular demands for a more inclusive government, the military announced the removal of President Morsi and the suspension of the constitution. On 4 July, Adly Mansour was sworn in as acting head of state. While the interim government promised swift elections, Morsi and a number of his supporters remained in incommunicado detention, and Egypt saw continuing protests in the country from both allies and opponents of the Muslim Brotherhood.

The future of Egypt's transition remains uncertain. It is hoped that the interim government has learned from Morsi's failures of limited change and a government more focused on its own ideology (and its own long-term rule) than on a national vision. However, it must also maintain respect for rule of law if there is to be the necessary foundation for democratic rule. At this stage it is unclear whether Egyptians will feel the benefits of a meaningful transition away from dictatorship.

Libya: building a state

Egypt's neighbour, Libya, was the next domino to fall, and this time the international community became involved. Demonstrations sparked in Benghazi in response to the 15 February arrest of human rights lawyer Fathi Terbil, who had been seeking justice for the 1996 mass killing at Abu Salim prison. Protests swiftly spread to other parts of the country, with calls for national (and international) rallies two days later. Following a brutal crackdown by the Libyan authorities, the UN Security Council took action, referring the situation in Libya since 15 February to the International Criminal Court (ICC) and imposing an arms embargo on Libya as well as a travel ban and asset freeze on Muammar Gaddafi, his family and senior regime officials (UNSC 2011a). The international response expanded over the following months – an international military intervention began, ultimately coordinated through NATO, and an arms embargo and no-fly zone were established (UNSC 2011b).[10] On 27 June, four months after the Security Council referral, the ICC issued an arrest warrant for Gaddafi, his son Saif al-Islam and military intelligence head Abdullah al-Senussi for crimes against humanity (ICC 2011). The conflict continued across the country until late October, when the National Transitional Council (NTC) announced that Gaddafi had been killed in Sirte.

Transitional justice discussions began while the eight-month-long conflict was still underway, with Libyan opposition and international policy makers alike stressing the need to find means to deal with Libya's past abuses as well as violations of international law which took place during the conflict. In an emergency session in February 2011, the UN Human Rights Council established an international commission of inquiry to investigate all alleged violations of international human rights law in Libya and provide recommendations on accountability measures (UNHRC 2011a). The commission issued two reports, raising such issues as truth-seeking, prosecution, compensation and other forms of reparations, and legal reform.[11] In an August 2011 memo on UN post-conflict deployment to the country, Ian Martin, then-UN Special Advisor to the Secretary-General on Post-Conflict Planning for Libya, raised the need for mechanisms to address national reconciliation, avoidance of reprisals, reparations and truth-seeking in a new Libya (Martin 2011). Soon thereafter, the Security Council referred to the importance of transitional justice in a resolution establishing the UN Support Mission in Libya (UNSC 2011c). This was reflected domestically in early 2012, when the NTC adopted a law on transitional justice, which established a Fact-Finding and Reconciliation Commission and provided for reparations. The Ministry for the Affairs of the Families of the Martyrs and the Missing was established, although there appears to be a deeper focus on the martyrs, which has not helped in matters of building trust among the broader pool of victims (Physicians for Human Rights 2013). In late 2013, Libya's General National Congress, the successor to the NTC, adopted a revised version of a formal transitional justice law that provides for, *inter alia*, a modified composition of the Fact-Finding and Reconciliation

Commission, as well as additional provisions on reparations and reaffirmation of the importance of criminal justice and vetting.

While many former regime figures are in detention in Libya today and await trial, a great deal of international attention has focused on how and where to try Saif al-Islam and Abdullah al-Senussi. Libyan authorities challenged the cases' admissibility before the ICC on the ground that its national system is actively investigating them, and that they are able to conduct the trials in-country (ICC 2012b; ICC 2013a; UNSC 2013). However, in July 2013, the ICC rejected the Libyan request to suspend the surrender of Saif al-Islam (ICC 2013b). Three months later, in response to Libya's admissibility challenge on the case of Abdullah al-Senussi (who unlike Saif al-Islam remains under the control of state authorities), the ICC found that Libya is both willing and able genuinely to carry out investigations in his case.[12] While primacy of jurisdiction favours domestic systems if they are willing and have the capacity, there are questions of whether a fair trial is possible in Libya. Concerns about this matter make the inclusion of capital punishment in Libyan law all the more troubling. The possibility of the death penalty also brings into question whether a Libyan trial would comply with international standards.

Yemen: an incomplete transition

In a very different context, Yemen was facing its own transition. Fuelled by domestic discontent in the absence of long-promised reforms, Yemenis began protesting in January 2011, calling for the ouster of then-President Ali Abdullah Saleh. Although he announced in early February that he would not seek re-election, protestors demanded that he step down immediately. The killing of scores of individuals around Change Square on 18 March – now known as 'Friday of Dignity' – enflamed the popular unrest, and led a number of officials in Saleh's government to resign; nevertheless, the president responded by cracking down and declaring a state of emergency. Seeking to achieve a peaceful transition of power and avert a civil war, the Gulf Cooperation Council (GCC) brokered an initiative between the ruling party and the opposition: power would be shared between them, elections would be called and Saleh would be granted immunity from prosecution in exchange for transferring power to his deputy. Although the immunity deal was one-sided, offered only to the president and his aides and not to the opposition, the president repeatedly refused to sign up to it.

In June 2011, Saleh was seriously injured during an attack on the presidential compound, and was taken to Saudi Arabia for medical care. During the period he was being treated, a UN assessment mission called for international, independent and impartial investigations; upholding the need for accountability and an end to corruption; and emphasising the need for national reparations programmes and institutional reforms (UNHRC 2011c). When Saleh returned several months later he said that he would step down 'in the coming days', although little happened immediately despite mounting violence. A Security Council Resolution passed in October 2011 and calling on all parties to sign a settlement agreement on the basis of the GCC initiative increased the pressure (UNSC 2011e). One month later, Saleh signed the deal.

More than two years after the protests began, Yemen's transition remained incomplete. The initiative's power-sharing arrangement established a 50/40 split between the ruling party and the opposition (with the remaining 10 per cent to other parties). As at the time of writing Ali Abdullah Saleh remained in the country, and he and his allies remained engaged in politics.

Taking into consideration the UN mission's recommendations, a Yemeni ministerial committee met in early 2012 to establish a commission to investigate violations in the wake of January's protests. Following extensive negotiations and consultations, President Abdo Rabbo Mansour Hadi – who had served as vice president under former President Saleh – issued a resolution establishing 'an independent and unbiased commission for investigating human rights violations committed in 2011'.[13]

Concurrently, domestic and international policy makers undertook consultations on the establishment of broader transitional justice programming, notably a truth commission together with reparations and preliminary institutional reforms. Provisions in early drafts of the Law on Transitional Justice and National Reconciliation relied heavily on the Moroccan experience, even to the point of echoing its name: the Equity and Reconciliation Commission. Civil society activists, already provoked by the immunity law, were further angered by what they saw as shortcomings in the draft, most importantly its explicit exclusion of criminal prosecutions, but also the limited extent of its consultation process. Partisans favouring broader consultation stressed the importance of discussing a potential truth commission at the upcoming National Dialogue process. Unsurprisingly, the period covered by the commission in the various drafts was deeply contentious, with one text proposing 1990 onward, and another removing the temporal parameters entirely.

In January 2013, President Hadi issued a new draft of the transitional justice law, renamed the Law on National Reconciliation and Transitional Justice. The most striking change was in the period of its mandate, amended to cover from January 2011 to February 2012. As of late 2013, the issue of transitional justice was being discussed within the framework of Yemen's National Dialogue process, with working groups established on transitional justice and on rights and justice (as well as others on related subjects such as armed forces and security or good governance). At the time of writing, however, it is unclear how the draft law and Yemen's process of dealing with its complicated past will proceed.

During the lead-up to the National Dialogue, President Hadi established two additional commissions, one to focus on issues of forcible dismissals from the civil, security and military fields in the southern governorates and the other to address the unlawful seizure of property in the same area. Established to address longstanding issues of concern to the south Yemenis, the bodies clearly also have a broader, confidence-building purpose: the decree stated that they were established 'with a view to creating national dialogue and reconciliation' and in recognition of public interest.

In late April 2013, a Yemeni court ordered an investigation into the responsibility of Saleh and several other former senior officials for the 'Friday of Dignity' incident. At the same time, the Attorney General ordered an inquiry into Saleh's alleged involvement in shelling the home of a prominent opposition tribal leader; at the time of the incident the sheikhs were meeting to mediate between the government and tribal members (Al-Jubari 2013). How far such investigations can proceed domestically in light of the immunity law remains uncertain: while prosecutions clearly fall within the prohibited framework of the law, the status of investigations is less clear. Moreover, even if such investigations cannot be used within Yemen, other states with jurisdiction to consider international crimes could use them within their own courts.

Bahrain: how much of a transition?

The small Gulf state of Bahrain has not experienced the change in government seen by other MENA countries, but it has been affected by the winds of change sweeping the region, with popular demonstrations early in 2011. On 17 February, government security forces attacked pro-democracy protestors gathered at Manama's Pearl Roundabout to voice opposition to the ruling al-Khalifa family. Four protestors were killed and hundreds injured, with three more killed and others wounded in the following days. One month later, and soon after troops from neighbouring Saudi Arabia entered Bahrain to support its military, security forces cleared the Roundabout, with the king declaring a 'state of national safety'. Special military courts were established (Royal Decree 18 2011), access to emergency medical care was restricted (with harassment and attacks on medical personnel accused of treating demonstrators) and state agencies dismissed employees who were absent from work during the period of the demonstrations.

In late June, Bahrain's monarch and head of state, King Hamad bin Isa al-Khalifa, announced that he was establishing a commission of inquiry – the Bahrain Independent Commission of Inquiry – to 'investigate and report on the events occurring in Bahrain in February/March 2011, and any subsequent consequences arising out of the aforementioned events, and to make such recommendations as it may deem appropriate' (Royal Decree 28 2011). Five months later, the Commission issued its nearly 500-page report.[14] It contained a number of strong findings, acknowledging, *inter alia*, that the security services used excessive force; that such behaviour was systematic; that it was questionable whether the military courts conformed to international standards; and that the lack of accountability of security officials had led to a culture of impunity. Recommendations included reviewing the convictions of the military courts, compensating the families of those who were killed, and investigating claims of torture and compensating those who were subject to it.

Although the report included a number of significant elements, the Commission did not identify those responsible, and larger systemic issues that enabled the violence remain unaddressed. Only a handful of policemen were sentenced for uprising-related violence. Subsequently, despite promised reforms, little was done, and violations on the ground continued. Talks between the government and the opposition to break a two-year deadlock bore no fruit. Thus far, the government's talk of change appears to be more rhetoric than reality.

Syria: an escalating conflict

At time of writing, Syria is rocked by a civil war and there appears to be no prospect of an imminent transition from more than 40 years of Ba'athist rule. Although demonstrations in early 2011 were minor compared to those elsewhere in the region, a government crack-down on protesters set in motion an apparently unstoppable escalation. Two years on, the UN estimates that more than 100,000 have been killed, with thousands more wounded, massive property destruction and millions displaced or refugees in neighbouring countries (UN News Service 2013). The violence has been exacerbated by the fragmentation of the opposition, the active participation of fighters from countries around the globe, and an absence of consensus among international policy makers.

Soon after the violence erupted, the UN Human Rights Council established a Fact-Finding Mission to investigate alleged violations, with a view to avoiding impunity and ensuring full accountability (UNHRC 2011b). Upon the promulgation of its report in August 2011, the UN High Commissioner for Human Rights briefed the Security Council in a closed session, urging it to consider referring the situation in Syria to the ICC (Pillay 2011). While the Security Council has held a number of sessions on the crisis, it has been plagued by internal divisions and unable to pass any resolution, other than one establishing (or renewing) the UN Supervision Mission in Syria. In the face of the Council's inaction, the General Assembly strongly condemned the Syrian government in May 2013 for violations of international human rights and humanitarian law, and stressed the importance of ensuring accountability and ending impunity (UNGA 2013). However, the Independent International Commission of Inquiry – the successor to the Fact-Finding Mission – operated throughout this period and issued several reports to date.[15] In the wake of the mass killing in al-Qusayr in June 2013, the Human Rights Council called on the Commission to carry out an investigation into the incident. The Council also explicitly emphasised the need for transitional justice processes to address the Syrian context:

> … [r]eaffirms that the Syrian people, on the basis of broad, inclusive and credible consultations, should determine, within the framework provided by international law, the process and mechanisms to achieve justice, reconciliation, truth and accountability for gross violations, as well as reparations and effective remedies for victims, while underlining the relevance of referrals to the appropriate international criminal justice mechanism under appropriate circumstances (UNHRC 2013).

As is the case in Libya, transitional justice proposals for Syria circulated early, with opposition, the UN and international stakeholders alike emphasising the need to address Syria's recent past (UNHRC 2011d; United States Institute for Peace 2012; Public International Law and Policy Group 2012). While crafting a fixed transitional justice programme for Syria would be premature and counterproductive in the longer term, commonalities became apparent early that may reflect key priorities for a new Syria, and important lessons learned for its authorities to keep in mind.[16] Truth-seeking, for example, has been raised by Syrians and internationals alike. Institutional reform will be essential in a post-Assad era. Dismantling Syria's labyrinthine security systems and rebuilding a weakened judicial system will take time, but will signal an intention to address past abuses at their roots. Care should be taken not to duplicate the Iraqi model of conducting a blanket purge of the Ba'ath Party – one which ultimately weakened the systems that were in dire need of strengthening through reform. Caution should also be taken in ensuring that transitional justice programmes (for Syria or any other country) are based on and reflective of genuine national priorities. Proposals that do not reflect broader national buy-in will likely be haunted by legitimacy challenges, harming their efficacy and encouraging a perception that hoped-for change is merely old wine in new skins.

Finally, it is striking – but perhaps unsurprising – that several countries in the region largely remained on the sidelines despite the uprisings taking place all around them. This has been the case for both Lebanon and Palestine, which have their own complicated legacies that have yet to be addressed. Each is in a delicate situation with its own weakened authorities, and some might suggest that neither really has its own coherent government to overthrow. Additionally, both have intertwined pasts – as well as presents – with one or more of their neighbours, heightening fears that domestic uprisings could lead to the renewal of what outside observers often perceive as perpetual conflict. Nevertheless, changes in the region are certain to influence each of them.

Regional affinities, regional challenges

Transitions in the MENA region began in very diverse circumstances – tribal states, supposed democracies and acknowledged dictatorships. Despite the variance of experiences and of contexts in a region that is far from homogenous, there are a number of common factors that can be seen across the region. Truth-seeking has been identified as a key priority for all of the transitioning contexts, whether through national or international commissions of enquiry or by establishing more specific truth commissions. At the time of writing, three countries across the region – Tunisia, Yemen and Libya – have proposed or promulgated laws to establish formal truth commissions, while interlocutors in more volatile contexts such as Syria have flagged this as a key priority once the situation has stabilised.

Criminal justice has largely been supported by local stakeholders, although not universally and not without controversy. Yemen explicitly took prosecutions off the table in its draft transitional justice law, and troublingly established a one-sided immunity deal. All of the trials in which Ben Ali was charged to date were necessarily held *in absentia*, given his absence from the country. While such trials are permissible under civil law legal systems, there are concerns that they may impair a defendant's right to a fair trial. Regional interest in domestic prosecution has not necessarily translated into greater support for the ICC – indeed, only Tunisia among the uprising countries has ratified the Rome Statute. Unfortunately, the ICC's 2012 decision that it did not have competence to determine whether Palestine was a state for the purpose of the Court's Statute – and thus that it would decline the 2009 Palestinian declaration granting the Court jurisdiction (ICC 2012a) – did little to help the body's perception in the region. While some commentators have raised concerns about the use of prosecutions as retributive and thus divisive in nature, policy makers in the region may wish to consider that for many victims, the recognition and acknowledgement offered through these processes is understood to be reparative.

Given the tight grip that leaders and ruling parties had in many MENA countries, it is self-evident that institutional reforms – most critically of the security sector, judicial and electoral systems – is essential. Constitutional reforms are also being discussed and pursued in several countries in the region, and here much can be learned from the drafting of constitutions around the globe over the last several decades.[17] Initial legislative proposals in Tunisia, Libya and Egypt risked the exclusion of individuals from politics or the judiciary on the sole ground of party affiliation – a worrying indicator that the lessons of Iraq's de-Ba'athification have not been learned.

Reparations have been clearly identified as a priority, but substantial delivery will be difficult while information about the conditions of all victims remains absent. Urgent needs will still need to be addressed through interim measures, of course. However, truth-seeking bodies can play an important role in gathering information that can be used in making decisions about which forms of reparations are most beneficial and to whom they should be distributed. In contexts that are development-dependent, reparations can be especially tricky, as development aid and reparations should not be conflated.

Women across the region played an active role in the uprisings, and they must be fully included in efforts to deal with the complex legacies of their countries' pasts. Sexual and gender-based violence was prevalent in a number of the uprisings, and will have to be sensitively addressed in transitional justice mechanisms established in the region. Additionally, longer-term legacies of violence against women and systemic discrimination against women can – and must – be addressed through these processes. As was seen in the provision of compensation in Morocco, such efforts can provide significant opportunities to promote social transformation from traditional norms that discriminate against women.

Identity – ethnicity and religion in particular – has a highly politicised role in several MENA countries, morphing into an element of conflict for some. Challenges to state structures during the uprisings have opened up space for 'the destructive power of identity politics' (Chase 2013). Transitional justice tools can be used in divided societies to help establish new narratives, recognise victims across groups and promote trust among communities. However, particular care should be taken when crafting such mechanisms in these contexts. They need, *inter alia*, to be seen by all affected groups to provide accountability and to promote trust across communities, to be legitimate and to make state institutions more representative of society. Strategies such as plural or neutral oversight of mechanisms, use of non-discriminatory procedures, broad and inclusive outreach and consultation will be important not just in establishing sound initiatives, but in relaying the clear message that these measures will be built on foundations that promote the rights and dignity of all members of society.[18]

One interesting trend which has been seen in the region is the proposal for comprehensive legislation that seeks to incorporate a package of transitional justice approaches – truth-seeking, reparations, prosecutions and institutional reform – in a single law. As addressed previously, Tunisia, Yemen and Libya took this approach. While this strategy is understandable in seeking to maximise transitional justice gains during the broadest windows of opportunity, it can have complications as well. Such laws may be perceived (rightly or otherwise) as the sole opportunity for crafting national programmes to deal with the past and, as such, debates around them may be all the more pivotal. Moreover, this approach can lead to a context in which the broader societal understanding of transitional justice may be limited to those approaches contained within the specific law – a problematic context for legislation that may be more selective.[19]

Whether from an interest in truth-seeking or criminal justice, reparations or institutional reform, domestic interlocutors across the region have expressed strong views in favour of nationally controlled mechanisms to deal with the past, rather than relying on international or even hybrid processes. Support and technical assistance from outside advisors was (largely) welcome, but ultimately the mechanisms themselves must be nationally staffed and driven.

Looking to the future

Although the political transition in the MENA region is still in its infancy, a number of important lessons can already be drawn from these experiences.

Resist the temptation to borrow too heavily from other contexts. Transitional justice experiences are imperfect things, and every country has faced challenges in implementing good programming in this area. There are important lessons which other contexts can contribute, of course, helping to inform policy makers and civil society elsewhere who may face similar challenges. However, given the different needs and experiences in each country, national stakeholders should avoid adopting 'out-of-the-box' models, and instead carefully consider their own context, developing principled and informed approaches that make the most sense for them. The stakes are too high, and the openings to address them too few, to put these opportunities at risk by simply transplanting what has worked in another context.

Take time when needed. Establishing credible and legitimate processes to deal with complicated legacies of the past is never a speedy process. Policy makers need to strike a careful balance between undertaking sufficient consultation to ensure that mechanisms being established are durable and meaningful, and taking action while the window of opportunity remains open. Identifying short-, medium- and long-term programming options can be useful strategies in delivering a clear message that the new state is committed to dealing with the legacy of past abuse; developing means to address urgent needs; and crafting longer-term programming in a way that can maximise its impact, inclusiveness and legitimacy. As the UN Secretary-General noted in his 2011 report, 'There is also growing evidence that transitional justice measures that evolve over time and involve strong national ownership result in greater political stability in post-conflict settings' (UNSC 2011d: p 6 para 18).

Build on other experiences. Like the mainstream human rights field, the transitional justice field has historically engaged more extensively with civil and political rights than with the full spectrum of rights. It has much thinner experience in areas such as economic crimes and corruption, raising concerns that an impunity gap may remain due to the narrow focus on a more limited set of rights.[20] This can be problematic in contexts across the MENA region where citizens have made clear before and after the uprisings that economic and social rights are critical. Difficulties in realising rights such as rights to an adequate standard of living, to housing and to work were contributing factors to the uprisings, and policy makers in the region must craft transitional justice programming which addresses these core issues. Asset recovery processes will raise their own challenges, not least in determining how best to use any recuperated money or other resources.

Buy-in is essential. Consultation and outreach are needed in all transitional justice contexts, but will be all the more critical for those whose past is deeply autocratic. This should, of course, include the victims, who have what the UN Secretary-General has described as a 'special status in the design and implementation of such processes'.[21] Moreover, new authorities in the region would do well to recognise that success at the ballot box does not translate into a blank check to determine how the legacy of past violence should be addressed. Fears of an old regime being replaced merely with a 'new form of top-down politics that mimic – structurally, albeit not ideologically – what was overthrown during the Arab uprisings of 2010–11' should be meaningfully addressed (Chase 2013). Direct channels of communication with NGOs, victims' organisations and the broader public will help to build stronger mechanisms, identify priorities and promote local ownership. They should be established at the outset, and in a way that recognises that civil society is not monolithic, by including, for example, those in rural areas or representing women, youth and marginalised communities. Resources for implementing transitional justice mechanisms will be limited. Making the best use of them will be vitally important.

Dealing with the past does not end with a report. Transitional justice processes such as truth-seeking bodies, tribunals and reparations programmes are essential if societies in the region are to build new foundations for their future. Reports and judgments will be recorded in history books. But they must be ever-present building blocks if broader social change is to be cemented. Education and other forms of memorialisation are important elements that will need to be included. Teaching the youth of today about past violence and about larger social commitments to prevent its recurrence will be key in building a better future.

It is still early days for the MENA transitions, the outcomes of which are fraught with uncertainty. Even in Tunisia, where progress has been the most apparent, it is unclear whether the achievements to date will survive the vagaries of politics – and, if so, to what extent. In Egypt, the heady idealism of early 2011 has morphed into a tenacious pragmatism focused at least as much on holding onto the progress to date as on developing it further. Yemen and Syria are still in flux, their transitions incomplete and their state-building capacity limited, albeit to vastly different degrees.

These contexts will provide a plethora of challenges for local activists seeking to deal with the legacies of violence. Managing expectations will be onerous – for no country will have unlimited time, funding or resources – but it will be important. Despite the uncertainties, however, one thing is clear: just as the field of transitional justice is helping to shape the transitions in the MENA region, so too will the regional uprisings change the field of transitional justice.

Notes

1 Particular thanks are owed to scores of courageous local activists across the region with whom we have worked over the last two years, and who played an essential role in bringing about the change we are witnessing. Deep gratitude is also offered to the International Center for Transitional Justice's (ICTJ's) current and former Middle East and North Africa specialists, as well as its past and present thematic experts, who have supported efforts towards accountability in the region. Michelle Bouchebel and Jeannie D'Agostino generously provided research support. Responsibility for flaws is wholly my own.

2 The Higher Political Reform Commission, subsequently merged with another body to become the High Commission for the Protection of the Objectives of the Revolution, Political Reform, and Democratic Transition.

3 National Fact-finding Commission on Abuses Committed from 17 December 2010 to the End of Its Mandate, formally established by Law 8 (2011) of 18 February 2011.

4 National Commission for the Investigation of Bribery and Corruption, formally established by Law 7 (2011) of 18 February 2011.

5 For background on the criminal justice efforts in Tunisia, see Human Rights Watch, 'Tunisia: Q&A on the Trial of Ben Ali, Others for Killing Protesters', 11 June 2012, available online at www.hrw.org/news/2012/06/11/tunisia-qa-trial-ben-ali-others-killing-protesters.

6 See in particular Decree 97 (2011) of 24 October 2011 and its amendments implemented through Law No 26 (2012).

7 National Fact-Finding Commission on the 25 January Revolution, at ffnc-eg.org/main.html.

8 The report is available at ffnc-eg.org/assets/ffnc-eg_final.pdf.

9 For background on the trial of Mubarak, see Human Rights Watch, 'Egypt: Q&A

on the Trial of Hosni Mubarak', 28 May 2012, available online at www.hrw.org/news/2012/05/28/egypt-qa-trial-hosni-mubarak.

10 UN Security Council resolution 1973 (2011)established the no-fly zone, enforced the arms embargo and further froze the assets of the Libyan authorities or individuals/entities acting on their behalf, and also authorised member states to take all necessary measures to protect civilians.

11 June 2011 report available online at www2.ohchr.org/english/bodies/hrcouncil/docs/17session/A.HRC.17.44 _AUV.pdf, and March 2012 report available online at www.ohchr.org/Documents/HRBodies/HRCouncil/Regular Session/Session19/A.HRC.19.68.pdf.

12 See http://www.icc-cpi.int/en_menus/icc/press%20and%20media/press%20releases/Pages/pr953.aspx

13 Presidential Resolution No 140 (2012) Pertaining to the Formation of the Commission of Investigation on Human Rights Violations for the Year 2011, 22 September 2012, available online at www.yemen-nic.info/sectors /politics/trans/law13.php.

14 *Report of the Bahrain Independent Commission of Inquiry*, 23 November 2011, available online at www.bici.org.bh /BICIreportEN.pdf.

15 Reports and updates available on OHCHR's Syrian Arab Republic homepage: www.ohchr.org/EN/countries/MENARegion/Pages/SYIndex.aspx.

16 See Ch 3.

17 US Supreme Court Justice Ruth Bader Ginsberg paid particular note to the positive rights model provided by the Constitution of South Africa. See ABC 2012.

18 For more on this subject, see Arthur 2009b.

19 Particular thanks should be noted to Habib Nassar, with whom I have had several valuable discussions on the issue of comprehensive legislation in our work across the region.

20 For more on this subject, see Carranza 2008.

21 See the internal note 'Guidance Note of the Secretary-General: United Nations Approach to Transitional Justice', 10 March 2010, para 6. On file with author.

Bibliography

ABC (2012) 'Ginsburg Likes South Africa as Model for Egypt', 3 February, available online at abcnews.go.com/blogs/politics/2012/02/ginsburg-likes-s-africa-as-model-for-egypt.

Al-Jubari, R (2013) 'Court in Sana'a and General Attorney Order Investigations of Former President Saleh and Company', 29 April, available online at www.yementimes.com/en/1672/news/2284/Court-in-Sana%E2%80%99a-and-general-attorney-order-investigations-of-former-President-Saleh-and-company.htm.

Arthur, P. (2009a) 'How "Transitions" Reshaped Human Rights: A Conceptual History of Transitional Justice', *Human Rights Quarterly* 31.

Arthur, P. (2009b) 'Identities in Transition: Developing Better Transitional Justice Initiatives in Divided Societies', ICTJ, November, available online at ictj.org/sites/default/files/ICTJ-Global-Divided-Societies-2009-English.pdf.

Bahrain Independent Commission of Inquiry (2011) 'Report of the Bahrain Independent Commission of Inquiry', 23 November, available online at www.bici.org.bh/BICIreportEN.pdf.

Carranza, R. (2008) 'Plunder and Pain: Should Transitional Justice Engage with Corruption and Economic Crimes?', *International Journal of Transitional Justice* 2, available online at ictj.org/sites/default/files/IJTJ-Global-Justice-Corruption-2008-English.pdf.

Chase, A. (2013) 'Restructuring Arab States: Do Fractured Politics Require the Tools of Transitional Justice?', *e-International Relations*, 8 January, available online at www.e-ir.info/2013/01/08/reconstructing-arab-states-do-fractured-politics-require-the-tools-of-transitional-justice.

Human Rights Watch (2012a) 'Egypt: Q&A on the Trial of Hosni Mubarak', 28 May, available online at www.hrw.org/news/2012/05/28/egypt-qa-trial-hosni-mubarak.

Human Rights Watch (2012b) 'Tunisia: Q&A on the Trial of Ben Ali, Others for Killing Protesters', 11 June, available online at www.hrw.org/news/2012/06/11/tunisia-qa-trial-ben-ali-others-killing-protesters.

ICC (2011) 'Pre-Trial Chamber I issues three warrants of arrest for Muammar Gaddafi, Saif Al-Islam Gaddafi and Abdualla Al-Senussi', ICC-CPI-20110627-PR689, 27 June, available online at www.icc-cpi.int/en_menus/icc/situations%20and%20cases/situations/icc0111/press%20releases/Pages/pre_trial%20chamber%20i%20issues%20three%20warrants%20of%20arrest%20for%20muammar%20gaddafi_%20saif%20al.aspx.

ICC (2012a) 'Situation in Palestine', Office of the Prosecutor, 3 April, available online at www.icc-cpi.int/NR/rdonlyres/9B651B80-EC43-4945-BF5A-FAFF5F334B92/284387/SituationinPalestine 030412ENG.pdf.

ICC (2012b) 'Application on behalf of the Government of Libya pursuant to Article 19 of the ICC Statute', 1 May, available online at www.icc-cpi.int/iccdocs/doc/Application%20on%20behalf%20of%20the%20Government%20of%20Libya%20pursuant%20to%20Article%2019%20of%20the%20ICC%20Statute.pdf

ICC (2013a) 'Libya's application to Pre-Trial Chamber I', 2 April, available online at www.icc-cpi.int/iccdocs/doc/doc1575650.pdf.

ICC (2013b) 'ICC Appeals Chamber rejects the Libyan authorities' request to suspend the surrender of Saif Al-Islam Gaddafi to the Court', 18 July, available online at www.icc-cpi.int/en_menus/icc/press%20and%20media/ press%20releases/Pages/pr934.aspx.

June 2011 report available online at www2.ohchr.org/english/bodies/hrcouncil/docs/17session/A.HRC.17.44 _AUV.pdf, and March 2012 report available online at www.ohchr.org/Documents/HRBodies/HRCouncil/Regular Session/Session19/A.HRC.19.68.pdf.

Martin, I. (2011) 'United Nations Post-Conflict Deployment to Libya', 22 August, available online at www.innercitypress. com/martin1unlibya1icp.pdf.

Physicians for Human Rights (2013) *Libyan Human Identification Needs Assessment and Gap Analysis*, March, available online at http://physiciansforhumanrights.org/library/reports/libyan-human-identification-needs-assessment-and-gap-analysis.html.

Pillay, N. (2011) 'Statement by Ms. Navi Pillay, UN High Commissioner for Human Rights to the Human Rights Council 17th Special Session on "Situation of human rights in the Syrian Arab Republic" in Geneva', 22 August, available online at www.ohchr.org/en/NewsEvents/Pages/DisplayNews.aspx?NewsID=11321&LangID=E

Presidential Decree 40 (2011) of 19 May 2011.

Presidential Decree 41 (2011) of 26 May 2011.

Presidential Decree 54 (2011) of 11 June 2011.

Presidential Decree 69 (2011) of 29 July 2011.

Presidential Decree 97 (2011) of 24 October 2011.

Presidential Decree 106 (2011) of 22 October 2011.

Presidential Resolution No 140 (2012) Pertaining to the Formation of the Commission of Investigation on Human Rights Violations for the Year 2011, 22 September 2012, available online at www.yemen-nic.info/sectors /politics/trans/law13.php.

Public International Law and Policy Group (2012) 'Planning for Syria's 'Day After' – A Framework for Transitional Justice in Post-Assad Syria', April, available online at

gallery.mailchimp.com/91ab76eaf4f3105e695b69fac/files/PILPG_Report_A_Frame work_for_Transitional_Justice_in_Post_Assad_Syria.pdf.
Royal Decree 18 (2011).
Royal Decree 28 (2011), available online at www.bici.org.bh/wp-content/uploads/2011/08/RoyalOrder28of2011.pdf
Royal Decree 29 (2011), available online at www.bici.org.bh/wp-content/uploads/2011/08/RoyalOrder29of2011.pdf.
UN News Service (2013) 'UN chief, United States Secretary of State, urge political solution to Syrian crisis', 25 July, available online at reliefweb.int/report/syrian-arab-republic/un-chief-united-states-secretary-state-urge-political-solution-syrian.
UNGA (2013) 'The Situation in the Syrian Arab Republic', A/RES/67/262, 15 May, available online at www.un.org/ga/search/view_doc.asp?symbol=A/67/L.63.
UNHRC (2011a), Resolution S-15/1, Situation of human rights in the Libyan Arab Jamahiriya, 25 February, available online at www2.ohchr.org/english/bodies/hrcouncil/docs/specialsession/15/A.HRC.RES.S-15.1_en.doc.
UNHRC (2011b) Resolution A/HRC/RES/S-16/1, 29 April, available online at www2.ohchr.org/english/bodies/hrcouncil/specialsession/16/docs/A%20-HRC-RES-S-16-1.pdf.
UNHRC (2011c) 'Report of the High Commissioner on OHCHR's visit to Yemen', A/HRC/18/21, 13 September.
UNHRC (2011d) 'Report of the Independent International Commission of Inquiry on the Syrian Arab Republic', A/HRC/S-17/2/Add.1, 23 November, available online at www.ohchr.org/Documents/Countries/SY/A.HRC.S-17.2.Add.1_en.pdf.
UNHRC (2013) Resolution, A/HRC/23/L.29, 11 June, available online at daccess-dds-ny.un.org/doc/UNDOC/LTD/G13/146/50/PDF/G1314650.pdf?OpenElement.
UNSC (2011a) Resolution 1970, 26 February, available online at www.icc-cpi.int/NR/rdonlyres/ 2B57BBA2-07D9-4C35-B45E-EED275080E87/0/N1124558.pdf.
UNSC (2011b) Resolution 1973, available online at www.un.org/News/Press/docs/2011/sc10200.doc.htm.
UNSC (2011c) 'Security Council Creates United Nations Support Mission in Libya, Adopting Resolution 2009 (2011)', 16 September, available online at www.un.org/News/Press/docs/2011/sc10389.doc.htm.
UNSC (2011d) 'The rule of law and transitional justice in conflict and post-conflict societies: Report of the Secretary-General', S/2011/634, 12 October, available online at www.unrol.org/doc.aspx?d=3096.
UNSC (2011e) Resolution 2014 (2011), 21 October, available online at daccess-dds-ny.un.org/doc/UNDOC/GEN/N11/559/61/PDF/N1155961.pdf.
UNSC (2013), 'Statement to the United Nations Security Council on the Situation in Libya, pursuant to UNSCR 1970 (2011)', 8 May, available online at www.icc-cpi.int/iccdocs/otp/Prosecutor-statement-to-UNSC-08-May-2013.pdf.
United States Institute of Peace (2012) '*Report* of The Day After Project: Supporting a Democratic Transition in Syria', August, available online at www.usip.org/the-day-after-project.

Chapter 3

Transitional justice in the wake of the Arab uprisings: between complexity and standardisation

Habib Nassar

The popular uprisings that started in Tunisia and have spread around the Middle East and North Africa (MENA) were in many ways fueled by demands for justice and accountability for human rights abuses. Transitional justice has thus emerged as a priority for those societies undergoing political transitions, with the international community joining in. But the Arab Spring is not the first instance of efforts to deal with past human rights atrocities in the region. Indeed, while the repressive regimes that were in place in most MENA countries left very little space for justice and accountability, this did not prevent victims' groups and civil society organizations from campaigning for transitional justice and lobbying the authorities for measures to address victims' rights. Taking advantage of small windows of opportunity offered by political liberalization in a context such as Morocco in the late 1990s and early 2000s, they even succeeded in obtaining a few gains such as the establishment of a truth commission and a reparations program. In post-Saddam Hussein Iraq, the rise to power of political parties representing groups brutally victimized by the former regime opened the door to the adoption of a series of measures aimed at addressing past atrocities. By contrast, in the Algerian and Lebanese post-conflict contexts, victims' groups, despite their relentless mobilization, have not yet succeeded in their efforts at advocating for truth and justice.[1]

While the post-Arab Spring contexts of countries such as Egypt, Tunisia, Libya and Yemen have little in common with Morocco's 'controlled' political liberalization process or Iraq's war-torn society, there are nonetheless important lessons to be drawn from the earlier efforts at justice in the MENA region. In order to identify these, it is first necessary to explore the regional factors and legacies that need to be taken into account when developing transitional justice policies or strategies in the present MENA context. This can also inform our understanding of the progress of transitional justice in the region as detailed in other parts of the book. The chapter then outlines and draws conclusions from the transitional justice efforts in the MENA region that preceded the Arab Spring, before concluding with an analysis of the effects of the emergence of an international transitional justice industry that pushes relatively standardized solutions that neither integrate the lessons of earlier experiences in the region, nor seem to take account of the complexities of the current Arab transitions.

A multi-composite legacy in a complex environment

Ambiguous transitions

While regime change appears to be complete in Tunisia with the collapse of the police state instituted by Zine al-Abidine Ben Ali over the years, the organization of elections in October 2011 and the rise to power of those who opposed the former regime, the rupture with the past has been less clear in other countries in the region. In particular, the balance of power and indeed the direction of the transition more generally remain uncertain in Egypt. There, the Muslim Brotherhood-affiliated Freedom and Justice Party's victory in the legislative and presidential elections led to a post-election period marked by an intense power struggle between the Brotherhood, a loose coalition of opposition parties often referred to as liberals and the army. The army has been considered the main 'regulator' of political life in Egypt since the 1952 revolution, a role that it sought to continue to play by removing the Freedom and Justice Party's President Morsi from office after only one year and calling for new elections and a new constitution. In Yemen, although Ali Abdallah Saleh has stepped down, he and his clan have not given up power. Saleh's party, the General People's Congress, controls half of the government portfolios, and members of his family and former associates still control parts of the army and the security apparatus despite increasing efforts by current president Abdo Rabbo Mansour Hadi to exclude Saleh's men from commanding positions. In addition, the country's stability remains fragile amid heightened tensions between the central government in Sana'a and centrifugal forces including southern separatists, the northern Houthi rebellion and the local branch of al-Qaeda, known as Al-Qaeda in the Arabian Peninsula. In Libya, the regime of Muammar Gaddafi collapsed after months of fighting, yet the government in Tripoli has not managed to expand its authority to substantial parts of the country's territory that remain under the control of local militias who fought against the former regime. At the same time, separatist voices are becoming increasingly loud in Cyrenaica, the eastern part of the country. And in Syria, what started as a popular peaceful uprising against the Assad regime has degenerated into a multilayered conflict marked by a superposition of internal fights and regional proxy wars.

Each of these 'transitions' has thus given rise to a specific balance of power and particular political constraints that no serious transitional justice plan could ignore. Indeed, the conditions resulting from the ambiguous transitions in each country are already shaping the justice choices that have been and are being made. Thus, while Tunisians have generally had enough space to initiate a national dialogue on transitional justice that did not seek to exclude any option, justice choices made so far in Yemen, Libya and Egypt have been limited by such factors as deep political divisions, the survival and ongoing influence of surviving elements of the former regime and the omnipotence of armed militias that do not hesitate to challenge the authority of central governments.

The legacy of crony capitalism and corruption

The end of the Cold War and the subsequent decline of ideologies such as pan-Arab nationalism, anti-colonialism and socialism that served as ideological foundations for many regimes inevitably undermined the legitimacy of ruling parties and their leaders across the Arab region.[2] In this context of weakening legitimacy, autocratic rulers sought new means to reassert their grip on power and consolidate their authority. As part of this effort, they gradually expanded control over their country's economy through privileges and tax 'favors' granted to their families, cronies and sectarian groups while also developing new patron-client networks and ties with the business elite and urban merchants.

The wave of economic liberalization policies that were enacted in the region in the early 1990s and that sought to transform government-controlled economies which had been in place for decades has no doubt facilitated the development of the 'crony capitalism' model in Egypt, Tunisia, Syria and, to a lesser extent, Yemen. This model has seen rulers' families and their entourage take advantage of the privatization of public services and state-owned enterprises in sectors such as telecommunications, oil, banking, tourism and audiovisual media to expand their control over key segments of the economy and to increase their personal fortunes. Indeed, in countries such as Tunisia or Syria it became almost impossible for private entrepreneurs to conduct their business without associating themselves with a member of the rulers' family or one of their cronies.

Over the years, the extraordinary economic influence and wealth garnered by rulers and their families helped them to assert control over the country's economy and thus to consolidate their political power. The growing economic nepotism combined with the prevalent political cronyism in countries such as Egypt, Syria, Yemen, Libya and Tunisia led to the emergence of what could be defined as quasi-monarchical republics or 'presidents for life' (Owen 2011: 1–11) in which sons (or sons-in-law) were groomed to succeed their fathers, and 'ruling families' enjoyed special privileges often comparable to those of royal families in absolute monarchies.

Furthermore, in countries like Egypt, Tunisia and Syria, corruption networks and systems of repression overlapped with each other and were tightly intertwined. Human rights abuses were used to facilitate corruption schemes (Beau and Craciet 2009)[3] and the use of corruption served to fuel the repressive machinery of the regime and replenish its slush funds. Hence, security apparatuses and the military in general were directly involved in business and often implicated in corruption.

The entangling of political and economic power, between corruption networks and systems of repression, is so tight in many MENA countries that no meaningful transitional justice process could overlook the economic dimension of authoritarianism in the region. More particularly, how could a truth-seeking mechanism understand and expose the 'root causes of conflict or repressive rule' (United Nations 2010) and the structural bases of power without taking into account corruption practices and the expansion of crony capitalism since the early 1990s?

Legacies of division and exclusion

Many of the Arab Spring countries have been marred for years by sectarian strife and deep political divisions. In countries such as Bahrain and Syria, what started as peaceful movements for reform and change in 2011 quickly degenerated into conflict with strong sectarianism overtones. These conflicts find part of their roots in long histories of injustice and discrimination against specific ethnic, linguistic and religious groups, as well as of particular regions. More particularly, in many countries in the MENA region, rulers have used and are using political, economic and cultural marginalization of entire regions or communities as a form of collective punishment against groups deemed disloyal to the central government, and thus as a way of consolidating their own power bases. They have also excluded minority groups from minority life and have deprived them of economic power as a way of controlling their ability to advance their claims.

In the Aleppo governorate in Syria, the mostly Sunni Muslim population was for decades excluded from the public services and development programs by the Assads' Alawite-dominated regime. In northern Syria, hundreds of thousands of Kurds were unlawfully stripped of their citizenship and deprived of their lands. In Morocco, the Rif region's mostly Amazigh population was seen by King Hassan II as rebellious; the king thus sought to isolate them from the rest of the country by depriving these areas of essential infrastructure and roads that would link them to other parts of Morocco and of public services as well as development subsidies critically needed to reduce poverty and illiteracy. The same happened in Yemen, where the southern secessionist regions have been politically and economically marginalized by Sana'a following the reunification of the country in 1990 and the north-south civil war of 1994. In Tunisia, the Gafsa Mining Bassin was deliberately neglected as a response to anti-poverty demonstrations that took place in the area in 2008. All of these actions underline major challenges for transitional justice in the region, since it must overcome often deep societal divisions and contribute to reconstructing the social fabric damaged by collective punishment policies and the deliberate marginalization of entire communities or regions. In this context, it is vital for the justice processes to avoid reproducing old patterns of exclusion by ensuring that all components of society participate in the design and implementation of transitional justice plans.

A multilayered and decades-long legacy of widespread human rights violations

While countries like Tunisia and Egypt are confronted with legacies of serious human rights abuses committed by state agents including widespread torture, arbitrary detention and the killing of peaceful demonstrators, other countries that have witnessed armed conflict such as Libya, Yemen and Syria have to address large-scale abuses and crimes that in certain cases constitute crimes against humanity. Moreover, patterns of violations committed in these conflict contexts are not only characterized by their magnitude and gravity but are also distinguished by the type of perpetrators implicated in the crimes since both state and non-state actors are involved. In Syria, for example, the Independent International Commission of Inquiry on the Syrian Arab Republic has documented gross human rights violations committed by government troops, pro-Assad militias known as the Shabiha and rebel forces composed of a myriad of armed groups (Independent International Commission of Inquiry on the Syrian Arab Republic 2013). Complicating things still further is that Syrian belligerents have received arms, logistical assistance and financial support from a range of foreign governments and external actors, which in turn implies that they are at least to some degree indirectly responsible for the human rights atrocities committed.

While the focus of the international media has been on human rights abuses that occurred during the Arab uprisings, most transitioning societies in the region are also confronted with decades-long legacies of human rights violations.[4] The violations of the Gaddafi regime for example started with the coup d'état that brought him to power in 1969. In Tunisia, determining what period should be investigated by the truth commission envisaged by the Transitional Justice Bill was one of the most contentious issues addressed during the National Debate on Transitional Justice.[5] While Islamist forces were generally in favor of investigating human rights abuses that have occurred since the country's independence in 1956, some pro-secular forces sought to limit the scope of investigation to the Ben Ali years in an effort to avoid exposing human rights abuses that took place under his predecessor, Habib Bourguiba, who is revered by many in Tunisia for his social reforms and secularization efforts. In the Transitional Justice Law passed by the National Constituent Assembly on 14 December 2013, Tunisians finally opted to address violations of human rights that occurred since January 1955.[6] In Syria, any investigation into the legacy of human rights abuses by the Ba'ath regime would not be complete if it did not address, for example, the 1982 Hama massacre, considered to be one of the bloodiest episode in Syria's modern history, or cases of enforced disappearance of political opponents that date back to the 1970s and 1980s. In fact, most transitional justice initiatives developed by Syrian activists in the past two years do attempt to address the Hama events of 1982 and the enforced disappearance phenomenon that started in the 1970s.

The scale, gravity, scope and nature of past abuses as well as the type of perpetrators implicated (state versus non-state, national versus international actors) have no doubt shaped the transitional justice debate in the MENA region and will be decisive in some of the choices to be made in the future. This multifaceted legacy of violations is all the more complex given that transitioning societies in the region are confronted with abuses over a span of several decades often involving a succession of authoritarian regimes and conflicts. Most transitional justice precedents in the rest of the world have dealt with the legacy of a single regime or of one particular conflict. That is, even when confronted with a long history of violence and repression, most transitioning societies have so far opted to deal with their most recent history of abuse.[7] The trend among transitioning societies in the Arab region to address or propose to address legacies of abuse left over time by various regimes and conflicts will require a great deal of creativity and innovation that the various transitional justice models and blueprints promoted today by international institutions do not appear to offer.

Economic growth, but at the price of social cleavages and violations of economic and social rights

The past two decades have been marked by economic growth in countries such as Egypt, Tunisia, Morocco and, to a lesser extent, Syria. This growth was a result of multiple factors, including growing foreign investment attracted by the privatization of important sectors such as telecommunications, banking and oil. It also resulted from support in the form of loans and international aid from foreign government and international financial institutions such as the International Monetary Fund and the World Bank – support that has increased since the 1990s. Similarly, transfers of money from MENA expatriates in Europe and the Gulf oil-producing countries increased significantly in the 1990s and 2000s.

However, this growth should not obscure the other side of the coin: in most of these countries, there has also been a significant increase in corruption (as outlined above) as well as increasing inequality in the distribution of wealth and, as a result, widening social cleavages (Khoury 2011: 43–6, esp. 44). This is because neoliberal economic policies adopted in MENA countries led to lower wages, growing levels of unemployment among university graduates[8] and increased restrictions on workers' rights, all of which have fueled anger and frustration among the low-income populations.[9]

While violations of civil and political rights have generated calls for justice and accountability across the region, dealing with legacies of violations of Economic, Social and Cultural (ESC) rights as well as addressing economic crime and corruption have also emerged as a priority for Arab Spring protesters and transitioning governments. It is no coincidence that the self-immolation of Tunisian Mohamed Bouazizi and the popular uprisings that followed in Tunisia and across the region prominently decried favoritism, unemployment and poverty in addition to police abuse and other socio-political injustices. Indeed, the main slogan of the Tunisian uprising – 'Jobs, Freedom, Human Dignity' – and of the Egyptian revolution – 'Bread, Freedom, Human Dignity' – underline the degree to which economic and social issues are a major concern on Arab streets. This concern has only deepened as revelations about endemic corruption of government officials and embezzlement of public funds have emerged over time.[10]

The centrality of socio-economic concerns to the Arab Spring uprisings seems to indicate that transitional justice in the region could well have a broadened purview compared to precedent experiences in the rest of the world. While no one expects transitional justice to provide solutions to economic problems, its mechanisms cannot ignore the economic and social grievances that affect most transitioning societies in the region. Dealing with systems of repression and police states in the region requires an understanding of their economic dimension and a response to the economic and social grievances they caused.

The regional transitional justice precedents

Addressing legacies of mass human rights abuses in the MENA region is not a concern that has only emerged in the wake of the Arab Spring. The region has witnessed successive wars, waves of violence and repression throughout its history, and it is striking to observe that one of the first international initiatives to deal with massive abuse and violence was the establishment of the Beirut International Commission by European powers in 1860. Following the 1860 sectarian violence that erupted between the Christians and Druze populations in Syria and Mount Lebanon – which were then part of the Ottoman Empire – European powers created the Commission, which was composed of representatives of France, Britain, Austria, Prussia and the Ottoman Empire, to bring peace back to Syria and Mount Lebanon and recommend accountability measures for the perpetrators of atrocities committed during the conflict and reparations for the victims. While many of the measures recommended by the International Commission, which formally met in Beirut 51 times between 5 October 1860 and 23 May 1862 (Daou 1996: 20), became a dead letter, this experience probably constitutes the first attempt at international peace-keeping and justice that is recognizably similar to what we now know as transitional justice (Bass 2008: 153–232).

In the region's contemporary history, a number of countries have put in place a range of measures aimed at dealing with past violations. Countries like Algeria and Lebanon have opted for amnesties, paying very little attention to the victims of human rights atrocities in the process.[11] Others, such as Morocco, chose to examine four decades of repression through the establishment of a truth commission that was also tasked with the development of a reparations program for the victims. In Iraq, the 2003 war and the collapse of the regime of Saddam Hussein was followed by a series of accountability measures that focused on perpetrators through prosecutions of former officials and lustration mechanisms. While each of these experiences is necessarily particular to the specific political context in which it took place, important lessons relevant to current MENA transitions can nonetheless be drawn from them.

Algeria: choosing stability over justice

Following the cancellation of the results of the 1992 parliamentary elections, Algeria slid into a violent civil war between the army and armed Islamist groups. The decade long 'dirty war', as many Algerians came to call it, left more than

100,000 dead and over 6,000 missing as a result of atrocities committed by both sides (Human Rights Watch 2005).

The Algerian government, which has largely been controlled by the armed forces since the 1990s' conflict, chose to favor 'national reconciliation' and peace over justice and accountability. Thus, a series of amnesty measures were adopted by the Algerian authorities, culminating with the adoption via referendum of The Charter for Peace and National Reconciliation in 2005, which provided amnesties to members of the armed groups who surrendered to the authorities (Presidential Order No 06-01, Articles 4–17 2006) and immunity from prosecution to the army and security forces (Presidential Order No 06–01, Art 45 2006) who had been involved in grave human rights violations such as torture, extrajudicial killings and enforced disappearances. It also granted compensation to the families of those who disappeared during the conflict and government aid to the families of members of armed groups who benefitted from the amnesty. In a subsequent presidential decree, compensation to the families of those who disappeared during the so-called 'national tragedy' was conditioned on the issuance by the judiciary of a death declaration judgment (Presidential Order No 06–01, Art 37 2006) which in essence meant that for compensation to be paid, the family would have to accept that the disappeared person(s) was dead without further investigation.

The provisions of the Charter were vocally denounced by Algerian victims' groups and international human rights organizations, particularly because impunity was granted to perpetrators of very serious human rights atrocities while the rights of victims and their families to know the truth about what happened and the fate of their missing loved one(s) were ignored. No serious measures were ever taken to investigate the fate of those who went missing. The Algerian President Abdelazzi Bouteflika appointed in September 2003 the Ad Hoc Inquiry Commission in Charge of the Question of Disappearances. The Commission's mandate was to investigate and determine the whereabouts and fate of the disappeared. It was headed by Farouk Ksentini, a lawyer who was also the president of Algeria's National Human Rights Commission (Commission nationale consultative de promotion et protection des droits de l'homme). Despite serious allegations from civil society and victims' groups about the independence of the Commission, many families of victims decided to cooperate with it and submitted individual claims and data they had gathered. Yet, in spite of this cooperation, the Commission, which was operational until March 2005, never published its report and did not share its findings with the families of the disappeared. Ksentini, who claims that he submitted a confidential report to the President, contented himself with declaring in a media interview that the Commission could conclude that state agents were responsible for the disappearance of 6,146 individuals (Benchabane: 2005). No names or information on the whereabouts of the disappeared or the circumstances of their disappearance were ever published.

Despite hostility from the Algerian state and the lack of support they enjoy within Algerian society, survivors and families of the victims of the 'dirty war' have continued their fight for truth and justice. Victims' groups such as Collectif des

Familles de Disparus en Algerie, Djazairouna and Soumoud have never stopped their protests and advocacy efforts for truth and justice in Algeria. However, their chances of success in the current context remain very limited. Algeria has regained stability in the last decade. But as long as the current regime – with its links to the military, which is complicit in the abuses – remains in power with no reform or change, there will be no political will to address the 'dirty war's legacy of human rights atrocities. In the absence of a real political transition, the voices of the victims will remain unheard.

More generally, it appears that Algeria will remain a prisoner of its past, incapable of turning the page of the 1990s' war, as long as impunity prevails and no official effort is made to establish the truth about past abuses. Thus, it is highly problematic that, at present, instead of acknowledging state responsibility in war atrocities, the government continues to praise the armed forces and security services 'for safeguarding Algeria' during the 'national tragedy'.[12] The resistance of the authorities to any form of self-questioning or introspection about their role during the 'dirty war', combined with a relentless glorification of the army's role during the conflict and a concomitant rejection of opposition demands for reform (under the pretext that the 'saviors' of the nation know what is in Algeria's interest) has only contributed to reinforcing Algeria's political immobilism. It seems then that the regime's instrumentalization of the 'national tragedy' has undermined any prospects of change and reform.

Thus, the country appears to be caught in a vicious circle. On the one hand, tens of thousands of Algerian citizens who were victimized during the conflict are denied their rights by an ossified regime that has been incapable of change or reform. On the other hand, the regime's refusal to meaningfully deal with its past and acknowledge victims' rights have significantly contributed to hindering any form of reflection that could have helped to open the door to a reform process. While in Morocco, which we will examine next, political liberalization and transitional justice have sustained each other, it seems that Algeria's official policy of denial and the prevailing political immobilism have mutually fed each other.

Algerian officials present their 'national reconciliation' policy as a model for conflict resolution and transitional justice that can be replicated in other contexts Mordjane 2009). The temptation is indeed strong for other regimes in the region, especially army-controlled regimes, to follow the same path of glorifying the military for their messianic role as protectors and saviors of the nation, a role that exempts them from accountability. The first signs of such an approach are already emerging in Egypt in the wake of the military coup of 3 July 2013. Still, the efforts of the Algerian regime to bury past abuses and sweep the suffering and demands of tens of thousands of its citizens under the carpet have failed. President Bouteflika's frustration and angry reaction to a demonstration by the families of the disappeared is a thundering testimony to such failure: 'You make me feel ashamed in [the rest of] the world; you are like weepers with your photos' (Collective des Familles de Disparus en Algerie 2009).[13]

Morocco's equity and reconciliation process: transitional justice with no transition

Between its independence, in 1956, and the 1990s, an especially repressive political system was in place in Morocco, one that resorted to violence and human rights abuse to silence political dissent and social protests. More particularly, under the reign of King Hassan II, thousands of political activists were targeted by state violence. Security services did not hesitate to resort to enforced disappearance, extrajudicial executions, torture, arbitrary detention and forced exile to crush the opposition. It also used forms of collective punishment against entire regions of the country that were deemed 'unsubdued' by the monarchy. This period has come to be known as the 'Years of Lead'.

In the early 1990s, Amnesty International's regular reports on the human rights situation in Morocco, as well as the revelations made by French journalist Gilles Perrault in his book *Notre ami le roi* (Perrault 1990), broke the silence that up until then had surrounded the Years of Lead, particularly the network of secret detention centers. Faced with international pressure generated by these revelations and the changing international environment marked by the end of the Cold War and the steady emergence of Islamism in the Arab region, King Hassan ordered the release of thousands of political prisoners and introduced timid reforms (Vermeren 2006: 85–97). The political liberalization process initiated by the king led to a rapprochement with left-wing parties and the appointment in 1998 of Abderrahmane el-Youssoufi, a long-time political opponent, as prime minister.

At the same time, the king was confronted by growing demands from victims and their families for the truth about the fate of those who were 'disappeared', as well as for reparations. He asked Morocco's national human rights commission, the Advisory Council on Human Rights (known by its French acronym CCDH)[14] to examine the pending cases of disappearances 'in order to clear them once and for all' (quotes in Freeman and Opgenhaffen 2005). The investigations conducted by the CCDH in the 1990s on cases of enforced disappearance led nowhere. However, the CCDH recommended the establishment of a body to compensate the victims of certain categories of abuse. Aware that a solution to the problem of the victims could no longer be postponed, and in a gesture of goodwill towards left-wing groups who were among those who suffered the most from the Years of Lead's brutal repression, Hassan established the Independent Arbitration Panel (IAP) a few weeks before his death in July 1999, with the limited mandate of delivering monetary compensation to victims of enforced disappearance and arbitrary detention. The panel members were appointed by the new King Mohamed VI and started their work in September 1999.

The IAP, which was operational between 1999 and 2003, eventually distributed up to USD 100 million in compensation, to approximately 7,000 individuals. But victims and their families were very critical of the Panel, whose mandate was denounced as being too limited and whose procedures and compensation criteria were seen as lacking in transparency and consistency. Victims represented by the Forum for Truth and Justice – an NGO established in 1999 by a group of former political prisoners to advocate on behalf of victims – called for a more comprehensive justice process that would go beyond a purely monetary approach and would expose past human rights violations as well as reveal the truth about what happened.

In 2001, the Forum, together with two of the most important Moroccan human rights groups, the Moroccan Association for Human Rights (AMDH) and the Moroccan Organization for Human Rights (OMDH), convened a national civil society symposium to discuss appropriate responses to the grave human rights abuses of the past. The participants in the symposium agreed on plans to establish a truth commission to look into the grave violations and the creation of a comprehensive reparations program. But participants were divided on the question of accountability, with groups led by AMDH favoring retribution while the others were generally in favor of an approach that would focus on truth and reparative justice rather than prosecutions. As a result of these divergent opinions, no position was taken on the question of accountability by the symposium participants, who decided to postpone *sine die* their decision on the issue.[15] The three conveners of the meeting did, however, submit a proposal for a truth commission to King Mohamed. After intense advocacy efforts and long negotiations between the king's advisors and Driss Ben Zekri, a founder and former Secretary-General of the Forum for Truth and Justice[16] who had been appointed by the king as Secretary-General of the CCDH in 2001, Mohamed established the Equity and Reconciliation Commission (known by its French acronym IER) in November 2003, and tasked it with investigating human rights abuses, delivering reparations to victims and recommending measures to prevent the repetition of past abuses and to promote reconciliation. The IER was inaugurated by Mohamed at the royal palace of Agadir in January 2004 and its statute was adopted by royal decree later that year.

The IER mandate limited the scope of its investigation to enforced disappearance and arbitrary detention that occurred between the country's independence in 1956, and 1999, the year of Hassan's death.[17] Yet the commission interpreted its mandate as including looking into extrajudicial killings, violent suppression of peaceful demonstrations, sexual abuse, torture and forced exile (IER, Final Report, Volume I, 62–97). Although the IER could not name individual perpetrators,[18] it was authorised to look into the responsibility of state institutions in past human rights violations (Dahir (Royal Decree) No 1.04.42, Art 9, point 3 2004).

The IER handed its final report to the king in November 2005. It was officially released by the monarch in January 2006 at a ceremony at the royal palace to which representatives of the victims were invited. During the ceremony, the king made a speech insisting on the importance of forgiveness in Islam.[19]

The report documented thousands of human rights abuses, including extrajudicial killings, enforced disappearance, arbitrary detention, torture, sexual violence and forced exile. The IER did not make any significant revelation about the past that prior reports published by human rights groups, as well as dozens of books written by former political prisoners, had not already disclosed. It did, however, expose for the first time the fact that the violent suppression of anti-poverty demonstrations in 1965, 1981, 1984 and 1990 in several Moroccan cities including Casablanca caused a substantial number of victims whose bodies were secretly buried by security forces. While it did not extensively investigate the abuses committed by insurgency groups during the internecine fighting that took place in the wake of the country's independence in 1957–1958, it was the first time an independent report exposed violations committed by these groups.

Although progress was made in the investigation of enforced disappearance cases, many of these remain unresolved, including high-profile cases such as the abduction of opposition leader Mehdi Ben Barka in Paris in 1965 and trade unionist Hussein Al-Manouzi in Tunisia in 1972. Also, it is particularly striking that human rights abuses in the disputed territory of Western Sahara were largely overlooked by the IER in its final report, which only mentions the conflict in passing although it has left thousands of victims since it began in 1975.

As noted earlier, the mandate of the IER forbade the commission from naming the perpetrators. Thus, the report focused on the responsibility of state institutions and security forces in the violations. Moreover, Hassan II, the supreme ruler of Morocco during the Years of Lead, is strikingly absent from the IER report other than references to his magnanimity in opening the door to reforms in Morocco and initiating efforts to deal with past violations.

While it is true that the IER did not make any new revelations about past abuses or name perpetrators, its report offers an official account of what happened and constitutes a recognition endorsed by the king of the state's responsibility for violations during the Years of Lead.

The IER also dedicated one volume to reparations, in which it explained the philosophical and legal basis of the reparation program and its criteria. In addition to an individual reparations program, the IER recommended the development of a collective reparations program for the regions that suffered the most from the repression of the Years of Lead. The reparations program was probably one of the most successful aspects of the IER experience. It provided individual reparations to almost 9,000 individuals (National Human Rights Council 2009: 54–62).[20] Special attention was given to women victims, who were granted additional reparations to take account of their vulnerable situation in Morocco's patriarchal society. A collective reparations program was also instituted to benefit 11 regions (National Human Rights Council 2009: 62–74) which suffered from collective punishment such as deliberate deprivations of public services, infrastructure and development, or which were harmed by the presence of a former secret detention center as well as efforts to conceal the existence of such centers, which led to the isolation of the entire areas where they were located.

As we can see from this brief description of transitional justice efforts in Morocco, the figure of the monarch, whether Hassan II or Mohamed VI, has been omnipresent throughout the gradual process initiated in the early 1990s to deal with past violations. Every measure taken to address past human rights abuses has been presented as a generous gift bestowed upon the Moroccan people by the king. Although the establishment of the IER was clearly the result of years of mobilization by victims' groups and civil society, the creation of the Commission, the appointment of its members, the issuance of its statute and the publications of its final report were all presented as royal gestures of magnanimity. The centrality of the king's image in this process is strongly symbolized by the portraits of Mohamed VI and Hassan II hanging above the heads of victims who testified before the IER during the public hearings the Commission organized in various parts of the country.

The absence of a transition or regime change explains this distinctive characteristic of the Moroccan transitional justice experience. The process took place within the same system that was responsible for the abuses of the past. It started under King Hassan II and was continued by his son who succeeded him. Although it occurred as a result of a political liberalization process, it was never the result of a radical change as was, for example, the case for its Latin American precursors.

Morocco's process thus emerges as a very good example of a transitional justice process with no transition. As such, the Moroccan transitional justice experience may serve as a model for the Arab region's monarchies which, with the notable exception of Bahrain, seem to have resisted the after-effects of the Arab Spring. Indeed, despite its controlled character and the central role the king played throughout the process, the transformative effect it had on Morocco's monarchy cannot be denied. Recognizing, albeit implicitly, the responsibility of the monarchy in past human rights abuses constituted a seminal moment for Morocco. More particularly, admitting that the monarchical institution and the *Makhzen*[21] were involved in past wrongdoings has profoundly impacted the very essence of Morocco's quasi-divine right monarchy in which the king, who also holds the title of Commander of the Faithful, is considered infallible.[22]

Acknowledging past abuses and the monarchy's responsibility in these violations has no doubt cleared the way for more profound change and an acceleration of the liberalization process in Morocco. Aware of such potential, the IER included in its final recommendations a full plan for political and institutional reforms. While the process of implementation of the IER recommendations on institutional reform was slow in the years that immediately followed the release of its final report, it is not a coincidence that many of these recommendations were incorporated into Morocco's new constitution approved via referendum in July 2011 in the wake of the Arab uprisings. In a way, the IER had paved the way for the constitutional reform. While the new constitution is still problematic in a number of respects, especially with regard to the king's executive powers and prerogatives, which remain unchecked, many significant amendments, especially in the area of human rights protection, were particularly welcome (Silverstein 2011). While the IER's transformative effects have been slow and often imperceptible, it has no doubt contributed to advancing victims' rights, particularly the right to truth and the right to reparation. Indeed, despite several gaps, significant progress has been made in the area of truth-seeking. As for reparations, Morocco's innovative approaches in the areas of gender and collective reparations could provide others in the region with important lessons on how to design a comprehensive reparations program. More broadly, while lessons from the overall Moroccan process of transitional justice with no transition might not appear particularly relevant to countries that have witnessed regime change in the context of the Arab Spring, there is no reason why it could not serve as a model to start addressing victims' rights in countries such as Jordan or the Gulf monarchies, where change remains a slow and top-down process controlled by the royal palace.

Iraq: lack of legitimacy and perceived victor's justice

Following the 2003 US-led invasion of Iraq and the fall of Saddam Hussein's regime, several measures were put in place by the occupying forces and the interim Iraqi authorities to address the human rights atrocities of the former Ba'ath regime. These measures included criminal justice initiatives, reparations programs and vetting efforts. But the measures were adopted hastily and involved very little consultation with the various segments of Iraqi society, which was deeply divided as a result of years of sectarian conflict, ethnic-based atrocities and marginalization and exclusion.

The trials of former senior officials by the Supreme Iraqi Criminal Tribunal (SICT) as well as the de-Ba'athification program remain the highlights of Iraq's initiatives aimed at dealing with the Ba'ath regime's legacy.

The SICT is a domestic special court established initially under the auspices of the Coalition Provisional Authority (CPA) to try Iraqi nationals or residents accused of serious crimes such as genocide, war crimes and crimes against humanity that occurred between 1968 and 2003 (Law of the Supreme Iraqi Criminal Tribunal, Law No 10, Art 1, para 2). Although the tribunal was an Iraqi court, it was at first regarded as an American creation (Sissons 2006) as a result of the direct involvement of the US-dominated CPA in its establishment. Cases investigated and tried before the tribunal included the Dujail killings,[23] for which Saddam was sentenced to death and then executed on 30 December 2006, as well as the Anfal Campaign,[24] for which other Iraqi former senior officials were convicted, such as Ali Hassan el-Majid, popularly known as 'Chemical Ali', who was sentenced to death.[25]

The trials before the SICT were marred by serious flaws, including violations of the right to a fair trial. The ostensible interference of the Iraqi government in the court's proceedings[26] and the lack of security that surrounded the trials impacted negatively on the perception that many Iraqis had of the court despite efforts by some of its judges to preserve the integrity of its proceedings. Many Iraqis denounced what appeared to them as victor's justice.

However, it is probably Iraq's de-Ba'athification program that constitutes one of the most divisive measures of the post-Saddam period.[27] While vetting measures are essential to restore society's confidence in state institutions, the wholesale approach adopted in Iraq to exclude former Ba'ath party members from government has only contributed to deepening sectarian divisions and impairing the functioning of the state. As a result, tens of thousands of Ba'ath party members were excluded from state agencies with very little consideration for due process. Instead of examining civil servants' records to check whether or not they were or could have been involved in human rights abuses or corruption, most of them were dismissed as a result of their mere affiliation with the Ba'ath party. This heavy-handed, indiscriminate approach has resulted in Sunni government employees being disproportionately targeted, and has caused resentment among Iraq's Sunnis who perceive de-Ba'athification as a form of political revenge and a tool to exclude them from power. As such, it has contributed to the sectarian tensions in the country rather than helping to dampen them.

Furthermore, de-Ba'athification has seriously impaired the functioning of many government institutions and of the security services, often by depriving them of experienced personnel under the simple pretext that they were former Ba'ath party members, this despite the fact that under Saddam Hussein, it was a quasi-requirement to be a party member to obtain a government job.

Similarly, Law No 3 of 2006, which established the Martyrs Foundation as a body to provide reparations to 'the victims of the extinct Ba'ath' party,[28] was particularly divisive as it expressly denied reparations to all those 'who worked with the former regime in its various institutions' (Law No 3 of 8 January 2006, Art 6, para 1), were loyal to it or were Ba'ath party members.

In considering transitional justice in post-Saddam Hussein Iraq, it seems clear that the move by the Iraqi interim authorities (often under pressure by the US-led CPA officials) to put in place measures aimed at dealing with past human rights atrocities and the legacy of Hussein's regime without undertaking significant public consultations and without the meaningful participation of Iraq's civil society and political forces, was fatal to the process. Indeed, no measure could stand the legitimacy test in Iraq's deeply divided society without an inclusive process that ensured that all segments of Iraq's political, sectarian and ethnic mosaic participate in the design of transitional justice plans. In the final analysis, the perception of political revenge fueled by the lack of consultation and the appearance that justice measures were being unilaterally imposed and instrumentalized by one side only contributed to delegitimizing the process, encouraging division between Iraq's sectarian groups and undermining political efforts to stabilize the country.

The transitional justice industry meets the Arab Spring

Following the wave of popular uprisings that have spread across the region, transitioning MENA societies are now confronted with the huge task of dealing with the complex legacies of decades of repression and human rights abuses. It is important to underline that these multifaceted legacies are not necessarily more complex than many other transitional justice processes in the past decades. More particularly, with the exception of a country such as Syria – which is witnessing an ongoing conflict – the complicated political environments in which MENA societies and transitioning authorities are having to operate is not fundamentally less favorable than many other contexts where transitional justice has taken place over the past three decades. However, a major difference between these earlier transitional justice experiences and those in the MENA region is an over-standardization of the proposed solutions and the rigidity with which an ever-growing international transitional justice industry is approaching the region's complexities.

The booming transitional justice industry

Unlike previous occurrences of transitional justice in Latin America, Central and Eastern Europe and Africa, MENA transitioning societies are confronted with an unprecedented proliferation of international actors seeking to play a role in national transitional justice processes, and pushing a relatively uniform set of transitional justice plans that rarely match the intricacies of the post-Arab Spring contexts. This has led to a situation where national actors are far from controlling transitional justice initiatives, since they are faced with what resembles an unprecedented global transitional justice industry (Theidon 2009). Indeed, what has really characterized the post-Arab Spring transitional justice landscape is the horde of international actors that have deployed their personnel in the region to promote transitional justice and offer their expertise. In addition to several intergovernmental organizations, a multitude of international NGOs and even for-profit businesses such as consulting companies and law firms have engaged in transitional justice in the region. While support provided by international actors has been generally welcomed by the transitional authorities in dire need of technical advice and funding, the proliferation of international interventions in the field of transitional justice has not come without the downsides envisaged by the UN Secretary-General in his 2004 report *The Rule of Law and Transitional Justice in Conflict and Post-Conflict Societies* (United Nations 2004), which criticized the emphasis the international community puts 'on foreign experts, foreign models and foreign-conceived solutions to the detriment of durable improvements and sustainable capacity'.

The most obvious manifestation of this is the succession of international transitional justice conferences in the MENA region and countless visits by foreign experts. There is no doubt that such activities have significantly contributed to nourishing transitional justice debates in several countries with comparative experiences, from which important lessons can be drawn. Indeed, many of the transitional justice efforts described by Anne Massagee in Chapter 2 were developed with the support and sometimes at the initiative of international actors. Thus, the first Libyan transitional justice law was developed 'under international auspices' during the revolution, when parts of the country were still under the control of Gaddafi forces and the conflict was still ongoing. The same phenomenon is repeating itself in the Syrian context, where several full transitional justice plans and draft laws have been developed at the initiative of international actors even before a regime change has taken place and without any clarity about the outcome of the ongoing conflict, the nature of the arrangement or the circumstances that may end the conflict, as well as the balance of power that would characterize the transition.

The larger point here is that plans and legislation proposals that fail to take full and proper account of the realities, circumstances and constraints of the transitions risk compromising or even damaging local justice efforts. Indeed, developing transitional justice plans before the transition has effectively started or while conflict remains ongoing precludes the essential local consultations without which any plan, no matter how comprehensive and sophisticated, will lack the legitimacy and local ownership required to ensure the success of a transitional justice process. Referring back to the earlier section on the Iraqi experience of transitional justice, to avoid the mistakes committed in Iraq, it is indispensable to conduct local consultations on transitional justice as soon as the situation permits and for the findings from these consultations to inform the transitional justice plans that are developed. This is especially the case in strongly divided societies such as in Syria. Yet if we look at the Syria transitional justice proposals currently 'on the market', none envisages the organization of national consultations once the conflict is over. Is this because there is a fear that such consultations would question the central role of international actors and complicate or delay their ability to intervene in the process?

Furthermore, as a result of the relative lack of coordination of interventions led by international actors, national actors have been receiving sometimes contradictory advice regarding transitional justice. For example, on the issue of including economic crimes in the mandate of a truth commission, Tunisian officials and civil society actors received contradictory recommendations emanating from within the same international institution, with some of its experts enthusiastically recommending their inclusion and others strongly advising their Tunisian counterparts against it.[29] At the same time, the requirement to meet with and manage so many international actors distracts national civil society groups and government officials from their own work and activities, to some degree turning them into support actors for their international counterparts. The lack of coordination has also led to a great deal of duplication of efforts in the assistance brought by the international community (Institute for Integrated Transitions 2013).

Standardization of policies and mechanisms

The efforts by international actors to rush national actors into the adoption of transitional justice measures and draft laws that do not match the realities of the transition and lack the legitimacy that could only be acquired through consultation with and the participation of local stakeholders and concerned parties such as the victims can be seen as part of a larger trend in transitional justice; that is, a trend toward increasing standardization of policies and mechanisms promoted by international actors who do not hesitate to propose ready-to-use formulas, much like a fast-food restaurant would serve ready-to-eat meals. This standardization is probably the result of a series of factors.

There is no doubt that the precipitous growth in the number and diversity of international actors anxious to show that they can rapidly develop plans and deploy their resources in the field in a more efficient manner than others often comes at the expense of quality and thoroughness and moreover favors the use of pre-packaged solutions and cookie-cutter approaches.

Another factor is the consolidation over the years of the normative framework of transitional justice. The multiplication of international treaties dealing with aspects of transitional justice, the evolving jurisprudence of international human rights bodies and the plethora of United Nations guidelines and other authoritative documents have contributed to a 'normatization' of the field. The development of new norms in the area of transitional justice is a positive step as it contributes to curtailing impunity and reinforces the protection of victims' rights. But the process can go too far, particularly when the practice is to standardize the mechanisms and policies that serve to implement the norms. Thus, for example, the right to know is the norm, while truth commissions are just an implementation mechanism for that norm; yet, truth commissions themselves are often presented as the norm or standard.

Standardizing policies and mechanisms generates a rigidity that precludes transitional justice from fully addressing the regional and national real-world complexities that were described in the first section of this chapter. The key point is that rather than thinking that a truth commission is the only way to satisfy the right to know, transitioning societies in the MENA region should be creative in the mechanisms and policies they develop in order to capture the multi-composite legacies of the past and the complexities of the existing and future environments. For instance, without a dose of creativity and innovation that would allow local actors to think outside the increasingly rigid framework that transitional justice is sadly becoming, it will be impossible to design the appropriate strategies to deal with the economic dimension of the region's repressive systems. Furthermore, the parachuting of standardized formulas into a particular context means that they are poorly suited to the realities and complexities of each situation, and underlines that policy making is no longer in the hands of the local concerned parties but may be moving gradually into the hands of international technocrats. Clearly, such disempowerment does not bode well for the long-term success of these transitional justice efforts.

Conclusion

While each country in the Arab region has its own specific challenges, and while it is important to avoid treating the region as a homogenous block, there is no doubt that the monarchical republics or 'president for life' (Owen 2012: 1–11) systems that were most affected or swept aside by the Arab uprisings shared a number of characteristics that transitional justice practitioners have to take into account. For instance, Economic, Social and Cultural rights violations, both at the individual and collective levels, have been widespread and have constituted an integral part of the repressive machinery of most autocratic regimes in the region. Such violations have also been pervasive in most conflicts in the MENA region and have underpinned many of the sectarian divisions across the region. Thus, any effective mechanism to deal with the past and achieve justice must take violations of ESC into account. Similarly, the tight entanglement of corruption networks and systems of repression in place in the MENA region means that it is impossible for transitional justice mechanisms to overlook economic crimes and corruption when investigating and exposing systems of repression.

Before turning to the pre-packed solutions that international experts are often keen to promote, local transitional justice actors should look at how other countries in the region dealt or failed to deal with some of the complexities that they were confronted with in their efforts to design the right transitional justice policies. Morocco, for example, offers a sophisticated approach to dealing with economic and social marginalization of communities through collective reparations programs. Iraq's failures offer crucial lessons for countries with divided societies, such as Libya, Syria and Yemen, on how essential it is for every segment of the society to be consulted and involved in the design and implementation of transitional justice policies, and how critical it is for justice mechanisms to be inclusive to prevent delegitimization and perceptions of victor's justice. As for Algeria or Lebanon,[30] the ongoing struggle of the victims and their families clearly demonstrate that a country cannot turn the page of the past by simply ignoring the pleas of tens of thousands of its citizens and leaving them behind.

The MENA region is in dire need of foreign solidarity and assistance. However, it cannot be said often enough that international actors should stay away from promoting ready-to-use formulas. Instead, they should focus on strengthening local capacity and providing national actors with the tools to create, design and implement their own transitional justice policies. Also, instead of pushing for the development of full transitional justice plans while the *ancien regime* is still in power or the outcome of a conflict is still uncertain, internationals should encourage the organization – once the situation on the ground permits – of public consultations and broad participatory processes that would reinforce local ownership and thus the effectiveness of transitional justice programs.

Notes

1 See Ch 5 for a detailed discussion of Lebanon and its non-pursuit of transitional justice, as well as the repercussions of this.

2 Similarly, following the 1978 Camp David agreement and the quasi-normalization of ties between Egypt and Israel, Egypt's regime could no longer use the threat of war with Israel to win the population over.

3 Journalists and political dissidents who exposed corruption were harassed by security services and often prosecuted and arbitrarily detained. In this regard, the case of Tunisian journalist Taoufik Ben Brik is particularly telling. He was harassed and jailed in the 1990s and 2000s for exposing government corruption and the economic problems in Tunisia. Arbitrary detention and unfair trials have also been utilized in many instances to pressure individuals perceived as business competitors of Ben Ali's family or cronies.

4 Some in the region have even called for transitional justice policies that would also deal with abuses of the colonial era.
5 See, e.g. the report of the Technical Commission in charge of Supervising the National Dialogue on Transitional Justice on the Open Day of Dialogue with Human Rights Organizations and Victims Groups, 25 August 2012 (on file with author).
6 Article 17 of Tunisia's Transitional Justice Law.
7 Countries that chose to examine a longer period of their history through their transitional justice process yielded mixed results. Morocco's Equity and Reconciliation Commission, which was tasked with examining abuses that occurred between the country's independence in 1956 and 1999, faced huge difficulties when investigating events from the 1950s and 1960s.
8 A phenomenon at least partly generated by the freeze in government hiring. In Morocco and Tunisia this led to the emergence of the Diplômés Chômeurs movement that was very present in the Arab Spring protests.
9 Many in the region are deeply resentful about the role international financial institutions have played in promoting economic liberalization policies and privatization while turning a blind eye to corruption and human rights violations. Loans granted by these financial institutions to the former regimes have often been denounced in the region as an 'odious debt' that should not be paid back.
10 The publication in late 2009 of *La Régente de Carthage*, a book by French journalists Nicolas Beau and Catherine Graciet, which revealed a series of corruption scandals in which Ben Ali and his family were involved, as well as the release by WikiLeaks on the eve of the Tunisian uprising of US government cables exposing the corruption of the president's family, have contributed to fueling public anger in the country.
11 See Ch 5 for more details on the Lebanese experience.
12 These are the terms used by the Charter for Peace and National Reconciliation (Presidential Order No 06-01 of 27 February 2006, Section Six) to define the involvement of the military and the state institutions in the 'dirty war'.
13 Quote found in press release from 2 November 2009, available online at www.algerie-disparus.org/cfda1/index.php?option=com_content&view=article&id=308:55eme-anniversaire-du-declenchement-de-la-revolution-es-familles-de-disparus-continuent-de-faire-honte-au-president-bouteflika&catid=63:communiques&Itemid=139.
14 Established by King Hassan in 1990. Following the 2011 constitutional revisions, the institution's name has become the National Council on Human Rights.
15 Until this day, Moroccan civil society remains divided on the issue of accountability and prosecutions. The AMDH remains the leading group calling for the prosecution of perpetrators of past abuses.
16 Ben Zekri was a former political prisoner.
17 Officially, the end date was linked to the establishment of the IAP, which occurred right before Hassan's death.
18 Article 6 of Dahir (Royal decree) No 1.04.42 of 10 April 2004 approving the IER's statute.
19 Royal speech of 6 January 2006 marking the end of the IER's mandate.
20 In addition to financial compensation, victims received reparations in the form of healthcare assistance, social reintegration and the settlement of administrative problems. In total, approximately 16,000 victims from the Years of Lead received some form of individual reparations either through the IAP or the IER process.
21 Term used in Morocco to define the royal elite.
22 Morocco's Alaouite Dynasty is also believed to be descended from the Prophet Mohammed.
23 Dujail is a small town in Iraq where 148 people were killed in retaliation for an alleged assassination attempt against Saddam Hussein in 1982.

24 The Anfal Campaign was the genocidal operation launched by the regime against the inhabitants of Iraq's Kurdish region in the north of the country in 1988.
25 Ali Hassan el-Majid received several death sentences in subsequent cases including for the mass killing of Shi'a Muslims in the wake of the 1991 intifada. He was executed in January 2010.
26 Such interference included the removal of judges under the pretext of de-Ba'athification. Also, some judges, including presiding judge Rizgar Amin who resigned in 2006, complained about government pressure and direct interference in cases.
27 On de-Ba'athification, see Sissons and Al-Saiedi 2013.
28 These are the words used to describe the mission of the Martyrs Foundation.
29 Tunisian officials, who asked to remain anonymous, shared their confusion with the author in a conversation in Tunis in October 2012.
30 See Ch 5 on Lebanon.

Bibliography

Bass, Gary (2008) *Freedom's Battle* (Knopf).

Beau, Nicolas and Craciet, Catherine (2009) *La régente de Carthage: Main basse sur la Tunisie* (La Découverte).

Benchabane, A. (2005) 'Me Farouk Ksentini au Forum d'El Youm: Le maintien de l'état d'urgence est justifié', El-Watan, 13 April, available online at www.europarl.europa.eu/meetdocs/2004_2009/documents/fd/faroukksentiniforum_/faroukksentiniforum_fr.pdf.

Collective des Familles de Disparus en Algerie (2009) Press Release 2 November, available online at www.algerie-disparus.org/cfda1/index.php?option=com_content&view=article&id=308:55eme-anniversaire-du-declenchement-de-la-revolution-es-familles-de-disparus-continuent-de-faire-honte-au-president-bouteflika&catid=63:communiques&Itemid=139.

Daou, Father Antoine (1996) *The 1860 Events in Lebanon and Damascus, The Beirut International Commission 1860–1862*, Volumes I and II (Moukhtarat, Beirut).

Dahir (Royal decree) No 1.04.42, Art 9, point 3.

Freeman, Mark and Opgenhaffen, Veerle (2005) *Transitional Justice in Morocco: A Progress Report* (International Center for Transitional Justice, November).

Human Rights Watch (2005) *Impunity in the Name of Reconciliation*, September, available online at www.hrw.org/reports/2005/09/02/impunity-name-reconciliation.

Independent International Commission of Inquiry on the Syrian Arab Republic, Sixth Report, A/HRC/24/46, 16 August 2013 (released on 11 September 2013.

Institute for Integrated Transitions (2013) *Inside the Transition Bubble – International Expert Assistance in Tunisia*, April.

Khoury, Rami (2011) 'The Long Revolt', *The Wilson Quarterly*, Summer 2011, 43-6.

King Mohamed VI (2006) Royal speech of 6 January, available online at www.ier.ma/article.php3?id_article=1531.

Law of the Supreme Iraqi Criminal Tribunal, Law No 10, Art 1, para 2.

Law No 3 of 8 January 2006, Art 6, para 1.

National Human Rights Council (2009) *Follow-up Report on the implementation of [the] Equity and Reconciliation Commission Recommendations*, Rabat.

Owen, Roger (2012) *The Rise and Fall of Presidents for Life* (Harvard Press).

Perrault, Gilles (in collaboration with Christine Daure-Jouvin) (1990) *Notre Ami le roi* (Gallimard).

Presidential Order No 06-01 of 27 February 2006, Articles 4–17, Aiming to Implement the Charter for Peace and National Reconciliation.

Presidential Order No 06-01 of 27 February 2006, Article 45, Aiming to Implement the Charter for Peace and National Reconciliation.

Presidential Order No 06-01 of 27 February 2006, Article 45, Aiming to Implement the Charter for Peace and National Reconciliation, Article 37.

Silverstein, Paul (2011) *Weighing Morocco's New Constitution*, Middle East Research and Information Project, 5 July, available online at www.merip.org/mero/mero070511.

Sissons, Miranda (2006), 'And Now from the Green Zone … Reflections on Iraq Tribunal's Dujail Trial', 20(4) *Ethnics & International Affairs'*, Winter, 505.

Sissons, Miranda and Al-Saiedi, Abdulrazzaq (2013) *A Bitter Legacy: Lessons of De-Baathification in Iraq* (International Center for Transitional Justice, March).

Theidon, Kimberly (2009) 'Editorial Note', 3(3) *The International Journal of Transitional Justice* 295.

United Nations (2004) *The Rule of Law and Transitional Justice in Conflict and Post-Conflict Societies, Report of the Secretary General*, 23 August, available online at www.unrol.org/files/2004%20report.pdf.

United Nations (2010) *Guidance Note of the Secretary-General: United Nations Approach to Transitional Justice*, March, available online at www.unrol.org/files/TJ_Guidance_Note_March_2010FINAL.pdf.

Vermeren, Pierre (2006) *Histoire du Maroc depuis l'indépendance* (La Découverte, Paris).

Chapter 4

Difficult but ultimately rewarding: lessons from transitional justice in Latin America

Andrew G. Reiter

As societies in the Middle East and North Africa (MENA) engage in transitional justice following the Arab Spring, it is important to look elsewhere in the world for lessons that may inform their efforts. Perhaps no region provides a more applicable, broader set of lessons than Latin America. Widely recognized as a global leader in transitional justice efforts, Latin America now has three decades of experience in engaging its authoritarian and violent past. Countries throughout the region have implemented a diverse array of transitional justice mechanisms in response to a wide range of past human rights violations. These decisions have often been controversial and highly contested, were undertaken in continuously evolving political environments, and have achieved various levels of success. Latin America thus presents a unique opportunity to draw important lessons regarding the implementation and effectiveness of transitional justice.

Moreover, the experiences from the region have the potential to particularly inform the current challenges and decisions facing the MENA region. Both regions share a similar history of deeply entrenched authoritarian rule. Libya's Muammar Gaddafi had been in power for over 40 years before he was captured and killed by rebel forces in 2011. Similarly, Egypt's Hosni Mubarak (1981–2011), Tunisia's Zine al-Abidine Ben Ali (1987–2011) and Yemen's Ali Abdullah Saleh (1978–2011) reigned for decades in their countries before the popular protests at the heart of the Arab Spring movement forced them from office. Syria's Bashar Assad, who is the midst of a deadly struggle to maintain power in the face of an increasingly growing armed opposition in a context that has descended into civil war, has ruled since 2000, when he assumed the presidency upon the death of his father, Hafez Assad, who had ruled since 1971.

There are clear parallels between this experience and that of Latin America. In the early 1980s, virtually the entire region – from Central America and the Caribbean, to the Andes and the Southern Cone – was authoritarian, ruled by a combination of dictators, military juntas and one-party regimes. As in the Middle East and North Africa, many of these regimes had been in power for decades and particular individuals dominated politics. Military juntas came to power in Brazil in 1964, Ecuador in 1972, Uruguay in 1973 and Argentina in 1976. General Augusto Pinochet seized power in a coup in Chile in 1973. Alfredo Stroessner was one of the world's longest reigning dictators, having taken control of Paraguay in 1954. Other dictators, such as Jean-Claude Duvalier (Haiti), Hugo Banzer (Bolivia) and Manuel Noriega (Panama), had firm control of national politics.

Much like the Arab Spring, Latin America also experienced a rapid wave of transitions away from authoritarian rule, in the midst of a larger global wave of democratization coinciding with the end of the Cold War.[1] By the early 1990s, nearly all of Latin America was nominally democratic; dictators were ousted and militaries were forced to return to their barracks. In addition, in many cases, these transitions were accompanied by mass, public protests. Demonstrations against the military junta in Argentina were emblemized by the Mothers of the Plaza de Mayo, who peacefully demonstrated for years in an effort to find their missing children who had been 'disappeared' by the regime. In the midst of economic crises and the military's humiliating defeat in the Falklands/Malvinas War against the British in 1982, the Mothers were joined by thousands of other protestors, forcing the regime to call elections and step down from power. Similarly, the Diretas Já movement in Brazil, organized under the common demand for direct elections of the president, grew dramatically in strength in the early 1980s, culminating in mass protests of well over one million people that compelled the military regime to relinquish power in 1985 (Porto 2003).

In addition to their common experiences with authoritarian rule and rapid transitions, Latin America and the MENA region also share a history of open armed conflict and extensive intervention by international powers, particularly the United States. In the MENA region, this is best exemplified by the combined operations of the United States, United Kingdom and France to support Libyan rebels in their efforts to oust Gaddafi in a civil war that killed an estimated 30,000. A civil war now rages in Syria, where around 100,000 are estimated to have been killed so far in just over two years of fighting. The rebels have found shelter in Turkey, have received arms from Qatar and Saudi Arabia, and have been provided vehicles, armor and other supplies from the United States, United Kingdom and France. Moreover, past links in the region, such as the well-known US military support of Mubarak's regime in Egypt, and current relationships, for example the coordinated drone campaign by the United States in Yemen today, will certainly shape transitional justice decisions.

Latin America's experience mirrors this in many ways. El Salvador (1979–1992) and Guatemala (1960–1996) experienced full-fledged, deadly civil wars (killing an estimated 75,000 and 200,000 respectively), with military governments supported by the United States combating guerrilla movements funded and armed by the Soviet Union and Cuba. In neighboring Nicaragua, the left-wing Sandinista movement toppled the regime of dictator Anastasio Somoza Debayle after a long struggle in 1979, only to be challenged itself for the next decade by the Contras, a collection of right-wing paramilitaries based in Honduras and supported by the United States. Colombia has attempted to implement transitional justice in the midst of its ongoing, nearly 50-year-long civil war, involving multiple guerrilla groups and paramilitary organizations. Efforts to engage in transitional justice have been complicated by the heavy participation by these actors in the international cocaine trade, which has drawn the involvement of the United States. Much like Iraq in 2003, the United States even intervened directly in Latin America, launching a full-scale invasion of Panama in 1989 to oust Noriega and install a new regime. Not surprisingly, Panama has enacted a range of transitional justice mechanisms to engage human rights violations committed under Noriega and previous dictators, but has largely refrained from examining any abuses committed by the US forces during the invasion.

In sum, Latin America's long experience with transitional justice enables it to provide many lessons for any countries beginning to engage their violent or authoritarian pasts, but striking parallels between Latin America and the MENA region make these lessons particularly applicable in examining transitional justice efforts in the wake of the Arab Spring. After a brief overview of transitional justice processes in Latin America, this chapter draws on those parallels to discuss four key lessons from the region that can inform transitional justice in the MENA region. It concludes by arguing that Latin America's experience suggests that the engagement with transitional justice will, in the long term, almost certainly be beneficial for the MENA region, despite the length and difficulty of the tasks the region faces.

Latin America's transitional justice experience

Transitional justice in Latin America is impressive for its breadth and depth. Every country with an authoritarian regime or civil war in its past has actively pursued a transitional justice agenda, and most have taken a comprehensive approach and enacted a wide range of mechanisms.[2] Of all of its approaches, Latin America is perhaps best known for trials. The new democratic regime in Argentina famously put the military junta on trial in 1985, convicting five important leaders of the previous regime. In 1995, Bolivia successfully extradited from Brazil, tried and convicted former dictator Luis García Meza, sentencing him to 30 years in prison. Uruguayan courts have successfully convicted two former dictators – General Gregorio Conrado Álvarez and Juan María Bordaberry – for human rights abuses committed during authoritarian rule. Former Chilean dictator Augusto Pinochet spent 503 days under house arrest in London after being indicted by a Spanish court under the principle of universal jurisdiction for crimes committed during his reign (Roht-Arriaza 2005) and spent the remainder of his life under house arrest and awaiting trial by Chilean courts for human rights abuses. Amid a corruption scandal, Peruvian dictator Alberto Fujimori left office in 2000 and took exile in Japan. In 2005, he made an ill-fated attempt to return to power, only to be detained in Chile and eventually extradited to Peru, where he was tried and is now serving a 25-year sentence for human rights violations (Burt 2009).

Latin America can also be considered a global leader in truth commissions. Argentina's National Commission on the Disappearance of Persons (1983–1984) was one of the world's earliest and most prominent truth commissions that served as model for subsequent attempts at uncovering truth around the globe. There have been over a dozen additional truth commissions implemented throughout the region since, including one directly established by the UN in El Salvador as part of its brokering an end to the civil war in 1992 (Buergenthal 1994). Most recently, in 2012, a truth commission in Brazil began investigating human rights abuses committed under its past military regime that left power in 1985.

Yet, while Latin America is well known for its pursuit of justice and truth in recent decades, amnesties have also played a key role in transitional justice processes throughout the region (Olsen et al. 2010). Many outgoing regimes passed self-amnesty laws to cover their abuses before leaving power, such as in Argentina, Chile and Brazil. In Uruguay, democratic leaders enacted a sweeping amnesty for past human rights violations in 1985, and it has been upheld via popular referendum twice (1989, 2009) since (Lessa 2012). In addition, amnesties were central to peace processes to end armed conflict in Central America, and the controversial Justice and Peace Law in Colombia (2005) allows demobilizing paramilitaries to receive reduced sentences in exchange for confessions to crimes and the payment of reparations (Theidon 2007).

In addition, many Latin American countries have enacted reparations programs, either in response to truth commission recommendations or to comply with court orders, including large-scale efforts in Argentina, Brazil, Chile and Peru (Lean 2003; Laplante and Theidon 2007). Vetting of the military was an important part of the peace process in El Salvador (Zamora and Holiday 2007); and, in Argentina, informal *impugnación* procedures allow civilians to challenge promotions in the military and police forces, the appointment of judges and those who seek to hold elected office (Barbuto 2007). In the wake of mass crimes, many countries have also created new institutions, such as human rights ombudsmen offices (Uggla 2004), in an effort to safeguard citizens' rights in the future. Finally, demand for memorialization of past crimes has been extensive throughout the region (Jelin 2007), creating what some have termed a full-fledged 'market' for memory in Latin America (Bilbija and Payne 2010).

In sum, Latin America has implemented a wide range of transitional justice processes in an equally wide range of circumstances over nearly three decades, putting it in a unique position to provide important lessons for the pursuit of transitional justice elsewhere in the world. The following sections discuss four key lessons learned from these experiences that are particularly informative for transitional justice processes following the Arab Spring. First, Latin America demonstrates the inevitability and importance of unique national circumstances in shaping transitional justice responses. Second, the region reveals that these will not be short-term decisions; rather, engaging the past should best be viewed as a process, not an outcome (McAdams 2011), taking place over decades instead of months. Third, transitional justice is not solely a national phenomenon, but is influenced by a variety of international actors. Fourth, engaging the past is not easy. Latin America demonstrates the intrinsic challenges and potential pitfalls of pursuing transitional justice in uncertain political environments. Finally, the chapter concludes by reflecting on the overall effectiveness of transitional justice as an endeavor. Despite the complexity and difficulty inherent in the first four lessons, I argue that Latin America illustrates the positive value of transitional justice: in the long term, it appears to be worth it.

Lesson 1: local context matters

As noted in the introductory section, Latin American countries engaging in transitional justice have done so under a wide range of circumstances. Former authoritarian regimes varied considerably in their duration, loci of power, and levels and types of repression used against their populations. Additionally, some faced little organized resistance to their rule, while others were engaged in full-scale armed conflict. The subsequent transitions to democracy or out of war were in some cases abrupt, with leaders seeking exile or militaries retreating to their barracks. Yet, in other cases, transitions were gradual and tightly controlled by former authoritarian elites who continued to dominate politics well after relinquishing power. These variations demonstrate the importance of local context in understanding the transitional justice responses of new democracies and the relative success of those responses.

While there is important within-region variation, countries in Latin America have typically pursued and achieved more accountability for and greater truth of past human rights violations in situations where past abuses were high, relatively one-sided and perpetrated by key individuals who no longer hold significant political power (Nino 1996; Pion-Berlin 1993). In contrast, countries emerging from less repressive regimes where authoritarian actors or institutions retain significant post-transition power, or where abuses were committed by both sides in an open conflict, have typically pursued amnesties and other less-contentious transitional justice mechanisms, and any major attempts at justice have been destabilizing.

For example, the recent trial of Fujimori in Peru, while momentous, was not entirely surprising. He had ruled Peru for a decade, creating a brutal police state led by the feared National Intelligence Service. Yet he left power abruptly, amid accusations of holding fraudulent elections and embroiled in scandals involving bribery of politicians, embezzling state funds and money laundering, protecting drug lords and arming Colombian guerrillas. In addition, the nature of his resignation (faxed from exile in Japan) left him with few political allies and little influence in Peru (Burt 2009). In addition to Fujimori, his security chief, Vladimiro Montesinos, and several members of the Grupo Colina death squad are also serving prison sentences for a variety of crimes committed during the regime.

Tunisia represents a similar case in the MENA region. It has been relatively free of its authoritarian shadow, as Ben Ali fled the country for exile in Saudi Arabia. The new regime has pursued trials of Ben Ali, several government officials and numerous high and low-ranking officers in the security forces for abuses committed during the uprising and protests in 2010–2011. A Tunisian court sentenced

Ben Ali in absentia to 35 years in prison in June 2011, and a year later a second court sentenced him to life imprisonment for inciting violence and murder. Like with Fujimori, Ben Ali's political influence has been significantly eroded and Tunisia can expect to be able to successfully pursue more accountability in the coming years for crimes committed during his regime.

Many would argue that the impetus for the new democracy in Argentina to pursue trials of the former leaders of the military junta and implement a major truth commission quickly after the transition was the severity of repression under the previous regime – an estimated 9,000 to 15,000 people were killed and disappeared by the military in its 'Dirty War' against subversion (Pion-Berlin 1993). While armed resistance was present in the early years of the regime, in the form of two guerrilla groups – the Montoneros and the People's Revolutionary Army – the violence was disproportionately one-sided. Moreover, the failure of the military to successfully manage the economy or win the Falklands/Malvinas War left it largely disgraced as it left power (Roniger and Sznajder 1999). Demand for truth and justice, therefore, was high in society following the transition. Indeed, the first democratic president, Raúl Alfonsín, ran and won while publicly condemning the junta's self-amnesty law. While military resistance limited early attempts at justice, Argentina has taken a comprehensive approach to transitional justice, and successfully implemented a wide range of mechanisms in several waves over the past three decades.

The new regime in Libya is following a similar path, due to the National Transitional Council's defeat and overthrow of the Gaddafi regime in 2011, in which Gaddafi was captured and killed. The approach to transitional justice to date has been broad. Green Square in Tripoli was renamed Martyr's Square to mark a clean break with the past regime and commemorate those who died in the fighting. The new government has also captured and is beginning trial proceedings against Gaddafi's son, Saif al-Islam Gaddafi, his former intelligence chief Abdullah al-Senussi (both of whom are wanted by the International Criminal Court (ICC)) and dozens of other Gaddafi-era officials. Furthermore, the beginning of a truth commission – the Fact-Finding and Reconciliation Commission – is underway, which will investigate human rights violations going back to Gaddafi's rise to power in 1969. In December 2012, the Commission hosted a truth-seeking and reconciliation conference in Tripoli in partnership with the UN Support Mission in Libya and the UN Development Programme, which included experts from past truth commissions around the world (including Peru). As with Argentina, we can expect a continued comprehensive approach to transitional justice in Libya that will play out over many years, with the added benefit that Gaddafi loyalists are relatively weak and unable to resist efforts, unlike the Argentine military.

In contrast to those cases, estimates are that as few as 400 were killed in a much more populous Brazil during its two-decade long military regime (Archdiocese of São Paulo 1986). The transition in Brazil was also gradual. The 1985 presidential elections were conducted through an indirect, electoral college process and the military exerted significant influence on politics during the term of José Sarney

(1985–1990). True democracy did not return to Brazil until direct presidential elections were finally held in 1989, following the adoption of a new constitution in 1988. The 1979 amnesty law passed by the military regime remains intact today (Abrão and Torelly 2012), and it was not until 2012 that a truth commission was established.

Similarly, in neighboring Chile, the number killed by Pinochet's regime was comparatively low and the worst repression occurred in the early 1970s, immediately following the coup. The regime was also viewed as a success by many Chileans, having steered the economy effectively throughout the 1980s avoiding what, for most Latin Americans, was a 'lost decade' of negative economic growth. In addition, Pinochet retained firm control over the democratic transition process. He remained commander-in-chief of the armed forces, made himself a senator-for-life and secured the loyalty of key judges through appointments (Correa Sutil 1997). While accountability has occurred in Chile, it took many years and several unique factors for it to emerge, and the 1978 amnesty law passed by Pinochet's regime still remains in force.

The case of Yemen follows a similar pattern to Brazil and Chile. The transition in Yemen was highly controlled by Saleh. The new president, Abdo Rabbo Mansour Hadi, was Saleh's vice president and the only candidate on the ballot in the recent election, and Saleh continues to serve as the head of the main political party, the General People's Congress, in the country. It is thus not surprising that no efforts have been made to investigate the past in Yemen, and that the amnesty, demanded by Saleh and his party as a precondition for the political transition, remains intact. Ironically, the most significant initiative of political memory was a museum, opened by Saleh in February 2013 to commemorate his own 33-year rule. It would not be surprising to see Saleh attempt to block any significant transitional justice efforts in Yemen in the future. But, as with Pinochet, this will likely not last forever: as new evidence emerges, external actors exert influence and domestic civil society strengthens, new debates on transitional justice will occur and Saleh's amnesty, and freedom, will be challenged.

Those Latin American countries emerging from armed conflict took a similar negotiated approach to transitional justice. In Guatemala, the UN-brokered peace process contained several amnesty laws, which were subsequently incorporated into the 1996 National Reconciliation Law. The UN endorsed the amnesty as necessary for securing peace between the warring sides and ending a bloody, 40-year civil war that particularly harmed a vulnerable indigenous population in what some have called an 'ethnocide'. Similarly, amnesty was central to the 1992 peace accord that ended the civil war in El Salvador (Braid and Roht-Arriaza 2012). Security concerns during the tenuous peace process were paramount and the amnesty was broadened in 1993, with President Francisco Flores declaring that: 'The prosecution of war crimes would have led to another war' (Martinez 2005). Perhaps no state has relied on amnesty more than Colombia, which has extended nearly a dozen amnesties to various guerrilla and paramilitary groups involved in its civil war dating back to the 1950s (Chernick 2003). Some of these amnesties have been extremely successful in demobilizing individual fighters and, at times, entire armed groups, such as the 19th of April Movement in 1990, which transformed into a political party. Recent attempts have relied on similar tactics in negotiating with the country's various right-wing paramilitary groups, and the state offered guaranteed lenient sentences as part of the peace process. Overall, amnesty has been extremely effective in securing peace in Latin America, and no major civil wars recurred after peace was negotiated. At the same time, however, amnesties have served to prevent accountability in many of these cases and block attempts to engage the past.

Syria represents the MENA case that is most like the civil wars in Central America: after more than two full years of fighting, neither side appears to be near victory. The state has used high levels of violence and committed numerous atrocities against civilians in its effort to cling to power, while the rebels are growing in strength and are now armed and supported by foreign powers and have themselves committed numerous atrocities. Current conditions in Syria suggest that negotiation will be difficult. After all, Assad and his regime are internationally isolated and there is little hope for exile (Crawford 2012). With any exit options removed, Assad may eventually be killed by his foes as Gaddafi was in Libya. In such a scenario, former officials of the Assad regime would likely face trial, and there would be an earnest and successful effort to enact a wide range of transitional justice mechanisms to engage the abuses of Assad's regime, during and before the uprising. Any abuses committed by the rebels would largely be ignored. Yet there is still a chance for a negotiated settlement, especially if Assad is killed or significant splits emerge within the military or ruling regime. The international community would likely seize any such opening to end the bloodshed, and an amnesty would probably be a key component of the process (Quinn and Joshi 2013) and would prevent any other serious transitional justice efforts in the short term.

The most prominent example of transitional justice in the MENA region, that of Egypt, illustrates a unique mix of the factors exhibited in Latin America mentioned above. Mubarak was forced to resign after a 30-year rule due to mass protests in 2011, and he, along with his sons and other top officials of his regime, faced trial shortly after. Mubarak was convicted in June 2012 of not putting a stop to the killing of protesters by the Egyptian security forces during the protests, but the verdict was overturned in January 2013; a retrial began in May 2013 but was adjourned until June 2013 (BBC 2013).

Yet at the same time, the Egyptian military has tightly controlled the transitional justice process (Reiter 2011; Abou-El-Fadl 2012). Accountability has been limited to economic crimes or crimes committed during the protests, not human rights abuses committed during the past three decades of military rule. Efforts to reform the security forces and remove those closely linked to the Mubarak regime have been limited and opaque to the public. The military also pre-empted calls for a truth commission by establishing its own special commission to investigate violations that occurred during the protests. As expected, the commission's findings, released in April 2012, held Mubarak's National Democratic Party solely responsible for the attacks on protesters (International Center for Transitional Justice 2013). It is likely that this pattern will hold for a while; but protests continue to occur over these issues, and as civil society grows, democracy deepens and the military's power gradually erodes, we will almost certainly see a revisiting of the past in Egypt like we did in Argentina. The early beginnings of this process may already be apparent, as a government report, leaked in April 2013, alleges that military officers killed, tortured and abducted Egyptians during the 2011 uprising (Human Rights Watch 2013).

In sum, the key lesson from Latin America is already becoming apparent in the Middle East and North Africa: local contexts matter. The nature of authoritarian rule, the extent of violence and the way in which transitions occurred have all served to shape transitional justice processes in predictable ways, leading to a wide range of outcomes.

Lesson 2: engaging the past is a never-ending process

The second lesson from Latin America builds on the first – while local contexts matter, local contexts also change. Because of Latin America's early transitions in the third wave of democratization, we have, in some cases, now up to three decades in which to examine transitional justice processes. One startling observation is that even in those countries that transitioned 30 years ago, transitional justice is still in the news today. There has been a process of continual reopening of wounds over time in the region. As new information comes to light and political conditions change, we constantly witness new attempts to engage the past. While the continual reopening of old wounds can be unsettling, many contend that the process is healthy for society and a key component of deliberative democracy (Payne 2008), and that the value of transitional justice lies in the process of engaging it (McAdams 2011).

No case in Latin America better illustrates this than Argentina, which has experienced dramatic swings in its transitional justice approach in the decades since its transition (Engstrom and Pereira 2012). While the regime quickly overturned the military's self-amnesty and pursued sweeping trials, including of the junta itself, dissent within the military forced a new amnesty in 1987; and a series of presidential pardons in 1989 set those who had been convicted free. In the 1990s, the state shifted its focus to addressing victims, creating the National Commission for the Right to Identity in 1992, which works with National Genetic Databank to track down children disappeared by the military regime. Millions of dollars in reparations were also paid out during the decade to victims of the Dirty War (Guembe 2006). But the public confessions of former naval officer Adolfo Scilingo in 1995, in which he revealed details of the 'death flights' that the military regime used to dispose of prisoners over the ocean, helped to shift the debate in favor of accountability (Payne 2008). A few years later, trials began again in Argentina and picked up steam in the ensuing decade, making Argentina the clear regional (and perhaps global) leader in human rights trials. Members of the junta who had been pardoned have since been reconvicted in this new round of justice (Sikkink 2011).

In contrast, Chile represents a case where transitional justice underwent a gradual evolution. A truth commission – the National Commission on Truth and Reconciliation – was created shortly after the transition in 1990 and issued a report a year later. In the mid-1990s, the National Corporation for Reparation and Reconciliation operated and provided reparations to victims of Pinochet-era abuses. A new truth commission was established in 2003 – the National Commission on Political Prison and Torture – to examine crimes not covered by the first commission. The detention of Pinochet in London in 1998 then served as a catalyst to spur the circumvention of the 1978 amnesty to begin trials within Chile (Pion-Berlin 2004), trials that continue today.

In many other cases in the region, transitional justice has been and continues to be revisited as human rights movements and courts strengthen, and new information comes to light. The amnesty-dominated negotiated transition in Guatemala, for example, has been challenged in recent years. The recent discovery of millions of documents relating to past human rights violations is now being used by human rights activists to pursue trials (Doyle 2005). The former police chief of Guatemala has been prosecuted, and General Efraín Ríos Montt, former head of the military regime, was convicted of genocide on 13 May 2013, though the Constitutional Court annulled the verdict shortly thereafter and ordered a retrial. Brazil's launching of a truth commission in 2012, more than two decades after its transition, was the result of a concerted push by many activists within the country to reopen past crimes. In Uruguay, creative judges linked former dictator Juan María Bordaberry to the assassination of two Uruguayan legislators in Argentina in 1976 as part of Operation Condor, in which the military regimes of the Southern Cone cooperated to combat dissidents. Ruling that the amnesty in place did not apply since the killings took place outside of Uruguay, Bordaberry was convicted in 2010 and sentenced to 30 years in prison (BBC 2010). He died under house arrest.

In short, Latin America demonstrates the long timeline of transitional justice and its ability to play a central role in politics for years, even decades after a transition. Countries in the MENA region are already experiencing the long process of transitional justice firsthand. Libya is in the very early stages of a truth commission process; one that is likely to continue to be an issue over the next few years. Likewise, the start of the trial of Gaddafi's sons in Libya has been pushed back several times, and in May 2013 was postponed again until September 2013, and future delays would not be unexpected (Reuters 2013).[3] In Egypt, the trial of Mubarak dominated national politics from his removal from office in 2011 to his conviction in June 2012. Yet an appeals court overturned his sentence and a retrial is slated for April 2013, dragging the issue further into the future. In both cases, if Latin America is to serve as a lesson, judicial activity will continue in fits and starts over the coming years.

More broadly, countries in the MENA region are highly susceptible to a reopening of the past as time goes on. New facts are almost certainly going to come to light. Many of the regimes in the region were secretive, in power for a long time and tightly controlled. It is highly likely that we do not know the full extent of abuses. As archives are discovered, documents are leaked and memoirs are written, new attempts at transitional justice will surely follow. While Saleh retains strong control over the transitional justice process now in Yemen, for example, new evidence of previously unknown past abuses or corruption could change public perception dramatically and spur new efforts to engage the past.

Moreover, many of these countries are undergoing their first attempts at democratization and the transitions are so far incomplete. If these societies continue to liberalize over the coming years, courts will become stronger and social movements more active, and we will be likely to see renewed transitional justice efforts. In Egypt, for example, democracy remains unconsolidated and the military retains significant power. If anti-democratic forces weaken over time, we will almost certainly witness society engage in new rounds of transitional justice mechanisms.

The MENA region is thus currently in the early stages of what will likely be a long journey towards confronting its past. If Latin America serves as a lesson, this process should be beneficial, in the long run, for the region. After all, even delayed initiatives in Latin America have coincided with positive developments in democracy and the rule of law. Whether mechanisms implemented many years later contributed to deepening democracy and a stronger rule of law, or were instead a result of improvements in these areas, or both, they were not destabilizing. Reopening old wounds over time, even many years after a transition when conditions are perhaps more opportune, can be an effective way to engage the past.

Lesson 3: the importance of foreign influence

The third key lesson that Latin America can teach the Middle East and North Africa is that transitional justice decisions will not be solely national. A wide range of international actors have had significant influence on transitional justice in Latin America. In many cases, international actors have pursued transitional justice where domestic actors have not, or they have served to prompt national action. At other times, these actors have prevented mechanisms from taking place or have taken control of processes out of the hands of the state in which the crimes were committed.

In Latin America, international courts have served to override domestic amnesties, hold trials where domestic states were unwilling to do so and spur domestic action. As noted above, the Spanish court case against Pinochet was central to the eventually beginning of trials in Chile. The Inter-American Court of Human Rights has also played an important role, ruling against amnesty laws in Peru, El Salvador, Chile and Brazil.[4] Recently, US courts have begun to play a role, as human rights activists bring cases against Latin Americans who committed human rights violations and are now living in the United States. In December 2012, for example, Inocente Orlando Montano, El Salvador's Vice-Minister for

Public Security from 1989–1992, pleaded guilty to immigration fraud and three counts of perjury in a US district court.

The United States has also played a very direct role in shaping transitional justice processes in several cases, namely by removing the ability of Latin American states to engage their own pasts. In its 1989 invasion of Panama, US forces captured Noriega and whisked him off to the United States to stand trial for drug trafficking and money laundering. He was convicted in 1992 and served in prison until he was eventually extradited to France in 2010 (Reichstein 2008). Panama was thus not able to deal with Noriega itself until 2011 when France granted him a conditional release and extradited him to Panama, where he is currently serving a 20-year sentence. More recently, the United States has exerted significant influence on Colombia's attempts to demobilize paramilitaries. While initial demobilizations under the Justice and Peace Law precluded extradition to the United States for drug trafficking, the Colombian government, under pressure from the United States, reversed course in 2008. Over a dozen senior leaders of the United Self-Defense Forces were sent to the United States to stand trial for drug trafficking under the argument that they were still committing crimes from prison, and thus not complying with the law.

Similar international actors have had an important effect already in the MENA region and will likely continue to do so. Most prominently, the ICC's indictment of Saif al-Islam Gaddafi and former intelligence chief al-Senussi has led to a showdown between the court and Libyan government, which wants to try those two individuals itself.[5] The ICC has ordered Libyan authorities to hand them over, but as at the time of writing, Libya has not complied. The effect of the indictments may be to spur a legitimate domestic trial of these two individuals, but if pressure continues, the result may be that the ability to enact justice is removed from Libya's hands. ICC influence is also likely to shape any attempts to engage the past in Mali, where investigations are underway. On the other hand, the ICC will likely not influence future transitional justice efforts in Syria because of Russian and Chinese efforts on the UN Security Council to block ICC intervention in the case.

Foreign states have also been important for transitional justice processes in the region. The amnesty that helped usher Saleh's removal from power in Yemen was part of a framework designed by the Gulf Cooperation Council, a precedent that is in the interest of the six monarchies which make up the council to set (Reiter 2012). The effect of this is to block any attempts at justice in the short term. Saudi Arabia is also notable for providing refuge for Ben Ali from Tunisia, and acting to suppress protests in Bahrain, likely linking itself to any future transitional justice efforts in either country. In addition, the United States will probably work to ensure that transitional justice efforts do not destabilize Yemen and in turn hinder US drone operations in the country, and it would have a keen interest in not seeing abuses committed by Mubarak's regime – a regime the United States heavily supported militarily and financially – too exposed. Finally, foreign powers that aided Libyan rebels and continue to aid Syrian rebels will undoubtedly resist efforts in the future to examine crimes committed by the opposition in the assaults on the Gaddafi and Assad regimes. Overall, foreign states will be heavily involved in transitional justice in the region and, in most cases, will serve to prevent or delay particular initiatives that go against their interests. In sum, like many phenomena in the world, transitional justice is becoming increasingly globalized; and current and future initiatives in the MENA region will undoubtedly be affected by a variety of actors outside of national borders.

Lesson 4: this will not be easy

If Latin America is to serve as an example, the MENA region has a difficult road ahead. The long history of transitional justice in Latin America has been fraught with contention. For example, in the early 1990s, courts in Chile began opening cases into Pinochet-era human rights violations under the concept of the 'Aylwin Doctrine' (named after President Patricio Aylwin) which held that the 1978 amnesty could only be applied after a case was heard and the defendant's commission of the crimes in question was verified. In response, while Aylwin was on a state visit to Scandinavia, the Council of Generals held an emergency meeting in Santiago, replete with soldiers in full camouflage and combat gear carrying bazookas, and armored vehicles patrolling the streets (Human Rights Watch 1994). This act of intimidation served to restrain domestic efforts to hold members of the military accountable.

In a similar case, a group of junior officers (the Carapintadas) in Argentina orchestrated a series of revolts in the late 1980s in the face of the increasing spread of trials for military-era crimes. These military threats led the government to pass the Law of Due Obedience in 1987, which exempted all members of the military under the rank of colonel for any past crimes under the argument that they were simply obeying orders (Payne 2000). In El Salvador, former soldiers revolted numerous times in 1995–1996, demanding payments and compensation promised to them in the 1992 accord. At one point, 500 soldiers occupied the Legislative Assembly, holding deputies hostage.

In Guatemala, contention over the past surrounded efforts to uncover the truth and led to a direct clash between religious and secular leaders. In the aftermath of the civil war, two competing truth commissions operated, one mandated by the UN and the other operated privately by the Catholic Church (Sanford 2003). The commission led by the Church – the Recovery of Historical Memory Project – issued its final report in 1998 (Archdiocese of Guatemala 1999). Two days later, Bishop Juan Gerardi, who had released the report, was found beaten to death in the garage of his home. In 2001, three army officers were convicted of his assassination.

These types of contentious debates surrounding transitional justice have already arisen in the Middle East and North Africa. Tens of thousands of youth protesters marched in Yemen in opposition to the amnesty law, forcing an eleventh-hour amendment that restricted the law's coverage, allowing Saleh's civilian and military aides to be held accountable for criminal or terrorist acts. An active opposition has publicly opposed many of the new Egyptian government's opaque and incomplete transitional justice responses. Religion has also played an important role in the region, with ultraconservative Islamist Salafis using strong rhetoric and mass protests in an attempt to influence the framing of the new constitutional and other reforms in Egypt, and resorting to open violence to challenge the transition itself in Tunisia. In Libya, violence has often occurred in the other direction, with frequent accusations of revenge attacks on former Gaddafi supporters.

The MENA region should be prepared for significantly more contention and debate, and even violence, surrounding transitional justice decisions in the coming years. Still-powerful actors tied closely to previous regimes, such as the military in Egypt, may react harshly if transitional justice efforts attempt to move too far too fast in engaging the past, and may work to block such efforts completely. The Supreme Council of the Armed Forces in Egypt has already demonstrated its power and willingness to intervene in political affairs. Following the transition, it fought to ensure that military courts retained the right to try civilians in the drafting of the new constitution, and has used these courts to prosecute its opponents (Moniem 2013). Then, in July 2013, in a move aided and supported by Mubarak loyalists, the military removed the country's first democratically elected president, Mohamed Morsi, from power in a military coup (Hubbard and Kirkpatrick 2013). The events suggest that the military will continue to work to prevent any serious efforts to engage past abuses in Egypt, at least for the foreseeable future.

Similarly, those with strong views on how new regimes should be shaped, such as the Salafis and other movements, may use pivotal transitional justice debates as political opportunities to mobilize and influence public opinion. Finally, because of the strong public protest element of the Arab Spring, populations (particularly youth) now know the usefulness of protest as a political tool. We can thus expect continued mass protests by young populations, such as has happened in Yemen and Egypt, over controversial transitional justice decisions.

In the end, if the MENA region follows the pattern of Latin America, we can expect there to be many contentious moments that generate significant debate over and, at most, delay specific initiatives; but we should not expect such events to derail the long march of transitional justice in the region.

Conclusion: it will be worth it

The lessons drawn from Latin America perhaps paint a bleak picture for the future of transitional justice in the MENA region. The Latin American experience is one of unique national circumstances leading to constant clashes among domestic and foreign actors taking place over decades, with no end in sight. These efforts have dominated national political agendas, created tensions between countries, consumed the courts, drained financial resources, and, in some cases, even threatened the very transitions that made transitional justice possible. It is reasonable to ask: was all of this worth it?

The answer appears to be yes, particularly in the long term. Despite tensions, debates, threats and even fights surrounding transitional justice, liberalization and democratization continued relatively unabated in the region, and indeed may even have been strengthened by the implementation of transitional justice mechanisms (Olsen et al. 2010). Coups did not occur and authoritarianism did not return. While it took many years in some cases, former authoritarian actors have been fully subordinated to democratic leaders and constrained by the rule of law. Prominent perpetrators have been held accountable across the region, despite strong popular support, early guarantees of amnesty or even temporary exile. Victims have also slowly uncovered the truth about the past and found missing relatives. In many cases, they have extracted meaningful reparations from the state and fought for new rights to be protected by new laws, constitutions and government offices. Social movements have successfully pushed for days of commemoration, official apologies and the construction of meaningful monuments and memorials throughout the region.

In sum, the Latin American experience indicates that the long journey of transitional justice, on which MENA countries are just beginning to embark in the wake of the Arab Spring, appears to be worth it. Each country is starting from its own place and burdened by its unique past. The road they will take will be long and difficult, and almost certainly lead to serious tensions domestically and internationally. But in the end, if Latin America serves as a useful comparison, the region will almost certainly be better off for engaging its past rather than ignoring it.

Notes

1 For an overview of transitions in Latin America, see: Hagopian and Mainwaring 2005.
2 For a concise overview of important scholarship on the Latin American transitional justice experience and what we have learned from it, see: Olsen et al. 2011.
3 For discussion about the circumstances of the detention of Saif al-Islam Gaddafi and the implications of where and how he should be tried, see Ch 10.
4 See *Barrios Altos v Peru* (2001), *The Massacres of El Mozote and nearby places v El Salvador* (2012), *Almonacid-Arellano et al. v Chile* (2006), *Gomes Lund v Brazil* (2010).
5 See Ch 10 for discussion of this issue.

Bibliography

Abou-El-Fadl, Reem (2012) 'Beyond Conventional Transitional Justice: Egypt's 2011 Revolution and the Absence of Political Will', 6(2) *International Journal of Transitional Justice* 318.

Archdiocese of Guatemala (1999) *Guatemala: Never Again!* (Orbis Books).

Archdiocese of São Paulo (1986) *Torture in Brazil: A Report* (English translation of *Brasil: Nunca Mais*), translated by Jaime Wright (Vintage Books).

Barbuto, Valeria (2007) 'Strengthening Democracy: Impugnacíon Procedures in Argentina', in A. Mayer-Rieckh and P. De Greiff (eds), *Justice as Prevention: Vetting Public Employees in Transitional Societies* (Social Science Research Council) 40.

BBC (2013) 'Ousted Egyptian President Hosni Mubarak's Retrial Starts', 11 May, available online at www.bbc.co.uk/news/world-middle-east-22491510.

BBC (2010) 'Uruguay's Ex-Ruler Bordaberry Jailed for 30 Years', 11 February, available online at http://news.bbc.co.uk/2/hi/8511204.stm.

Bilbija, Ksenija and Payne, Leigh A. (eds) (2010) *Accounting for Violence: The Memory Market in Latin America* (Duke University Press).

Braid, Emily and Roht-Arriaza, Naomi (2012) 'De Facto and De Jure Amnesty Laws: The Central American Case', in Francesca Lessa and Leigh Payne (eds), *Amnesty in the Age of Human Rights Accountability: Comparative and International Perspectives* (Cambridge University Press) 182.

Buergenthal, Thomas (1994) 'The United Nations Truth Commission for El Salvador', 27(3) *Vanderbilt Journal of Transnational Law* 498.

Burt, Jo Marie (2009) 'Guilty as Charged: The Trial of Former Peruvian President Alberto Fujimori for Human Rights Violations', 3(3) *International Journal of Transitional Justice* 384.

Chernick, Marc W. (2003) 'Colombia: Does Injustice Cause Violence?', in Susan Eva Eckstein and Timothy P. Wickham-Crowley (eds), *What Justice? Whose Justice?: Fighting for Fairness in Latin America* (University of California Press) 185.

Correa Sutil, Jorge (1997) '"No Victorious Army Has Ever Been Prosecuted ...": The Unsettled Story of Transitional Justice in Chile', in A. McAdams (ed.), *Transitional Justice and the Rule of Law in New Democracies* (University of Notre Dame Press) 123.

Crawford, Jamie (2012) 'Is Assad Seeking Asylum?', CNN, available online at http://security.blogs.cnn.com/2012/12/05/is-assad-seeking-asylum/?hpt=hp_c1.

Doyle, Kate (2005) 'The Guatemalan Police Archives', available online at www.gwu.edu/~nsarchiv/NSAEBB/NSAEBB170/.

Engstrom, Par and Pereira, Gabriel (2012) 'From Amnesty to Accountability: The Ebb and Flow in the Search for Justice in Argentina', in Francesca Lessa and Leigh Payne (eds), *Amnesty in the Age of Human Rights Accountability: Comparative and International Perspectives* (Cambridge University Press) 97.

Guembe, María José (2006) 'Economic Reparations for Grave Human Rights Violations: The Argentinean Experience', in Pablo de Grieff (ed.), *The Handbook of Reparations* (Oxford University Press).

Hagopian, Frances and Mainwaring, Scott P. (eds) (2005) *The Third Wave of Democratization in Latin America: Advances and Setbacks* (Cambridge University Press).

Hubbard, Ben and Kirkpatrick, David D. (2013) 'Sudden Improvements in Egypt Suggest a Campaign to Undermine Morsi', *The New York Times*, 10 July, available online at http://www.nytimes.com/2013/07/11/world/middleeast/improvements-in-egypt-suggest-a-campaign-that-undermined-morsi.html?pagewanted=all&_r=1&.

Human Rights Watch (2013) 'Egypt: Release Report on Abuse of Protesters', 12 April, available online at www.hrw.org/news/2013/04/12/egypt-release-report-abuse-protesters.

Human Rights Watch (1994) 'Chile, Unsettled Business: Human Rights in Chile at the Start of the Frei Presidency', Vol VI, No 6, available online at www.hrw.org/sites/default/files/reports/CHILE945.PDF.

International Center for Transitional Justice (2013) 'Background: A History of Repression, Cautious Optimism', available online at http://ictj.org/our-work/regions-and-countries/egypt.

Jelin, Elizabeth (2007) 'Public Memorialization in Perspective: Truth, Justice and Memory of Past Repression in the Southern Cone of South America', 1(1) *International Journal of Transitional Justice* 138.

Laplante, Lisa J. and Theidon, Kimberly (2007) 'Truth with Consequences: Justice and Reparations in Post-Truth Commission Peru', 29(1) *Human Rights Quarterly* 228.

Lean, Sharon F. (2003) 'Is Truth Enough? Reparations and Reconciliation in Latin America', in John Torpey (ed.), *Politics and the Past: On Repairing Historical Injustices* (Rowman & Littlefield Publishers) 169.

Lessa, Francesca (2012) 'Barriers to Justice: The Ley de Caducidad and Impunity in Uruguay', in Francesca Lessa and Leigh Payne (eds), *Amnesty in the Age of Human Rights Accountability: Comparative and International Perspectives* (Cambridge University Press) 123.

Martínez, Benjamín Cuéllar (2005) 'Los dos Rostros de la Sociedad Salvadorena', in Gilda Pacheco Oreamuno, Lorena Acevedo Narea and Guido Galli (eds), *Verdad, justicia y reparación: desafíos para la democracia y la convivencia social* (IDEA/IIDH).

McAdams, A. James (2011) 'Transitional Justice: The Issue that Won't Go Away', 5(2) *International Journal of Transitional Justice* 304.

Moniem, Dallia (2013) 'The Return of Military Trials in Egypt', *Africa Review*, 9 January, available online at www.africareview.com/Special-Reports/The-return-of-military-trial-in-Egypt/-/979182/1661532/-/k3np8dz/-/index.html.

Nino, Carlos S. (1996) *Radical Evil on Trial* (Yale University Press).

Olsen, Tricia D., Payne, Leigh A. and Reiter, Andrew G. (2011) 'Transitional Justice in Latin America', 13(3) *International Studies Review* 558.

Olsen, Tricia D., Payne, Leigh A. and Reiter, Andrew G. (2010) *Transitional Justice in Balance: Comparing Processes, Weighing Efficacy* (United States Institute of Peace Press).

Payne, Leigh A. (2008) *Unsettling Accounts: Neither Truth nor Reconciliation in Confessions of State Violence* (Duke University Press).

Payne, Leigh A. (2000) *Uncivil Movements: The Armed Right-Wing and Democracy in Latin America* (The Johns Hopkins University Press).

Pion-Berlin, David (1993) 'To Prosecute or to Pardon? Human Rights Decisions in the Latin American Southern Cone', 15(1) *Human Rights Quarterly* 105.

Porto, Mauro P. (2003) 'Mass Media and Politics in Democratic Brazil', in Maria D'Alva Kinzo and James Dunkerley (eds), *Brazil Since 1985: Politics, Economy and Society* (ILAS) 288.

Quinn, J. Michael and Joshi, Modhav (2013) 'Settling Syria Why a Negotiated Peace is Possible – And Likely', *Foreign Affairs*, 6 February, available online at www.foreignaffairs.com/articles/138833/j-michael-quinn-and-madhav-joshi/settling-syria.

Reichstein, Matthew (2008) 'The Extradition of General Manuel Noriega: An Application of International Humanitarian Law to Answer the Question, "If So, Where Should He Go?"' 22(2) *Emory International Law Review* 857.

Reiter, Andrew G. (2012) 'Yemen Loses a Dictator, but Not His Shadow', Op-Ed, *The Christian Science Monitor*, 23 February, available online at www.csmonitor.com/Commentary/Opinion/2012/0223/Yemen-loses-a-dictator-but-not-his-shadow.

Reiter, Andrew G. (2011) 'Failed Transitional Justice in Egypt', *International Policy Digest*, 16 October, available online at www.internationalpolicydigest.org/2011/10/16/failed-transitional-justice-in-egypt/.

Reuters (2013) 'Gaddafi's Son Saif al-Islam Appears Briefly in Court', available online at www.reuters.com/article/2013/05/02/us-libya-gaddafi-idUSBRE9410WS20130502.

Roht-Arriaza, Naomi (2005) *The Pinochet Effect: Transnational Justice in the Age of Human Rights* (University of Pennsylvania Press).

Roniger, Luis and Sznajder, Mario (1999) *The Legacy of Human-Rights Violations in the Southern Cone: Argentina, Chile, and Uruguay* (Oxford University Press).

Sanford, Victoria (2003) *Buried Secrets: Truth and Human Rights in Guatemala* (Palgrave Macmillian).

Sikkink, Kathryn (2011) *The Justice Cascade: How Human Rights Prosecutions Are Changing World Politics* (Norton).

Theidon, Kimberly (2007) 'Transitional Subjects: The Disarmament, Demobilization and Reintegration of Former Combatants in Colombia', 1(1) *International Journal of Transitional Justice* 66.

Uggla, Fredrik (2004) 'The Ombudsman in Latin America', 36(3) *Journal of Latin American Studies* 423.

Zamora, Rubén (with David Holiday) (2007) 'The Struggle for Lasting Reform: Vetting Processes in El Salvador', in A. Mayer-Rieckh and P. Grieff (eds), *Justice as Prevention: Vetting Public Employees in Transitional Societies* (Social Science Research Council) 80.

Chapter 5

The costs of avoiding transitional justice: lessons from Lebanon

Ora Szekely

The Lebanese civil war ended in 1990 following 15 years of carnage that left 150,000 dead, over one million wounded and thousands more missing. But despite the trauma and destruction produced by the war, no process of transitional justice was instituted in Lebanon. A blanket amnesty was granted to all those who had participated in the war. The national focus was to be on reconstruction (if not actual restoration) rather than self-examination. This approach has had mixed success at best. The negotiated settlement that ended the war was known as the Taif Agreement (or the National Reconciliation Accord). It provided for some redistribution of power among Lebanon's various sects, essentially under Syrian custodianship, but did not provide any sort of framework within which the Lebanese could confront the atrocities carried out during the war and reconcile with one another. The militias largely disarmed and rebranded themselves as political parties, which both allowed the war to end and guaranteed that the post-war Lebanese order would remain dominated by the very men who had waged the civil war in the first place. That Lebanon has not experienced (as of this writing) a second major civil war (despite a number of smaller conflicts among the Lebanese and at least one larger war with Israel) is less a result of systemic reform or internal reconciliation than of a combination of Syrian hegemony and simple exhaustion.

While the political divisions in the country today are somewhat different than they were in 1975, the larger issues remain generally the same – a conflict in a neighboring state (then Israel/Palestine, now Syria), leading to an influx of refugees (then Palestinians, now Palestinians and Syrians), in combination with sectarian political rivalry (then the Sunni and Palestinian left versus the Maronite right, now the Shi'ite parties versus the Sunni parties), and the question of what Lebanon's position should be vis-à-vis the wider Arab conflict with Israel (which remains largely the same). That these issues remain so dangerous suggests that Lebanon is a powerful illustration of the essential truth behind the cliché that 'those who forget their history are doomed to repeat it'.

This chapter will attempt to address a number of questions raised by the Lebanese experience: How can Lebanon's approach to post-war transition, that is, the (re)integration of its militias and their leaders into the government and the rejection of a transitional justice process in favor of sweeping the civil war and its costs under the rug, inform ideas about transitional justice in the context of the Arab Spring? In particular, what lessons can countries, currently undergoing their own transitions from authoritarianism, as addressed elsewhere in this volume, learn from Lebanon's post-war transition? This chapter will begin with a brief history of the civil war in Lebanon, followed by a discussion of the Taif Agreement and the political order it established. It will then continue on to a discussion of five 'lessons from Lebanon' for other Arab Spring states making their own transitions from authoritarianism and/or civil war to new systems of government.

The war

The Lebanese civil war was the product of both long-standing political tensions and more recent economic, political and regional pressures. Since gaining its independence in 1943, Lebanon has practiced a form of consociational democracy predicated on the division of power between its confessions, or religious groups. In the context of nationalist mobilization against the French Mandate during the Second World War, an unwritten bargain was struck between the Maronite and Sunni political elites, known as the National Pact. The presidency, the most powerful political position in the government, would be reserved for a Maronite Christian, while the position of prime minister would be reserved for a Sunni and that of speaker of parliament for a Shi'ite. Seats in the parliament would be reserved for Christians and Muslims at a ratio of 6:5. Positions in the military and bureaucracy were likewise apportioned according to sect (Traboulsi 2007:105–6; Salibi 2003).

However, by the 1970s, Lebanon's demographics had changed. Higher Christian emigration and lower birth rates had produced a Christian minority, leading to an increasing sense among Lebanon's Muslims (particularly the Sunnis) that this division of power was no longer fair. At the same time, poverty, pronounced income inequality, lack of economic or educational opportunity and general state neglect in the largely Shi'ite south and the Bekaa Valley led to rising Shi'ite discontent and political mobilization (Ajami 1986). Moreover, the long-standing tensions over whether Lebanon was an Arab country oriented politically and culturally toward the East or an independent country oriented toward the West (which had already produced a brief civil conflict in 1958), had begun once again to boil over (Salibi 2003).

This was compounded by tensions over the presence of 300,000 Palestinian refugees in the country's crowded and under-served refugee camps. Out of fear of the demographic consequences of granting citizenship to a large group of Sunni refugees (mostly on the part of the Maronite elite), the Palestinians had been marginalized both politically and economically since their arrival in 1948, barred from over 70 professions, and severely constrained in terms of where they might live and work.[1] These conditions proved fertile ground for Palestinian radicalization; by the late 1960s, Fatah was using South Lebanon as a base for military operations against Israel, and found the camps to be an excellent source of new recruits. The Maronite right objected to the Palestine Liberation Organization's (PLO's) presence in Lebanon, viewing it as a threat to Lebanese sovereignty and security (not to mention their own position), while the Sunni and Druze left was both ideologically sympathetic to the Palestinian cause and optimistic that the PLO might help further their own political ambitions vis-à-vis a weakening of Maronite power in Lebanon. And, as always, all of the various political factions were supported and egged on by outside sponsors eager to promote their own political programs in what was then the only free marketplace of ideas in the Middle East. On the eve of the civil war, Lebanon was a country of 3.5 million being asked to serve as a political testing ground for a region of 300 million; seen from this perspective, particularly given the weakness of the Lebanese state, Lebanon never stood a chance.

The war itself began on 14 April 1975, with the massacre of Palestinian refugees by Maronite militiamen on a bus in the Beirut neighborhood of Ayn Rummaneh. It was to drag on for 15 years. In some ways, it was less a single conflict and more a series of smaller, overlapping wars. The earliest phase, from 1975 to 1976, pitted the PLO and its leftist allies in the Lebanese National Movement (LNM) against the rightist militias, primarily the Maronite Lebanese Forces (also known as the Phalange); it ended with Syrian intervention against its former Palestinian clients to save the Christians and preserve the status quo, beginning 29 years of Syrian military engagement in Lebanon. The Israeli invasion in 1982 marked a second major round of conflict, which pitted the Israelis and their Maronite Lebanese Forces (LF) (also known as the Phalange) allies against the PLO, accompanied by a secondary conflict, called the Mountain War, between the Druze and Christians on Mount Lebanon. In 1985, the War of the Camps broke out between the Shi'ite Amal militia and some of the Palestinian factions who had managed to hang on in Beirut after 1982. The latter half of the 1980s saw fighting in South Lebanon between Hizbullah and the Israelis and their Lebanese puppet militia, the South Lebanon Army (SLA), and in Beirut between different factions of the PLO. In 1988 and 1989, Christian infighting between the Lebanese Forces and a faction of the army led by General Michel Aoun was devastating for East Beirut, while in the south, fighting raged between Amal and Hizbullah.

These periods of extreme violence were separated by periods of simmering conflict, characterized by sniper fire, bombings, abductions, shelling and occasional massacres. By the end of the war, nearly every faction had fought nearly every other faction and fighting had also broken out within every major faction. All sides had committed atrocities. These included multiple massacres and liquidations of entire refugee camps and villages. The most well-known are probably the massacres at Sabra and Shatila refugee camps in Beirut in September 1982 by the Christian militias with the acquiescence of the Israel military, but there were many others, including massacres in the same camps by Amal in 1985 and

1986, in Christian villages on Mount Lebanon by LNM forces, in Druze villages by Christian forces and in the south by SLA forces (Y. Sayigh 1997; Hanf 1993; Fisk 2002).

In addition to the massacres, a range of other atrocities were also committed against civilians. These included bombardment of civilian areas by all the various factions as well as the Syrians and the Israelis; execution by sniper fire; car and suitcase bombings of civilian areas; kidnappings, both for ransom and for political reasons; 'identity card murders', in which those presenting the 'wrong' kind of ID card at a militia checkpoint were shot on the spot for being a member of the wrong religious group; torture; and sexual assault. Villages (especially in the mixed areas of Mount Lebanon) were 'ethnically cleansed' of Christians or Druze, as were mixed neighborhoods in Beirut. Massive numbers of (primarily Shi'ite) refugees poured into Beirut to escape the fighting in the south. By the end of the war, tiny Lebanon, smaller than Connecticut in the United States, had been carved up into ethnic cantons, and multi-sectarian Beirut was divided by barbed wire, checkpoints and sniper fire. The economy had essentially collapsed. There had been no new parliamentary elections since before the war. A quarter of Lebanon's population, and half of Beirut's, had left. It was in these desperate circumstances that negotiations to end the war were held in the autumn of 1989, in Taif, Saudi Arabia.[2]

The Taif Agreement

The Taif Agreement was signed by the surviving members of the Lebanese parliament on 22 October 1989. It was not immediately clear that the Taif Agreement would prove any more permanent than the many failed negotiations that had preceded it; exactly a month after it was signed, the newly elected president, Rene Mouawad, was assassinated by a car bomb. Nor was Taif welcomed by all parties; in particular, it was rejected by many of those opposed to the Syrian presence in Lebanon.[3] But, by 1991, it had been sufficiently implemented that the war could be said to have ended.

The Taif Agreement had a number of important consequences. The first was for Lebanon's political system, where changes were for the most part in content, not structure, and left many of the inequalities of the pre-war era in place. It did provide for a redistribution of political power within the existing Lebanese system, to the benefit of what was by that point the Muslim majority (broadly conceived). Most importantly, the Sunni post of prime minister was strengthened at the expense of the Maronite post of president, and the number of seats in parliament was increased and split evenly between Muslims and Christians. Overall, however, it was the Sunnis who were overwhelmingly the beneficiaries of the redistribution of power under Taif; the Shi'ites remained under-represented.

The Agreement also included an attempt to institutionalize cross-confessional power sharing. Districts were redrawn such that parties who had formerly had to appeal only to their 'own' constituents now had to win votes from other confessional groups as well. But while this has forced parties to put those outside their normal constituency on their electoral lists, this has mainly been a cosmetic change and has not resulted in a serious shift in the confessional nature of Lebanon's politics. A mechanism for the eventual abolition of consociationalism was discussed; a council was to be appointed to oversee this transition, though it did not propose a timeline (Taif Agreement, section 1, sub-section II, article G). One outcome might have been a bicameral system with a non-sectarian lower house and an upper house that would provide proportional representation for Lebanon's sects and ensure that minorities retained a voice, as described in the 1926 Constitution (Traboulsi 2007: 244). However, this council was never established, and consociationalism as the bedrock of Lebanese democracy remained intact.

The second major effect of Taif was the official disarmament of 'all the Lebanese and non-Lebanese militias' (Taif Agreement, section II) under the auspices of the Syrian military (see below). Nearly all of the Lebanese militias did indeed disarm, or at least surrender their heavy weaponry. Some fighters were incorporated into the Lebanese military and security forces; others transitioned into civilian life. The major exception to this process was Hizbullah, which was allowed to remain armed because it was termed a 'national resistance' rather than a militia. (Even today, at Hizbullah rallies, one can see signs saying 'the resistance is NOT a militia'.[4]) Hizbullah's allies among the Palestinian parties, particularly the Popular Front for the Liberation of Palestine – General Command (PFLP-GC) also retained many of their arms, although they do not represent a significant military force.

A third effect was the establishment of a 'Pax Syriana' in Lebanon. In essence, it established Syria as hegemon in Lebanon, the guarantor of security and final source of authority. In 1991, Syria and Lebanon signed a 'Treaty of Brotherhood and Cooperation', further cementing this principle. The Syrian military remained in Lebanon until 2005, when massive demonstrations following Prime Minister Rafiq Hariri's assassination forced them to withdraw. During those 15 years, although there was a Lebanese president at Baabda Palace, a Lebanese prime minister and elections held for the Lebanese parliament, a powerful veto was exercised by the Syrian military intelligence headquarters in the Bekaa, headed by Ghazi Kanaan. His authority was backed by 15,000 Syrian troops and a massive network of informants. Anti-Syrian parties were banned and driven underground, election results were strongly controlled and even Hizbullah's resistance activities in South Lebanon had to be coordinated with the Syrian-controlled Lebanese government. Dissidents (ranging from members of the rightist Lebanese forces to the Communist Party) were arrested, tortured and disappeared. The Syrian occupation also proved to be a drain on the economy, as funds were siphoned out of Lebanon and into Syria (Blanford 2006).

At the same time, however, Syrian domination also produced more stability than Lebanon had seen in two decades, and provided an umbrella under which reconstruction, championed by Prime Minister Hariri, could begin. In some ways, the Syrian occupation represented a period of stasis; the war was over and reconstruction was underway, but the political tensions which led to the conflict were never addressed, nor were the atrocities of the war confronted on a national level. This is reflected in the fact that after the Syrian withdrawal, Lebanese politics became almost instantly divided into an anti-Syrian camp (composed of most Sunni and some Christian parties) called the March 14th coalition, after the date of the largest of the anti-Syrian protests, and a pro-Syrian coalition (composed of the Shi'ite parties and the other Christian parties), called March 8th, after the date of the largest pro-Syrian protest.

The Taif Agreement did not provide for structural reform of the Lebanese political system, or initiate a serious national conversation about the communal and economic tensions which had produced the Lebanese catastrophe in the first place. The promised council to transition Lebanon into a non-sectarian system never materialized. While power was reallocated somewhat, consociationalism remained the basis of the Lebanese political system and confessional identity the primary frame through which Lebanese citizens experienced their interactions with the state. Moreover, the Taif Agreement left many of the same political players in place. In many cases, the leadership of the political parties remained as it had been before and during the war, even among the parties driven underground, with the same families and individuals dominating political life (sometimes from abroad) regardless of what they had done during the war (discussed further below).

The most important thing that Taif did not do, however, was provide a framework for transitional justice. There were no truth and reconciliation commissions in Lebanon, no public tribunals and no chance for the survivors of the war's atrocities to confront those who had committed crimes against them. A cornerstone of Taif was a general amnesty for all acts committed during the war, declared by parliament in August 1991 (Barak 2007: 54). Nor was there any official government investigation into the human rights abuses committed during the war – many of them by men who were themselves members of the Lebanese government. In 2000, at the urging of a Lebanese NGO called the Committee for the Relatives of the Kidnapped and Missing, Salim al Huss' government established a commission of inquiry to investigate the fates of the more than 17,000 victims of kidnappings and disappearances during the war. In its report on the commission, however, Amnesty International was less than optimistic, stating that 'What is worrying is the lack of independence of the membership of this commission, the lack of terms of reference and the exceedingly short reporting timeframe' (Amnesty International 2000: 1).

What all of this meant for Lebanon, therefore, was that the aftermath of the war was everywhere, but unacknowledged and un-reconciled. What, then, are the lessons that other states in the region can draw from Lebanon's post-war transition? What lessons should the states currently undergoing transitions in the context of the Arab Spring learn from Lebanon?

Lesson 1: cosmetic changes are not enough

The first major lesson concerns the importance of institutional reform. True, the precise tensions that sparked the war in 1975 – political conflict between the Sunni/Druze left and Christian right, and tension over the presence and behavior of the PLO in Lebanon – are no longer the major issues in Lebanese politics. But the shaky political structures that allowed those tensions to pull the Lebanese house down on itself remained, and remain, unrepaired. In terms of its institutions of government, Lebanon is not much better equipped to handle political and sectarian conflict in the 2010s than it was in the 1970s.

The readjustment of the National Pact under the Taif Agreement did little to address the fundamental structural problems inherent in the Lebanese system. This failure, combined with the re-entrenchment of sectarian identity as the basis for political claims-making, has had real consequences for Lebanon. The state remains weak and decision-making fragmented, meaning that it is unable to confront new challenges as they arise. The paralysis that followed the July 2006 war is one example; the crisis created by the onset of the Syrian civil war is another. By the summer of 2012, events in Syria had already begun to raise political tensions in its smaller neighbor. The presence of anti-regime Syrian refugees and activists in predominantly Sunni Tripoli, where resentment remains over the Syrian treatment of the city during its invasion and occupation in the mid-1970s, raised tensions with the small Alawite community in the city, leading to armed clashes (BBC 2012). The Syrian-backed parties, notably Hizbullah and Amal, have remained thus far loyal to their patron, increasing the already substantial tensions between them and the anti-Syrian Mustaqbal party – a Sunni party dominated by the Hariri family. During the summer of 2012, strikes, road closures, tire burnings, rising street crime, power outages caused by the weakened electrical grid, and occasional armed clashes produced a generalized sense of insecurity and highlighted the weakness of the Lebanese state (*The Daily Star* 2012a; *The Daily Star* 2012c). Had the structural weaknesses that led to the civil war been addressed, the current crisis might have been easier to negotiate.

For some of Lebanon's neighbors, this is more or less a moot point. Libya, for instance, where voter turnout exceeded 60 per cent in the 2012 elections, has clearly begun the process of shifting away from the *Jamahiriya* system of government pioneered by Muammar Gaddafi. But for others, the danger of simply replacing political content while retaining the same structures remains an issue. In Egypt there were concerns that the Morsi government, in collusion with the military, was consolidating its power in ways not conducive to a democratic transition. In July 2013, Morsi and his government were removed from power by the military (albeit in response to massive popular protests against the Muslim Brotherhood). In short, the military retains much the same level of power it held during the Mubarak era. At the same time, the strength of the executive relative to the legislative and judiciary makes it unsurprising that a new military-backed strongman has emerged. Without significant structural reforms to address the distribution of power in the system, Egypt remains vulnerable to a cycle of coups and semi-authoritarian governments and its transition runs the risk of collapsing in on itself, much as Lebanon's did.

Lesson 2: foreign sponsorship comes with strings attached

Nearly all of the Lebanese factions have demonstrated, at one point or another, a predilection for seeking foreign aid as a way of gaining an advantage over their domestic adversaries. During the war, many of the Christian militias received aid from Israel, while Amal and later Hizbullah received backing from Syria and Iran, respectively. Egypt sponsored the Nasserites, Iraq the Ba'athists, and so on. The PLO was both a recipient of foreign aid and a provider of it, mostly to neighborhood defense militias in West Beirut. Even after the war ended, this dynamic continued: with Syria's ascendance as hegemon in Lebanon, its clients (primarily Amal and Hizbullah) gained an advantage, while Saudi Arabia has acted as a financial and political benefactor for the Sunni Mustaqbal party and Iran provides Hizbullah with both money and weapons.

There are undeniable advantages to foreign patronage. During the war, all parties benefitted from the weapons and funding their sponsors provided. After the war ended, Syria helped ensure that its clients would do well in elections in Lebanon during its years as guardian there. Iran has poured millions of dollars into Hizbullah, allowing it to construct a massive social service network in Lebanon and fund the reconstruction of homes and businesses damaged and destroyed during the July 2006 war. Saudi Arabia even paid to have expatriate voters from communities likely to support the March 14th parties flown back to Lebanon to vote in the 2009 election.

But the Lebanese experience also demonstrates that foreign sponsorship can be a double-edged sword. To begin with, sponsors can and do change sides, sometimes at the most inconvenient of times. In 1976, when it appeared that the PLO and its leftist allies were on the verge of defeating the Christian militias and establishing a new order in Lebanon, Syria turned on its former Palestinian clients and sent forces into Lebanon to protect the Christians and deny the PLO and the Lebanese left their victory. In 1982, in the midst of the Israeli invasion that would ultimately result in the PLO's expulsion from Lebanon, Syria agreed to a ceasefire with Israel and confiscated the PLO's weapons stores in Damascus with the aim of ending the fighting as quickly as possible (Y. Sayigh 1997).

More importantly for the post-war transition and the prospects for transitional justice, however, external sponsorship can have unfortunate domestic political consequences: it both increases the chances that regional rivalries will translate into local conflict and stands to increase distrust between local parties, thus damaging prospects for local dialogue and reconciliation. Both of these effects are clearly present in Lebanese politics.

The Lebanese civil war was strongly shaped by the regional rivalry between Syria and Israel, a rivalry played out by their respective clients. Since the end of the war, in addition to the conflict between Israel and Hizbullah playing out on Lebanon's southern border, the strategic rivalry between the Iranian-Syrian regional axis and the Saudi regional axis has increasingly shaped domestic Lebanese politics, as the former backs the March 8th alliance, and the latter, March 14th. This has had the effect of amplifying and exacerbating even minor neighborhood disputes.

Likewise, sponsorship by foreign governments has clearly increased the suspicion with which all parties in Lebanon view their opponents. To the March 14th bloc, Hizbullah's relationship with Iran is deeply problematic, at least in part because of the religious doctrine concerning the Supreme Leader of Iran's authority over Shi'ites outside of Iran. In an interview during the 2009 electoral campaign, a member of the Kataeb party's politburo expressed explicit concern to the author over what would happen if, for instance, the Supreme Leader of Iran ordered Hizbullah to attack Israel, over the objections of the Lebanese government (Kostanian 2009). Conversely, the cooperation between Israel and some of the Christian factions during the civil war means that they will always be viewed with distrust by some parties. Amal's close relationship with Syria is still cause for suspicion to some in the March 14th alliance, while the Mustaqbal's association with Saudi Arabia is likewise cause for suspicion to many in March 8th. While there is no shortage of suspicion and hostility in Lebanese politics, allegations of foreign sponsorship do little to improve the situation.

This should serve as a warning to both political parties and armed factions elsewhere in the region. Many have already appealed to outsiders for aid: the rebels in Libya obviously relied heavily on NATO assistance during the war, and Salafist and Islamist parties in Tunisia and Egypt are widely rumored to have received campaign funding from backers in Qatar and Saudi Arabia (much as the Hariri family and their Mustaqbal party do in Lebanon) (Kirkpatrick 2011; Lacroix 2012). Due to the ongoing civil war, this is a particularly relevant issue for Syria. Hizbullah has come to the aid of the Assad regime (at least partly as a proxy for Iran), and it has also received arms from Russia. The United States has offered diplomatic support to the more mainstream segment of the rebel movement, the Free Syrian Army (FSA), and has been training FSA fighters in Jordan which has also supported some segments of the FSA (Gordon and Landler 2013). On the other hand, a different segment of the rebel forces, the Al Nusra Front, has ties to Al Qaeda.

This support has its advantages – external military support will likely be necessary for the FSA to survive, much less overthrow, the Assad regime. But it also carries risks. It almost certainly helped to prolong the civil war in Lebanon, and there is a danger that it could do the same in Syria. Of course, to those facing defeat, prolonging the war is obviously preferable to the alternative, but external support also stands to prolong conflicts by turning them into proving grounds for their own ideologies and the political projects of the sponsoring states rather than those of their local clients. Al Qaeda's involvement will almost certainly do so. And in the long run, especially in peace time, outside support may reduce the political legitimacy of the recipients of that support. Those who suggest that the Islamist parties in Tunisia and Egypt, for instance, have received support from the Gulf States do not make this allegation out of admiration. And the various militant groups in Syria certainly risk losing both credibility and autonomy if they rely too heavily on foreign support.

Lesson 3: blanket amnesties are risky

A third lesson which Lebanon's transition offers its neighbors is that, as a means of dealing with the crimes committed during a civil war, the blanket amnesty can be a very dangerous choice. While it can make it easier in the short term to convince the various parties to disarm, it can also leave those who committed atrocities in positions of power and prevent national reconciliation from taking place.

There are very practical reasons why a blanket amnesty may be an appealing option.[5] For one thing, it takes less time than establishing a truth commission or a war crimes tribunal, which may be significant if there is an immediate danger of hostilities restarting. This was very much a concern in Lebanon, given that many previous ceasefires and peace agreements had failed. Moreover, the amnesty fit Lebanon's tradition of resolving conflict in such a way that there was 'no victor and no vanquished' (Hanf 1993; Haugbolle 2010). And practically speaking it allowed the leaders of militias which had committed atrocities (which was nearly all of them) to disarm their forces without worrying that they would find themselves on trial.

In this sense, the Lebanese approach mirrors that taken in Chile and other Latin American dictatorships in which military dictators were allowed to step down without fearing that they would find themselves in front of the very firing squads to which they had subjected their political adversaries. But in Lebanon, the militia leaders did not, for the most part, quietly retire or assume purely ceremonial positions. Rather, many remain active in politics, with the crimes they committed or the massacres they ordered largely unaddressed.

Compounding the problem, the amnesty was not applied universally. The leaders of the Christian militias did face some consequences. Samir Geagea, leader of the Lebanese Forces, was the only major militia-leader prosecuted and jailed for his actions during the war. He was tried and convicted in 1994. Similarly, Amin Gemayel, leader of the Kataeb party, and Michel Aoun, went into exile in France (El-Khazen 2001). Feeling unfairly singled out, many Christians boycotted the elections held over the following decade in protest, which did little to contribute to a process of national reconciliation and left the government further divided (Hijazi 1992; *New York Times* 1992). This suggests that if a blanket amnesty *is* to be applied, it should at the least be applied evenly.

Perhaps a better model is the policy pursued in the zone formerly occupied by the Israeli Defense Forces (IDF) after the Israeli withdrawal in 2000. Despite fears of Hizbullah reprisals against those who had lived in the Christian enclave established by the IDF and guarded by its proxy, the SLA, in fact there were none.

Those who had fought with the SLA were instead handed over to the Lebanese military, tried by the Lebanese courts and for the most part given sentences of less than two years. Those who had traveled to Israel (mostly women in search of medical treatment) were in general not sentenced at all. Only high ranking SLA commanders or fighters who had fled to Israel in 2000 and remained there received lengthy sentences, mostly in absentia (Norton 2007: 32–3). This process was far more transparent than that established under the Taif Agreement and has allowed for a far greater degree of security and mutual reconciliation in the south, where there are still large Christian communities. A process of transitional justice based on targeted and relatively transparent prosecutions, as opposed to blanket amnesties which are in practice unevenly granted, may prove to be more effective for Lebanon's neighbors during their own period of transition.

The question of whether and how to hold former regime members accountable is clearly an issue for the Arab Spring states. Some former dictators have been tried in the courts: Hosni Mubarak and his son Gamal have been put on trial in Egypt, while Tunisia's Zine al Abedine Ben Ali was convicted in absentia. While Muammar Gaddafi was executed by rebel fighters, his son Saif al Islam will likely stand trial in Libya (though the International Criminal Court (ICC) has claimed jurisdiction). But other members of the former regimes remain free: Ahmed Shafik, a former prime minister under Mubarak, came within three points of winning the 2012 presidential election. Moreover, trials of former rulers that do not also hold to account members of the security services or military who committed atrocities, or those in the government who gave the security services their orders, carry similar risks in the blanket amnesty approach. As Lebanon's experience demonstrates, impartially confronting abuses committed during conflict or under the former regime and removing those who committed them from power is an important part of the transition.

Lesson 4: militias can choose to change

If the fate of the leaders of militant groups is significant in shaping post-war politics, so is the status of the organizations themselves. While the demobilization and reintegration of individual fighters is important, so is the transition of the larger organizations of which they were a part. Likewise, while leaving individuals who had committed atrocities during the war in positions of power was in and of itself problematic, allowing the organizations themselves to evolve from militias into political parties has proved to be a source of stability. Of course, armed movements exercise a great deal of agency in this matter. They face a choice: will they remain armed, maintain an adversarial relationship with the state and so risk being marginalized, or compromise their stated principles in order to participate in the political process? The state, too, must decide whether these organizations will be allowed to participate in politics.

In negotiating this issue, Lebanon has been somewhat successful. While it is true that the leadership of many of Lebanon's militias remained the same following the civil war, the organizations themselves have largely disarmed. The Lebanese formula of 'no victor, no vanquished' meant that most of the Lebanese militias were able to transition relatively smoothly into peacetime political parties, which is, of course, what many of them had nominally been to begin with (Hanf 1993).

While disarmament was certainly important for its own sake, it also signaled willingness on the part of Lebanon's various factions to play by the rules of the game as laid out in the Taif Agreement and to integrate themselves into the post-war political order. This was not, of course, accomplished immediately; during the 1990s, many Christian parties were banned and their leaders exiled. But by the beginning of the next decade, many had begun to re-engage with Lebanese politics and, crucially, none responded to their exclusion with military force.

Interestingly, perhaps the most striking post-war transition was that undergone by the one faction which was allowed to remain armed under the provisions of Taif: Hizbullah. (The organization was designated a 'national resistance movement' rather than a 'militia'.[6]) Hizbullah's post-war evolution offers important insight into the choices which radical movements may face in other contexts. From its inception in 1982 until the end of the war, the organization's official policy was that it objected out of principle to the National Pact, and advocated instead the establishment of an Islamic state in Lebanon (though it did not advocate forced conversion of non-Muslims) (Ranstorp 1994: 305). The party therefore refused *a priori* to engage with the Lebanese political system. With the end of the civil war, however, and the national elections of 1992, Hizbullah faced a choice: to maintain its stance against the Lebanese state and risk being marginalized in the post-war order, or to compromise and risk internal discord.

After consulting with Iran, Hizbullah convened a committee to decide the issue, which voted 10–2 in favor of participation in the elections. This marked the beginning of Hizbullah's process of 'Lebanonization' (Azani 2009; Norton 2007). By 1998, it had replaced the old slogan on its flags, 'the Islamic Revolution in Lebanon', with a new one, 'the Islamic Resistance in Lebanon'. It reformatted its newspapers and radio stations, changed some of its propaganda materials and in general moved to rebrand itself as a primarily Lebanese organization, oriented toward the Lebanese state and embedded within the Lebanese political system (Alagha 2002: 171; Azani 2009: 129).

All has not been smooth sailing since then; the Hariri assassination in 2005 and the July 2006 war raised tensions with other political actors in Lebanon and led some to question whether Hizbullah truly prioritized Lebanon's interests above its own (or Iran's). The sit-in by March 8th supporters outside of parliament from December 2006 to May 2008, culminating in an armed takeover of West Beirut by Hizbullah and its allies, confirmed some of the party's opponents' darker suspicions about its real preferences. In other words, it has, at times, behaved much like Lebanon's other political parties.

In sum, both the successful disarmament of the civil-war era militias and Hizbullah's engagement with the Lebanese political system suggest that if it is possible to bring militias in states like Libya (and maybe eventually Syria) into the post-war order as political parties, it may pay to do so; having those parties embedded in the system is perhaps preferable to leaving them, discontented and still armed, outside of it. In Libya, the risks posed by these militias are clear: the presence of so many armed groups does little to strengthen the state's legitimacy and has created an atmosphere conducive to violence. The Al-Qaeda-linked militants who attacked the US Consulate in Benghazi are only one example (although this incident also led an angry mob, already frustrated with the prevalence of armed groups in the country, to attack the bases of several Islamist factions in response) (*NBC News* 2012).

On the other hand, the approach taken by the National Transitional Council (NTC), the organized leadership of the revolution in Libya, indicates the benefits that a successful transition can bring. The military leadership of the NTC largely refrained from sitting for elections themselves (including its leader, Mahmoud Jibril) but did coordinate a network of smaller parties, civil society groups and NGOs in forming the National Forces Alliance, the moderate umbrella party which won the 2012 election. This echoes the experience of those Lebanese parties which were able to successfully transform into political parties in the post-war environment.

Lesson 5: memory and memorialization matter

The last of the five lessons Lebanon offers its neighbors is perhaps the most cautionary of all. The civil war, its troubled aftermath and the current weakness of the Lebanese state all speak to the importance of the formation of shared historical narratives to successful post-war transition and the implementation of transitional justice. But in Lebanon, the significance of these shared narratives is made most evident by their absence.

The official Lebanese 'amnesia' vis-à-vis the civil war (Barak 2007; Haugbolle 2010) exists in tandem with a profound popular awareness of the war and its aftereffects. While there is little by way of official state commemoration or acknowledgement of the war, memorialization does occur within individual communities. This means that the way the war is commemorated varies a great deal from community to community. Visiting different neighborhoods in Beirut, one encounters what appear to be memorials to several entirely different civil wars. In Sassine Square in Christian East Beirut, there is a large memorial to Bachir Gemayel, scion of the Gemayel family and leader of the Kataeb, who was assassinated in 1982 shortly after his election as president. In the Palestinian refugee camps, posters of fighters (and civilians) killed (or massacred) by that same militia still dot the walls. In Shi'ite South Lebanon, the most prominent memorials are to those who died fighting the IDF and SLA, and the wars fought in Beirut and on Mount Lebanon feel largely absent. Even those sites which perhaps could have been framed as significant to the country as a whole have been claimed, to one degree or another, by particular parties. At the ruins of the notoriously brutal Khiam prison in South Lebanon, where prisoners from across South Lebanon were held by the SLA and IDF until 2000 (and which was kept as a museum until it was destroyed by Israeli bombing during the July 2006 war), the gift shop sells pictures of prominent Hizbullah leaders. Even at the far less politicized memorial to the victims of the Qana massacre, which is focused for the most part on the victims and their families, the guide made certain to mention that speaker of the parliament and Amal leader Nabih Berri had helped to fund its construction.

If those memorials which do exist are in some ways a missed opportunity to promote reconciliation, or at least acknowledge a common experience of the war across sectarian lines, this is doubly true of the lack of memorialization which exists in other areas. Downtown Beirut is an extreme example; the reconstruction of the city center largely erased most visual reminders of the shared wartime experience of the city's inhabitants. There is still no memorial denoting the 'green line' dividing East and West Beirut which once ran directly through downtown, or to the many people killed by sniper fire crossing from one side of the city to the other.

A more concrete problem, though, has been the lack of a standardized national history curriculum in Lebanon's schools. Despite the fact that the Taif Agreement stipulates that a common curriculum should be created, this has not happened. Lebanese secondary schools, which in any case tend to be segregated by confession, use a wide range of history texts offering different historical perspectives, which in any case do not cover the civil war (*The Daily Star* 2012b). This has contributed to the reinforcement of sectarian narratives and has done little to encourage a shared understanding of Lebanon's history or to promote either the confrontation of uncomfortable historical truths or national reconciliation. That higher education in Lebanon (with the notable exception of the American University of Beirut) remains segregated by sect serves to further reinforce divergent understandings of Lebanon's history. Outside the educational system, this effect is further amplified by the Lebanese media, which is itself heavily divided along sectarian lines; five of Lebanon's seven major news stations (Al Manar, Future TV, LBC, OTV and NBN) are closely affiliated with a particular political party or faction, and tend to provide a version of the news that is heavily shaped by that party's perspective.

The reinforcement of divergent narratives regarding the civil war and the concomitant failure to create a shared understanding of Lebanon's history has not helped the process of Lebanese national reconciliation. It has served both to reinforce the political salience of sectarian identity and to strengthen the barriers between communities. Moreover, the lack of a shared understanding of the history of the war has made it all the easier for those looking to leverage inter-communal mistrust (through ethnic outbidding or externalization of local dissent) to advance their own position within 'their' community to do so. But, most importantly, failure to acknowledge a shared responsibility for the Lebanese national tragedy (and a shared experience of suffering) has proved a barrier to the establishment of a strong sense of Lebanese identity. This contributes to the country's continued fragility and vulnerability to internal conflict, and should therefore serve as a warning to Lebanon's neighbors. While most of the transitions prompted by the Arab Spring have not yet reached a stage where these issues seem pertinent, eventually they will have to deal with the question of how to understand and memorialize these events. Particularly in Libya, Syria and Bahrain, where protests took on a sectarian tone, the construction of an inclusive and shared understanding of these events will be crucial to political stability and successful democratization.

Conclusion

In December 2006, with the government deadlocked and downtown Beirut paralyzed by a massive March 8th sit-in, Byblos Bank, one of the largest banks in Lebanon, put out a commercial that had nothing to do with banking. A series of men and women stand in front of various national flags, wearing their 'national dress'. The man in the denim jacket standing in front of an American flag says 'I am American'. The man in the kuffiyeh stands in front of a Palestinian flag and says 'Ana Filustini'. Other actors appear representing France, India, Japan, Oman, Serbia, South Africa, Japan, Iran, the United Arab Emirates and Colombia. Then, in front of a Lebanese flag, a young man says, in Arabic, 'I am Sunni'. Another says 'I am Druze'. A young woman says 'I am Maronite'. And another man says 'I am Shi'ite'. With each phrase, there is a sound like a gunshot and the Lebanese flag behind them spasms and drops toward the ground. Each actor looks down, either in shame or in grief. The screen goes black, and text appears (in Arabic) reading, 'When will we be Lebanese?'

This advertisement, intended as a rebuke to the Lebanese, should perhaps also be treated as a warning to Lebanon's neighbors. While there is undoubtedly a great deal of pride in Lebanese identity across all of Lebanon's sects, it is an identity often refracted through a sectarian lens, and whose meaning at the political level is strongly conditioned by sectarian concerns. This dynamic has in turn contributed to the weakness of the Lebanese state since the departure of the Syrian military, and to Lebanon's continued vulnerability to contagion from regional upheavals.

Could this have been avoided through a more effective process of transitional justice? Perhaps. Open acknowledgement of the crimes committed by individuals and organizations might have facilitated a national healing that has largely been absent, at least at the official level (though civil society organizations have in part filled the vacuum). Lebanon's approach – to mildly reform the pre-war political system, apply a blanket amnesty and avoid any sort of broad national conversation about the events of the civil war – has left many of the pre-war communal tensions and state vulnerabilities more or less unchanged, if somewhat reshuffled. This has only been exacerbated by the continued involvement of neighboring states in Lebanon's politics. Taif's major success was in convincing (or forcing) the various militias to disarm and either convert or revert to political parties (a process for which the amnesty was arguably necessary). But while this compromise successfully allowed the shooting to stop in the short term, in the long term, leaving their leaders in positions of political power has meant that those who committed war crimes are in some cases quite literally sitting in parliament. It has also meant that the state remains weakened and divided, and vulnerable to future conflicts.

What lessons, then, can those of Lebanon's neighbors now undergoing their own transitions from authoritarianism and/or civil war take from its experiences? Some of the points raised above clearly apply more directly to some states than others. For instance, those states which have experienced full scale civil war (that is, Libya and Syria) face a more difficult task in incorporating armed factions into the new state than those who have had more peaceful transitions, and are more likely to face challenges similar to Lebanon's with regard to the role of former combatants in the new government.

On the other hand, some of the above lessons can be applied more broadly. The question of how and to what degree to reform earlier political systems is clearly an issue for all of the states currently in transition in the Middle East, though thus far some have engaged in a more serious process of reform than others. Tunisia, Egypt and Libya have all begun or completed the process of drafting – or in Tunisia and Egypt's case, redrafting – new constitutions, and even Morocco has made significant reforms. Other states, notably Yemen, have not done so, despite a change in the executive. Likewise, Jordan's promised reforms have yet to be implemented and do not, in any case, represent a major overhaul of the system.

Finally, nearly all of the states currently facing transitions from authoritarian regimes will need to decide how and whether to prosecute members of the former regime, whether for war crimes or other human rights violations. But what Lebanon's experience suggests is that while this is an important, if painful, process, equally as important is a broader, national process of reflection and reconciliation.

Notes

1 For more detail on the Palestinian experience in Lebanon see R. Syigh 1979; Y. Sayigh 1997; Brynen 1990.

2 For further history and analysis of the civil war, see El-Khazen 2000; Hanf 1993; Salibi 2003; Winslow 1996.

3 Chief among these was General Michel Aoun, the Christian head of the army, who, against convention, had been appointed prime minister by Amin Gemayel in 1988. Aoun objected both to the sanctioning of the Syrian presence in Lebanon and to the weakening of the presidency (and therefore the Maronite position) which Taif proposed (Traboulsi 2007: 241–2). Beginning in 1989, he launched a last offensive against the Syrians in West Beirut and then against the rival Christian militias. Aoun's final defeat in October marked the end of the conflict, and the real beginning of the implementation of the Taif Agreement.

4 The author saw one such sign at a Hizbullah rally in Beirut in May 2009.

5 For discussion of the issue, see Ch 6.

6 The other major exception was the SLA, an Israeli puppet militia that remained active until the Israeli withdrawal in 2000. However, it existed outside the bounds of the Lebanese state and was termed illegal under Taif. The SLA was dissolved in 2000.

Bibliography

Ajami, F. (1986) *The vanished Imam: Musa al Sadr and the Shi'a of Lebanon* (Cornell University Press).

Alagha, J. (2002) *The Shifts in Hizbullah's Ideology: Religious Ideology, Political Ideology, and Political Program* (Amsterdam University Press).

Amnesty International (2000) *Lebanon: Commission of Inquiry into 'disappearances' must be effective and public*, available online at www.amnesty.org/es/library/asset/MDE18/001/2000/es/6f2d4c8b-f873-11dd-a0a9-2bd73ca4d38a/mde180012000en.pdf.

Azani, E. (2009) *Hezbollah: the story of the party of God: from Revolution to institutionalization* (Palgrave Macmillan).

Barak, O. (2007) '"Don't Mention The War?": The Politics of Remembrance and Forgetfulness in Postwar Lebanon', 61(1) *The Middle East Journal*, 49.

BBC (2012) 'Deadly clashes over Syria in Lebanese city of Tripoli', 21 August, available online at www.bbc.co.uk/news/world-middle-east-19329633.

Blanford, N. (2006) *Killing Mr. Lebanon: the assassination of Rafik Hariri and its impact on the Middle East* (IB Tauris).

Brynen, R. (1990) *Sanctuary and survival: the PLO in Lebanon* (Westview Press; Pinter Publishers).

El-Khazen, F. (2001) 'Lebanon – Independent No More: Disappearing Christians of the Middle East', 3(1) *Middle East Quarterly*, available online at www.meforum.org/16/lebanon-independent-no-more [Accessed September 29, 2012].

El-Khazen, F. (2000) *The breakdown of the state in Lebanon, 1967–1976* (Harvard University Press).

Fisk, R. (2002) *Pity the Nation: The Abduction of Lebanon* (4th edn, Nation Books).

Gordon, M.R. and Landler, M. (2013) 'Move to Widen Support for Syria Rebels Gains Speed', *The New York Times*, available online at www.nytimes.com/2013/04/11/world/move-to-widen-support-for-syria-rebels-gains-speed.html.

Hanf, T. (1993) *Coexistence in Wartime Lebanon: Decline of a State and Rise of a Nation* (IB Tauris).

Haugbolle, S. (2010) *War and Memory in Lebanon* (Cambridge University Press).

Hijazi, I. (1992) '2 More Lebanese Ministers Quit to Protest Election', *The New York Times*, available online at www.nytimes.com/1992/08/26/world/2-more-lebanese-ministers-quit-to-protest-election.html.

Kirkpatrick, D.D. (2011) 'Tunisia Election Faces Financing Questions', *The New York Times*, available online at www.nytimes.com/2011/10/23/world/africa/tunisia-election-faces-financing-questions.html.

Lacroix, S. (2012) *Sheikhs and Politicians: Inside the New Egyptian Salafism* (Brookings Institute).

NBC News (2012) 'Protesting Libyans storm militant compound in backlash against armed groups', available online at http://worldnews.nbcnews.com/_news/2012/09/21/14018495-protesting-libyans-storm-militant-compound-in-backlash-against-armed-groups.

New York Times (1992) 'Major Christian Party to Boycott Lebanese Voting', available online at www.nytimes.com/1992/08/16/world/major-christian-party-to-boycott-lebanese-voting.html?src=pm.

Norton, A.R. (2007) *Hezbollah: A Short History* (Princeton University Press).

Ranstorp, M. (1994) 'Hizbullah's Command Leadership: Its Structure, Decision-Making and Relationship with Iranian Clergy and Institutions' 6(3) *Terrorism and Political Violence* 303.

Salibi, K. (2003) *A House of Many Mansions: The History of Lebanon Reconsidered* (IB Tauris).
Sayigh, R. (1979) *The Palestinians* (Zed Books).
Sayigh, Y. (1997) *Armed struggle and the search for state: the Palestinian national movement, 1949–1993* (Clarendon Press; Oxford University Press).
The Daily Star (2012a) 'Assir holds Beirut rally in support of Syrian uprising', available online at www.dailystar.com.lb/News/Politics/2012/Aug-10/184160-assir-holds-beirut-rally-in-support-of-syrian-uprising.ashx#axzz27drgJU30.
The Daily Star (2012b) 'Mikati: History curriculum no place for narrow interests', available online at www.dailystar.com.lb/News/Local-News/2012/Feb-28/164870-mikati-history-curriculum-no-place-for-narrow-interests.ashx#axzz27Lm4bucO.
The Daily Star (2012c) 'Striking contract workers seal entrance to EDL', available online at www.dailystar.com.lb/Business/Lebanon/2012/Jul-24/181721-striking-contract-workers-seal-entrance-to-edl.ashx#axzz27drgJU30.
Traboulsi, F. (2007) *A History of Modern Lebanon* (Pluto Press).
Winslow, C. (1996) *Lebanon: war and politics in a fragmented society* (Routledge).

Chapter 6

Risks and rewards: lessons from Central and Eastern Europe's transitional justice experiences

Klaus Bachmann, Robert Stewart and Kirsten J. Fisher

The preceding chapter is in many ways a cautionary tale about the dangers of not undertaking backward-looking transitional justice in countries dealing with the aftermath of atrocity. In the same vein, the Arab Spring has seen many calls for the perpetrators of past human rights violations to be punished and for as many victims as possible to be compensated. However, as this chapter shows, there can be inherent risks to this approach that ought to be acknowledged and heeded. The Central and Eastern European (CEE) transitions were reluctant to apply large-scale punishment and vetting, and refrained even from organizing trials for high ranking perpetrators. Exploring the CEE context and its different approach provides important lessons for Arab Spring countries. Indeed, as this chapter demonstrates, under certain circumstances, avoiding retribution and not fighting impunity (or at least limiting each of these) can in fact have positive practical consequences for democratization, economic restructuring and societal healing. The chapter also reveals the often-ignored potential risks of retribution and of security sector reform, explores the pros and cons of vetting through the use of secret service records and considers the implications of compensating or not compensating victims. While the chapter stops well short of arguing that post-atrocity accountability (in the form of prosecutions or otherwise) should be abandoned for impunity and political amnesia, it acts as a reminder that there are significant hidden risks to backward-looking justice that must be acknowledged and heeded, and that attempts must be made to circumvent them.

Since this chapter aims to draw lessons from CEE transitions for Arab Spring countries, it first details the very different backdrops – temporal and political – against which these transitions transpire. Despite these differences, important lessons can be drawn from the CEE experiences since the differences can allow us to see such things as patterns, causal relationships and possible repercussions of actions that might otherwise be missed.

Two ways from dictatorship

Any comparison between the transitional justice experiences of such Arab Spring countries as Tunisia, Egypt, Libya, Morocco and – perhaps – Syria on the one hand and the transitions of the countries of CEE two decades ago must take into account two huge differences in their external environments. First, CEE countries started their transitions when the Washington consensus was almost unchallenged. Therefore, they underwent transition with a clear and comprehensible roadmap that plainly pointed the way from authoritarianism and a planned economy to pluralist democracy and a market economy. The choice of what direction to go was thus clear both for transitional governments as well as for the public: they could either share in the economic and social decay of the shrinking Soviet empire or 'go West'. When the pro-Western orientation of most CEE governments prevailed in elections, transition soon came to be embedded in a new legal framework which consisted of rules established by the European Community (later the European Union) and the Council of Europe. As a result, the human and civil rights culture of these organizations proliferated in the transitional societies, providing additional constraints for large-scale retribution and extra-legal punishment. Only later would domestic protests against the direction of transition emerge, as the social cost of market reform became apparent. In the Arab Spring countries, however, the relative consensus regarding the way forward and the stabilizing effect of external actors and legal frameworks are notably absent, particularly since, in many of these countries, 'going West' is strongly contested.

The second difference in their external environments relates to trends in transitional justice: regime change in CEE countries took place when the international political environment was dominated by a discourse regarding restorative justice. Thus, when Poland began to democratize, the thinking about transitional justice tended to be primarily concerned with the tension between punishment and amnesty, and the recognition of related dilemmas inherent in periods of political flux (Teitel 2003: 76). At this time, there was also a principled focus on nation building in the aftermath of authoritarianism. Today, international actors like the United Nations, the United States, the European Union and the international human rights community demand punishment for perpetrators, 'coming to terms with the past' and reckoning with past atrocities of the regime. Arguably, the global agenda has become dominated by two concepts: that perpetrators must be punished and that victims must be compensated. This retributive agenda only occasionally meets resistance – generally unsuccessful, for instance when local communities oppose demands from international institutions in the name of reconciliation, respect for local customs and values or in the name of stability and peace. This can be seen, for instance, in the situation between Serbia and the International Criminal Tribunal for the former Yugoslavia (ICTY) (Subotić 2009: 38–82), between local communities in Uganda and the International Criminal Court (ICC) (Djukić 2007: 691–8; Wegner 2012) and between the African Union and the ICC in the Al-Bashir case (Abdulai 2010). In these examples, the 'peace versus justice' debate is prominent, with one side arguing that there can be no real peace without justice – and the understanding of justice that they are drawing upon is generally understood as retribution. This is different from when CEE started to democratize.

Transitional justice after communism in CEE countries: neither punishment nor amnesty

There is no academic consensus about when transition in CEE countries actually started. The same is not true regarding when the first communist government fell: Poland in 1989. In Poland, like in most other CEE countries, transition was negotiated between opposition movements and the leadership of the communist parties, with mediation from the Church or the military. Romania was an exception to this rule with its sanguinary, civil war-like putsch. The different transitions had, to some extent, been triggered by the Polish example, which quickly became paradigmatic since it seemed to demonstrate that a peaceful regime change was possible and would not provoke a military intervention by the Soviet Union (unlike what happened in the German Democratic Republic (GDR) in 1953, in Hungary and Poland in 1956, in the Czechoslovak Socialist Republic (CSSR) in 1968 and in Poland in 1981).[1] This was a powerful incentive for the reform-minded part of the nomenklatura in CEE to engage in transition negotiations with the moderate part of the opposition and to resist communist and anti-communist hawks on both sides. The Polish example and the quiet encouragement for reform from Moscow (or at least tacit acceptance) provided the proof of what now had become possible.

In terms of transitional justice, CEE transitions had even more in common. No single member of the *ancien régime* was prosecuted for crimes committed before 1989. As in Poland, there was neither punishment nor formal amnesty. Vasil Bilak, one of the protagonists of the Czechoslovak post-Stalinist regime that had quashed the Prague Spring after inviting Soviet tanks to the country, was accused of treason in 2001, but his trial was suspended for lack of prosecution evidence. Former party leader Gustáv Husák had died in 1987, similar to his Hungarian counterpart János Kádár, who died in 1989, before he could be held accountable. Some of East Germany's communist leaders were prosecuted and received light sentences, but Erich Honecker, the GDR's stubborn head of the State Council who bore most responsibility for human rights violations, was allowed to escape to Chile with his family (Bruce 2009). The only exception to the lack of punishment of high-ranking communist leaders was the sham trial and subsequent execution of Romanian dictator Nicolae Ceauşescu in December 1989 (Stan 2009). Except for the short but gory civil war in Romania, CEE transitions remained peaceful.

This lack of prosecution was not for want of evidence of crimes committed by the *ancien régime*. In Germany, a parliamentary committee under the auspices of former dissidents collected information detailing atrocities, torture and secret police informers, but its proceedings were academic and its final report was voluminous – it amounted to several thousand pages – which made it inaccessible for use by the media and the public (Enquetekommission 1990). In Poland, a much smaller committee, called the Rokita Commission, investigated more than 100 disappearances of opposition members and delivered its findings to the public prosecutor, but it was then dissolved and the findings relatively ignored (Dudek and Rokita 2005). Prosecution inquiries into past atrocities in Hungary and Czechoslovakia revealed new evidence about torture, extra-legal killings, death squads and corruption – all of which had been public secrets before 1989 – but punishment for such crimes nonetheless remained the exception to the rule – that is, there was no retribution, but neither was amnesty declared. Indeed, in some countries, such as the Czech Republic and Hungary, the communist system was declared criminal, while in others, such as Poland or Latvia, laws were put in place that forbade communist ideology and the denial of communist crimes. But despite these moves, those who had worked to put in place the system and who had defended it with sometimes great cruelty remained unpunished.

The hostage dilemma and the influence of external hegemons

Whenever an autocratic ruler is threatened by popular upheaval and confronted by a united opposition that wants to oust him, a dilemma emerges which is very similar to the one between a hostage and its kidnapper once the ransom has been delivered: how to guarantee the kidnapper enough security such that he will give up the hostage without hurting him (or, in the case of a ruler, that he will feel sufficiently confident about his security that he would give up power). This hostage dilemma is easier to solve in some transitional settings than in others, particularly when both sides have recourse to third party enforcement and contractual agreements such as amnesties or constitutional veto rights which prevent the new government from changing the rules of the game after the dictator has lost power (Nalepa 2010).

The hostage dilemma in CEE transitions was solved in a totally informal way. No agreements about impunity were signed, and no speeches were made about reconciliation and unity. The *ancien régime* was weak enough to agree to a negotiated transition, but it was strong enough to prevent punishment of its leaders. No formal amnesty was necessary – both sides knew their strengths and weaknesses and both sides had silently agreed to construct the new institutional architecture in a way that would guarantee impunity to the *ancien régime*, since otherwise the regime supporters would lack incentives to agree to the deal. In Poland, the new and the old regime exchanged power for legitimacy, but the old elite kept enough economic power and institutional safeguards to secure a safe withdrawal from political power. In order to understand this mechanism, it is necessary to look at the wider context.

In all CEE transition countries, transition took place under close observation from powerful hegemons. Until the Warsaw Pact dissolved and the Soviet Union collapsed in 1991, opposition movements and the ruling establishment had strong incentives to avoid destabilization and to keep transition peaceful. This in turn helped to mute the possibility of any attempts at large-scale or elite-targeted vengeance, punishment or even intimidation. It is a significant reason why both sides treated one another as partners rather than antagonists, rivals or enemies. After the Soviet Union had collapsed – with Russia becoming independent and the Soviet Union's Western parts separating – transition was monitored by the

North Atlantic Treaty Organization (NATO) and the European Community (later the European Union). The new governments were put under heavy pressure to refrain from any destabilizing measures which could endanger peace, democratic transition and economic recovery, pressure that was particularly applied during the negotiations about trade liberalization, EU association and membership. In regards to transitional justice, external actors pushed unity, reconciliation and forgiveness over punishment and retribution. Soviet, European or US politicians did not refer to human rights in the name of the fight against impunity. Domestically, the fear of a repetition of the violent Romanian revolution helped to keep popular demands for retribution down.

Such constraints are and were almost absent in Arab Spring countries. Except for the short-lived upheaval in Bahrain (which was suppressed by Saudi Arabian troops), there is no regional hegemon able or willing to constrain popular demands for the punishment of the *ancien régime*. Nor is there a strong incentive comparable to membership in the European Union or NATO which could or would constrain the new governments from action against members of the old regime. Countries which might have been in a position to push Egypt and Tunisia toward a specific transitional justice policy, such as the United States or France, were to some degree caught by surprise when Ben Ali and Hosni Mubarak were forced to step down and were wary of being seen as pushing particular policies in a context where existing distrust and hostility toward the West was being exacerbated by the rise of Islamism.

Regarding the hostage dilemma, the United States, United Kingdom and France pushed for an International Criminal Court mandate in Libya; but once the ICC prosecutor had indicted Muammar Gaddafi, US diplomats began to seek a safe refuge for him probably as a result of realizing that the ICC's move had made him more likely to fight to the bitter end, while giving him a way out might encourage him to end the bloodshed earlier (*Guardian*, 29 March 2011). In Egypt, the military junta continued to oversee the country throughout the transition from the Mubarak era and was able to limit the scope of punishment to Mubarak's inner circle. And in Tunisia, the military protected the police from victims' claims by referring their lawsuits against policemen from civil to military courts.[2]

This analysis shows that the mode of transitional justice pursued – retributive or restorative – can depend strongly on the dominant discourse regarding a particular mode of transitional justice as well as the strength of the old regime's influence after transition and the role played by external hegemons. Indeed, these factors are seemingly much more important than the character of the *ancien régime* in terms of its legitimacy and the degree of liberalization before transition (Schmitter 1994: 57–74; Nedelsky 2004: 65–115); and while the gravity of crimes committed and the oppression carried out by an *ancien régime* are relevant in some circumstances (Moran 1994: 95–105), they are not overall decisive factors. Put simply, when perpetrators are punished in a transition, it is not only because they deserve it, because their legitimacy failed or because of the character of their regime. Rather, a principal factor is that they can be punished. In other words, even a reckless and brutal dictator may evade punishment in a negotiated transition whereas a relatively benevolent one may be severely punished if he is quickly overwhelmed and ousted by the opposition.

Security sector reform and vetting

Security sector reform is an important aspect of transition for countries with a legacy of authoritarianism and human rights violations by police, the military and intelligence services. Organizational models must be replaced and organizational cultures must be changed to prevent a continuation of the old norms and practices and to promote faith in the sector going forward among the citizenry. Given that massive and systemic human rights violations are primarily carried out by state security forces in authoritarian political contexts, transitional justice has a particular interest in promoting reform of abusive security structures and more generally the construction of an effective security sector that respects human rights (Patel 2010: 3). In many ways, security sector reform is an ambiguous concept that covers a wide range of issues and actions related to reorganizing public sector security agencies. With that ambiguity comes much debate about how best to accomplish successful reform. Transitions must usher in models that stress transparency, accountability and citizen involvement, and must do so in a careful and patient manner, 'in order to avoid backlash among security services' (Planty 2012). Since 'one of the major drivers of popular outrage in the Arab world has been and continues to be the repressive and brutal tactics of the security sector', security sector reform is a priority for Arab Spring countries (Hanna 2013). At the same time, such reform remains nascent in the Middle East and North Africa.

In contexts of transition from authoritarianism to peace and democracy, there is a particular interest in the relationship between accountability and reform since 'prosecutions of leaders of security forces or armed groups for war crimes or violations of international human rights and humanitarian law criminalizes this kind of behavior, demonstrates that no one is above the law, and may act as a deterrent and contribute to the prevention of future abuses' (Patel 2010: 3). Yet pursuing accountability for leaders can be a major challenge. For example, after the hostage dilemma is solved during a negotiated transition it can often be extremely difficult, or at the very least legally or politically very tricky, for the transitional government to pursue punishment of high-ranking perpetrators because they enjoy some kind of formal or informal impunity. Sometimes, these guarantees may be revoked, as happened in Argentina when courts started to summon army officers in cases involving disappearances (Nino 1996). But, this is often only possible after the old boys' networks have lost power completely, which can take a long time. Of course security sector reform involves much more than just leaders. Thus, while new transitional governments usually take the same approach of filling strategic positions with people loyal to the new order, it is not clear whether a few political appointees loyal to the new government can make a difference if they have to work in a hostile environment where information can be manipulated and clandestine networks maintain secret channels for information sharing and decision-making.

In Central and Eastern Europe, almost all transitions started with the dissolution or abolition of the secret police and the creation of new services from scratch. Transitional governments were much less radical with respect to the police, although the police force was often as discredited, ridiculed and hated as the secret services due to its relatively high visibility and close contact with the population. There are several reasons for a reluctance to deal radically with the police, some of which stem from the experience with the disbanding of the secret services. Perhaps most important is that secret service agents do not disappear after they are dismissed. In Poland, Romania and, to a lesser extent, Eastern Germany and the Czech Republic, many agents joined the private security sector, which usually expands exponentially after transition due to the increased threat perception of the population.[3] But unregulated private security markets under transitional conditions provide fertile ground for unscrupulous entrepreneurs operating in the grey zone of legality to open new, sometimes less-than-savory security companies that actually contribute to instability by rivaling the state security forces. At the same time, disbanded secret agents can be recruited by organized crime and by the secret services of hostile foreign governments. Thus, they start to use the skills and knowledge that they acquired in their professional lives against the new political order, constituting possibly an even greater threat to stability than if they had not been fired.

The same trade-offs can be seen relative to radical police force reform: while purges of high ranking officers and large-scale screening of rank-and-file personnel may increase the transition's credibility and public confidence in the security services, such purges also mean that there are less experienced police officers available when they are needed. More fundamentally, security sector reform destabilizes law enforcement agencies by erasing institutional memory and compromising work routines, which may be counterproductive for a transitional government struggling with the generalized socio-political instability and economic challenges that so frequently characterize transitional contexts. The destabilizing effects risk spreading even further given that large-scale screening of police and military officers can run into legal difficulties, with screening verdicts and dismissals challenged in court and overturned by judges, many of whose loyalty to the new order may also be doubtful. In turn, such developments risk inflaming divisions within society and thus undermining transitional justice efforts. Divisions can also arise from radical security sector reform under transitional conditions by virtue of the fact that it creates incentives for the creation of pressure groups, lobbies and political parties which will strive to protect the interests of ousted police officers and fight for their rehabilitation. When such lobbies occupy pivotal or veto player positions in the political system, they may even manage to undo purges, causing deep societal cleavages with negative repercussions for political stability and democratic consolidation.[4]

Importantly, the challenges arising from security sector reform in transitional contexts can occur against a backdrop of a generalized sense of increased insecurity among the populace. In Poland, for example, the years after 1989 saw relatively stable (and, compared to Western Europe, relatively low) crime rates; but the percentage of respondents who regarded their country as 'dangerous' and treatment of criminals as 'too lenient', and who, as a result, demanded the reintroduction of capital punishment, increased markedly between 1988 and 1992 (Bachmann 2006: 13–33). Contributing to this are challenges that can arise in the criminal justice system – for example, in 1990, Poland saw a huge wave of violent protests sweep through its prisons, which were triggered by a debate about amnesty but whose true cause was corruption behind the prison walls. Similar events have already taken place in Tunisia and Libya. More particularly, in the first half of 2011, several waves of spectacular prison breaks took place across Tunisia. In the following months, there was a series of smaller escapes from provincial prisons in both countries, caused by corruption but also the demoralization and disorientation of the prison staff (Gouëset 2011). These incidents have strongly contributed to already existing popular anxiety and feelings of insecurity (Gouëset 2011; Fish and Michel 2012; Weslati 2011).

Related to security sector reform is vetting. Vetting refers to processes of assessing the integrity of individuals, including their adherence to relevant human rights standards, to determine their suitability for public employment (International Center for Transitional Justice (ICTJ)). Countries undergoing transitions to democracy and peace can use such processes to exclude abusive or incompetent public sector employees from public service. Controversial issues in vetting include whether it is right to employ vetting practices that make use of archives of information from the old secret services compiled using abusive methods and which include records of 'collaborators' with the old regime (who were known as 'informal collaborators' in East Germany and 'agents' in Poland and the Czech Republic). A comprehensive process of security sector reform in the Arab Spring countries will likely have to include vetting. That being said, actual progress on vetting in the Arab Spring countries is still preliminary.[5] The remainder of this section offers some lessons from CEE countries, where vetting was used relatively extensively, to inform more comprehensive vetting processes that may happen in Arab Spring countries in the future.

As with most transitional justice policies, there was considerable debate in CEE countries regarding the advantages and disadvantages of vetting practices that involved opening secret services archives. Opponents of these vetting practices usually put forward arguments about unity and reconciliation and were concerned that opening the archives to the public would increase interpersonal conflicts, rip families apart and sow hatred and an urge for vengeance. They also pointed to the doubtful value of files and testimonies of former secret service officers. Accepting them as evidence would, they said, give supporters of the *ancien régime* the power to discredit the new democrats in court (since many of them had been followed by the secret services and thus had extensive records), ultimately weakening the new democracies. Indeed, opponents often regarded vetting as a late victory of secret service agents over their former victims (Śpiewak 2000). In response, supporters of these vetting practices usually invoked the need for transparency and claimed that secret old boys' networks could more easily survive and threaten the new order if the files were kept secret. The underlying reason for supporters' demands often flowed from their longing for a fresh, untainted start and for a break with a dirty past, predicated on a new order without any elite continuity (Śpiewak 2000).

Actual vetting experiences of CEE allow us to draw some general conclusions, many of which show that the concerns and arguments put forward by both supporters and opponents were unfounded. First, in most trials involving secret informers in CEE, their controlling officers proved loyal to them. The officers either negated or downplayed the role of their agents, even when documentary evidence contradicted their court testimonies. There was therefore no real danger that networks of secret police officers would systematically discredit proponents of the new order. This exculpatory practice was often facilitated by lack of evidence, since the secret police archives had either been cleansed during transition or taken over by the new government's secret services (and were thus kept secret). Second, a conclusion can be drawn from the CEE experiences that vetting cannot really be avoided. That is, if there is no official, legal vetting procedure, it will take the form of extra-legal accusations which are frequently based on leaked (or even forged) documents, whose accuracy will then be assessed in civil courts through libel complaints or lawsuits against media, which often publish leaked evidence. Such informal processes may be more damaging than an official vetting process. A third observation from CEE is that there is no real threat of civil war or even an increase in interpersonal conflicts arising from vetting. Indeed, Poland went through extensive 'wild' vetting, which was then followed by limited vetting procedures based on several laws passed during the second half of the 1990s. Vetting was a hot topic in the media when the archives were closed, as well as when documents about high-ranking politicians were leaked, but it quickly ceased to be an issue of public interest once the archives were open and the media were flooded with information from the files. The lesson here is that opening the archives depoliticizes the issue rather than increasing its salience.

Overall, vetting contributed to regime stability and transparency in the Czech Republic and Eastern Germany, where it was carried out immediately after the fall of the *ancien régime* and went hand in hand with (mostly administrative) repression of supporters of the old order. In Poland, vetting was used to try to discredit political opponents since it took place at a time when supporters of the former communist regime no longer had any power, the successor party had already governed the country for four years and a huge part of the archives had already been destroyed or taken over (and sealed off) by the new secret service. The collateral damage to new political forces in Poland as a result of how vetting was carried out there provides a striking illustration of the unintended consequences of putting vetting off.

Governments that consider vetting should keep in mind that looking through the archives for secret collaborators is more likely to provide ammunition against their own supporters from the past struggle than against the remnants of the ousted regime. Moreover, if vetting is carried out without retribution against those who controlled the informers and commanded the controlling officers, it will be seen as hypocritical by the public if informers – who were often coerced into treason and may be seen as perpetrators as much as victims – are publically exposed and punished when those who pulled the strings from above go free and unpunished. This is what happened when Poland engaged in large-scale vetting during the late 1990s, where secret police officers and their superiors were hardly ever targeted by prosecutors. The situation was different in the Czech Republic and East Germany, where vetting was accompanied by attempts to punish officers and politicians and remained almost undisputed by the public. Yet vetting was not without its challenges in these countries, since vetting procedures and attempts to dissolve the civil secret service in 1990 and later the military secret service in 2007 led to the breakdown of these services' networks of agents abroad and to the exposure of the identity of agents, which in turn severely damaged the services' ability to cooperate with allies and recruit new agents. This experience could also be useful for the countries of the Arab Spring, which should keep in mind that even when a secret service is abolished by a transitional government and then rebuilt from nothing, some elements of its institutional memory, such as files and information on secret informers, will remain. Thus, vetting can reveal information that makes it possible for hostile foreign governments to identify and eliminate a transitioning country's agents; since actual and potential informers will be aware of this risk, the services' ability to keep agents or recruit new ones will be affected.

End impunity, compensate the victims – or not?

The new, informal, global consensus on transitional justice requires states in transition to do two things: to 'end impunity', which is seen to mean punishing perpetrators, and to compensate victims. In CEE transitions only a few perpetrators were punished. But CEE governments were also reluctant to compensate victims. As with the reluctance to punish perpetrators, this was a result of social, political and economic constraints, particularly lack of resources and the need to concentrate what resources were available on stimulating economic recovery. The latter point underlines that both a perpetrator-centered and a victim-centered policy take resources away from reconstruction. Indeed, victim-centered policies are often even more costly since the number of victims is usually much higher than the number of perpetrators. In considering victim-centered policies, Arab Spring countries should also remember that victimhood (just like perpetratorhood) is not a stable and objective concept, but one which emerges from public discourse, legal definitions and incentives for people to define their past roles. Thus, it is up to truth commissions, parliaments or governments to decide the period for which victims will be compensated and, more fundamentally, what definition of victimhood will guide the process. The broader the definition and the longer the period for which compensation is given, the higher the financial cost of compensation and the putative negative impact on reconstruction. The definition and scope used in Poland meant that victims of post-war communist expropriation were not compensated, and that compensation for other victims was largely symbolic (unlike in the GDR and the Czech Republic).

Arab Spring countries are now facing many of these same dilemmas when deciding how far into their past to go in compensating victims.[6] A key issue in this debate is the financial cost of victim compensation, unlike the debate in CEE countries. This is because CEE countries were able to cover a large part of their reconstruction effort from external sources, through foreign debt reduction, International Monetary Fund (IMF) and World Bank loans and structural funds from the European Union. Arab countries have a more limited ability to access these sources of money, and there is no golden EU membership shining at the end of the transition tunnel. This, in turn, means that there will be relatively fewer funds available to compensate victims.

Arab Spring countries should also take into account the unintended political consequences of victim-centered policies. Perhaps most fundamental is that combining large-scale punishment with large-scale victim compensation risks creating a political system marked by a deep and possibly long-lasting divide between 'victims' and 'perpetrators', which will make stable parliamentary majorities extremely difficult to achieve and mean significant delays in reconstruction and problems for transitional justice policy making more generally. It also risks creating divisions within society along the same lines. Moreover, just as perpetrator-centered policies are shaped by an inherent paradox – that the higher the number of perpetrators, the more difficult it is to prosecute and punish them, especially if the judiciary is dominated by members of the old elite – so are victim-centered policies, since the higher the number of victims, the more difficult it is to compensate them. From the point of view of a transitional government, the easiest policy in practice is one that punishes relatively few perpetrators and compensates a small number of victims, if any. Such a policy may blur rather than deepen socio-political cleavages, facilitating reconstruction and economic development as well as political cooperation more generally. That being said, such a policy will not be popular, and hard to defend on moral grounds. Clearly, then, the issue of compensation represents a political minefield for Arab Spring countries, even more than it did for CEE countries.

Conclusion: excluding whom, when and how?

The experience of transitional justice in CEE offers multiple useful lessons for Arab Spring countries. In general, the CEE experience suggests that prudence is important when carrying out screening, security sector reform and vetting. Undertaking immediate, hasty reforms may increase societal fears in a period that is already unstable, triggering fear and societal demands for more punishment as well as undermining the efficiency of law enforcement. Carrying out reforms in such a way also provides incentives for the strengthening of 'old boys' networks' as well as the creation of pressure and revenge groups and risks pushing officers of the *ancien régime* into organized crime and dubious private security companies. The challenge then is to balance fighting impunity with protecting the transitional society from the risks inherent in backward-looking transitional justice policies. A possible solution might be to discharge high-profile, high-ranking officers and to carry out selective punishment as a kind of symbolic purification that in theory at least offers a fresh and untainted start by allowing society to symbolically break with a bad past, but without harming economic development or undermining the stability of the political system. Of course, as some of the CEE cases show, institutional reform is often undervalued in transitions, since the general public and the political sphere are both dominated by strong emotions and popular demands for retribution. Yet such reform, if carried out in a considered way, offers the possibility of solving some of the dilemmas of transitional justice set out in this chapter. For example, instead of firing police officers and rebuilding the security sector from scratch, it might make more sense to rotate officers into new positions and embed them within new institutions, which may provide better results in terms of helping to avoid instability, crime surges and feelings of insecurity among the population.

This points to probably the most important lesson that CEE transitions can offer to the Arab Spring countries: attempts to avoid radical exclusion of certain individuals and groups in the early stages of transitional justice create a lot of tensions, but may pay off in the long term. The observation is true of elites as well as supporters of the *ancien regime*, since ostracizing them can risk increasing in-group solidarity and nurturing strong grievances against the new political order. Outside the system, they may be more dangerous to the new order than inside it. Of course when news about the former elite's crimes and abuses become better known, they arouse public outrage that is usually accompanied by demands for punishment, with victims crying out for justice and reparations. It is a difficult balance to weigh, between, on the one hand, restraint and caution that might provide (minimally) a strong foundation for negative peace and, on the other, backward-looking justice that promotes and reinforces the values of the new society including human rights, the rule of law and equality before the law.

The importance of a cautious and considered approach is illustrated by contrasting some CEE experiences: in the Czech Republic and the GDR, strong and broad vetting and screening measures created lasting cleavages, undermined the party system and fueled the creation of strong and radical political parties. Meanwhile, in Poland, where the former nomenklatura was quickly reintegrated, the post-transitional cleavage between communists and anti-communists evaporated after 10 years (Grabowska 2004). More particularly, the swift reintegration of supporters of the *ancien regime* meant that they were deprived of any community of interests and any incentives to resort to collective action.

As this chapter has shown, the external environment which in many ways dictated the particular course of transitional justice in CEE was significantly different than that in the Middle East and North Africa (MENA) region, in terms of the existence of a clear and comprehensible path forward, an external hegemon offering encouragement along that path and the dominant transitional justice trend. These factors made possible a large-scale restorative transitional justice process in CEE countries, marked by institutional reform, integration of former regime supporters and the slow replacement of judges, prosecutors and police. Ultimately, a wholesale environmental change occurred, involving the laws, institutions and educational and training system, as well as more fundamentally the societies' norms, values and incentive structure. Such broad-based change will possibly be more difficult for Arab Spring countries struggling over such fundamental issues as the place of religiosity in the public sphere and shared values and norms – a struggle that undermines their ability to choose and then to follow a particular path forward. Its prospects are also affected by the fact that the region has and continues to be the site of militarily driven, short-term incursions by external actors as opposed to the relatively slow and sustained external nurturing that characterized the CEE countries' transitions. Perhaps as a direct result of these caveats, it is even more important for Arab Spring countries to draw lessons from the CEE countries' experience. These lessons, which are characterized by caution, careful rebuilding of institutions and the need to at least question the retributive tendencies that dominate at present, can contribute to strengthening the possibility for transitional justice's success in helping to move these countries toward a more democratic and rights-based future.

Notes

1 The only call for military intervention from other states of the Warsaw Pact came in Romania in 1989, but this was ignored by all other members of the pact, including the USSR.

2 Klaus Bachmann interviews with human rights activists in Tunis, December 2012.

3 Awareness of crime and the resultant fear (Cohen 2002) often rises during transition, even when crime rates are relatively low and stable. Fueling this is the fact that the media, enjoying new freedom from censorship, can focus on crime and high level corruption, topics that attract customers to the media outlets but which simultaneously undermine popular trust in the new order and make people feel uncomfortable, especially when they are not yet acquainted with this kind of aggressive journalism (Koralewska 1987).

4 The term 'veto player' is a reference to actors whose consent is needed in order to continue the decision-making process (for example in regards to legislation); without the consent of the veto player, the process is halted and thus the status quo remains in place. See Tsebelis 2002.

5 In Egypt for example, the National Democratic Party of ousted president Hosni Mubarak was disbanded and its assets nationalized by a court order. In Tunisia, the same happened to the long-ruling Constitutional Democratic Rally after former dictator Zine al-Abidine Ben Ali had fled to Saudi Arabia.

6 See Ch 2 for more details on this issue, particularly in relation to Tunisia, where the process is most advanced.

Bibliography

Abdulai, E.S. (2010) 'The Standoff between the ICC and African Leaders: The Debate Revisited', in The Foundation for Law, Justice and Society (ed.), *Oxford Transitional Justice Research: Debating International Justice in Africa* (The Foundation for Law, Justice and Society and The Centre for Socio-Legal Studies, University of Oxford), available online at www.csls.ox.ac.uk/documents/Abdulai_African_Leaders_Final_OTJR.pdf.

Arieff, A. (2011) *Political Transition in Tunisia*, CRS Report for Congress, Congressional Research Service 7-5700 RS21666 (9 April 2011), available online at www.crs.gov.

Bachmann, Klaus (2010) *Repression, Protest, Toleranz. Wertewandel und Vergangenheitsbewältigung in Polen nach 1956* (Atut und Neisse Verlag).

Bachmann, Klaus (2006) 'Die List der Vernunft. Populismus und Modernisierung in Polen', 11/12 *Osteuropa* 13.

Borodziej, Włodzimierz and Garlicki, Andrzej (2004) 'Okrągły Stół: dokumenty i materiały', 2 *Warszawa: Zapol* 6.

Bruce, Gary (2009) 'East Germany', in Lavinia Stan (ed.), *Transitional Justice in Eastern Europe and the Former Soviet Union. Reckoning with the communist past* (Routledge) 15.

Cohen, Stanley (2002) *Folk Devils and Moral Panics* (30th edn, Routledge).

Czarnota, Adam (2007) 'The Politics of the Lustration Law in Poland 1992–2006', in Alexander Mayer-Rieckh and Pablo de Greiff (eds), *Justice as Prevention. Vetting Public Employees in Transitional Societies* (Social Science Research Council) 222.

de Greiff, Pablo and Duthie, Roger (eds) (2009) *Transitional Justice and Development: Making Connections* (Social Science Research Council).

Djukić, Dražan (2007) 'Transitional Justice and the International Criminal Court – in "the interests of justice"?' 89(867) *The International Review of the Red Cross* 691, available online at www.icrc.org/eng/assets/files/other/irrc-867-dukic.pdf.

Dudek, Antoni (2009) *Zmierzch dyktatury* (Instytut Pamieci Narodowej – Komisja Ścigania Zbrodni przeciwko Narodowi Polskiemu).

Dudek, Antoni (2004) *Reglamentowana Rewolucja. Rozkład dyktatury komunistycznej w Polsce 1988–1990* (Arcana).

Dudek, Antoni and Rokita, J.M. (eds) (2005) *Raport Rokity. Sprawozdanie Sejmowej Komisji Nadzwyczajnej do Zbadania Działalności MSW* (Arcana).

Enquetekommission (1990) 'Aufarbeitung von Geschichte und Folgen der SED-Diktatur in Deutschland', available online at www.stiftung-aufarbeitung.de/die_stiftung/errichtungsgesetz.php.

Fish, M. Steven and Michel, Katherine E. (2012) 'What Tunisia did right', *Foreign Policy*, 2 November, available online at www.foreignpolicy.com/articles/2012/11/02/what_tunisia_did_right.

Freeman, Mark and Opgenhaffen, Veerle (2005) *Transitional Justice in Morocco: A Progress Report* (The International Center for Transitional Justice), available online at www.ictj.org/sites/default/files/ICTJ-Morocco-Progress-Report-2005-English.pdf.

Garlicki, Andrzej (2003) *Karuzela. Rzecz o Okrągłym Stole* (Czytelnik).

Gibson, James L. (2005) *Overcoming Apartheid. Can Truth Reconcile a Divided Nation?* (Cambridge University Press).

Gouëset, Catherine (2011) 'Tunisie: mystérieuses évasions de prisonniers', *L'Express*, 6 May, available online at www.lexpress.fr/actualite/monde/tunisie-mysterieuses-evasions-de-prisonniers_989891.html.

Grabowska, Mirosława (2004) *Społeczne podstawy polityki w Polsce po 1989* (Scholar).

Hanna, Michael Wahid (2013) 'Security-Sector Reform: The Seven Pillars of the Arab Future', The Century Foundation, at http://tcf.org/blog/detail/security-sector-reform-the-seven-pillars-of-the-arab-future.

Hayner, Priscilla (2011) *Unspeakable Truth. Transitional Justice and the Challenge of Truth Commissions* (Routledge).

Huntington, Samuel P. (1991) *The Third Wave. Democratization in the Late Twentieth Century* (University of Oklahoma Press).

Huyse, Luc and Dhondt, Steven (with Paul Depuydt, Kris Hoflack, Ingrid Vanhoren) (1991) *Onverwerkt verleden. Collaboratie en repressie in Belgie 1942–1952* (Leuven).

International Center for Transitional Justice (nd) 'Vetting', available online at http://ictj.org/our-work/research/vetting.

Judt, Tony (2005) *Postwar. A History of Europe since 1945* (Penguin Books).

Kitschelt, Herbert, Mansfeldova, Zdenka, Markowski, Radosław and Toka, Gabor (1999) *Post Communist Party Systems: Competition, Representation and Inter-Party Cooperation* (Cambridge University Press).

Koralewska, Jadwiga (1987) *Autorytaryzm, lęk, konformizm. Analiza społeczeństwa polskiego końca lat siedemdziesiątych* (Polska Akademia Nauk).

Kowal, Paweł (2001) 'Dlaczego doszło do Okrągłego Stołu? Przyczyny zmian politycznych w Polsce w latach 1989–1990 w opiniach polityków, aktywnych uczestników tego okresu', in Tomasz Szarota (ed.), *Komunizm: ideologia, system, ludzie* (PAN) 156.

Kubik, Jan and Linch, Amy (2006) 'The Original Sin of Poland's Third Republic: Discounting "Solidarity" and its Consequences for Political Reconciliation', 153(1) *Polish Sociological Review* 9, 13.

Lagrou, Pieter (2000) *The Legacy of Nazi Occupation. Patriotic Memory and National Recovery in Western Europe* (Cambridge University Press).

Machcewicz, Paweł (ed.) (2002) *Polska 1986–1989. Koniec systemu. Materiały międzynarodowej konferencji. Miedzeszyn, 21–23 października 1999* (Trio).

Markowski, Radosław and Wnuk-Lipiński, Edmund (eds) (2001) *Transformative Paths in Central and Eastern Europe* (IPS PAN, Friedrich Ebert Foundation).

McManus-Czubinska, Claire, Miller, William L., Markowski, Radosław and Wasilewski, Jacek (2004) 'Why is corruption in Poland "a serious cause for concern"?', 41 *Crime, Law & Social Change* 107.

Moran, John (1994) 'The Communist Torturers of Eastern Europe. Prosecute and Punishment or Forgive and Forget?' 27(1) *Communist and Post-Communist Studies* 95.

Nalepa, Monika (2010) *Skeletons in the Closet. Transitional Justice in Post-Communist Europe* (Cambridge University Press).

Nedelsky, Nadya (2004) 'Divergent Responses to a Common Past: Transitional Justice in the Czech Republic and Slovakia', 33(1) *Theory and Society* 65.

Nedelsky, Nadya (2004) 'Czechoslovakia, and the Czech and Slovak Republics', in Lavinia Stan (ed.), *Transitional Justice in Eastern Europe and the Former Soviet Union. Reckoning with the Communist Past* (Routledge) 37.

Nettlefield, Sara (2011) *Courting Democracy. The Hague Tribunal's Impact on Bosnia-Herzegovina* (Oxford University Press).

Nino, Carlos (1996) *Radical Evil on Trial* (Yale University Press).

Osęka, Piotr (2004) 'Okrągły Stół. Taktyki negocjacyjne władzy i opozycji', in Włodzimierz Borodziej and Andrezej Garlicki, *Okrągły Stół: dokumenty i materiały*, Vol 1 (Zapol) 5.

Paczkowski, Andrzej (2002) 'Droga do, mniejszego zła. Strategia i taktyka obozu władzy lipiec 1980–styczeń 1982' (Wyd. Literackie) 206, 246.

Patel, Ana Cutter (2010) 'Transitional Justice, DDR, and Security Sector Reform', *Research Brief* (International Center for Transitional Justice), available online at www.ictj.org/colombia-justicia-priorizacion-2/sites/default/files/ICTJ-DDR-SSR-ResearchBrief-2010-English.pdf.

Planty, Donald J. (2012) 'Security Sector Transformation in the Arab Awakening', United States Institute of Peace, available online at www.usip.org/publications/security-sector-transformation-in-the-arab-awakening.

Schmitter, Philippe C. (1994) 'Democratic Dangers and Dilemmas', 5(2) *Journal of Democracy* 57.

Śpiewak, Paweł (2000) *Spór o Polskę 1989–1999* (PWN).

Stan, Lavinia (2009) 'Poland', in Lavinia Stan (ed.), *Transitional Justice in Eastern Europe and the Former Soviet Union. Reckoning with the Communist Past* (Routledge) 76.

Stan, Lavinia (2009) 'Hungary', in Lavinia Stan (ed.), *Transitional Justice in Eastern Europe and the Former Soviet Union. Reckoning with the Communist Past* (Routledge) 102.

Stan, Lavinia (2009) 'Romania', in Lavinia Stan (ed.), *Transitional Justice in Eastern Europe and the Former Soviet Union. Reckoning with the Communist Past* (Routledge) 128.

Subotić, Jelena (2009) *Hijacking Justice. Dealing with the Past in the Balkans* (Cornell University Press).

Teitel, Ruti (2003) 'Transitional Justice Genealogy', 16 *Harvard Human Rights Journal* 69.

Tsebelis, George (2002) *Veto Players: How Political Institutions Work* (Princeton University Press).

Wegner, Patrick (2012) 'Where to With Transitional Justice in Uganda? The Situation After the Extension of the Amnesty Act. Justice in Conflict', available online at http://justiceinconflict.org/2012/04/22/where-to-with-transitional-justice-in-uganda-the-situation-after-the-extension-of-the-amnesty-act/.

Welsh, Helga A. (1994) 'Political Transition Processes in Central and Eastern Europe', 26(4) *Comparative Politics* 379.

Weslati, Slah (2011) *Democratie ou guerre civile? Chronologie de la Révolution Tunisienne* (Nirvana).

Wiatr, Jerzy J. (2006) *Europa postkomunistyczna. Przemiany państw i społeczeństw po 1989 roku* (Scholar).

Wiatr, Jerzy J. (2003) 'Polska droga do demokracji', in Jerzy J. Wiatr, Jacek Raciborski, Jerzy Bartkowiak, Barbara Frątczak-Rudnicka and Jarosław Kilias, *Demokracja Polska 1989–2003* (WydawnictwoNaukowe Scholar) 13.

Williams, Kieran, Fowler, Birgit and Szczerbiak, Aleks (2011) 'Explaining lustration in Central Europe: A Post-Communist Politics' Approach', SEI Working Paper 62, available online at www.sussex.ac.uk/sei/wp62.pdf.

Part Two

Issues pertaining to Arab Spring transitional justice

Chapter 7

Challenges of representation and inclusion: a case study of Islamist groups in transitional justice

Line Khatib

The rise to political prominence of Islamists – Muslims seeking political power in the name of Islam – as a result of the Arab Spring in countries such as Egypt, Tunisia and probably Syria once (or if) the regime is eventually ousted, causes some concerns to the pro-democracy movement in the region. Indeed, despite these mainstream Islamists'[1] recent assertions that they are fully committed to international norms regarding human rights and liberal democratic rule,[2] many observers continue to argue that Islamist political movements are not liberal democratic actors.[3] In particular, liberal activists and the youth whose demonstrating has practically propelled the collapse of the previous authoritarian regimes fear that Islamists have taken advantage of the Arab Spring movement and the mass demonstrations only to instate repressive regimes *à l'Islamique* this time around, and more generally to push their conservative Islamic agenda. At the very least, they dispute the sincerity of the Islamists' wish to transition the countries they lead into liberal democracies that respect and defend human rights and individual freedoms, or to participate politically as part of the opposition in the move toward liberal democracies.[4]

The position of the mainstream Islamists vis-à-vis human rights and liberal democratic rule in turn has important implications for transitional justice in the region, since transitional justice as understood and practiced up to now is not politically neutral but is rather an element of liberal peace-building. Indeed, as Ruti Teitel claims, transitional justice is 'intimately tied to the fashioning of a liberal political identity' (Teitel 2003: 225).[5] There thus seems to be a tension between the Islamists and the goals of transitional justice.

With this tension in mind, the present chapter will examine the accuracy of the perception that Islamists are bad liberal democratic actors. It will ask whether the region's Islamists, apparently one of, if not the, main socio-political force to contend with in the present and likely the future phases of the Arab Spring, can oversee and constructively take part in transitional justice and thus bring about societal healing through processes predicated on liberalism. In particular, can they avoid undermining freedom of speech and freedom of the press, and defend gender and minority group rights (all rights that the Islamists themselves claim to respect in their electoral programs)?

To answer these questions, this chapter will first briefly examine the content of the putatively Islamist political discourse in order to shed some light on the Islamists' political vision and socio-political mindset. In doing so it looks at the complex issues of culture, democracy and religion and how these concepts are understood by Islamists, as well as how these understandings impact the process of justice. It will then look at some of the actions, proposed policies and laws that Islamists have promoted while in power and will discuss the relationship between these and transitional justice. This part of the chapter will focus on three themes that highlight the tension between liberal and illiberal conceptions of rights and the public sphere – women's rights, freedom of expression and factionalism – and three countries – Tunisia, Egypt and Syria. In Egypt, the focus will be on how the previously governing Islamists – the Freedom and Justice Party – defined women's rights and the possible impact on transitional justice.[6] The chapter will also discuss how the Tunisian Islamist Ennahda party delineated freedom of expression. Finally, the impact of the current events in Syria on a possible transition towards democracy and justice will be the subject of the final section. The argument throughout the chapter is that the main challenge when it comes to Islamists overseeing transitional justice and participating politically in a constructive manner is that their ideology is a hybrid between religio-political ideals based upon the founding texts and corpus of Islamic law and a modern democratic political vision. Islamists therefore incorporate 'traditional' elements that are at odds with the values fundamental to liberal democracy, and in so doing compromise the ability of transitional justice to successfully achieve its goals.

There are several points to keep in mind while reading this chapter:

(1) The chapter posits that many human rights standards first articulated by liberals have acquired a universality independent from their original 'European' field of meaning and historical specificities.[7] The Arab Spring movement and the demands of the protestors for basic civil liberties and democratic rule have arguably confirmed this assumption.

(2) The chapter is concerned with the reconstruction of the public sphere by actors who have not contributed to the injustices of the previous regimes, and yet who might recreate a political system and a political culture that are in tension with 'universal' concepts of justice.[8] Moreover, while the cases examined in the chapter are hardly exhaustive, they illustrate the overall pattern in the region vis-à-vis Islamists at the time of writing.

(3) The chapter touches upon one aspect of the process of vetting in its examination of Islamists and their discourse and actions.[9] Vetting is frequently defended as a way of punishing perpetrators of past wrongs as well as transforming institutions in order to safeguard the democratic transition and to prevent the recurrence of human rights abuses. Yet this chapter's focus on Islamists (rather than the old authoritarian regimes) means that it is only concerned with the latter aim: the prevention of the recurrence of human rights abuses and the possibility of institutional reform.[10]

The Islamists' political imagination: an overview

This section briefly describes the content of putatively Islamic political thought, and gives examples from the discourse of the Ennahda Party and the Egyptian Muslim Brothers.[11] It is important to underline that this section does not mean to argue that Islam is an anti-democratic or pro-democratic ideology.[12] It simply explores the political theory that Islamists have advanced in order to shed light on major illiberal concepts within today's Islamic political discourse.

Setting international norms of justice as the criteria by which to assess the possibility of democratic reform is controversial and politically contested for obvious reasons, the most prominent being whether or not international justice is a concept that should be upheld by all, and whether a 'cultural', relativist vision of justice should be supported instead. While this has been the overall stance of Arab Islamists over the past decades, many within the Islamist front have recently rhetorically committed themselves to liberal democracy as a conceptual and institutional necessity. In so doing, they have rendered the earlier Islamist-liberal debate as to whether international norms are truly universal largely moot.

Having said this, however, a closer look at their discourse shows that Islamists across the region continue to stress the specificity of local needs and contexts, arguing that certain Islamic mores should still color Arab democratic institutions. For instance, the Egyptian Muslim Brothers continue to make it clear that only the three monotheistic religions (Islam, Christianity and Judaism) are allowed to be practised in public and to establish places of worship.[13] This is illustrated by a comment from Dr Fareed Ismail, a prominent member of the Muslim Brotherhood and member of the Constituent Assembly tasked with overseeing the drafting of the new Egyptian constitution. When Ismail was asked about the Baha'i faith and their rights in Egypt, he argued that the state in Egypt is Muslim and that since Baha'ism is not one of the three established monolithic religions, Baha'is do not have the right to establish places of worship and cannot display their beliefs publically, especially because doing so would disrupt 'public order' (ON TV 2012). Another member of the Constituent Assembly and a spokesperson for the Freedom and Justice Party, Dr Dawud al-Baz, argued that according to Islam one does not have the right to be Baha'i or homosexual, views that he and other Islamists assume should in turn frame the constitution and define public space in Egypt (ON TV 2012).

What these claims show is that despite their promises to respect international norms of human rights (Gulfnews.com 2013), Islamists in power in the Arab Spring countries have been sometimes unwilling to uphold internationally recognized human rights standards and instead adhere to particular religious, cultural and local values that are portrayed as timeless. In so doing, they are hindering the process of transitional justice because their specific conservative and 'cultural' Islamic interpretation of human rights discriminates between women and men and between the different religious sects. It also curtails freedom of speech and faith, as will be demonstrated in more detail later in the chapter.

Some observers may argue against this claim by saying that Islamization of the state does not change the rules of the political and economic game, since 'the influence of Islamism is more superficial than it seems' (Roy 1994: 25–27). Yet it is important to note that the configuration and framework of liberties and rights have a significant impact on the process leading to justice, on society's accepted norms in the long run and on the democratic transition's final outcome. In other words, the Islamization of the nascent democratic state, in light of the overall pious tendencies of society in the region, will have a significant impact on the socio-political realm in the longer term and beyond the Islamists' immediate years in power. This is particularly the case as Islamists sometimes seek to use such means as constitutional and legal reform to instate their beliefs.

Indeed, the problem with the political rise of Islamists from the point of view of transitional justice is that while international law is a cluster of concepts and standards with strong liberal undertones, Islamists are fundamentally illiberal movements which advance pragmatic and modern yet illiberal discourses and policies. In particular, their understanding of justice, human freedom and human rights is based upon how they choose to interpret the Islamic sharia (Islamic law). Therefore, while Islamic jurisprudence (*fiqh*) can be reasoned in a way that advances a liberal discourse, the majority of today's ulamas and Islamists still adopt conservative interpretations of the sharia, especially when it comes to deniability of the existence of God, the separation of the political realm from life's other realms for Muslims, the sacrosanct place of monotheistic religion within society, the role of women within the family unit and the subaltern status of minorities within the *Umma* (the nation).

The dual game being played by the Islamists can be seen in the political programs that Ennahda and the Egyptian Freedom and Justice Party outlined during the 2012 election campaigns, where both promised *huriyat al-itiqad* (freedom of faith) and *huriyat al-tabeer* (freedom of expression), as well as the same citizenship rights to all, women and men, majority and minorities. They also both expressed their commitment to the concept of 'citizenship' (*muwatana*) and its role in safeguarding peace and unity. And yet the Freedom and Justice Party wrote in its party platform that '*thaqafat al-Sha'b*' (the ethos of the people) is 'Islamic' and that the meaning of citizenship (which they assert is a 'high human concept') is determined by the identity and the culture of the Egyptian people, which, it says elsewhere within the document, is 'Islamic'.[14] Indeed, in the section '*al-mabade' al-assiasiya*' (political principles), there is a contradiction between points 2 and 3. While point 2 avows citizenship rights for all, point 3 promises women their complete rights 'as long as these do not contradict the principles of Shari'a, and in a way that achieves balance between her rights and her duties' (author's translation). The Ennahda Party has made similar declarations. In its 'fikr' section (thought), it asserts its commitment to Islam and promises to consider the Islamic creed as its foundation in all areas of life.[15] Thus, although freedoms and rights are said to be guaranteed, the Islamic culture and 'public morals' will in fact continue to characterize and truncate all sorts of universal freedoms.

It is important to note that up until the revolutionary movement of the Arab Spring, Islamists' focus was on criticizing the leaders who were in charge. Their overall rhetoric stressed Islamic ethics and portrayed leaders as sinners lacking the virtues of Islamic leaders. During the Arab Spring, Islamists shifted their focus to emphasize their own commitment to human rights and democratic rule. But, as argued above, their programs in fact reveal a continued commitment to a traditional view of Islamic ideals, and thus a belief that democratic political leaders should govern by the sharia (interpreted by the established ulamas). The rule would be 'democratic' in the sense that it is controlled by the sharia, the shura (advisory committee), and *ijma* (consensus), with the caveat that shura and *ijma* cannot overrule the sharia.[16] Thus, democracy always remains within the confines of Islamic law, understood according to the interpretation of the established ulamas.[17] It is enough to watch programs on Egyptian TV channels focusing on the new constitution – meaning the constitution drafted by the Morsi government – to see that discussions are restricted as soon as the role of religion within society is brought up, probably because it risks challenging the fundamental assumption that *din al-dawla huwa al-Islam* (the religion of the state is Islam). Moreover, none of the discussants and experts on the topic of the new constitution challenge the idea, not even daring Egyptian intellectuals such as Yusri Fuda and university professors such as Rabab al-Mahdi.

It thus seems that Islamists either do not have a clear understanding of fundamental human rights, or that human rights and freedoms are consciously used as empty signifiers for election purposes. No matter which one of these two suppositions is the right one (or whether it is a combination of the two), the result is that Islamists promote 'Islamic' limits on civil rights because, ultimately, they do not aim to protect individual rights and freedoms but rather a more communal notion of justice. Their discourse seems to show that only the justice of the sharia (and not also freedom *from* the sharia) can defeat political repression and tyranny, as its precepts define the virtues of the leader and the community of believers. Olivier Roy explains, '[e]thics, and not democracy, is the watchword of protest … this is how one must interpret the weakness of democratic demand [by Islamists] in a Muslim country' (Roy 1994: 10–11). The Islamic political imagination subscribes to the non-separation of the religious, legal and political spheres.[18] The sharia should be the source of the law and human rights, and the setter of individual and society's behavior.

Another key element in Islamists' political vision is the concept of *tawhid* (oneness or fusion) (Roy 1994: 13), which says that there is but one God. This oneness acts as an ideal that inspires the relationships between God and society, between the individual and the state and between society and politics. The ideal undermines the ostensibly democratic tendencies in Islamists' vision, since it shows that they are in fact committed to the fusion of individuals into a perfect society of the pious and moreover that the blurring of borders between society and the state is not only possible but commendable. The fusion of society and the state means that all have been Islamized, in the sense that all are acting within the confines of Islamic law (even Christians and Jews living in a majority Muslim society) and thus that justice will finally be achieved for all. In this *imaginaire*, democracy is the rule of the people by the people who view ethics and the law through an Islamic lens. Needless to say, this contradicts notions of universal human rights and ultimately endangers the possibility of effective transitional justice.[19]

In the following section, the chapter will focus on the constitutional articles, policies and actions of Islamists. It will claim that despite playing the democratic game (by standing for elections and accepting to share political power with leftist and liberal parties), and notwithstanding their expressed commitment to democratic rule and human rights, Islamists that won elections in Arab Spring countries such as Tunisia and Egypt drafted illiberal constitutions and bills that would hinder freedoms. This argument is supported by examining relevant events and constitutional articles that illustrate the overall trend.

Pragmatic politics, democracy and the possibility of successful transitional justice in Egypt, Tunisia and Syria

In any transitional justice context, the way in which human rights are presented and events characterized is crucial in determining how violations committed by previous regimes are confronted and how the institutional, social and cultural reconstruction of society will take shape. Therefore, it is important to consider how the emerging Islamist political forces address or propose to address the culture and legacy of repression created by decades of human rights violations. This section will examine how these new political forces have sought to break with their respective countries' repressive past, by asking such questions as: Do they work to establish a political culture that respects human rights, as they say they will? And, how do they reconstruct the public sphere, empower disenfranchised groups such as women and the impoverished, and challenge past silences and lies? In other words, what sort of actions have they been undertaking (in the case of Syria) and what policies are they or were they actually proposing (in the case of Egypt and Tunisia) and how have they reconfigured their own discourse (presented above) into 'just' and 'democratic' social norms? This selective yet representative examination of Islamists' actions and policies will tell us about the possibility of transitional justice succeeding. It will shed light on Islamists' deeply held understandings of what a democratic regime means, the boundaries of political power and the legitimacy of civil liberties and human rights.

Tunisia's Islamists: on the question of freedom of expression

On 14 January 2011, following weeks of protests, Tunisian President Zine al-Abidine Ben Ali's authoritarian regime fell after 23 years in power. It was hoped that the departure of Ben Ali would put an end to political repression, systematic torture and forced exile for dissidents, and would start an era of respect for human rights and for the rule of law. The democratic elections brought in the Islamist Ennahda as governing party.

From the outset, Ennahda's proposed constitutional changes seemed to be at odds with its promises to uphold human rights and transition the country towards a full-fledged democracy (*Arabic News Digest* 2012). More particularly, the party has not demonstrated its commitment to all those rights that are considered to be at the core of transitional justice. Thus, it is not promoting a context that safeguards freedom of expression and women's rights. Indeed, a number of Tunisian civil rights activists, artists and journalists have complained that the Ennahda government has indulged the demands of the Salafis (an Islamic movement with a purist interpretation of Islam) and has, as a result, curtailed individual freedoms and liberties (*Arabic News Digest* 2012). Even Tunisia's interim President, Mr Marzouqi, reportedly said: 'The Ennahda movement is trying to grab all the vital points of the nation; they are adopting the same methods of the deposed president, Ben Ali' (*Arabic News Digest* 2012).

Three main articles of the draft Tunisian constitution from August 2012 clearly encroached on international norms vis-à-vis human rights: Article 5, which was meant to regulate the media; Article 28, which delineated the status of women; and Article 3, which called for the criminalization of religious offenses (Marks 2012). Even though all three articles impinged on international norms, this section's focus will be on Article 3 only. This is because Article 3, which criminalized criticism of religion and thus any public expression of atheism as well as any attack on that which is considered sacred, was the most problematic as it would have had a significant impact on all other rights and freedoms including those affected by Article 5 and Article 28. More particularly, Article 3 set considerable limits on how Tunisians were to approach issues such as public morals, women's rights, inheritance, divorce, adoption and sex. The article stated that 'The state guarantees freedom of religious belief and practice and criminalizes all attacks on that which is sacred'. Considered sacred are such things as God and belief in God, the prophets, the sacred books and places of worship. Insulting religion, deriding God or representing the prophet Mohamed would be considered an offense. The question is, how would judges decide on such matters? Would the background of the judge set the limits/extents of the accused's individual's liberty? The nebulous nature of the article was problematic; it left the door wide open to potential abuses of power and it suggested that not all speech is equally protected, particularly not that of atheists. Further questions arising from the article include whether or not scientific research that denies the existence of God could be distributed in Tunisia, whether evolution theory would be taught in schools and whether heterosexuality is considered to be a 'sacred' issue.

The Ennahda Party proposed Article 3 after what it considered to be provocations by Tunisian atheists regarding Tunisians' 'cultural sensitivities' (Hassassi 2012). These provocations included the airing of a film by Tunisian director Nadia El-Fani originally titled *No God, No Master*. The film was considered blasphemous to religion and, as a result, disruptive of 'public order and public morals' (it had stirred members of the Tunisian Salafi movement to riot in the country) (Hassassi 2012). In another incident, the Iranian film *Persepolis* aired on the Nessma TV channel:

> The film … shows a depiction of God … which prompted a mob attack on Nessma's Headquarters. Karoui [the head of the television channel] could have faced up to three years' imprisonment under Article 48 of the old Press Code for libeling a religion and up to five years under Article 121(3) of the Penal Code for distributing information that could do harm to 'public order or good morals'. Ultimately, Karoui was forced to pay a fine of 1200 TND ($750). Those charged with attacking Nessma's headquarters and intimidating or assaulting staff members were asked to pay a fine of only 9.6 TND ($6) (Barrie 2012).

In another incident, nudity was considered morally offensive. Christopher Barrie writes, 'the same article of the Penal Code was relied upon to sentence Nasreddine Ben Saida who was detained pretrial and fined 1,000 TND ($625) for allowing the publication, in his *Attounissia* newspaper, of a picture of German-Tunisian footballer Sami Khedira in an embrace with a nude model (Barrie 2012; see also Human Rights Watch 2012).

Apparent in these incidents is an inability to shed some of the most repressive laws that restricted freedom of speech during Ben Ali's era. Yet rescinding these laws are the first steps to take in order to reconstruct the public sphere, both literally and figuratively, and to promote a different political culture from the previous one. Not doing so arguably reflects an inability to vet past attitudes about basic human needs and rights. Christopher Barrie explains, 'To some extent, the faltering process of media reform can be attributed to the failure to adopt the new Press Code as elaborated in November 2011 by the National Committee of Information and Communication Reform (INRIC). One must, however, ask why, despite commitments to the contrary, the government and justice system have so consistently failed to implement this new law or pay heed to the recommendations of the INRIC' (Barrie 2012). Monica Marks' remarks provide some insight into Barrie's question:

> Considering the pitched nature of these controversies, however, civil society has remained puzzlingly mute concerning Article 3, which may well present the most problematic portion of the draft constitution. Although 7,000 women and men marched through downtown Tunis to protest against women's perceived complementarity in Article 28, no such protests against Article 3 have taken place. Groups that would typically be expected to oppose Article 3, like the Tunisian League of Human Rights, journalists' associations, and secularly oriented political parties, have kept silent … (Marks 2012)

This refusal to take to the streets in order to protest Article 3 alludes to the repressive political discourse to which both the previous regime and the Islamists adhere, where limitations on civil liberties are the rule given their nebulous nature. In this case, activists appear to prefer to stay home rather than challenge or to be seen as challenging the Islamic faith. Not protesting the article seems to demonstrate the persistence of a repressive political culture, supported by a repressive legal tradition.[20] According to Sarah Whitson, Middle East and North Africa director at Human Rights Watch, '[a]s long as these repressive Ben Ali-era laws are on the books, authorities will have the temptation to use them whenever politically convenient' (Human Rights Watch 2012).

The August 2012 iteration of the constitution has since been superseded by another draft that at the time of writing is expected to form the basis for negotiations leading toward a permanent constitution.[21] This new draft deletes the articles discussed above in favor of more vague formulations on the issues of the status of women, religion and the media. While these formulations seem to be evidence of compromise on the part of the Ennahda Party with its secular political opponents, they should not be seen as the last word on the party's commitments regarding human rights and democracy. This is because of the important divisions within Ennahda, whose intellectual leadership is willing to compromise on these issues with its secular political opponents yet whose base is considerably more radical and considers that the leadership has departed from its Islamist mission (Khalaf 2013). As the distance increases between the leadership and the more radical base of the party, and as the country's powerful Salafist movement – with its more puritanical interpretation of Islam – gains in strength and thus increasingly becomes the power nexus with which compromise is necessary rather than the secular political parties, it does not seem at all clear that Ennahda will be able or will want to protect the values essential to transitional justice. Indeed, the fact of its movement on these values between one draft of the constitution and subsequent drafts illustrates that its new positions are very soft, contextual and even opportunistic.

Unless the new regime definitively commits itself to these new positions and demonstrates its commitment by defending them in the long term, it is difficult to see Tunisian society moving past the repressive era by addressing past human rights abuses, fostering individual and national reconciliation, and establishing justice – all basic requirements of a successful transitional justice process. More particularly, although Tunisia's Islamists have promised to break free from the Ben Ali era and redress previous grievances, it is possible that not everyone will be able to partake in this process to the fullest extent. This is because for the Islamists, *fusion* and *oneness* (see the discourse section above) are the ideals of current prominent Islamists – thus, Tunisian culture should come together on the basis of the majority's Islamic ideals, despite the fact that not all Tunisians are Islamists.

Egyptian Islamists: women's rights

In Egypt, a new era is emerging, which could put an end to the three decades of Hosni Mubarak's rule with its harsh repression, arbitrary detention and widespread torture.[22] By June 2012, Egyptians were voting for a new president in what turned out to be the country's first democratic and free elections ever. On 30 June 2012, Mohamed Morsi, the leader of the Freedom and Justice Party – the political wing of the Islamist Egyptian Muslim Brotherhood – became president.[23] During his campaign for the presidency, Morsi promised the Egyptian people a liberal democracy with everything that democratic rule supposedly entails, and one that respects individual freedoms and civil rights (Levs 2012).[24] Indeed, he stated that there is no such thing as an Islamic democracy: 'There is democracy only ... The people are the source of authority.' When asked about the role of women, he asserted that 'women's rights are equal to men' (Levs 2012).

But many observers were fearful that the Muslim Brotherhood did not necessarily mean to keep its promises. Some have argued that President Morsi represents the older, more conservative wing of the Muslim Brotherhood and has endorsed a strict Islamic vision that appeals to the more conservative segments of the Egyptian people, such as the Salafis. Indeed, Morsi's drafting of the Muslim Brothers' platform of 2007, in which he inserted clauses excluding women and minorities from access to the presidency, firmly established his image as a conservative.[25] The Constituent Assembly, formed by Morsi and the People's Assembly (dominated by Islamists) to draft a new Egyptian democratic constitution, was criticized as many of its members and observers complained that the chosen body was dominated by the Muslim Brothers and was not representative of Egyptian society (ON TV 2012). This Islamist domination led Constituent Assembly members to resign, one of whom argued at the time that 'it is clear that the constitution is being shaped in order to satisfy one specific group who is codifying the concept of the religious state in order to seize power' (Ahmad al-Buhayri et al. 2012, author's translation).

The impact of such codification could have been disastrous for women's rights, as Dalia Ziada wrote at the time:

> After the long speech they [Morsi's advisers] gave about how Morsi will empower the civil society and that the Muslim Brotherhood will respect human rights including women's rights, a colleague of mine raised his hand to ask a question. 'I saw in your booklet that you respect human rights and women rights according to Sharia', my colleague asked. 'Is it different from the rights mentioned in the international conventions that Egypt has signed?' The answer given by one of the leaders of Morsi's campaign was shocking. 'Sharia values women more than the international conventions', the Morsi adviser said. 'Do you know that according to Sharia the woman may choose not to breastfeed her child or clean the house until her husband pays her for doing this?' he added confidently, to much laughter in the room. This simple

> conversation, more than anything, sums up how the Muslim Brotherhood views women's rights and what the status of women is likely to be under its rule (Ziada 2012).

For mainstream Egyptian Islamists, challenging past silences and lies and establishing a culture that respects human rights and individual freedoms do not appear to include women. Indeed, in the proposed draft constitution of summer 2012 whose drafting was undertaken by an assembly led by a majority of Islamists, Article 36 states, 'the state works to ensure the equality of men and women in political, economic, cultural and social sectors of life and all other sectors without undermining the precepts (*ahkam*) of the Islamic law … The state also works to help her succeed in managing her duties towards her family and her work' (al-Qumsan 2012).

In the draft constitution that was finally ratified in December 2012, Article 36 was integrated into Article 10 which indirectly states the same thing. The article reads, 'The family is the basis of society, founded on *religion*, ethics and patriotism. Both the state and society commit to upkeep the authenticity of the Egyptian family … and the state undertakes to fully subsidize mother and child care services, and to help the woman balance between her duties towards her family and her work' (emphasis added; author's translation). The problem with this sort of clause is that interpretations of religion continue to subjugate women to a different role than that of men, as clearly – and perhaps naively – stated by Morsi's campaign advisor, and as made clear within these articles. Both the advisor's answer and Article 10's implications raise concerns about the possibility of redressing women's grievances and moving towards women achieving their full citizenship rights. Some feminists and activists even feared that rights and changes achieved during the last 20 years may have been reversed as Article 10 demonstrates unwillingness, and perhaps even an inability, to uphold internationally defined standards. This dichotomous understanding of gender roles reflects similar norms upheld during the Mubarak era and is an example of the sort of positions to be shed to prevent delaying the transitional justice process and democratization.

That clause 36 of the constitution was changed before it finally became law does not alter the fact that the document shows a dubious commitment to human rights on the part of the Freedom and Justice Party. Indeed, even more so than the draft of the Tunisian constitution cited above, the December 2012 Egyptian constitution accorded an important place to sharia law as 'principal source of legislation' (Article 2), with the religious scholars of al-Azhar to interpret that law (Article 4) (Youssef 2012). As regards women's rights in particular, it did not improve upon the already dubious protection provided under the previous constitution, assigning women the role of the 'other' in society (Al-Ali 2012).

It seems therefore that the current major Egyptian Islamist political forces do not consider women to be victims of the previous repressive regime and do not feel that their rights need to be incorporated within the national reconciliation agenda.[26] In their view, the public arena would remain the domain of men. More importantly, primordial and dichotomous structures would continue to be proclaimed as organic and timeless, and so remain 'naturally' untouched and unproblematic. What this means for women and how their possible inclusion within the political system after decades of exclusion will change the Egyptian Muslim Brothers has yet to be seen. One might argue in such a context that the main issue is not whether democracy is really at the heart of the new political forces – whether or not Islamist – but rather what democracy entails if it is understood to be individual freedom and civil rights within the confines of the Islamic faith. Again, the implications for the aim of transitional justice to create societal cohesion through inclusion are significant.

Syria: violence, human rights abuses and factionalism[27]

In Syria, breaking with the past will entail respecting the rule of law, refraining from using the supposed threat of factionalism and Sunni sectarian domination to justify government repression and refraining from using violence as a political tool in the name of retribution. Accordingly, this section will explore whether the main Islamist actors on the ground, namely Islamist factions within the Free Syrian Army (FSA) – militants fighting the incumbent regime – aim to establish a culture that respects human rights, as well as whether they can reconstruct the public sphere, empower disenfranchised groups and challenge past silences and lies. In so doing, we will discuss whether transitional justice can be expected to be part of Syria's near future if and when the regime falls.[28]

Like Tunisia and Egypt, Syria has witnessed the revolutionary commotion of the Arab Spring. Protestors took to the street and demanded political change, the end of corruption, justice and the rule of law. Soon, however, regime repression ensued. Thousands were imprisoned, tortured and killed just for protesting. The FSA emerged after months of peaceful protesting with the avowed aim of defending the protestors. These men, many of whom are deserters from Syria's official army, could no longer stand by and carry out the regime's orders. Moreover, many within Syria also believe that the regime left Syrians with no other choice but to resist with force. But, as the FSA secures more territory and gains more power within a context that has now degenerated into civil war, it becomes more important than ever to scrutinize its actions.

In examining its defense strategy, one wonders where the exact line is between defense and revenge. After all, some of the FSA brigades and individual members' actions are troubling to many within Syria and beyond, including those that support and have contributed in one way or another to the Syrian uprising. This is partly because some of the militant factions seem to have Islamized (eg al-Nusra Front militia, Suleiman al-Farsi brigade), meaning that their members are now fighting the Bashar regime in the name of Sunni Islam. This is despite the fact that Sunnis represent only one faction within Syria's diverse society. Furthermore, a majority of Syrians, some of whom also happen to be Sunni, prefer an entirely secular system.[29]

Indeed, many Syrian observers, European security officers, as well as Syrian citizens in general are afraid that some FSA members are not only religiously radicalizing but also turning to political Islam (that is, Islamizing). A number of incidents have stirred these fears.[30] One involved the beheading of a *shabiha* (a pro-regime mercenary who is part of pro-regime ghost militias) accused by members of the al-Nusra front militia of raping and murdering a girl (*Los Angeles Times* 2012). Another incident occurred in the city of Aleppo: 'the FSA-affiliated Tawheed Brigade captured members of the Barri clan. Seated in a line on a dirty floor, they faced the cameraman, one by one. Most of their faces were bloodied. Ringleader Zeyno Barri, stripped to his underwear, looked forlorn and humiliated – and like a man who knew the end was near' (Hanano 2012). In early September 2012, another Islamist group called The Suleiman al-Farisi brigade killed as many as 20 soldiers. Handcuffed and bloodied, they were apparently executed as members of the brigade stood around their bodies (Holmes and Solomon 2012). Fears are especially rising given that radical Islamists such as Abu Baseer al-Tartusi, a British resident, are in Syria and helping with the uprising (Maher 2012).

Increased religious radicalization of the fight is thus a real threat. The violent rebels and the incidents described reveal that human rights violations are no longer the exclusive preserve of the regime – they are also part of the rebels' actions and thus risk adversely affecting Syrian society in the future as well as potentially compromising the ability of the rebels to legitimately oversee a transitional process. They also suggest that the aftermath of the uprising could have a factional face, especially given that many of the *shabiha* are accused of being of the Alawi Muslim sect, while the vast majority of the FSA are Sunni Muslim. Indeed, the battle against Syria's regime is taking a factional face. This is because the Bashar regime is wrongly[31] seen by the public masses as Alawite, and thus as at odds with the country's Sunni majority. Given this perception, the violence involved is providing 'the kind of sectarian animus that al-Qaeda relied on to escalate its activities in Iraq. And the increasingly wanton violence Assad's regime is unleashing on rebels and innocent bystanders alike is producing the sort of ghastly images of massacred and mutilated bodies that – once transformed into al-Qaeda recruitment propaganda – helped radicalize and motivate outraged European Muslim youth to take up combat in Afghanistan, Iraq and Algeria' (Crumley 2012; see also Maher 2012). Indeed, a number of Syrians have pointed out that almost every family in Syria is directly touched by the violence. Some Sunni families have lost loved ones because of the regime actions, while some Alawis have suffered similar losses as a result of actions by the militant rebels. To those affected, the rebellion has turned into a polarizing battle between Syria's factions rather than between a repressive regime and pro-democracy forces.

Further complicating the situation is that some of the rebels who are committing human rights crimes are doing so in the name of Islamism. This would seem to greatly compromise their ability eventually to play a constructive role in efforts to re-unify Syrian society across ideological lines through transitional justice processes that are fair and respectful of due process and of victims' rights. Indeed, will restorative justice – which is concerned with healing the community as a whole by involving all stakeholders, including victims and perpetrators (Hayner 2011: 86–106; Cooper 2001: 205–15; Minow 2000; Fisher 2012: 146–8) – even be possible within the community? More broadly, one is left to wonder how a new culture of reconciliation and new, more inclusive institutions will emerge if violent, repressive means similar to those employed by the Assad regime to maintain power are used to bring about change, and are justified based on factionalism, that is, Islamism.

What does seem clear is that the scale and ferocity of the militarized rebellion is both a symptom of the deep physical and psychological violence visited on Syrians over the past 40 years of repressive rule, as well as a sign of how significant the wounds that will have to be healed are. Such healing is of course rendered even more difficult the longer the present status quo continues, with war between the regime forces and the FSA leading to ever more war crimes and atrocities as well as a deepening of divisions and hatreds. Such factionalism undermines the possibility of eventually achieving a shared understanding of events, while the large number of individuals and families that have become involved on one side or another poisons the possibility of future efforts to promote peace and stability in the country. A further challenge arises from the fact that many Syrians talk about eventual justice from a retributive standpoint as opposed to a restorative one, which would seem to point toward the likelihood of continuing finger-pointing and mutual accusations – probably along communal lines – rather than shared efforts to reconcile. All of these factors underline the challenge for Syrians in ultimately coming together under a situation of respect for the rule of law and human rights, and make clear the very serious difficulties that will eventually face transitional justice processes in the country.

Conclusion

This chapter posits that the Arab Spring movement has shown that international principles of human rights, citizenship, equality, justice and democracy are the frame of reference in the Arab region. While these concepts are currently theoretically praised by Islamist and secularist parties alike, the actual larger implications of what they mean and the trade-offs they involve remain to be fully developed within the present Arab political context. Indeed, this chapter demonstrates that the *madani* (civic), democratic and respectful-of-human-rights policies that Egypt and Tunisia's Islamists promised within their electoral programs have subtle caveats within them and have, moreover, lost some of their meaning when put into practice. The issue of real commitment to human rights is even more stark in Syria, where opposition Islamist militias within the FSA have committed human rights abuses in the name of God. This chapter argues that the reason behind these discrepancies is an Islamic political imagination that incorporates traditional interpretations of the Islamic creed while also attempting to conform to a liberal democratic vision.

Of course, Islamists have clearly changed their stance from only a few decades ago when the London-based Islamic Council came up with the Islamic Universal Declaration for Human Rights – a document that did not really grasp the concept of individual freedoms – and when the recognized Islamic authority on human rights, Sheikh Muhammad al-Ghazali, issued a religious decree authorizing the killing of Muslims who want to suspend the sharia.[33] That being said, however, no major Arab thinker, scholar, journalist or observer taking an active part in the Arab Spring has yet disputed the sanctity of the sharia within a possible constitutional framework. Thus, while the Arab Spring has allowed for more transparency, and people are debating issues of democracy, the fundamental question as to whether someone who is born a Muslim can repudiate their religion or stray from its dictates is still a taboo subject. This in turn impacts upon countless other issues within society; for example, Christian and Muslim citizens cannot inter-marry, women and men are not treated as equals and minorities are treated as subalterns. The conservative ulamas remain dominant forces therefore, both in countries where the Islamists form the government and in those in which they do not. Under these circumstances, one wonders if transition towards liberal democracy and a culture founded on human rights can proceed, even incrementally and gradually. Of course, in saying this, it is clear that events in the region remain highly dynamic, and moreover that it is difficult to take into account all the factors that influence the political and social spheres in Arab Spring countries. Yet this should not dissuade us from continuing to scrutinize events and actions as well as parse policies, to move beyond the rhetoric and seek to fully understand the complicated and often contradictory impulses of the Islamists as they navigate between 'tradition' and the values fundamental to liberal democracy. As this chapter has shown, doing so will also tell us a great deal about whether or not transitional justice can be successful in the region in the long term.

Notes

1 The 'mainstream Islamists' is a reference to the major Islamist actors and not to the small, extremist groups who are also Islamists but who have not and who have little chance of achieving widespread political success, nor to the Salafi groups. Future uses of the term 'Islamists' in this chapter refer to these mainstream Islamists unless otherwise specified.

2 For instance, Mohamed Morsi, the then-president of Egypt and the former leader of the Egyptian Muslim Brotherhood, asserted during the 67th meeting of the UN General council (27 September 2012) that Egypt is committed to establishing a democratic rule that guarantees human freedoms and rights.

3 This chapter assumes the interconnection between transitional justice and democracy as the only system of governance that makes it possible to rebuild social trust and to promote reconciliation.

4 For an exhaustive account of the intellectual genealogy of transitional justice, see Teitel

2003. According to Teitel, transitional justice is 'the conception of justice associated with periods of transitional change, characterized by the legal responses to confront the wrongdoing of repressive predecessor regimes' (p 69).

5 For further discussion of this point, see the introductory chapter.

6 Emphasis is on women's rights, although freedom of expression and freedom of the press are major issues that Egyptians are debating at the time of writing; however, space constraints make it impossible to explore these issues.

7 As is also argued in Ch 8.

8 Indeed, some might argue that they are already doing/have already done this.

9 Vetting is defined as 'processes for assessing an individual's integrity as a means of determining his or her suitability for public employment. "Integrity" is used here to refer to "a person's adherence to relevant standards of human rights and professional conduct, including her or his financial propriety"'. And 'screening public employees or candidates for public employment to determine if their prior conduct (including, most importantly from a transitional justice perspective, their respect for human rights standards) warrants their exclusion from public institutions' (ICTJ 2007: 17).

10 See Ch 6 for further consideration of the topic of vetting.

11 The Egyptian Muslim Brothers are the parent organization for the Freedom and Justice Party, which was the ruling political party in Egypt until July 2013.

12 All monotheisms include both democratic and non-democratic values within their founding texts.

13 Only the three Abrahamic religions (al-adyan al-samawiyya) are recognized in the draft constitution, which was finally ratified in December 2012 (arts 3 and 43). Other belief systems are not considered 'religions' according to the ruling party in Egypt. See *France 24 online* 2012. See also comments made by the Minister of Information, Salah Abd al-Maqsud, to the al-Hurra channel during an interview with journalist Tareq al-Shami on 7 September 2012.

14 See sections 'ri'ayat huquq al-muwatana' ['the safeguarding of citizenship rights'] and 'almabade' al-asasiya al-lati nas'a li-tahqiqiha' ['the fundamental principles we aim at attaining'], available online at www.fj-p.com .

15 See 'al-riyada al-diniya' ['the precedence of religion'] available online at www.ennahda.tn/ الريادة الدينية.

16 This is often stated by Islamist thinkers such as H. al-Banna, A. Maududi and R. al-Ghannoushi.

17 See, eg the official website of the Ennahda Party, available online at www.ennahdha.tn (Arabic), especially under the section 'Fikr' ('thought'). See also www.Ikhwanweb.com for a glimpse into the political vision of the Egyptian Muslim Brothers.

18 Olivier Roy writes: 'There exists unquestionably what one might call an "Islamic Political Imagination" (in the sense of a horizon of thought), which recurs in the corpus of the ulamas and is explicit in the texts of the salfists…and the Islamists': Roy 1994: 13.

19 Even when it comes to establishing Islamic human rights, Ann E. Mayer states in her seminal book on Islam and human rights that Islamic thinkers who aim to establish Islamic human rights 'are reluctant to state openly that following Islamic criteria entails departures from the norms of international law': Mayer 1991: 98. Quoted in Tibi 1994: 277.

20 It is important to note that this is not the stand of all Islam's ulamas; a few, such as Egyptian judge Muhammad al-Ashmawi, Syrian Islamic thinker, Muhammad Habash and Sudanese legal scholar, Abdullahi al-Naim, argue that there is no compulsion in Islam.

21 A translation of the latest draft of the constitution is available at www.constitutionnet.org/files/tunisian_consititution14_dec_2012-english-undp.pdf .

22 Of course, such processes are never smooth – witness the removal of the democratically elected Freedom and Justice Party from office by the Supreme Council of the Armed Forces in July 2013.
23 Morsi won 52% of the votes. The other candidate, former Hosni Mubarak official Ahmed Shafik, took 48% of the votes.
24 Mohamed Morsi had asserted his commitment to a liberal democracy on many occasions, including on television, for instance in an interview with Yusri Fuda on his famous programme *Akher Kalam.*
25 This discourse was criticized by a few Muslim Brothers within Egypt, such as Abd al-Muneim Abu al-Futuh (Abdel Moneim Aboul Fotouh), and by the Syrian Muslim Brothers' superintendant at the time, Sadr al-Din al-Bayanuni. For an account of events as to the rise of the MB to power in Egypt, see Coleman 2012.
26 A point that is explored in more detail in Ch 8.
27 Even in Libya, where 99% of the population is Sunni Muslim, the nascent process of national reconciliation, the halting of human rights abuses and the process of democratic construction are being challenged. Salafis, adhering to a purist interpretation of the Islamic creed, have undertaken the destruction of historic Sufi sites in the cities of Tripoli, Misrata and Zlitan. This attests not only to the lack of law and order at this point of the transition towards democracy, but also to the culture of intolerance to which Libyans have to respond if they are to create democratic institutions. See Sadiki 2012.
28 The FSA is part of the Syrian National Council, which is a main opposition coalition; given their membership in this Council and as a result of their significant presence on the ground, they could be expected to play a significant role in any post-Assad regime scenario. If, however, the regime does not fall, it seems highly unlikely that transitional justice would take place in any shape or form.
29 Minorities in Syria – who form around 30% of Syrians – and a large part of the Sunni majority prefer a secular regime. Although there are no surveys and statistics to verify this statement, my own extensive fieldwork, in addition to interviews with Syrian intellectuals, sociologists and journalists, suggests that it is the case. One might also point to the Syrian National Council, which is a secular opposition movement that has expressed its deep commitment to the rule of law, the cause of human rights and civil liberties.
30 Many more abuses of power and horrific incidents have occurred since the writing of this chapter.
31 'Wrongly' because the regime is a ruling coalition dominated by a large Alawi family (and which has attracted many Alawis as a result, hence the perception that the regime is Alawi), but which also includes Sunnis, Christians and other Syrian factions. The reality is that anyone who wishes to be part of the ruling coalition and is willing to play the regime's game of corruption and repression can enter the coalition. An Alawi who refuses to play by the regime's rules is as ostracized as anyone else, while a Sunni who is willing to enable the power clique is as welcome as anyone else. Claims that Alawis have it easier in Syria might be a result of the corruption that allows those in power to favor those they know.
32 Author's own fieldwork.
33 It is not long ago that Bassam Tibi wrote, 'fundamentalist sheikh al-Ghazali who is considered to be the Islamic authority on human rights after the publication of the above referenced book, in June 1993 issued a Fetwa (religious decree) in which he authorizes killing every Muslim who publicly subscribes to suspending the shari'a. This Fetwa was given in a testimony during the trial of the killers of the Egyptian writer Faraj Fuda who was assassinated for having published books supporting secular views. The Fetwa of the Egyptian Sheikh al-Ghazali was used later also by Algerian fundamentalists to

legitimize their killing of intellectuals like the sociologist Mohammed Boukhobza and the essayist Taher Jaout. (In 1993, twelve leading Algerian intellectuals were slain.)': Tibi 1994: 289–90.

Bibliography

Al-Ali, Z (2012) 'The new Egyptian constitution: an initial assessment of its merits and flaws', *openDemocracy*, 26 December, available online at www.opendemocracy.net/zaid-al-ali/new-egyptian-constitution-initial-assessment-of-its-merits-and-flaws.

Al-Buhayri, A. et al. (2012) 'Itifaq al-Azhar wa al-Kanisa ala baqa' al-mada al-thania dun ta'dil, al-Masry al-Youm, N 3026, 25 September, available online at today.almasryalyoum.com….aspx?articleID=454527. Article last viewed October 2013.

Al-Qumsan, N. (2012) 'Dastur Misr al-Jadid lil-Rijal Faqat' ['Egypt's new Constitution for Men Only'], al-Watan online, 22 September, available online at elwatannews.com/news/details/51842.

Al-Tahhan, M. (2002) *al-Fikr al-siyasi al-Muaser: dirasa fi fikr al-ikhwan al-mulsimin* (Dar al-tawzi wa al-nashr al-islamiyya).

Arabic News Digest (2012) 'Tunisia's Totalitarianism', *The National* (UAE), 29 August, available online at www.thenational.ae/thenationalconversation/comment/tunisias-totalitarianism.

Barrie, C. (2012) 'Tunisian Media: al-Nahda Tightens its Control', al-Akhbar English, 6 September, available online at http://english.al-akhbar.com/content/tunisian-media-al-nahda-tightens-its-control.

Coleman, I. (2012) 'Is Egypt Headed for Islamist Rule?', i-CNN, 27 April, available online at http://edition.cnn.com/2012/04/26/opinion/coleman-egypt-islam/index.html).

Cooper, D. (2001) 'Collective Responsibility, "Moral Luck", and Reconciliation', in Alesandar Jokic (ed.), *War Crimes and Collective Wrongdoing: A Reader* (Blackwell).

Crumley, B. (2012) 'As Syrian Conflict Rages, France Examines Potential Terrorism Risks', *Time World*, 31 August, available online at http://world.time.com/2012/08/31/as-syrian-conflict-rages-france-examines-potential-terror-risks/.

Ennahda (2013) 'Ennahda official program', available online at www.ennahda.tn.

Fisher, K. (2012) *Moral Accountability and International Criminal Law: Holding Agents of Atrocity Accountable to the World* (Routledge). www.fj-p.com

France 24 Online (2012) 'Mawad Mukhtalaf Aleyha', 25 December, available online at www.france24.com/ar/20121225-مصر-دستور-مواد-اختلاف-قوى-مدنية-إسلامية.

Freedom and Justice Party (2013), Official website, available online at www.fj-p.com.

Gudrun, K. (1993) 'Islamist Notions of Democracy', 183(23) *Middle East Research and Information Report*, available online at www.merip.org/mer/mer183/islamist-notions-democracy.

Gulfnews.com (2013) 'Egypt Brotherhood rejects UN Women Charter', 17 March, available online at gulfnews.com/news/region/egypt/egypt-brotherhood-rejects-un-women-charter-1.1159395.

Hanano, A. (2012) 'FSA Rebels Accused of War Crimes Shape Syria's Future', *The National* (UAE), 29 August, available online at www.thenational.ae/thenationalconversation/comment/fsa-rebels-accused-of-war-crimes-shape-syrias-future#page1.

Hassassi, H. (2012) 'Campaign to Defend Artists Accused of Disturbing Public Order',

3 September, available online at www.tunisia-live.net/2012/09/03/campaign-to-defend-artists-accused-of-disturbing-public-order/.

Hayner, P. (2001) *Unspeakable Truths: Confronting State Terror and Atrocity* (Routledge).

Holmes, O. and Solomon, E. (2012) 'Video Shows 20 Syrian Soldiers Believed Executed', *Reuters*, 10 September, available online at www.reuters.com/article/2012/09/10/us-syria-crisis-execution-idUSBRE8890V420120910.

Human Rights Watch (2012) 'Tunisia: Seven years jail for mocking Islam', 6 April, available online at www.hrw.org/news/2012/04/06/tunisia-seven-years-jail-mocking-islam.

ICTJ (2007) *Justice as Prevention: Vetting Public Employees in Transitional Societies* (Social Science Research Council), available online at www.ssrc.org/workspace/images/crm/new_publication_3/%7B57efec93-284a-de11-afac-001cc477ec70%7D.pdf.

Ikhwan Web (2013), Ikhwan Web: The Muslim Brotherhood's Official Website, available online at www.Ikhwanweb.com

Khalaf, R. (2013) 'Nahda party reflects a divided Tunisia', 14 February, available online at http://www.ft.com/intl/cms/s/37efc52e-76a3-11e2-8569-00144feabdc0,Authorised=false.html?_i_location=http%3A%2F%2Fwww.ft.com%2Fcms%2Fs%2F0%2F37efc52e-76a3-11e2-8569-00144feabdc0.html%3Fsiteedition%3Dintl&siteedition=intl&_i_referer=#axzz2UVaR9wmQ

Levs, J. (2012) 'Islamic presidential candidate promises democracy', i-cnn, 15 June, available online at http://articles.cnn.com/2012-06-15/middleeast/world_meast_egypt-election-morsi_1_prime-minister-ahmed-shafik-islamic-muslim-brotherhood?_s=PM:MIDDLEEAST.

Los Angeles Times (2012) 'In Syria, Islamic Militants May Complicate Uprising', *LA Times* online, 25 August, available online at www.latimes.com/news/nationworld/world/la-fg-syria-foreign-fighters-20120826,0,7940241.story?page=1.

Maher, S. (2012) 'British Residents Join Syrian Uprising', *The Spectator*, 16 August, available online at http://blogs.spectator.co.uk/coffeehouse/2012/08/british-residents-join-syrian-uprising/.

Marks, M. (2012) 'Speaking on the Unspeakable: Blasphemy & the Tunisian Constitution', 4 September, available online at http://carnegieendowment.org/2012/09/04/speaking-on-unspeakable-blasphemy-tunisian-constitution/drbh.

Mayer, A. (1991) *Islam and Human Rights: Tradition and Politics* (Westview Press).

Minow, M. (2000) 'The Hope for Healing: What Can Truth Commissions Do?' in Rotberg, R. I. and Thompson, D. (eds) (2000) *Truth v. Justice: The Morality of Truth Commissions* (Princeton University Press).

ON TV (2012) 'Akher Kalam with Yusri Fuda', 25 September.

Roy, O. (1994) *The Failure of Political Islam*, translated by Carol Volk (Harvard University Press).

Sadiki, L. (2012) 'Libya: Testing Tolerance', aljazeera online, 4 September, available online at www.aljazeera.com/indepth/opinion/2012/09/201291125110843653.html.

Teitel, R. G. (2003) 'A Genealogy of Transitional Justice', 16 *Harvard Human Rights Journal* 69.

Tibi, B. (1994) 'Islamic Law, Human Rights, and Morality', 16(2) *Human Rights Quarterly* 277.

Youssef, N. (2012) 'Egypt's draft constitution translated', *Egypt Independent*, 12 February, available online at http://www.egyptindependent.com/news/egypt-s-draft-constitution-translated

Ziada, D. (2012) 'Egypt's Islamists: Much to prove on women's rights', Special for CNN, 28 June, available online at http://edition.cnn.com/2012/06/28/opinion/egypt-womens-rights/index.html.

Chapter 8

Transitional justice and the Arab Spring from a gender perspective

Elham Manea

Many scholars have focused on the question of gender in the Arab Middle East and North Africa (MENA) region. They have diverged, however, in the way they approach the issue and especially in the conceptions of women's rights and of women's place in society that underlie that approach. Some use an essentialist and particularistic approach, arguing that the conditions women experience should be understood within their religious and cultural contexts and therefore may not be compared with 'other' conceptions of 'women's rights'. Often they tend to see justice from a 'community' perspective, arguing that in 'different cultural contexts' the interests of the group take precedence over those of the individual. Among others, Charles Taylor (1994) offers a theoretical basis for this approach in arguing for a multicultural 'politics of recognition'.

Along the same lines, most Islamist groups claim that the concept of 'women's rights' is a Western invention that does not apply to an 'Islamic society'. They often take the argument a step further and state that a religious conception of justice better protects women's dignity. This argument often ignores 'equal rights' in its conception of justice and dignity.[1] The consequences of both perspectives tend to be outright violations of women's and children's rights. These include denial of access to public life, along with child marriage, female genital mutilation, forced marriage and unequal rights in marriage, divorce and custody of children.

Another approach, espoused mainly by scholars from the MENA, tends to avoid an essentialist view of the region and instead insists on a universal approach to women's rights.[2] It highlights how religion and culture have been used to justify the mistreatment of women and to perpetuate unequal power structures that favour patriarchal notions of family and society. Counting myself among this group of scholars, I have suggested (Manea 2010) focusing on the consequences of *not applying* international norms on women's rights. The approach tries to bring in the human face of the suffering that results when human rights are violated, not only on an individual basis but also on a larger social level. By illuminating the grave consequences of violating human rights, this approach turns the discussion around. Rather than trying frantically to answer the question of whether human rights are universal, a different question emerges: Why are these rights being violated in the first place?

This divergence in the perceptions of the gender question has become very relevant in the aftermath of the Arab Spring, specifically considering the processes of transitional justice in the MENA region. The key objective of transitional justice is to help societies rebuild following rights abuses in a process founded on *societal trust* and *inclusive participation*. This makes gender central to transitional justice, as women clearly must play a principal part in this process. What is not clear is the roles that women will be allowed to play, especially with the rise of Islamist groups who reject the notion of universal human/women's rights.

At the same time, the transitional justice processes in the Middle East represent an enormous opportunity from a gender perspective since fundamental societal norms and values, as well as the institutions and laws that both embody and propagate those norms and values, are being re-examined and debated in many of the region's transitioning societies. This chapter argues that, from a gender perspective, it does not suffice merely to add 'gender' to measures of transitional justice, exposing in the process the widespread occurrence of sexual violence targeting women during times of political instability (Bell and O'Rourke 2007: 24). Instead, the concept of transitional justice must be widened to include restoring gender justice and equality in states that systematically discriminate against women through their legal systems and societal norms. It is clear, however, that this restoration process remains under threat in the region, given the existing institutional and societal barriers to women's participation and, more recently, the rise of Islamist groups. Certainly, a great deal is at stake as the processes of transitional justice unfold following the Arab Spring.

First, this chapter argues that the mere participation of women in revolutions does not necessarily lead to concrete gains from a gender perspective. The history of the MENA region provides ample examples that testify to this. The following section describes how women participated in the Arab Spring; how, in many states, they were targeted for sexual crimes by the security apparatus and violently attacked by Islamist extremists and others; and how, more often than not, they have been excluded from the political and constitutional bodies created during the transitional periods. The chapter then argues that a transitional justice process should not focus only on measures that address the grave sexual violations that occurred in some of these countries. In fact, it must also focus on targeting the systematic gender discrimination engrained in Arab legal systems.

History of women's rights in the MENA region

Historical examples illustrate that the political, economic and social changes brought about by revolutions in different regions of the world have presented women with unique opportunities. Indeed, traditional social structures and values that have historically oppressed women are often altered, weakened or overthrown by revolutions. New structures that present opportunities for women's upward mobility are often created (Julià and Ridha 2001).

Nevertheless, such success 'might be ephemeral, a product of crisis mobilization'

(Jaquette et al. 1994; cited in Julià and Ridha 2001: 584). When women participate in such events, they often end up with the gender status they had before the war or revolution. In some countries their new experiences do not replace traditional values and roles in the post-war/revolution periods and a return to normality has often meant a return to the status quo regarding gender relations. Once again, women's choices, rights and lives tend to become circumscribed by tradition, religion and male prerogatives. The real outcome of these experiences, however, was what Julià and Ridha (2001: 585) call 'unsettling women for the good': the process can transform women's perceptions of themselves and their roles in society.

This trend is hardly new in the MENA region. In fact, throughout history Arab women have played an integral role in many independence movements and struggles against occupation, and in the process defied social stereotypes and the traditional constraints. The moment the situation started to normalize, however, the old social norms and traditional perceptions of women's roles tended to reassert themselves. Examples of this are plentiful.

During the 1919 Egyptian revolution for national independence, women of diverse social backgrounds actively participated in actions ranging from public and/or sexually segregated demonstrations to boycotts of British goods. Women of the upper and middle classes organized themselves into the Women's Central Committee of the Wafd Party, the most popular Egyptian party, which rallied for Egypt independence from British colonial rule. The Committee issued press releases explaining women's positions on various political issues and events. But despite this very public engagement by women, the 1923 Constitution was silent on women's political rights. The political elites simply ignored women's right to suffrage once Britain was ready to negotiate (Hatem 2011; cited in Joseph 2000: 34–40).

Just like the Egyptian women's movement, the Syrian women's movement during the anti-colonial struggle (1922–1946) set the goal of national independence as its first priority. Women's demands and voting rights were relegated to a secondary position. 'Independence comes first', was the slogan at the time. Indeed, as Nikki R. Keddi described, Syrian women activists hesitated to demand full female suffrage during the first Arab Women's Conference held in Cairo in December 1944: 'A Syrian women's leader said that Syrian women were more concerned with national goals than with women's goals. She and the main Lebanese leader, while expressing higher hopes, dared only to demand partial suffrage for educated women' (quoted in Manea 2011: 177). Only in 1949, three years after independence, were educated women given the right to vote; two years later that right was extended to all Syrian women.

The same pattern repeated itself in Algeria, albeit in connection with another issue: the reform of Algerian Islamic family law. Following Algerian independence in 1962, the rhetoric of equality permeated a political discourse that included statements about women. Women's participation in the anti-colonial war had left many Algerians expecting changes once the guerrilla war was over (Charrad 2001). Promises to make changes to women's status were connected to their participation in the war for independence. For example, in 1963, the minister of justice declared that 'because of her effective contribution to the struggle for national liberation' the Algerian woman had 'earned her right to the city' and her role was 'no longer a matter of debate' (quoted in Charrad 2001: 187).

The glorification of women aside, governments rose and fell and the promises to change Algerian family law in a way that would reflect gender equality were never fulfilled. Not until 1984 did the state finally promulgate a unified family law, which was very conservative. Family, according to this law, was perceived as an 'agnatic kinship structure in which the patrilineal male line had primacy and women were subordinate to both husbands and male kin' (Charrad 2001: 197).

A final example is the indispensable role that Kuwaiti women played against the Iraqi occupation of their country in 1990. Though the tradition of democratic experience dates back to the 1960s in this small Gulf emirate, women had no right to suffrage. However, after actively participating in the anti-occupation movement they expected nothing less than their political rights. They were the first to stage a demonstration against the occupation; they smuggled arms; they distributed anti-occupation statements; and they hid Kuwaiti men who were being hunted by the Iraqi forces (Manea 2011: 153–5).

Fatima al-Abdali, who stayed in Kuwait during the occupation and participated in the anti- occupation movement, described this experience:

> We expected that we would gain our rights immediately after the liberation [1991]; that it would become clear [after what we had done] that we, men and women, are equals . . . and we stayed silent afterwards during the period of re-building Kuwait thinking that the political leadership would surely give us our rights. . . . [But] when they started to prepare for the 1992 elections, we realized that the women's issue was [not a priority]. They said no. Stay. You have done your duty [during the occupation], now stay at home. This was the point that made us decide to engage in the political struggle to gain our rights. (Manea 2011: 155)

We will return to al-Abdali and to the Kuwait example later in this chapter.

Women and the Arab Spring: between participation and marginalization

Will this pattern of participation and exclusion/marginalization repeat itself after the Arab Spring? A qualified answer requires that we make a distinction between three phases.

- **First phase: before the Arab Spring.** Women's participation in the Arab Spring was preceded by strong female activism. In fact, female activists were involved in civil society activities and movements seeking reform and justice in their own societies. Here, justice had a national dimension (political and economic reforms) in addition to gender-specific demands relating to women's rights.

- **Second phase: the Arab Spring.** During this phase the active participation of women was intertwined with situations where women were targeted sexually by the security apparatus in several authoritarian states. This was coupled with a conservative and Islamist backlash against women in general and the demands they raised. These attacks, it should be emphasized, have continued into the transitional phase.
- **Third phase: transitional.** Many transitional governments have exercised measures that exclude women. Tunisia stands as the exception. The outcome underlines the importance of approaching transitional justice from a wider perspective, one that situates gender justice and equality at the heart of any transitional processes in MENA countries.

In the following discussion, these phases are explained in more detail.

Before the Arab Spring

Over the past decade, women have been instrumental in various civil society movements calling for reform and change. These initiatives and activities involved the demands of political and economic reform and justice for women.

In Egypt, Esraa Abdel Fatah, an Egyptian blogger, was credited for mobilizing the first strike that led to the creation of the 6th April Movement. She created a Facebook group to support a textile workers' strike on 6 April 2008 – and 77,000 followers attended the demonstration. That day marked the first time protesters demanding political change in Egypt joined the efforts of those demanding economic justice. Abdel Fatah was later arrested (Abdel Fattah; in Worden 2012: 73).

During this same phase, women in Egypt campaigned successfully for changes in provisions of the Islamic family law that gave women more rights in issues of divorce and child custody. Others lobbied, albeit unsuccessfully, for an end to the Coptic Church's ban on divorce (the church permits divorce and a second marriage only in cases where a spouse commits adultery or converts to another Christian sect or another religion).

In Tunisia, Seham ben Sedrin was a vocal activist, criticizing the human rights violations of President Zine al-Abidine Ben Ali's regime. In 2000, she was one of the first to publish an online independent magazine, *El Kalima*, which gained her the wrath of Tunisian police forces. Her magazine provided a rare venue where people could express their demands for political reforms and shed light on the human rights violations committed under the Ben Ali regime.

Women in Tunisia were also visible in demands for economic justice. In 2008 they participated in the first popular demonstration that soon swept the region, as crowds protested against unemployment, the cost of living, nepotism and the unfair recruitment practices of the major employer in the region, the Gafsa Phosphate Company (Al Jourchi 2008 and Amnesty International 2009).

Amel Grami, a Tunisian professor and a leading activist for women's rights, recounted the first time women participated in activities against the Ben Ali regime in 2008: 'women of the Mining Basin in the south of Tunisia organized protest marches'; at that time 'such an act could lead to their death' (survey by author, October 2012).

Further, Tunisian women were demanding more reforms and rights to augment the progressive nature of Tunisian family law. Sometimes their efforts met with hostility. For example, on 13 August 2006, the fiftieth anniversary of the progressive Tunisian Personal Status Code, the Society of Democratic Women demanded equality between men and women in inheritance rights, but were overwhelmed as quasi-government newspapers launched a defamation campaign in the media.

In Yemen, well-known human rights activists such as Huda Al Attas, Amal Al Basha, Tawakkol Karman (joint winner of the Nobel Peace Prize) and Arwa Othman were involved directly in campaigns demanding political and social justice. In 2009, for example, they were all involved in a campaign to support the villagers in Ja'ashin, an area in Ibb where the feudal sheikh evicted dozens of families after they refused to pay 'taxes' and instead insisted on paying the municipalities directly (Manea 2012).

Moreover, Yemeni women activists were involved in many campaigns to increase women's political participation, to end child marriage and to change laws that require approval from male guardians for women to travel, work or gain identity cards and passports.

Finally, in Syria since 2000, women activists, including Razan Zaitouna, Suhair al Atasi and Fidaa al-Hourani, were the public faces of political initiatives calling for political reform. Fidaa al-Hourani chaired the National Council of the Damascus Declaration for National Democratic Change, composed of 250 leading opposition members who joined together on 16 August 2005 and signed a declaration calling for democratic change in Syria through peaceful means. She was arrested in December 2007, along with 11 male leaders of the declaration, underwent a sham trial and was sentenced to two-and-a-half years in prison.

Again, demands for political and economic reforms at this stage were accompanied by activities that aimed to change gender-biased laws. In 2002 women activists in Syria succeeded in gathering 15,000 signatures in a campaign to change child custody laws in a way that would establish the child's welfare as the ultimate goal. Similarly, women's organizations joined in a campaign against 'honour killings' and called for a change in Article 548 of the Syrian Penal Code, which allowed men involved in honour killings to be granted suspended sentences or less than a year in prison (Manea 2011: 184–6).

The Arab Spring phase

As shown above, it is important to situate women's participation in the Arab Spring within a wider context. Its way was paved by consistent activism over the last decade by women who sought reform and change in their own societies.

It should not come as a surprise, therefore, that when the uprisings began on 17 December 2010, the day Mohammad Bu Aziz self-immolated in Tunisia, women's participation was highly visible.

Just like their male counterparts, the women had had enough of minimal economic opportunities, political stagnation, brutal police state methods, corruption and lack of accountability.

The slogans that cried out for freedom, dignity, employment, social justice, equality, democracy and an end to the patronage system united both men and women in their call for change: 'Women and men stood side by side, marched together, protected each other from government forces, and were united in calling for reform and regime change' (Haleh Esfandiari; quoted in Heideman and Youssef 2012: 1).

The following section delineates forms of women's participation, acts of violence targeting women and measures of exclusion that followed in the transitional periods. The focus will be on the four countries where protests led to the overthrow of the incumbent presidents.

Forms of participation

Women's participation in the Arab Spring has taken different forms and varied from one country to another.

In Tunisia, women – bloggers, journalists, activists, trade unionists, students and mothers – mobilized and took to the streets demanding Ben Ali's resignation, along with freedom and dignity (FIDH 2012: 8).

Their participation took different forms. Women mobilized using Facebook; they documented events through photos and videos; and they participated actively in meetings of unions, parties and organizations. They attended demonstrations and strikes, and coordinated their activities with various organizations. They also sheltered the wounded and those fleeing police brutality, and helped to protect some neighbourhoods when law and order broke down in Tunisia.

In Egypt, women from across the Egyptian social spectrum – young and old, Muslim and Christian, veiled and unveiled, poor and affluent – filled the streets (Hatem 2011: 36). With Egyptian men they demanded freedom, justice, social justice and bread. Young female activists were credited for mobilizing the 25 January protest, along with their male counterparts. For instance, Asmaa Mahfouz, a 26-year-old blogger and a member of the 6th April Youth Movement, is credited with launching a successful online appeal to Egyptian men and women to join her in Tahrir Square on 25 January (Mahfouz 2011; FIDH 2012: 16).

In Libya, the uprising was in fact sparked by a women's demonstration on 15 February 2011. Mothers, sisters and widows of men who had died in the Abu Salim prison in Tripoli in 1996 gathered in front of the Court of Justice in Benghazi to protest against the arrest of their lawyer and denounced the failure of the authorities to investigate the deaths and more broadly the corruption of the Gaddafi regime. The violent police repression that targeted these women led to massive protests in several Libyan cities (FIDH 2012: 26).

Libyan women played both traditional and non-traditional roles in the uprising and the civil war that later erupted. They travelled with men to the front lines to set up makeshift kitchens; they were positioned inside Gaddafi strongholds and smuggled guns; and they carried information from one town to another. They also organized relief efforts, supported the injured and families and took up arms and fought alongside men (Omar 2011; FIDH 2012).

Finally, in Yemen, women defied strict traditional norms and participated in the protests demanding an end to President Saleh's corrupt regime. On 28 February 2011, in Taghier Square in Sana'a, a female protester recounted that in January 2011 only a handful of women had been present in a flood of male protesters (interview by author, Sana'a, 28 February 2011). By February, however, thousands of women had started to join the demonstrations.

Well-known activists such as the journalist Tawakkul Karman, leader of the NGO Women Journalists without Chains, and now a joint winner of the Nobel Peace Prize of 2011, became the public face of the Yemeni youth uprising.

Again, participation took traditional and non-traditional roles. In February 2011 women described how they cooked for the participants in the sit-in strikes, collected donations to buy tents and blankets and tended to the wounded. They participated in the security committees in the occupied squares in Sana'a, Taiz, Aden and elsewhere, where some gave lectures on issues of civil society and civil and human rights. Others documented the events and broadcast them using television, blogs, Twitter, Facebook and YouTube videos (visit to Yemen by author, February 2011; survey by author, October 2012).

Acts of violence targeting women

During the uprisings, and after the successful toppling of Arab autocrats in Tunisia, Egypt, Libya and Yemen, acts of violence that specifically targeted women were committed. Members of the security apparatus in several states systematically targeted women with sexual violence. Moreover, some Islamist groups attempted to enforce their harsh interpretation of Islam on women activists and their lives, by taking advantage of the collapse of law and order or the tacit approval of the incumbent regimes, or by becoming part of the new transitional order. Both types of violence were conducted within a larger societal context characterized by increased violence against women.

Acts of violence by supporters of the regime, especially rape and sexual violence, were most widespread in Libya. There, women were sexually targeted by Gaddafi forces as a means to demoralize the opposition. In fact, during the civil war (February to October 2011), clear evidence shows that rape was used throughout the country as a weapon of war. In June 2011, investigators with the International Criminal Court (ICC) shared evidence that points to the Gaddafi regime using rape as a tool of repression. The regime had acquired large quantities of drugs, especially Viagra, for its soldiers in an apparent bid to make them more likely to commit sexual assault (United Nations News Centre 2011). During the same month, Libyan charities announced that they were 'getting reports that in the west of the country, which is particularly conservative, Col Muammar Gaddafi's forces have tended to rape women and girls in front of their fathers and brothers' (Harter 2011).

Women interviewed by FIDH (2012), an NGO supporting women's rights, reported that victims of rape risk being killed by male family members to 'wash away family dishonour'. FIDH (2012: 27–8) reported cases in which husbands of rape victims committed suicide and men killed their wives or daughters before leaving to fight, to avoid the risk of their being raped. In one case a man killed his young sister when Gaddafi's forces arrived.

Rape and sexual violence was also reported in Tunisia, albeit on a smaller scale. During the uprising women were subjected to various forms of police violence, including sexual harassment and rape. FIDH (2012: 8–9) documented reports of girls being raped by members of Ben Ali's Special Forces in Kasserine and Thela between 11 and 12 January 2012. Moreover, between 14 and 15 January, several women protesters were raped while held in detention in the Interior Ministry.

Having said that, it is important to emphasize that sexual violence was often used as a tool against women during the reign of Ben Ali. Women were arrested for their political opinions, ideas or religious observance. They faced brutal beatings and sexual abuse at the hands of police and prison guards and after their release they were often blacklisted, unable to pursue employment and education (International Centre for Transitional Justice (ICTJ) 2012).

In Egypt, following Mubarak's departure, women protesters and observers were threatened, harassed and sexually assaulted by mobs. Most significantly, they were targeted by violence perpetrated by the police and military. The 'virginity tests' episode is a well-documented case in point. In March 2011, the army arrested 18 women protesters in Tahrir Square; the women were then severely beaten, tortured and verbally abused. They were later transferred to a military detention centre where seven of them were stripped and forced to submit to 'virginity tests' administered by male army doctors. The then-head of Egypt's military intelligence admitted to the practice, claiming that 'the tests were conducted so that women could not later allege they had been raped' (FIDH 2012: 18).

In Yemen, sexual violence was not reported although some reported threats to use it. Nabila Al Zubair, a writer and a well-known civil society activist who was an integral part of the Yemeni youth uprisings, described it this way in October 2012:

> Before 21 March, 2011, the security organizations of Saleh's regime tried to kidnap women when they were leaving the sit-in square (in Sana'a) in an attempt to force their families to make them stop going to the squares. But

> because the tribes were present [in the squares and also as supporters of the two rival competing core elite factions], and they consider such actions to be a type of 'black shame' [which brings shame on those committing them], these attempts did not persist. (survey by author, October 2012)

Former President Saleh tried to exploit traditional norms and what he called 'Islamic values' to discredit the women who were participating in the uprising. On 14 April 2011, he said that 'Islam forbids men and women mixing in public places', and called on women 'to return home'. Finally, pro-government groups injured dozens of women who were taking part in the peaceful marches to celebrate Tawakkul Karman receiving the Nobel Peace Prize. Interestingly, male relatives of the women activists received phone calls asking them to 'control' their wives, daughters and sisters (FIDH 2012: 40).

The state security forces were not the only men to commit acts of violence and intimidation. Similar acts were also perpetrated by members of the Islamist groups that have tried to implement their version of Islamic sharia by force. In Tunisia, Salafi groups targeted women, especially teachers, professors and students at universities, using violence, intimidation and smear campaigns. In addition, they tried to impose the veil on unveiled students and teachers, using violence and intimidation (FIDH 2012: 11). A prominent professor at Zaytouna University had this experience. Using an alias, she described what happened:

> To my shock after the revolution, I came to campus to give my class lectures and was confronted by students and professors who demanded that I veil myself on campus. I refused to submit to their request. As a result, they banned me from teaching unless I wore the veil. It was a battle everyday as I walk on campus. Unfortunately, due to the ridicule and discrimination I have suffered on this issue, I have now begun to wear the veil as I teach my classes so I can keep my job and continue to educate my students. (Fatima [pseudonym] 2011: Appendix D)

The newly elected government, led by the Islamist Ennahda Party, was slow to react to these actions, leaving women without the protection of the law.

In Egypt, hundreds of the women who gathered on 8 March 2011 in Tahrir Square to call for a greater voice in Egypt's transitional process were attacked by mobs that included Islamists. Women found themselves outnumbered and surrounded by a counter-protest made up mainly of men, chanting 'the people want to bring down women' – a variation on the chant that became the cry of the Arab Spring: 'The people want to bring down the regime'. Men shouted the female protesters down with insults; some yelled at them saying, 'Go home, go wash clothes', or 'You are not married; go find a husband', while others said 'This is against Islam' (Davies 2011; Chick 2011).

Again, just as in Tunisia, the army was slow in its reaction to stop the harassment and attacks targeting this demonstration.

In Yemen, the Islah Islamist Party, a strong partner within the alliance opposing Saleh's regime, used force to segregate the men and women protesters during a sit-in. The measures began as a response to Saleh's comment denouncing any 'mixing between the sexes'. Women activists who opposed these measures were attacked, beaten and defamed. Arwa Othman, a pioneer activist, was one of these women. On 16 April 2011 she insisted on participating in a mixed demonstration, along with other well-known activists, both female and male. As a result, she and 18 of her colleagues, both male and female, were brutally attacked and beaten publicly (statement of 23 April 2011). The attack drew sharp criticism and condemnation from many political and civil actors in Yemen but the segregation continued. Gradually, the independent activists, both female and male, were side-lined. The case has made it clear to many that despite the 2011 protests, traditional structural inequalities still persist.

A final note is warranted here: acts of violence and intimidation against women were not restricted to the regime and Islamists; they were also committed by non-Islamist members of society. The most notorious example in this regard is the gangs of youth who sexually harassed and raped women in Egypt's Tahrir Square (Kingsley 2013).

The transitional phase: between inclusion and exclusion

With the exception of Tunisia, the same historical pattern – of participation followed by institutionalized exclusion – was repeated to a great extent in other countries.

Tunisia has often stood as an exception in gender affairs in the region, possibly because the state took measures to ensure women's emancipation long before others did so. One such measure was a progressive family law, introduced in 1956, that helped remedy structural gender imbalance within the family.

Building on past measures, in 2011 women lobbied the High Commission, which was set up to fulfil the goals of the revolution. They succeeded in introducing a provision in the new electoral law, requiring parity on electoral lists. Although all the parties respected this rule, few placed women at the top of the lists, limiting the effects of this provision. Nevertheless, women represent more than 27 per cent of representatives to parliament, the highest proportion in the region (FIDH 2012: 10). A word of caution is warranted here: the majority of women parliamentarians are members of the Islamist Ennahda Party and they often follow their party's conservative line on gender issues.

Besides Tunisia, the picture looks gloomy for women's representation in political bodies. Egypt stands as the worst case of exclusion. Not a single woman was appointed to either the Constitutional Review Committee or the Civil Consultation Committee, the latter referred to as the 'Council of Wise Men'. The Supreme Council of the Armed Forces (SCAF) also abolished a quota of 10 per cent women in parliament that was introduced during the Mubarak era. The result was felt immediately during the parliamentary elections at the end of 2011:

women had only 2 per cent of seats in the new parliament. Finally, out of 100 members in the Constituent Assembly, which was assigned the task of drafting a new constitution, seven are women, and five of those are members of Islamist parties and have expressed views at odds with gender justice and equality (FIDH 2012: 19–20; National Front of Egyptian Women (NFEW) 2012).

In Libya, the first declaration by the president of the National Transitional Council (NTC) after Gaddafi's forces were defeated raised questions about the NTC's commitment to gender justice. He announced that any legal provision that contradicted sharia law would henceforth be null and void, including laws limiting polygamy. Given that sharia law discriminates against women, the message was worrying for many women. Moreover, the electoral law adopted by the NTC did not contain a quota for the representation of women in elected bodies (FIDH 2012: 4). But the parliamentary elections in July 2012 brought a surprise: women won 17 per cent of seats in the new body. This was due to a 'zipper system' that called for male-female parity in parties' lists of candidates (Soguel 2012).

During the transitional period, Yemen has remained vague about women's participation in the transitional bodies. On the first national council, created after President Saleh stepped down, eight per cent of representatives were women. However, on the Technical Committee, which is tasked with preparing a national dialogue conference, 27 per cent of representatives are women (survey by author, October 2012).

Transitional justice from a gender perspective: justice, transitional and permanent

Transitional justice has often been described as a 'package of measures which societies emerging from violent conflict use to pursue accountability' (Bell and O'Rourke 2007: 24). More recently, however, and specifically since the post-1990 moves from authoritarian to liberal regimes in Eastern Europe and South Africa, the term has become synonymous with initiatives responding to an increasing variety of situations, including 'war, in a time of peace, political fragmentation, weak state, small wars, and steady conflict' (Bell and O'Rourke 2007: 24). Its main objective seems to be extending accountability into a post-conflict terrain. In this sense, transitional justice is 'both justice with an instrumental purpose (to effect transition) and a differentiated form of justice for a peculiar and time limited period' (Bell and O'Rourke 2007: 24).

However, as Bell and O'Rourke point out, both the legal standards upon which transitional mechanisms are based and the process of designing them have often ignored women, resulting in their exclusion. Exclusion takes the form of women's absence from the negotiation process and the transitional justice bodies created to tackle the grievances of the past. But even when women's input is guaranteed at the peace agreement stage, it is often more difficult to ensure that they can participate in negotiating the details of the transitional justice mechanism. Attempts to remedy this situation have resulted in 'adding gender' to the mechanism. This phenomenon has been most prominent in the legal treatment of sexual violence in conflict, after the transnational feminist mobilisation of the 1990s focused on the need to end impunity for violence against women. Its relevance to transitional justice was clear: it exposed the widespread and systematic occurrence of sexual violence in situations of violent conflict and the use and limits of law as a tool to address such violence (Bell and O'Rourke 2007: 26). As Bell and O'Rourke (2007: 26) describe it, this process entailed three steps:

> Firstly, to secure recognition of women's experiences of gender based violence in armed conflict as amongst the most serious crimes of war;
> Secondly, to bridge the gap between the legal standards and their enforcements by securing prosecutions for these war crimes; and
> Thirdly, to secure reform in courtroom procedures in order to ensure that victims of sexual violence were not re-victimized by the adversarial legal process.

The three steps are badly needed in Arab Spring countries where women were subjected to sexual violence as a 'war tool', as in the Libyan civil war, and an 'intimidation method', as occurred in Egypt and Tunisia before and after the uprisings. As one would expect, the process is not easy and still marred with ambiguity.

Only Tunisia has shown any interest in a mechanism of transitional justice that seeks to involve women. The International Committee for Transitional Justice (ICTJ), an international non-profit organization specializing in transitional justice, has pointed to Tunisia as the country most interested in including women's perspective in its national transitional justice programming. Meetings with victims, Tunisian officials and the ICTJ delegation have led to calls for measures ensuring accountability (ICTJ 2012).

But in countries like Libya and Egypt accountability for sexual violence has yet to be addressed. In Libya, the stigma of rape in a conservative traditional society has hampered efforts to document the sexual violence committed by Gaddafi's troops. One NGO, Voice of Libyan Women, has reported that considerable evidence, including mobile phone recordings, was destroyed in order to protect victims from being stigmatized. In addition, lawyers and human rights organizations in Libya told FIDH in January 2012 that they 'had become increasingly reticent to document crimes of sexual violence for fear of reprisals against victims' (FIDH 2012: 27–8). This reluctance is also evident in the new Libyan transitional regime, leading Human Rights Watch (2011b) to call on it publicly to 'investigate allegations of sexual violence perpetrated during the Libyan armed conflict and provide medical services, treatment, and support for survivors'.

In Egypt, trust in the new transitional political order has eroded as victims of sexual violence are denied justice. In fact, courtroom procedures often re-victimized the victims. For example, on 27 December 2011, a Cairo administrative court declared 'virginity tests' illegal, but a military court refrained from taking legal action against the perpetrators. The judge ruled that witness statements were 'contradictory'. The court ruling was considered a clear message to other women seeking justice: perpetrators of sexual violence would have impunity (FIDH 2012: 18; Cave 2012).

In short, so far, except in Tunisia, transitional justice measures to address sexual violence against women have not been developed.

Yet ensuring gender justice in transitional societies should not merely be a matter of 'adding gender' to the transitional justice mechanism. If gender justice is to be achieved, then the very concept of transitional justice must be expanded to include measures ensuring permanent justice for women.

In 2002 the first Arab Human Development Report identified three critical deficits in all Arab countries: lack of freedom, lack of women's empowerment and a deficit in human capabilities and knowledge relative to income. That the report specifically mentioned the lack of women's empowerment as a source of the region's problems did not come as a surprise.

In fact, that deficit is not the result of some arbitrary situation; it is the result of systematic discrimination perpetuated by the state.

Indeed, discrimination against women in many Arab states is enshrined in their legal systems (Tunisia and Morocco are the exceptions). The fourth Arab Human Development Report (United Nations Development Program (UNDP) 2006) is entitled *Towards the Rise of Women in the Arab World*, and explores the lack of women's empowerment in Arab states. It highlights this point (UNDP 2006: 189):

> If legally sanctioned discrimination means disparity in the rule of law in spite of the presumed equality in legal status of citizens, then Arab personal status laws, with regard to Muslims and non-Muslims alike, are witness to legally sanctioned gender bias. This stems from the fact that personal status statutes are primarily derived from theological interpretations and judgments. The latter originate in the remote past when gender discrimination permeated society and they have acquired a sanctity and absoluteness in that confused area where the immutable tenets of religious creed interact with social history.

Family laws may be less discriminatory in some Arab countries than in others. As a rule, personal status laws in North Africa are more progressive than those in the Arab East. However, certain characteristics are common to family law in all Arab states, with Morocco and, again, Tunisia being the exceptions (Manea 2011: 6). As the fourth Arab Human Development Report maintains, these characteristics include the notion that men are women's keepers and have a degree of command over their lives. This notion has been translated into laws that restrict women in several ways: they oblige husbands to support their wives financially and oblige their wives to obey them, and they grant men alone the right to unilaterally divorce their wives and the right to require their return against their wish in the event of revocable divorce. Other laws restrict women's ability to marry, move, work or travel freely without the consent of their male relatives or husbands (Manea 2011: 6–7).

Hence, a woman may have the right to be elected to parliament or to be chosen as a minister in a government cabinet, yet this same parliamentarian or minister may not be allowed to travel outside the country with a government delegation if her husband withholds his permission (Manea 2011).

Given the systematic nature of this type of discrimination it is only to be expected that some women activists started to call for the inclusion of issues relating to gender justice in any national dialogue. Yemen provides the best example here, as it has one of the most discriminatory family laws in the region. According to its Family Law No 20 of 1992, a wife owes her husband obedience in four particular situations: he chooses the place of residence, she fulfils his sexual desires, she follows his orders and undertakes her domestic chores, and she is not to leave their marital residence without his permission (Article 40). Moreover, the law sanctions child marriage. Article 15 states that a marriage of a child is permitted if she is considered 'fit' to be married.

Women activists participating on the Technical Committee, which is to prepare for the Yemeni National Dialogue Conference, insisted on, and succeeded in adding, 'women's rights' and 'child marriage' as subjects to be discussed and addressed during the conference (Technical Committee of the Conference of the Comprehensive National Dialogue 2012).

However, those who lobbied for this inclusion were accused of 'diverting attention' from the main issues for 'national dialogue' by introducing 'peripheral issues such as child marriage', as one journalist put it. Amal Al Basha, a member of the committee and a leading women's activist, responded to his accusation, saying that 'the conference seeks legal protection for vulnerable segments' of the population, along with 'the advancement of women' and an end to offences that violate children. She ended by saying that 'We in the committee identified the ramifications of these issues' (Darem 2012).

The ramifications are dire. According to a Human Rights Watch report on child marriage in Yemen, in 2005 the country was ranked fourteenth on a list of 20 worldwide hotspots for child marriage, with 53 per cent of girls married before age 18 and 14 per cent married before age 15 (Human Rights Watch 2011a: 15). These girls are often at risk of dying from complications of pregnancy. Studies have shown that girls in their teens are twice as likely as adult women to die from causes related to pregnancy and childbirth and that young girls between age 10 and 14 are five times more likely to die during delivery than mothers between 20 and 24. Not surprisingly, maternal mortality in Yemen is the highest in the MENA region, estimated at 210 deaths per 100,000 live births: 'Maternal mortality in Yemen is the cause of approximately 39 percent of all deaths for women of reproductive age, and child marriage is an important factor. Government data indicate that 74.2 percent of all maternal deaths occur in cases of girls or women who were married before they reached 20 years old' (Human Rights Watch 2011a: 27).

Indeed, it is the ramifications of systematic and state-sanctioned gender discrimination that make it imperative to include gender justice as a category in any mechanism for transitional justice. The aim should be to allow for the possibility of restoring justice in the daily lives of women, and thus make it permanent.

Challenges and opportunities: between the politics of survival and women's activism

Challenges to introducing issues of gender justice into transitional justice mechanisms include the politics of survival used by both the state and political actors and the principled position of Islamist parties against women's rights.

Arab states have often been trapped in the politics of survival, with clear consequences from a gender perspective. Politics of survival refer to the processes by which states shift their alliances with, and allocate and channel resources to, various political and social groups to ensure their hold on power, and to survive in a hostile regional environment (Manea 2011: 108).

States use two strategies to survive. First, leaders often make their alliances with social and political groups within the wider circle of the traditional/cliental base of power. In doing so, they have one clear purpose: to weaken competing political groups that prove threatening to their authority. And these alliances are by nature ephemeral – they shift along with the sands of politics. Second, leaders play the Islamist card, taking advantage of the phenomenon of political Islam. They endorse certain Islamist groups rather than others and forge political alliances with them. The main aim of this strategy is political: to deploy the support of these Islamist groups as a means of legitimizing their rule in a religious sense or/and delegitimizing that of their rivals (Manea 2011: 109).

These strategies have ramifications from a gender perspective. Gender rights and policies have often been held hostage to the political bargains of the political elites. This in turn suggests that the Arab state is neither liberal nor patriarchal in the way it pursues its gender politics. Rather, it is opportunistic, acting always in a Machiavellian manner. This has meant that only if it made sense politically to support women's emancipation would the state do so (Manea 2011: 193).

This pattern is unlikely to change in the new transitional period, especially as the existing political groups and parties, whether nationalists, leftist, liberal or secular, engage in the same pattern of politics. When the issue is women's rights, they have often acted opportunistically: they refrain from promoting gender justice for fear of antagonizing their conservative constituency. Kuwait offers an example of this type of politics (Manea 2011: 146–59).

Islamists, on the other hand, have often held a principled position against women's rights. They may vary in the limits they exert on women's rights, but they share a conservative view on women's role in society. Those holding this view subscribe to a biological distinction between man and woman that should, they believe, be reflected in differences in rights.

Hassan Al Banna, the founder of the Islamist Muslim Brotherhood, articulated this view: 'The distinction between man and woman in rights comes from their natural differences, which are unavoidable (inevitable), and in accordance with the difference in the task each is conducting, and for the protection of the rights given to each' (Al Banna (nd)).

According to this view, women are equal to men in dignity but not in rights. This belief is reflected in the Islamists' firm position against the demands of women's movements for changes in laws and policies that marginalize women. Their voting patterns testify to this (United Nations Development Program 2006). Given this background, the sweeping victories of Islamists in recent elections in some Arab countries, and more generally their rise to political prominence in almost all, gives rise to serious questions about the future of women's rights.

Clearly, the challenges to the inclusion of gender justice are huge. Nevertheless, it is important to include it as a category in the transitional justice process for one simple reason: women themselves have been the absent player in the politics of survival and the Islamist parties' positions against women's rights. The moment women started to lobby and organize themselves, their actions tended to have results.

This brings us to Fatima al-Abdali's statement about the Kuwait women's movement. It was when women realized that the political establishment did not place a priority on women's right to vote that they decided to engage in the political struggle to gain their rights. And, after a decade, they succeeded.

Of course, to a great extent these rights are in place only at the legal/institutional level and have not yet permeated throughout society. For example, no woman was elected in the two parliamentary elections in Kuwait (June 2006 and May 2008) after women gained the right to vote, even though women made up around 50 per cent of voters in the 2006 election and 55 per cent in 2008. But, just as the move toward legal reform was a process that took time, so we can expect that the societal norms and values will gradually come to reflect women's rights. Indeed, it was the tireless campaigning of women activists, and their use of new media forms, in addition to the support of liberal Kuwaiti political groups, that resulted in the historical election, in May 2009, of four women to the 50-member parliament (Manea 2011: 5).

Al-Abdali's statement also applies to the Yemeni women's movement. Thanks to their representation on the Technical Committee, and despite much protest and defamation, women succeeded in including the issues of women's rights and child marriage into the national dialogue on the transitional process. The outcome of this inclusion is still up in the air. But the main message of these examples is straightforward: *civil and human rights are not gifts to be handed down from the top by state or political actors; they have to be won through peaceful but relentless struggle. Women's rights are no exception.*

Conclusion

From a theoretical perspective, the inclusion of gender in the transitional justice process in the MENA region offers two main opportunities for the global discussion of transitional justice.

First, we must move beyond simply adding gender-specific measures to the processes of transitional justice and focus on restoring gender justice and equality. Efforts to pursue accountability should not be limited to crimes and atrocities perpetrated during times of violent conflict. They should not be limited in either their time, scope or measures. They should seek to establish justice in women's daily lives, and transform that justice from 'transitional' to 'permanent'. This requires thinking in terms of both the short and long term.

Certainly it is necessary to include women in the negotiation process, in the transitional justice bodies created to tackle the grievances of the past. It is also crucial to recognize women's experiences of gender-based violence in armed conflict as crimes of war, to bridge the gap between the legal standards and their enforcement in the prosecution of such war crimes and to reform courtroom procedures to avoid re-victimizing the victims of sexual violence. All these measures known to the transitional process are vitally important, especially as we have seen that, during the Arab uprisings, women were targets of systematic sexual violence and degradation. And, all too often, they were also excluded from the transitional bodies that were created after the fall of authoritarian Arab leaders.

Yet women's grievances in the MENA region are not limited to the periods of upheavals and uprisings that have swept the region since 17 December 2010. They relate to systematic and state-sanctioned gender discrimination cemented with cultural prejudice that has rendered women minors in their own societies. Women often do not experience fair and equal treatment during their daily lives. This should be addressed by measures that tackle the legal foundations of gender discrimination and the social prejudice permeated by education systems and the media. Efforts to move beyond the addition of gender-specific measures to the mechanisms of transitional justice processes should not be limited to the MENA region. They are relevant to similar conditions in other regions of the globe.

Second, a tension exists between the liberal foundations of the transitional justice movement and the non-liberal or reactionary social actors who are included in this process (a point that is also made in Chapter 7). This tension should be resolved by emphasizing the underlying universality of human rights represented in transitional justice. It should be resolved in a way that guarantees women's dignity and rights. These two – dignity and rights – exist together. The liberal foundations of transitional justice entail the inclusion of all important social actors in the process of rebuilding society. This is of course crucial to avoid risking and limiting the legitimacy and local ownership of the transitional process. However, the inclusion of Islamist groups in this process poses real questions about the guarantees of gender equality and justice, especially as such groups consider human rights a 'Western' concept that should not be applied to Islamic countries.

The answer to these challenges should refrain from essentializing Islamic societies. It should consider that these claims of particular notions of Islamic justice and rights are being contested not only by women and human rights groups in these societies but also within Islamic theology itself, which has produced alternative interpretations. The answer should also remind us how religion has been used in Western societies to justify grave violations of human rights, including the mistreatment of African Americans in the United States, the apartheid system in South Africa and gender inequality in Switzerland. Alternative interpretations paved the way towards restoring justice to traditionally marginalized groups. Culture does change. It is still in a process of change in the United States and Europe. Until 1967 homosexual relations were punishable by law in the United Kingdom. Today it is their marriage that seems to be contested. The marginalization of social groups, whether because of their gender, religion, colour, race or other factors, occurs around the globe. It happens in every society on this planet, western and eastern alike. It is because of this fact that human rights are universal. They set the rules of the game for any society, insisting on equality and justice before the law for every member of society. Questioning the underlying universality of human rights, which is the basis for the transitional justice process, will jeopardize its long-term goal of profound change and lasting justice. From a gender perspective, human rights should be the building block of any transitional justice process.

Notes

1 For an example of Islamist conception of rights in their translation into laws, see The Cairo Declaration on Human Rights in Islam, 5 August 1990. For overview and critique of the Islamist approach, see Moosa 2004.

2 Scholars who use this approach are many. For example, the authors of the Arab Human Development Report 2005, 'Towards the Rise of Arab Women', Fatima Mernissi's books on gender and Suad Joseph's scholarly research on the subject.

Bibliography

Al Banna, H. (nd) 'The Muslim Woman Tract', in Arabic, available online at www.ikhwanwiki.com/index.php?title=ملف:المرأة_المسلمة_حسن_البنا.pdf.

Al Jourchi, S.A. (2008) 'Tunisia: the mining bastion's rebellion opens the social file', Swissinfo (in Arabic), 18 April, available online at www.swissinfo.ch/ara/detail/content.html?cid=6592094.

Amnesty International (2009) 'Tunisia: releases welcome but repression must end', 5 November, available online at www.amnesty.org/en/library/asset/MDE30/016/2009/en/174a9f7a-d641-4142-9d30-abed81053344/mde300162009en.html.

Bell, C. and O'Rourke, C. (2007) 'Does feminism need a theory of transitional justice? An introductory essay', 1 *The International Journal of Transitional Justice* 23.

Cave, P. (2012) 'Egypt court clears doctor in "virginity test" case', *ABC News*, 12 March, available online at www.abc.net.au/news/2012-03-12/egypt-court-clears-army-doctor-in-27virginity-tests27-case/3882872.

Charrad, M.M. (2001) *States and Women's Rights: The Making of Postcolonial Tunisia, Algeria, and Morocco* (University of California Press).

Chick, K. (2011) 'In Egypt's Tahrir Square, women attacked at rally on International Women's Day', *Christian Science Monitor*, 8 March, available online at www.csmonitor.

com/World/Middle-East/2011/0308/In-Egypt-s-Tahrir-Square-women-attacked-at-rally-on-International-Women-s-Day.

Damascus Declaration for National Democratic Change (in Arabic), available online at www.nidaasyria.org.

Darem, F. (2012) 'Yemeni National Dialogue Conference aims at peaceful transition' (interview with Amal Al Basha), *Al Shorfa com.*, 29 October, available online at http://al-shorfa.com/en_GB/articles/meii/features/2012/10/29/feature-01.

Davies, C. (2011) 'Tahrir Square women's march marred by rival protest', *Guardian*, 8 March, available online at www.guardian.co.uk/world/2011/mar/08/rival-protesters-clash-women-tahrir.

'Fatima' [pseudonym] (2011) 'Women and the Arab Spring', Testimonies of Tunisian Women, Appendix D (Committee on Foreign Relations, United States Senate. Kindle Issue).

FIDH (Fédération internationale des ligues des droits de l'Homme) (2012) 'Women and the Arab Spring: taking their place?', March, available online at www.fidh.org/Women-and-the-Arab-Spring-The.

Harter, P. (2011) 'Libya rape victims face honour killings', *BBC News*, 14 June, available online at www.bbc.co.uk/news/world-africa-13760895.

Hatem, M. (2011) 'Gender and revolution in Egypt', 261 *Middle East Report* 36.

Heideman, K. and Youssef, M. (eds) (2012) *Reflections on Women in the Arab Spring* (Woodrow Wilson International Centre for Scholars, Middle East Program), available online at www.wilsoncenter.org/sites/default/files/International%20Women%27s%20Day%20 2012_4.pdf.

Human Rights Watch (2011a) 'How come you allow little girls to get married?', *Child Marriage in Yemen*, available online at www.hrw.org/sites/default/files/reports/yemen 1211ForUpload_0.pdf.

Human Rights Watch (2011b), 'Libya: transitional government should support victims', 19 September, available online at www.hrw.org/news/2011/09/19/libya-transitional-government-should-support-victims.

International Centre for Transitional Justice (2012) 'A struggle against invisibility: gender justice in Middle East and North Africa', 26 September, available online at http://ictj.org/news/struggle-against-invisibility-gender-justice-middle-east-and-north-africa.

Jaquette J., Chinchilla N., Crummett M. and Buvinic M. (eds) (1994) *Women and the Transition to Democracy: The Impact of Political and Economic Reform in Latin America* (Woodrow Wilson Center).

Joseph, S. (ed.) (2000) *Gender and Citizenship in the Middle East* (Syracuse University Press).

Joseph, S. and Slyomovics, S. (eds) (2001) *Women and Power in the Middle East* (University of Pennsylvania Press).

Julià, M. and Ridha, H. (2001) 'Women and war: the role Kuwaiti women played during the Iraqi occupation', 13 *Journal of International Development* 583.

Kingsley, P. (2013) 'Tahrir Square sexual assaults reported during anniversary clashes', *Guardian*, 28 January, available online at www.guardian.co.uk/world/2013/jan/27/tahrir-square-sexual-assaults-reported.

Mahfouz, A. (2011) 'Asmaa Mahfouz: The video that fuelled the Egyptian revolution' (with English subtitles), 18 January, available online at www.youtube.com/watch?v=RIuiWL TMonY&feature=related.

Manea, E. (2012) 'Sheikhdown: why tribes aren't the answer in Yemen', *Sada*, Online journal of Carnegie Endowment for International Peace, available online at http://carnegieendowment.org/sada/index.cfm?fa=show&article=47588&solr_hilite=.

Manea, E. (2011) *The Arab State and Women's Rights: the Trap of Authoritarian Governance* (Routledge).

Manea, E. (2010) 'Islam and human dignity: a consequence-based approach to human dignity and rights', in D. Deimann and S. Mugier (eds), *Entgegensprechen: Texte zu Menschenwürde und Menschenrecht*, Vol 1 (edition gesowip) 499.

Moosa, E. (2004) 'The Dilemma of Islamic Rights Schemes', *World & Knowledges Otherwise* 185.

Moosa, E. (2000–2001) 'The dilemma of Islamic rights schemes', 15(12) *Journal of Law and Religion* 185.

National Front of Egyptian Women (2012) 'Statement by the National Front of Egyptian Women on the Composition of the Constituent Assembly', *Al Ahali* (in Arabic), 11 September, available online at www.masress.com/alahaly/16197.

Omar, M. (2011) 'Women and the Arab Spring' (Committee on Foreign Relations, United States Senate. Kindle issue).

Organization of the Islamic Conference (1990) Cairo Declaration on Human Rights in Islam.

Soguel, D. (2012) 'Libyan elections give women a 17% starting point', *WeNews*, 18 July, available online at http://womensenews.org/story/the-world/120719/libyan-elections-give-women-17-starting-point#.UJkPZm_A_4Y.

Syrian Human Rights Committee (2008) 'Leaders of Damascus Declaration sentenced to two years and a half', 29 October, available online at www.shrc.org/data/aspxng/printpage.aspx?myLink=/data/aspx/d3/3743.xml.

Taylor, C. (1994) 'The politics of recognition', in A. Gutmann (ed.), *Multiculturalism: Examining the Politics of Recognition* (Princeton University Press) 25.

Technical Committee of the Conference of the Comprehensive National Dialogue (2012) Committee Facebook page/website, 6 November, available online at www.facebook.com/pages/140995129374601/ اللجنة-الفنية-لمؤتمر-الحوار-الوطني-الشامل.

Text of communique about the assault on activists and journalists during a women's march (16 April 2011) (in Arabic), on Afrah Nasser's blog, available online at http://afrahnasser.blogspot.ch/2011/04/blog-post_23.html.

United Nations Development Program (2006) *Arab Human Development Report 2005: Towards the Rise of Women in the Arab World* (United Nations).

United Nations News Centre (2011) 'Evidence emerging of use of rape as tool of war in Libya – ICC prosecutor', 8 June, available online at www.un.org/apps/news/story.asp?NewsID=38664&Cr=libya&Cr1.

Worden, M. (2012) *The Unfinished Revolution: Voices from the Global Fight for Women›s Rights* (Seven Stories Press).

Chapter 9

Egypt and the struggle for accountability and justice

Michael Wahid Hanna

In the wake of the Arab uprisings and the toppling of entrenched authoritarian regimes, notions of transitional justice have informed the discourse of the transitions from their start. But despite the ubiquity of transitional justice rhetoric, state practice has diverged sharply in Egypt, Libya and Tunisia. The particular circumstances of each of these heretofore chaotic transitions have impacted the ability of the countries to give careful consideration to issues of transitional justice. In fact, these divergences have clear political roots, in the sense that transitional justice responses have been bound up with, and limited by, the political trajectory of the post-authoritarian transitions in each of these societies. Transitional justice has been a key and lagging indicator of the overall health of the transition processes.

Egypt's troubled post-Mubarak history is perhaps most instructive in elucidating the obvious link between the tangled politics of this transitional period and the broad and diffuse desire for accountability. Transitional justice is an inherently political endeavor and is a function of a nascent or established political order's sense of purpose and, at times, legitimacy. Of course, as a political act or set of actions, transitional justice will manifest itself through varied and divergent modalities depending on the overarching political context. Further, transitional justice can also be politicized in a negative fashion to further factional gains or to achieve ulterior ends. The Egyptian example, to date, exemplifies politicized and limited transitional justice that is employed not to further the legitimate aims of transitional justice, such as the rule of law, accountability, truth-telling and national reconciliation, but to advance narrow interests and often as a means to inhibit systemic reform.

These deficiencies can be seen when examining the various modalities in which considerations of transitional justice have received an airing: prosecutions; security sector reform; vetting; preservation of historical memory and truth-telling; and victims' compensation. In each of these categories, the failures and squandered potential of Egypt's transition can be seen on a more granular level. Where transitional justice efforts have been undertaken, they have been marred by a lack of political will, selective application and the use of cynical, prophylactic measures to avoid more thoroughgoing and consequential processes of accountability and reform.

Apart from the normative value of accountability, the impact of impunity upon the success of a given transition and the ability to consolidate democratic gains is uncertain. Other transitional settings have seen democratic consolidation and success despite such questions being ignored. However, the broader global shift on the normative value of transitional justice has also created expectations of accountability and justice. Such expectations are clearly visible in the demands of the uprising and the turbulent post-Mubarak period. Raised expectations mean that it is important when comparing past examples to properly take context and shifts in that context (both national and international) into account, since not doing so risks missing the manner in which transitional justice discourse has become embedded in the ethos of the mobilized political class that has propelled continued protest and dissent. As such, the dashing of expectations could be a further spark for instability when added to the perpetuation of repressive state actions.

When compared to the idealistic starting point represented by the halcyon 18 days of Tahrir Square, the neglect and manipulation of transitional justice is disappointing. Furthermore, to the extent that transitional justice issues have arisen, they have been almost exclusively focused on the violence of the uprising, without a broader consideration of the decades of systematic repression that came before. This is an unfortunate outcome and a lost opportunity. More robust transitional justice efforts that sought to document state repression during the rule of Gamal Abdel Nasser and Anwar Sadat, in addition to a more comprehensive accounting of the full tenure of the Mubarak regime, would reinforce the moral and practical imperative of breaking with this checkered past.

However, while the arc of progress on transitional justice issues remains wholly inadequate, comparative cases suggest that the urge for accountability and truth is not necessarily an ephemeral, time-limited phenomenon.[1] As with the decades-long push for prosecutorial accountability in connection with Argentina's 'Dirty War', the political roots of transitional justice are clear and the durability of such grievances can be lasting if left unaddressed. Prior to the ouster of President Mohamed Morsi, opposition politicians in Egypt renewed their attention to the notion of transitional justice and began making public demands for a comprehensive transitional justice law (Salah 2013).

In fact, the post-Mubarak era itself produced new instances of repression and impunity that spurred a second wave of calls for transitional justice. Those calls will now be added to the already long list of proposals in the face of escalating, elective and unconscionable state violence targeting the supporters of the ousted president, Mohamed Morsi, and other dissidents who have broken with Egypt's military-led political order.

In the wake of the popular uprising and military coup that dislodged President Morsi and upended Egypt's political order, many appear willing to countenance renewed repression, with an eye toward enforced normalcy. However, with mass mobilization and political consciousness now a reality, many segments of Egypt's society may no longer be amenable to new forms of repressive stability. Indeed, many of the old modes of repression now threaten anew the stability of the state. With this new impetus, it is unlikely that the calls for accountability and justice will evaporate completely. Egypt's current-day rulers should be forewarned and the country's previous repressors should take no abiding comfort in the dismal state of current democratization and transitional justice efforts.

Prosecutions

As an elucidation of the failures of Egypt's transitional justice efforts, no category of transitional justice is as revealing as the post-Mubarak prosecutions. These uncoordinated and reactive legal actions were designed not as an exercise in accountability and reconstruction of the truth, but as a limited prophylactic to broader systemic reform. Prosecutions were used to divert demands for change that coursed through Egypt's streets by creating an air of responsiveness.

Broadly speaking, the post-Mubarak prosecutions can be divided into four discrete categories that represent differing motivations and divergent outcomes: (1) corruption prosecutions against the Mubarak inner circle; (2) prosecutions of police for excessive violence during the 18-day uprising; (3) the trial of Mubarak and his key associates at the Ministry of the Interior (MOI); and (4) extremely limited prosecutions of post-Mubarak police violence.

After the fall of Mubarak, prosecutorial efforts followed a bifurcated track, reflected in the systematic divergence between the successful prosecutions of regime insiders for corruption and the largely unsuccessful efforts to establish legal accountability for repressive and indiscriminate violence during the uprising. This divergence is indicative of the political interests that corrupted the early stages of prosecutorial efforts. In this sense, the interests of the then-ruling military council seamlessly dovetailed with the prosecutorial record and are suggestive of the priorities that governed that period of Supreme Council of the Armed Forces (SCAF) rule.[2]

In the years preceding the uprising much speculation had centered on the issue of presidential succession and the transparent efforts by Mubarak to engineer his son's ascension to the presidency. The controversy surrounding the possibility of a familial, dynastic succession created widespread political dissatisfaction that was shared by segments of the Egyptian armed forces. Many military leaders resented the president's entitled son, Gamal Mubarak, and were concerned about the ostentatious levels of corruption associated with the economic reform programs he championed. This corruption, many military players speculated, was of a scale and kind that risked aggravating public opinion and undermining support for the regime. Further, the circle of business insiders who benefited from this style of crony capitalism formed another rival power center within the regime that further threatened the position of the armed forces, which had seen its influence decline throughout the Mubarak years. The military, with its statist approach to its own vast business empire, was also suspicious of concentrated efforts at privatization, which had been a hallmark of the younger Mubarak and his associates.

Prosecutions of such figures, including Gamal Mubarak and his brother 'Alaa, represented a step toward consolidating military authority and neutralizing rivals, while also satisfying, to some degree, calls for accountability.

These corruption prosecutions happened at breakneck speed in the months following Mubarak's fall, raising important question regarding the fundamental fairness of the proceedings. Among those prosecuted and convicted were the Mubarak brothers, Safwat el-Sherif, the former secretary general of the National Democratic Party (NDP) and former speaker of the Shoura Council; Fathi Sorour, the former Speaker of the People's Assembly; Zakaria 'Azmi, President Mubarak's former Chief of Staff; Youssef Boutros Ghali, the former Minister of Finance; Rachid Mohamed Rachid, the former Minister of Foreign Trade and Industry; Ahmed 'Ezz, a former NDP official, steel tycoon and close associate of Gamal Mubarak; and Hussein Salem, co-owner of the East Mediterranean Gas Company and a confidante of former president Hosni Mubarak. These successful prosecutions were all linked by their focus on corruption and graft, which were politically palatable targets for the SCAF. The focus of the prosecutions on a handful of key officials allowed the military to distance itself from some of the excesses of the former regime without calling into question the broader legitimacy of the regime in which it participated and protected for decades. The reach of corruption investigations has more recently extended to the MOI, with 13 police officers and 16 civilian employees of the Ministry facing charges of corruption and the illegal use of public funds (*Ahram Online* 2013). The heavy focus on corruption was consistent with the limited approach to transitional justice issues when looking beyond the violence of the 18-day uprising.

In contrast to this hyper-efficient record on corruption, the judiciary has proven unable to effectively prosecute participants in regime repression aimed at crushing the uprising. While the MOI also represented a rival power center within the regime, the military was partly reliant on the disgraced police force to maintain law and order in the post-Mubarak period and was eager to cede domestic policing to the beleaguered ministry. For the military to redeploy and transfer responsibility for domestic security and policing back to the MOI, it needed some level of cooperation with the police. This logic, which colored the military's approach to prosecutions of police, also crippled the possibility of early efforts at security sector reform.

While the SCAF did not directly interfere with investigative and prosecutorial efforts, it did nothing to ensure cooperation of the security sector. With no direction or compulsion, the very institutions under investigation were left to subvert investigations through non-cooperation and destruction of evidence, essentially crippling prosecutorial efforts. The military has denied being involved in the destruction of evidence incriminating the MOI (Mohamed Abdel Razek 2013). Amnesty International has described this dubious prosecutorial track record in the post-Mubarak era as a 'festival of acquittal for all' (Amnesty International 2013), in which '[n]o senior official or security officer has been convicted or justly punished for directly and deliberately killing or injuring protesters' (Amnesty

International 2013). In the two years following the fall of Mubarak, only three police officers were successfully prosecuted for killing or injuring demonstrators. The successful prosecution of Mohamed el-Shenawi, who became known as the 'Eye Sniper', only happened because of the vigilance of demonstrators who captured graphic video evidence of his actions. The only two senior MOI officials to have been prosecuted successfully during this period were not connected to deaths during the uprising, but were convicted for their involvement in the February 2012 Port Said stadium disaster, in which over 70 fans were killed (Maher 2013). The two officials received 15-year jail sentences; however, they were convicted solely on charges of criminal negligence.

Overall, the track record of prosecutions of both rank-and-file police officers and senior officials has been abysmal, with acquittals being the norm. In private discussions with Egyptian judges, several have pointed to flawed evidence as the principal cause of these unsuccessful trials. However, while there is certainly merit to this argument, it cannot fully explain the failure to hold individuals accountable for the violence unleashed against protesters. While investigations have been compromised, the approach to prosecutions has been uncoordinated and ad hoc. No efforts have been made to divert resources to these trials. Similarly, the criminal justice process has been opaque and has lacked transparency. This compromised approach to accountability has further eroded the standing of the courts and fueled public frustration among reformists and activists.

The major exceptions to this pattern have been the prosecutions of the former Minister of Interior, Habib el-'Adly and the former president, Hosni Mubarak. The focus on el-'Adly has, despite his criminal complicity, distracted from the broader criminal culpability within the MOI. He has served as a convenient scapegoat in many respects, and has absorbed a disproportionate share of investigative and prosecutorial attention. This effect is even more in evidence with respect to the trials of the former president, in particular the central trial of the president and his key domestic security officials, including el-'Adly, for the violent suppression of protests during the uprising.

It was widely assumed that the SCAF would seek to shield Mubarak, a former military man, and provide him with a dignified exit out of respect for his institutional role and military service. While accountability for Mubarak was a key demand of the uprising and the mobilizations that continued after he was toppled, the decision to allow the prosecution to proceed had a prophylactic effect on transitional justice efforts. As opposed to establishing a governing rationale of accountability and an end to impunity, the chaotic trial process and the excessive, but understandable, focus on the former president had the paradoxical effect of stymying more broad-based transitional justice efforts. By offering up the former president, a figure that many assumed would go unpunished, the authorities diminished much of the impetus behind the accountability movement.

The prosecution itself produced an illogical verdict, which saw the senior operational commanders and officials within the MOI acquitted, while Mubarak and el-'Adly were convicted of negligence in failing to prevent the actions of their underlings. In essence, no individuals were ever found guilty for authorizing the systematic and violent repression of protests. Even these convictions were eventually dismissed on appeal, with a retrial now in its early stages.

In keeping with the limited scope of transitional justice to date, the criminal justice system has made no sustained efforts to seek accountability for the pre-uprising repression. The exceptions to this have been isolated, with the most high-profile criminal action involving the October 2011 conviction upon retrial of the two security officials who killed Khaled Said (*Guardian* 2011), an iconic figure whose death at the hands of police helped galvanize public anger in the months prior to the initial 2011 uprising. Additionally, five security officials were convicted in June 2012 by an Alexandria Criminal Court for the death of Sayed Bilal, a Salafi figure who was wrongfully accused of involvement in the January 2011 New Year's Eve bombing of the Qudayseen Church (*Egypt Independent* 2012). Other actions have been undertaken, resulting in fines for security officials accused of torture, but such efforts have not been designed or managed in any coherent fashion.

Security sector reform

In keeping with the near absolute impunity of the MOI for the use of excessive force and indiscriminate violence against protesters during Egypt's 18-day uprising, there has been little in the way of serious efforts to reform Egypt's corrupt and brutal police force. Of course, police brutality and venality are longstanding phenomena that numbered among the most significant factors that animated Egypt's beleaguered pre-uprising opposition forces and mobilized protesters at the beginning of the Egyptian uprising. The MOI has traditionally been the primary apparatus of repression in Egypt, as opposed to the armed forces, which were, save for several exceptions, the silent guarantor of regime stability. The MOI's profile and budget expanded rapidly during the 1990s as Egypt faced a low-level Islamist insurgency and growing militancy.

With the continuation of mass mobilization and protest, Egypt's streets have been the focus of sustained political activity and the airing of grievances. Combined with the disappointing results of Egypt's transition, such outpourings of frustration have proven combustible, with governmental authorities, whether the SCAF or the Morsi government, often keen to quash popular discontent. This trend has deepened since the ouster of Morsi, and the use of indiscriminate detention and force by the police has increased. With the utilization and deployment of an unreconstructed police force employing traditional methods of repression, a vicious cycle of protest and repression has taken shape throughout the post-Mubarak period. With the mainstreaming of political violence by civilian actors on all sides of Egypt's political divides, the ruling authorities have become dependent upon the very aggravating factor helping to fuel continued mobilization and outrage. This cycle was poignantly and tragically on display in the January 2013 violence that engulfed Port Said and which resulted in the deaths of over 30 people, mostly from gunfire and including two police officers.

The prevailing lack of political consensus throughout the transition period has also thwarted the possibility of security sector reform. As with many other monumental challenges facing Egypt, security sector reform is potentially destabilizing. In the case of the security sector, this stems from the retaliatory capacity that resides within the MOI. Cosmetic reforms and reassignments were carried out in the early post-Mubarak period when the State Security Investigations (*Mabahith Amn al-Dawla*), the lead actor in repressing political opposition and Islamist militancy, was dissolved in March 2011. Despite this dissolution and the reassignment of some personnel, it was succeeded by a National Security Apparatus (NSA) whose mandate has not been made public. More importantly, the MOI continues to act repressively and no attempts have been made to tackle the systemic cultural deficiencies and lack of professionalism that typify the institution.

As with the broader transition, which has focused on a procedural roadmap eschewing institutional reform, the MOI has emerged from this fraught period largely intact despite its tense relationship with the previously governing Muslim Brotherhood. The fortunes of the ministry have improved even further since the ouster of Morsi, and hardline actors within the security establishment have become the key figures. That relationship between the MOI and the Muslim Brotherhood was one of suspicion based on the past role of the MOI in repressing Islamist actors, particularly the Brothers, and the presumed ideological animus of sectors of the Ministry to its former foes. Despite this complicated relationship, the Muslim Brotherhood-led government lent its rhetorical support to the police force as it continued to face sustained opposition and protest. Coupled with the reluctance of the military to deploy as a domestic police force during Morsi's troubled tenure, the Muslim Brothers found themselves reliant on those that had repressed them only recently. While the present uncertainty in the country following the removal of the Muslim Brotherhood-led government makes it hard to predict the trajectory of security sector reform, the ascendancy of the Egyptian military, the revitalized role of the police and the staunch public support for a crackdown make the prospects for such reform non-existent in the near-term.

Vetting

While often controversial and prone to abuse, vetting can be an important tool for cultivating legitimacy in transitional politics and increasing popular confidence in nascent democratic institutions. However, since the sanctions for vetting are often an alternative to prosecutions and less onerous than criminal sanction, states have traditionally employed less stringent modes of adjudication. This creates abundant opportunity for over-broad application and victor's justice, often with an eye toward institutional and bureaucratic capture.

During Egypt's transitional period, vetting has been the subject of sustained and substantial attention. Initially, vetting was eschewed during the tenure of the SCAF. While the former ruling party was dissolved by court order in April 2011 and had its assets seized by the state, more ambitious approaches to vetting were the subject of heated debate that did not translate into concrete actions. The most high-profile vetting was the largely cosmetic restructuring at the MOI, which resulted in a limited degree of administrative reassignment and early retirement of employees.

However, the early debates on vetting were complicated by the overbroad approaches that formed the basis for those discussions. This was unfortunate and undermined the possibility of instituting properly tailored vetting that provided fair and transparent process while also providing broad scope and application.

The first option considered was a simple ban on the participation of former-President Mubarak's NDP in political life. This approach suffered from being overbroad and blunt with respect to relevant individuals, while failing to deal more broadly with the bureaucracy, where the NDP was represented in small numbers, and the security sector, where the NDP was not represented at all. The second approach, which was proposed by various political forces but ultimately rejected by the SCAF, was the amendment of *Qanun al-Ghadr*, the moribund law of treason first established in the wake of the Free Officers Revolution in 1952. At that time, the law was used as a tool to purge political enemies. The vagueness of the law, which delineated political offences as potential criminal acts, would have been ripe for misuse. As opposed to considering more systematic approaches to vetting, these ill-conceived ideas served only to confuse and thwart early efforts.

The lack of appreciable vetting during the period of SCAF rule likely fueled the more draconian approach that was eventually adopted as part of the flawed 2012 constitutional drafting process, which narrowly focused on NDP affiliation. As such, it provided sanctions without evidence of wrongdoing, while ignoring criminality and abuse carried out outside the narrow confines of the ruling party elite.

Article 232 of the December 2010 Constitution targets leaders of the dissolved ruling party.[3] The article bans such individuals from political work and prohibits them from running for presidential or legislative elections for a period of 10 years from the date of the adoption of the Constitution. The article goes on to define leadership as 'everyone who was a member of the Secretariat of the Party, the Policies Committee or the Political Bureau, or was a member of the People's Assembly or the Shoura Council during the two legislative terms preceding the 25 January revolution'.[4]

Objections to the lack of cognizable process associated with these provisions for political disenfranchisement caused concern among some members of the assembly. The representative of al-Azhar objected to the application of the provision to those who had not been 'found guilty of political corruption' (El-Din 2012). He further noted that it would be 'unfair for the constitution to ostracize a certain segment of society' (El-Din 2012).

Although these concerns were not reflected in the text of the Constitution, the Supreme Constitutional Court interpreted the provisions narrowly and their application might have been thereby limited in scope (Shalaby 2013). The court had ruled that the text of the article was only intended to include those individuals who served during the entire 10-year period set out in the article. Even such limited interpretation, however, would not have remedied the fundamental flaw of this approach to vetting, which is solely linked to association and has no connection to proof of involvement in abuse or criminality. The limitations suggested by the court might have also had the negative effect of allowing individuals who abused their authority to participate in political life. The increasingly polarized political climate and fears of political monopolization and institutional capture undermine any short-term possibility of broad-based institutional reform that would include systematic vetting. Further, with the 2014 Constitution that superseded the 2012 Constitution having stripped any mention of vetting from the text, such steps have no near-term prospects.

Preservation of historical memory and truth-telling

The course of transitional justice in Egypt has been tightly linked to the disappointing political progress of the post-Mubarak era. The instrumentalization of transitional justice as a political tool for institutional or factional gain has meant that it has been reactive, incomplete and ad hoc. The lack of a coherent vision for transitional justice has been exacerbated by the absence of a normative framework elucidating the rationale for undertaking transitional justice efforts. This muddled approach has undermined the truth-telling aspects of transitional justice. Even now, historical memory with respect to the 18-day uprising, remains a secondary concern. In fact, active efforts are underway to fabricate new historical narratvies and to create alternative histories of the uprising and the post-Mubarak period.

These shortcomings are exemplified by the haphazard and opaque manner in which prosecutions have been undertaken. There has been little consideration of transparency and openness with the public, nor have efforts been made to further understanding of the uprising and the modalities of repression and violence employed by the regime. This fragmentary and inconsistent record has done little to further accountability since the fall of Mubarak.

Although the possibility of establishing a truth and reconciliation commission has been mooted by civil society actors and human rights groups, the issue has yet to find appreciable political traction. However, two separate fact-finding commissions have been established since the fall of Mubarak. The National Fact-Finding Commission[5] on the January 25th Revolution was established on 16 February 2011 by Prime Minister Ahmed Shafik (Shafik 2011). The Commission was tasked with investigating the violent repression of protesters during Egypt's 18-day uprising. The Commission was comprised of five commissioners, three of whom were former senior judicial officials and two of whom were legal academics, supported by a larger technical team.[6]

The Commission released interim reports throughout February and March 2011[7] and a final summary report on 4 April 2011 (Fact Finding National Commission 2011b). This compressed schedule limited the depth of the Commission's work, as did its lack of subpoena authority and the limited cooperation afforded it by various security sector institutions. Despite these serious limitations, the Commission was able to conclude that security forces used live ammunition and that former regime members were implicated in the use of armed thugs to suppress protests on 2 February 2011 during the 'Battle of the Camel' (FFNC 2011b). Crucially, however, the report failed to ascribe command responsibility for the violence, and the preliminary nature of its findings, which were later referred to the office of the public prosecutor, provided only a fragmentary and incomplete account of state violence during the uprising.

This first attempt at establishing a historical record was limited by the still dominant role of the security services, but also by the failure of the Commission to carry out its given mandate. The Commission's approach indicated that it saw its work as a safety-valve, whereby it acknowledged generalized wrongdoing without ascribing accountability. Similarly, its recommendations were diffuse, lacking granular engagement with the events it was tasked with clarifying. The Commission made a summary of its final report public, but did not disclose the full version of that report.

Due to the limitations of the Commission's work and public frustration with mishandled investigations and prosecutions, President Morsi, after being sworn in as Egypt's first democratically elected president in June 2012, established a second fact-finding Commission (Morsi 2012), whose mandate was to examine the use of state violence against protesters in the period between 25 January 2011 and 30 June 2012, thus extending beyond the initial uprising to include later incidents of state violence during the transitional period. The Commission was comprised of 10 members (FFNC 2011a), including sitting officials, former officials and outside experts. Among the members was counselor Omar Marwan, who served as an adviser to the initial fact-finding commission established under the SCAF. The Commission also included six observers from the families of victims and the revolutionary youth (FFNC 2011a).

The Commission was tasked with gathering new evidence and ascertaining the identity of the perpetrators of violence and their accomplices. In a meeting with representatives from Amnesty International, several Commission members indicated positive progress and elaborated upon the methodology of the Commission's work, indicating that its focus was on uninvestigated incidents or cases still under appeal (Amnesty International 2013: 9–10). The Commission also sought to elucidate the pattern of acquittals of members of the security forces (Amnesty International 2013: 9–10). The final report of the Commission was completed and submitted to President Morsi on 8 January 2013. Notably, the report, or a summary version of it, has not been made public, limiting its impact and undermining the efforts at establishing a transparent and unimpeachable historical record. The report was submitted to the office of the public prosecutor, and withholding the report from the public has been justified as a precaution to avoid tampering with ongoing investigations. This may be a valid concern as it relates to cases of individual accountability, but the Commission's lack of transparency and its refusal to relay its main findings and conclusions to the public is ill-advised. Prosecutions are by necessity a limited tool, and the scope of the report's mandate is far broader than the set of cases that could practicably be investigated and prosecuted. At the very least, the Commission had a responsibility to communicate with the public directly, particularly since leaks of the key findings of the final report have been reported by various press outlets (Hendawi 2013).

With the accretion of numerous incidents of indiscriminte state violence and heavy-handed repression of dissent since Morsi's ouster, the framing of events and the construction of historical memory will continue to be a highly-contested public issue.

Victims' compensation

The iconic place of victims in the narrative of uprising transcends borders and fuels mobilization and protest. The special status of victims and the notion of victims' rights have recently received a boost from the experience of the ad hoc tribunals, specialized focus from multilateral bodies (UN GAOR 2006) and increased scholarly attention.[8] Those who have suffered physical or mental injury, emotional suffering, economic loss or the significant impairment of basic legal rights have now come to constitute a recognizable transitional justice category that includes those who have directly experienced violations, and their immediate family members. In terms of rights, one recent scholarly attempt at codifying the range of victims' rights suggests that victims should be afforded 'equal and effective access to justice, factual information concerning violations, and adequate, effective, and prompt reparations' (Bassiouni and Rotherberg 2008: 53).

In Egypt, the revered role of the 'martyrs' of the 18-day uprising continues to be sacrosanct for the protest movement and a rallying cry for continued mobilization. The iconography associated with the dead and injured continues to figure prominently in the staging of public protest. As the sphere of public dissent has shrunk, the protest movement has become increasingly balkanised, and the parallel protest movements now look to different sets of victims as representatives of the new class of 'martyrs'. In keeping with the broader and unfortunate trends of transitional justice in Egypt, however, victims of repression and abuse prior to the uprising still have yet to receive such concentrated attention or focus.

Even with regard to the victims of the initial uprising itself, transitional justice efforts have fallen short. As demonstrated above in the discussion of the ineffective and divergent prosecutorial approaches to regime violence and repression in connection with the 18-day uprising, it is clear that victims have not been afforded equal and effective access to justice. The opacity of the prosecutorial record and its ad hoc nature have also undermined the ability of victims to receive accurate and factual information regarding the violations. Furthermore, the circumscribed efforts to establish a historical record in the form of fact-finding commissions have remained of limited utility, particularly since the more comprehensive report commissioned by then-President Morsi and completed in 2013 has not been made public. While both fact-finding commissions have implicated security forces in the violent suppression of protests, the limited nature of the first report and the secrecy surrounding the second have hampered their effectiveness.

With respect to reparations, a compensation framework has been put in place to compensate the victims of the uprising and their families. The first step was the establishment of a victims' compensation fund by the SCAF in July 2011 (Ahram Online 2011b); the fund designated LE30,000 for families of those killed, LE15,000 for those with a disability due to injury and LE5,000 for those injured (Ahram Online 2011b). Disbursements began in the summer of 2011; however, in interviews conducted with victims and their families in spring 2012, administration of the compensation fund appeared to vary considerably, breeding resentment among those victims who felt that their claims had been ignored or improperly handled.[9] Despite purported efforts by the government to streamline the registration process and improve access to medical care, some victims have publicly expressed anger at the sums offered when compared to the severity of injuries, the excessive costs of treatment and the substandard levels of medical care provided (Sabry 2012).[10] In addition, some victims have expressed resentment at compensatory efforts in the wider context of impunity, which continues to define the post-Mubarak era (Ahram Online 2011a).

Such limited efforts at victims' compensation did not keep pace with the continued abuses of security forces in the post-Mubarak era despite legal expansion of the classification of victims, and have yet to even begin taking into account the abuses of the post-Morsi era. Efforts at expanded eligibility will be further complicated by the evolving nature of protest and violence and the dramatic shift in the political fortunes of the Muslim Brotherhood and their former opponents. The introduction of elements of civil strife, including violence between civilians, the rise of terrorism and the specter of cyclical violence, further cloud the prospects for expansion. Within this current polarized political context, efforts to expand the classification of victims will likely be politicized or curtailed because of the implications of such classifications for the current government.

Post-Mubarak violations consisted primarily of police abuse, but also included instances of military repression, including the violent dispersal of a predominantly-Christian October 2011 demonstration at the radio and television building in Cairo, popularly known as Maspero. The use of force by the military at Maspero resulted in 27 deaths. These victims were later included in the existing compensation scheme at the directive of the prime minister (Ahram Online 2011c), who further expanded the eligibility for compensation to include the victims of police violence, most notably those from the major clashes at Mohamed Mahmoud in November 2011 (Ahram Online 2011c), and the victims of the Port Said Stadium massacre on 1 February 2012. Executive decrees were issued by both the SCAF and then-President Morsi to expand those eligible for victim compensation. When coupled with the lack of appreciable official accountability in connection with any of these incidents, however, such administrative steps appear to be primarily a means to deflect attention and dilute anger.

These instances of state violence have been overshadowed by the more recent serial incidents of mass killings of pro-Morsi protesters in the wake of the military intervention that ousted Morsi from the presidency. The casualty figures from these violent dispersals now (at the time of writing) exceed the total number of previous victims and create an entirely new category of victimization and abuse. The scale of those incidents virtually guarantees a future cycle of retaliatory violence and attendant repression. A future in which insurgency and terrorism are serious possibilities bodes ill for the prospect of a rights-respecting culture and adherence to the rule of law.

As state violence continued under the watch of the Morsi government, raising the appearance of collusion between the executive branch and the MOI, the approach to state violence and police brutality became more complicated. With deepening political polarization and the growth of distinctly anti-Muslim Brotherhood protest, the fate of victims became far less certain. Recognition of the status of victims would have implicated the then-ruling Muslim Brotherhood and would, at the very least, have highlighted its inability to exert effective authority over the MOI. For example, the victims of the January 2013 police violence in Port Said, in which over 40 residents were killed, have not been accorded special status (Taha 2013). Commenting on this inconsistent approach, Ayman Abdel Meguid, the head of healthcare for the victims' fund, noted that '[w]e cannot add victims according to our whims. ... We receive presidential decrees telling us to add victims of certain clashes or incidents' (Taha 2013).

With the strengthening of the security sector and the potential for continuing instability following the ousting of Morsi, the impulse to hold the security sector accountable has suffered a further blow, both at the level of government and society. However, with the recurrent nature of mass mobilization, public protest, street violence and police brutality, the question of the status of victims is not one that will likely recede. In the immediate future, Egypt will continue to witness skewed and politicized approaches to dealing with the aftermath of state violence and criminality.

Finally, beyond the politically contested post-Mubarak period, the conception of victimization should be broadened to account for the decades of repression that preceded the January 25th uprising. Such a formal acknowledgment and perspective would offer long overdue recognition to those victims and would begin the process of grappling with the country's checkered past. It would also open up much-needed opportunities for redress and reparations.

Conclusion

The failures of transitional justice are neatly encapsulated in the fact that, more than two years after the fall of Mubarak, fundamental questions of fact regarding the uprising and the use of state violence remain murky and contested. Basic questions as to who was responsible and how and why protesters were murdered in the streets have not been answered. This near-past history remained a source of polarization and uncertainty, fueling popular discontent among activists and revolutionaries, buttressing misplaced doubts about state complicity among former regime loyalists and pushing unsatisfactory bargains by the reordered institutional powers. In short, transitional justice to date has been truncated and compromised, and these haphazard efforts have undermined the possibilities for genuine and much-needed national reconciliation. Each of the modalities of transitional justice – prosecutions, security sector reform, vetting, preservation of historical memory and truth-telling, and victims' compensation – demonstrates the critical political flaws that have hampered transitional justice, specifically, and democratization more broadly.

These failures have pertained to the very recent past, yet the constant struggles for factional supremacy have blocked off broader inquiry into the legacies and pathologies of repression and authoritarianism. Egypt has yet to delve deeply into examining the decades of misrule and abuse, and this incomplete interrogation has produced a limited understanding of how the country reached its current state and what is needed to produce systemic reform. With the reinvigoration of the security state and more permissive public attitudes to state violence in the wake of Morsi's July 2013 ousting, the prospect for more searching inquiry appears particularly dim.

This contentious and fragmented transitional period has produced an unstable state of affairs, with a newly mobilized political consciousness among certain sectors of society no longer amenable to the logic of blunt repression. In turn, this has led to a recurring cycle of protest and excess that shows no signs of abating, and which will likely increase in the post-Morsi period. This cycle has led to fresh calls for justice. As impunity endures and accelerates, and as calls for accountability are reinvigorated, the prospects for transitional justice remain real and vital. As such, if democratization eventually emerges from this period of turbulence and contestation, the deeply embedded ethos of transitional justice will likely persist. Such steps alone cannot ensure transition to and consolidation of democracy in Egypt without corresponding political and economic reforms, but they would certainly play a critical part in the struggle against repressive rule and the systematic violation of human rights. Needless to say, this disappointing chapter in Egypt's history continues with the possibility for future correction, as does the pursuit of justice and accountability.

Notes

1 As is noted in Ch 4.
2 The subsequent moves by the Egyptian military to remove President Morsi from office and its behavior after doing so would seem to indicate its determination to play an overseeing role that will have very significant consequences for what and how transitional justice measures are carried out.
3 At the time of writing, the 2012 Constitution has been superseded by a revised and controversial Constitution that was similarly passed by a popular referendum in January 2014. The newly-adopted constitution includes no provisions for vetting.
4 The language of the article created controversy with respect to the Grand Imam

of Al-Azhar, Sheikh Ahmed el-Tayeb, who had been a member of the NDP policy secretariat, although he had ostensibly resigned. The representative of Al-Azhar to the Constituent Assembly, Hassan El-Shafie, threatened to withdraw from the process in the face of accusations from the Muslim Brotherhood members that el-Tayeb was a remnant of the former regime who should be barred from public life. While the assembly appeared to come to notional agreement on the approach to el-Tayeb, it is possible that the provision will provide a legal platform for el-Tayeb's rivals to undermine his position.

5 For background on the Commission, see www.ffnc-eg.org/main.html.

6 For the full composition, see www.ffnc-eg.org/about.html.

7 The interim reports are available online at www.ffnc-eg.org/about.html.

8 'These parallel developments, as well as others within domestic legal systems, evidence a wide movement towards the recognition of the rights of victims of crime, whether domestic or international, or gross violations of human rights' (Bassiouni 2006: 203)..

9 Author interviews, Cairo, Egypt, May 2012.

10 'They kicked us out of the hospital and said none of us would receive any further treatment ... Most of us were carried out by family members and friends. We were screaming in pain' (Sabry 2012).

Bibliography

Ahram Online (2011a) 'Compensation Fund doesn't Impress Martyr's Families; They Demand Justice First', 26 June, available online at http://english.ahram.org.eg/NewsContent/1/64/15070/Egypt/Politics-/Compensation-fund-doesn%E2%80%99t-impress-martyr%E2%80%99s-familie.aspx.

Ahram Online (2011b) 'Compensation Funds to be Disbursed to Families of Victims of Egypt's Revolution: Tantawi', 31 July, available online at http://english.ahram.org.eg/NewsContent/1/64/17806/Egypt/Politics-/Compensation-funds-to-be-disbursed-to-families-of-.aspx.

Ahram Online (2011c) 'Mohamed Mahmoud and Maspero victims are revolution martyrs: PM', 12 December, available online at http://english.ahram.org.eg/NewsContent/1/0/29155/Egypt/0/Mohamed-Mahmoud-and-Maspero-victims-are-revolution.aspx.

Ahram Online (2013) 'Ex-Egypt Security Officials Slapped with Travel Ban', 10 April, available online at http://english.ahram.org.eg/NewsContent/3/12/68963/Business/Economy/ExEgypt-security-officials-slapped-with-travel-ban.aspx.

Amnesty International (2013) 'Rampant Impunity: Still No Justice for Protesters Killed in the "25 January Revolution"', available online at www.amnesty.org/en/library/asset/MDE12/004/2013/en/906ba6fd-9c4d-4845-adac-021318293a6a/mde120042013en.pdf.

Bassiouni, M. (2006) 6(2) *Human Rights Law Review* 203.

Bassiouni, M. and Rothenberg, D. (eds) (2008) *The Chicago Principles on Post-Conflict Justice*, International Human Rights Law Institute (Chicago, United States), Chicago Council on Foreign Relations (Chicago, United States), Istituto Superiore Internazionale di Scienze Criminali (Siracusa, Italy), Association Internationale de Droit Pénal (Paris, France)

Egypt Independent (2012) 'Five policemen sentenced to prison for Sayed Bilal murder', 21 June, available online at www.egyptindependent.com/news/five-policemen-sentenced-prison-sayed-bilal-murder.

El-Din, G. E. (2012) 'Constituent Assembly Okays Draft Egypt Charter in Night-Time Session', *Ahram Online*, 30 November, available online at http://english.ahram.org.eg/NewsContent/1/64/59505/Egypt/Politics-/Constituent-Assembly-okays-draft-Egypt-charter-in-.aspx.

Fact Finding National Commission, Main page, available online at www.ffnc-eg.org/main.html.

Fact Finding National Commission (2011a), Preliminary report, available online at http://www.ffnc-eg.org/about.html.

Fact Finding National Commission (2011b) 'Summary Final Report of the National Fact Finding Commission on the January 25th Revolution', 4 April, available online at www.ffnc-eg.org/assets/ffnc-eg_final.pdf.

Guardian (2011) 'Anger in Egypt as police who killed Khaled Said get seven years', 26 October, available online at www.guardian.co.uk/world/2011/oct/26/khaled-said-police-sentenced.

Hendawi, H. (2013) 'Egypt Government Inquiry Finds Police Shot Most of Nearly 900 Dead in Uprising', Associated Press, 13 March, available online at www.theprovince.com/touch/story.html?id=8090725.

Maher, H. (2013) 'Port Said Football Disaster was Premeditated: Egyptian Court', *Ahram Online*, 31 March, available online at http://english.ahram.org.eg/NewsContent/1/64/68153/Egypt/Politics-/Port-Said-football-disaster-was-premeditated-Egypt.aspx.

Prime Ministerial Decision No 294 of 2011, 16 February, available online at www.ffnc-eg.org/assets/file01.pdf.

Presidential Decision No 10 of 2012, 5 July.

Razek, M. A. (2013) تادنتسم مرف« ىف »ىسيسلا«ل نيعدملاو ةمكحملا ةلئسأ ..صنلاب سيلو ماعلا بئانلا بلط دعب جراخلا نم نيمأتلل راقملا انملتسا :قيرفلاو ..»ةلودلا أمن »زاهجلا« .. تارباخملاو ةيبرحلا مل رجت تايرحت Al-Yom al-Sabah, 16 April, available online at www1.youm7.com/News.asp?NewsID=1021626#.UW7ove2HwUc.twitter

Sabry, M. (2012) 'Egypt Boosts Aid to Wounded Protesters, but Many Still Suffer', McClatchy, 30 January, available online at www.mcclatchydc.com/2012/01/30/137350/egypt-boosts-aid-to-wounded-protesters.html

Fady Salah, F. (2013) 'NSF Calls for Transitional Justice Law' *Daily News Egypt*, 3 April, available online at www.dailynewsegypt.com/2013/04/03/nsf-calls-for-transitional-justice-law/.

Shalaby, E. (2013) 'SCC Returns Election Draft Law to Shura Council', *Daily News Egypt*, 18 February available online at www.dailynewsegypt.com/2013/02/18/scc-returns-election-draft-law-to-shura-council/.

Taha, R. M. (2013) 'Protests in Port Said over Exclusions from Victims' Funds', *Daily News Egypt*, 1 April, available online at www.dailynewsegypt.com/2013/04/01/protests-in-port-said-over-exclusions-from-victims-funds/.

UN GAOR (2006) 'Basic Principles and Guidelines on the Right to a Remedy and Reparation for Victims of Gross Violations of International Human Rights Law and Serious Violations of International Humanitarian Law, General Assembly Resolution 147, UN Doc A/Res/60/147, 21 March.

Chapter 10

Justice after the war: The International Criminal Court and post-Gaddafi Libya

Mark Kersten[1]

In contrast to other Arab Spring uprisings, the International Criminal Court (ICC) intervened in Libya and has subsequently played an important, if controversial, role in the country's political transition. This chapter provides a critical overview of key events pertaining to the ICC's role and impact in post-Gaddafi Libya. It offers some tentative conclusions on how Libya's experience with international criminal justice may affect the broader field of transitional justice.[2]

Libya has clearly indicated that its actions regarding post-Gaddafi accountability are aimed at maintaining its sovereignty and establishing itself as an equal member of the international community, able and willing to prosecute senior members of the Gaddafi regime. The ICC has striven to show that it is an effective institution that can have positive effects on conflict and post-conflict justice and accountability. However, as this analysis makes clear, the pursuit and politics of justice in post-Gaddafi Libya has been characterized by ongoing mistrust and rancour among key figures and actors. This animosity has been consistently stoked by a lack of interest among the concerned parties to seek, identify and pursue judicial avenues where their interests could converge and complement each other. Ultimately, this may hamper the objectives and interests of both the ICC and Libyans.

The chapter proceeds in three sections. Section one examines the capture of Abdullah al-Senussi in Mauritania and Saif al-Islam Gaddafi[3] as well as the controversies over where they should be tried. Section two details efforts to represent Saif, focusing in particular on the controversial arrest and detention of ICC defence counsel following their visit to Zintan in June 2012. Section three offers some reflections on the implications of the pursuit of post-Gaddafi justice on the field of transitional justice.

Saif and Senussi: will they stay or will they go?

The decision of where to hold post-conflict trials has always been politically contentious; the dilemmas it poses are part of the hardwiring of international criminal justice. Divorcing justice from the communities in which atrocities have occurred is replete with trade-offs and controversy (Simpson 2007: 30–53). Extracting evidence, protecting witnesses and contextualizing crimes becomes an immensely difficult process when adjudication takes place far away from where atrocities were perpetrated. But in many cases, post-conflict states do not have the resources or the judicial and political stability to adjudicate serious breaches of international criminal justice. This dilemma is captured by the ICC's principle of complementarity wherein the Court can only investigate and prosecute crimes when national authorities are unable or unwilling to do so.

Following the death of Muammar Gaddafi, Abdullah al-Senussi and Saif al-Islam Gaddafi were the only remaining individuals wanted by the ICC for their roles in the Gaddafi regime's brutal crackdown against civilians. The fate of Saif and Senussi became the locus of a potent and polarizing debate on where post-conflict justice in Libya should be served. This section provides background on both Saif and Senussi before delving into the polarizing fight over where to try them, a battle which has created an acrimonious rift between those actors who see The Hague as the only legitimate venue for trial and those who believe that Libya has the sovereign prerogative to try Saif and Senussi.

'The Senussi Sweepstakes'[4]

Abdullah al-Senussi was a key member of Gaddafi's most trusted circle of advisors, having served as both Libya's external and internal intelligence chief. As one observer suggests, 'Senussi's association with the worst excesses of the Libyan regime stretch back to the early days of Col. Gaddafi's dictatorial rule' (Sherlock 2011). With the exception of Muammar Gaddafi, Senussi may have been 'the most feared man in Libya' (Hilsum 2012a). Notably, Senussi is widely believed to bear responsibility for the infamous 1996 Abu Salim Massacre (where at least 1,200 Libyan prisoners were killed) and the Lockerbie bombing in 1988. Because of his position as the gate-keeper of the regime's secret, Geoffrey Robertson (2011a) called Senussi the 'crown jewel' of justice in Libya. For his role in the crackdown on Libyan demonstrators, the ICC issued an arrest warrant against Senussi for being an 'indirect perpetrator' on two counts of crimes against humanity – murder and persecution (ICC 2012k).

In March 2012 it was reported that Senussi had been arrested in a joint operation between French and Mauritanian officials in Nouakchott, Mauritania. Immediately following his arrest, Senussi's fate emerged as the centrepiece of what was described as a 'three-way custody battle' (Mark 2012) and an 'extradition race' (Hirsch 2012) between Libya, France and the ICC. In seeking Senussi's surrender, Libyan authorities took an aggressive and ultimately successful approach, applying concerted diplomatic pressure and offering Mauritania substantial incentives in order to gain custody of Gaddafi's right-hand man. Finally, on 5 September 2012, Senussi was extradited to Libya, 'on the basis of guarantees given by the Libyan authorities' (see Harding and Black 2012). It was reported that Senussi's transfer cost Libya $200 million (see Sydow 2012).

Saif in Zintan

Prior to the Libyan uprising – and even in its early stages – many observers and diplomats saw Saif al-Islam Gaddafi as a moderating force in Libya. The London School of Economics-educated Saif had been instrumental in Libya's rapprochement with the West, played a key role in negotiating the surrender of the country's weapons of mass destruction and nuclear programme, helped to secure compensation for victims of the Lockerbie bombing, and spearheaded efforts to de-radicalize and make peace with the Libyan Islamic Fighting Group (LIFG). As Lindsey Hilsum (2012b: 156) writes, in the 2000s 'it became clear that he was his father's heir apparent, and anyone who wanted to do business in Libya had to do business with him'. Consequently, many saw Saif as a reform-minded successor to his father, someone who could continue Libya's transformation from a pariah state to a legitimate and respected member of the international community.

It quickly became clear, however, that Saif was willing to play a significant role alongside his father. As with Senussi, the ICC issued an arrest warrant for Saif, accusing him of being an indirect co-perpetrator on two counts of crimes against humanity – murder and persecution. After fleeing Tripoli, on the night of 19 November 2011, Saif was arrested by a militia brigade from Zintan where he remains at the time of writing. The drama over where he and Senussi would be tried, however, had long since commenced.

Where to try Saif and Senussi?

Discussions on where to try Saif and Senussi began as early as August 2011, when the prospect of bringing senior Libyan officials to justice became a distinct possibility (see Bosco 2011; Jillions 2011; Kersten 2011a; Kaye 2011). The debate has been characterized by a polarizing battle between proponents of trying them in Libya, on the one hand, and those who believe that only the ICC should try them impartially and legitimately, on the other. Within these camps, however, is a curious constellation of actors and positions. Predictably, Libyan authorities have made clear their intentions to try Saif on Libyan soil with Libyan judges, while international human rights NGOs have insisted that Gaddafi's son be tried in The Hague (see Amnesty International 2011; Parliamentarians for Global Action 2011). However, somewhat paradoxically, the Office of the Prosecutor (OTP) has been supportive of Libya's claims to try Saif, while the Office of Public Counsel for the Defence (OPCD) has vociferously worked to demonstrate that a fair trial in Libya is all but impossible.

From the outset, the National Transitional Council (NTC) maintained that Saif would be investigated and tried in Libya. Doing so, it has been consistently claimed, is essential to establishing the country as a sovereign member of the international community (see, for example CNN 2012; Al Jazeera 2012). For example, in October 2011, a month prior to the arrest of Saif, Colonel Ahmed Bani, the military spokesman for Libya's interim rulers, explained why the ICC could not gain custody of Saif:

> We will not accept that our sovereignty be violated like that. We will put him on trial here. This is where he must face the consequences of what he has done. We will prove to the world that we are a civilised people with a fair justice system. Libya has its rights and its sovereignty and we will exercise them. (See Chulov 2011)

Libya's desire to try Saif should also be understood within the context of prevalent fears that surrendering Saif or Senussi to the ICC could undermine Libya's revolution and potentially destabilize the country. There is a concern that Saif could be found innocent or released after serving a short sentence if tried at the ICC. This concern is likely a result of a combination of the relatively minor charges against him at the ICC, his young age (41 years old as at the time of writing) and the possibility of a lenient sentence. Notably, the Libya Working Group, an assembly of experts on Libya, has opined that it would be politically impossible for the NTC to allow Saif to receive an innocent verdict because it would be seen to 'betray the revolution' (see Chatham House 2012a: 3). And, according to Geoffrey Robertson (2011b), an innocent verdict at the ICC is a real possibility: 'Saif has the makings of an arguable defense ... His judges would be independent and his conviction on the basis of proof beyond reasonable doubt would by no means be a foregone conclusion'. In contrast, Libya could charge Saif with additional offences, such as corruption, and impose the death penalty.

Remarkably, the OTP has, by and large, sided with the NTC's plans to try Saif, demonstrating a leniency that appears unprecedented in the history of the Court. During a November 2011 visit to Tripoli, Moreno-Ocampo capitulated to the inevitability of the NTC's demands to try Saif:

> The standard of the ICC is that it has to be a judicial process that is not organised to shield the suspect ... and I respect that it's important for the cases to be tried in Libya ... and I am not competing for the case. (See BBC 2012a)

Rather than standing by the orthodox standard of complementarity, whereby a state has to convince ICC judges that it is actively able and willing to prosecute the same individuals for the same crimes, the OTP has seemingly calculated that it is best positioned to argue that it contributed positively to Libya's pursuit of justice.[5] There are a number of plausible explanations for this position.

As suggested above, it is not a given that Saif would be convicted at the ICC. The Libya Working Group noted in February 2012 that '[t]here is speculation that the ICC does not want Saif to be put on trial in The Hague as they do not have a strong case against him' (see Chatham House 2012c). Timothy William Waters (2011) has argued, alternatively, that Moreno-Ocampo's acquiescence was a pragmatic response aimed at ensuring the cooperation of Libyan authorities so as 'to have any hope of influencing the process'. In this context, it is important to note that the ICC has received scant support from the international community which has been largely unconcerned with the pursuit of post-Gaddafi accountability, periodically reaffirming that the ICC and Libya should cooperate but that it is up to Libya to decide the fate of Saif and Senussi. Indeed, the general consensus among the states that intervened has been that Libya should prosecute Saif and Senussi, irrespective of the ICC's indictments (see Lynch 2011; McGreal 2012; Kersten 2013).

Rather than demanding the surrender of Saif and Senussi, the OTP has shifted its focus away from seeking custody of Saif or Senussi towards claiming that they can achieve 'positive complementarity' in Libya. In this context, Moreno-Ocampo argued that 'the ICC is still providing an important service, because we will ensure justice in Libya, whoever will do it' (see Papenfuss 2012). The OTP, moreover, appeared on numerous occasions at the side of NTC leaders, reaffirming the perception that his role is to support – and not challenge – Libya's efforts to try Saif. As Waters (2011) suggests, this may be a pragmatic calculation on the part of Moreno-Ocampo. Claiming some responsibility for bringing both Saif and Senussi to justice in Libya by couching arguments in the rhetoric of positive complementarity may soften the blow – and deflect criticism – of the ICC appearing largely impotent in contributing to accountability in post-Gaddafi Libya. Still, the attitude of the OTP has not been shared by all organs of the Court.

By working to defend the ICC's right to prosecute Saif and Senussi, it has been the Office of Public Counsel for the Defence (OPCD) which has most adamantly sought to ensure that Saif and Senussi be tried in The Hague. As a result, on a number of occasions the OPCD has taken aim at the OTP's acquiescence with Libya's demands to prosecute Saif and Senussi. Just days after Saif's arrest on 28 November 2011, the OPCD asserted that the OTP was employing double-standards with regards to its conception of complementarity:

> … it is in the general interests of the Defence that the standard and criteria for determining the existence of investigations and prosecutions be interpreted and applied uniformly throughout the different ICC cases: it would be unfair to apply a more stringent standard to cases in which admissibility is challenged by the Defence, whilst applying a more relaxed standard in the present case due to the apparent coalescence of Prosecution and State interests (ICC 2011c; see also Stahn 2012: 12).

The OPCD also took issue with Moreno-Ocampo's public comments and appearances with members of the NTC which, they argued, appeared to reaffirm the validity of the NTC's desire to prosecute Saif in Libya. In May 2012, the OPCD filed a motion with the ICC's Appeals Chamber to disqualify Moreno-Ocampo from the Libyan case due to 'an objective appearance that the Prosecutor is affiliated with both the political cause and legal positions of the NTC government' (ICC 2012c para 28). While the motion was ultimately unsuccessful, just four days before the end of Moreno-Ocampo's tenure as Chief Prosecutor the Appeals Chamber issued a scathing ruling which claimed that the Prosecutor's behaviour was clearly inappropriate in light of the presumption of innocence. 'Such behaviour not only reflects poorly on the Prosecutor but also, given that the Prosecutor is an elected official of the Court and that his statements are often imputed to the Court as a whole, may lead observers to question the integrity of the Court as a whole' (ICC 2012h).

Libya's admissibility challenge

In May 2012, Libya filed an admissibility challenge at the ICC in which the government argued that because it was actively investigating and willing to prosecute Saif and Senussi, ICC judges had an obligation to rule in favour of Libya's admissibility challenge (ICC 2012b). At the same time, Libya unveiled a refurbished courtroom in Tripoli (see Al Shalchi 2012) and a prison custom-made for Saif (Stephen 2012b). The application, and the commitment to demonstrating that it was actively investigating and willing to prosecute Saif and Senussi, is an indication of the Libyan government's interest in having the ICC and the international community more broadly endorse Libya's efforts at achieving transitional justice.

Prior to Senussi's extradition from Mauritania to Libya, it was widely believed that Libya's admissibility challenge would be fundamentally undermined by the fact that it did not have custody of Senussi and that Saif remained in the custody of a Zintani militia. With Senussi's extradition to Libya, a significant obstacle to Libya's admissibility challenge was removed. However, the Court rejected Libya's admissibility challenge in Saif's case, relying heavily on the fact that Gaddafi's son remains in the custody of a Zintani brigade and not the central government.[6] Yet while the admissibility challenge has precipitated a fascinating political and legal debate which will undoubtedly have implications on the future functioning and practices of the ICC, it should not deter from a recognition that other options were available with regards to prosecuting Saif and Senussi.

A missed opportunity

The polarizing battle between proponents of a trial in Libya versus those advocating justice in The Hague deflected attention away from existing alternative legal and political options, which could have served the interests of all parties. Two distinct options could have satisfied the interests of both the ICC and Libya: an *in situ* trial and a sequencing of trials. Unfortunately, neither was sufficiently explored.

The Rome Statute envisages the possibility of *in situ* trials under Article 3(3), which states that proceedings may take place 'elsewhere, whenever [the

ICC] considers it desirable'. Indeed, the potential of holding trials away from The Hague has been explored by the ICC in other contexts.[7] Such trials have numerous advantages: their proximity to the victims, witnesses and evidence; acting as a demonstration that justice is being done; contributing to the building of the rule of law by training lawyers and providing a material legacy; and maintaining the standards of international criminal justice (see Kaye 2011; Kersten 2011a).

The OTP initially saw the option of an *in situ* trial favourably and presented it to the NTC during a visit in November 2011 to discuss the fate of Saif. On the eve of the visit, ICC spokesperson, Fadi El Abdallah, suggested that a trial by ICC judges in Libya was indeed a viable option (see Murphy 2011). The OTP subsequently reported that it had offered such an option to the NTC (ICC 2012b). Importantly, holding an *in situ* trial in Tripoli (or perhaps even Zintan) could have satisfied the need of both parties. The NTC would be able to reaffirm itself as a sovereign entity able to hold fair trials as well as demonstrate its commitment to international law. The ICC would hear a key case and demonstrate that it was sensitive to the desire of Libyans to see justice served where crimes occurred rather than divorcing proceedings from victims and survivors. Nevertheless, the NTC rejected the possibility of an *in situ* trial and stated that it would only accept a trial in Libya, by Libyan judges (see Murphy 2011; Stephen 2012a). Rather than defending this option and presenting its benefits to the Libyan public or the international community, the possibility of an ICC trial in Libya appears to have been subsequently ignored by the ICC, international human rights NGOs and the Libyan government itself.

During the November meeting, the OTP also suggested that the ICC and the NTC could sequence prosecutions. Sequencing, envisioned under Article 94 of the Rome Statute, would entail the ICC trying Saif and Senussi for the alleged crimes outlined in their indictment and subsequently transferring them to Libya to be tried for other alleged crimes (see Stahn 2012: 325–49). As Carsten Stahn writes, the sequencing of trials could have been 'settled on a negotiated basis, i.e. through consultation and agreement' (2012: 340). The trial at the ICC would have provided time for Libya to stabilize the country and build an independent judiciary capable of subsequently trying Saif and Senussi domestically for crimes beyond the ICC's temporal jurisdiction (see Robertson 2011b). Moreover, sequencing could have ensured that alleged crimes committed before and after 15 February 2011[8] were investigated and prosecuted. However, as with an *in situ* trial sequencing remained insufficiently explored.

Of course, neither an *in situ* trial nor a sequencing of trials is a perfect or risk-free option; each has its own drawbacks. But these were real options which could have avoided the animosity of the current debate regarding the fate of Saif and Senussi by potentially satisfying the interests of all actors involved – not to mention the interests of justice. While Libya may not have looked upon any option other than a local trial favourably, it is important to note that the ICC did very little to communicate or demonstrate its work locally or to establish any kind of local presence during the conflict (Chatham House 2011: 10). This point was noted by the director of Lawyers for Justice in Libya, Elham Saudi (Chatham House 2011: 10):

> The press and NGOs were in Libya and were gathering evidence but there was no visible presence of the ICC. People were not clear as to what should happen after the indictments and did not understand why, for example, the BBC was in Libya but the ICC was not.

The ICC thus had little leverage when it came to influencing where Saif and Senussi would be tried. The Court appeared alien to Libyans and, as a consequence, many find absurd the notion of handing over prized detainees from the Gaddafi regime to a Court that had a minimal presence during their struggle against Gaddafi.

But there should be no confusion: the polarizing nature of the debate regarding where to try Saif and Senussi was not inevitable. It was an extension of the fact that the OTP, international human rights groups and the international community did not effectively communicate the existence of other options. As Saudi adds:

> It is not an either or of having a trial in The Hague or a trial in Libya. There's a multitude of options in between as well and that's where the education is lacking and the ICC is failing because they have an active responsibility and a positive duty to inform Libyans of all their options and to assist them in achieving those options. (See BBC 2012b)

The OPCD detention debacle

From the moment the former heir to the Libyan regime was captured, efforts to represent Saif have been fraught with controversy and characterized by an accumulation of mistrust, bitterness and animosity between the OPCD and the OTP and between the ICC and Libya. Nothing demonstrated this reality as vividly as the detention of four ICC staff members from June to July 2012.

On 7 June 2012 four staff members of the OPCD – Melinda Taylor (Australia), Helene Assaf (Lebanon), Alexander Khodakov (Russia) and Esteban Peralta Losilla (Spain) – were arrested following a meeting with Saif al-Islam Gaddafi in Zintan. The four staff members had been granted access to Saif by the office of Libya's General Prosecutor but were detained by members of the Zintani militia which had held custody of Gaddafi since his arrest. Describing their arrest, Ajmi al-Atiri, a commander from the Zintani brigade, explained: 'We tricked the ICC team by presenting them with one of our men who we told them was deaf and old and illiterate but he is actually a wise man who can speak four languages including English' (see Shuaib and Al Shalchi 2012). In describing the actions of the ICC staff as 'a homeland security issue', al-Atiri further claimed that numerous blank documents, a coded letter to a close confidante of Saif, Mohammed Ismail, as well as spying and recording devices, had been retrieved from the lawyers. The four were arrested, it was maintained, because their actions threatened Libyan national security. It subsequently came to light that at least some members of the NTC were seeking to leverage the staff's freedom. On 12 June, NTC spokesperson Mohammed al-Hareizi declared that Taylor was free to leave in exchange for information regarding the location of Ismail:

> We want this guy. It is very important to catch this guy because this guy is very, very, very danger[ous] for us … We don't have anything against this woman. Just we need some information from her, after that she will be free. (See Al Arabiya 2012a)

In response to these developments, ICC President Judge Sang-Hyun Song declared that ICC staff enjoyed immunity from arrest and prosecution in their capacity as the defence counsel for Saif and demanded that Libyan authorities 'take all necessary measures to ensure their safety and security and to liberate them' (ICC 2012g). Following this initial reaction, the Court became engaged in a series of negotiations with Libyan authorities aimed at guaranteeing the return of Taylor and her staff. Additionally, the Australian government and, in particular, Foreign Minister Bob Carr and Australia's ambassador to Libya, David Ritchie, played an intimate role in efforts to have the ICC staff released. For its part, the international community was largely silent. A week after the arrest of the ICC staff, NATO Secretary-General Anders Fogh Rasmussen, on an official visit to Australia, declared: 'I strongly regret that certain groups in Libya have arrested or withheld representatives of the International Criminal Court. I would urge them to release these individuals as soon as possible' (see Al Arabiya 2012b). More than a week after the arrest of the ICC staff and in response to pressure from Russian Foreign Minister Sergei Lavrov, who believed that the staff's detention was in violation of UN Security Council Resolution 1970 (see RIA Novosti 2012), the Security Council finally issued its own statement where it 'express[ed] serious concern over the detention' of the staff and 'urge[d] Libyan authorities at all levels and all concerned to work towards immediate release of all the ICC staff members' (Security Council 2012b). Notably, the Council's statement did not demand that Libya release the staff members, nor did it criticize the arrest and detention of an international delegation that enjoyed diplomatic immunity.

In working for Taylor's release, Carr began to publicly voice criticism of the ICC for not having adequate protocols and procedures in place for lawyers working in fragile, highly volatile contexts (see ABC 2012; *Telegraph* 2012). He consequently suggested that the ICC apologize for any 'misunderstandings' it had caused. The notion of an apology was criticized by a number of observers. Amnesty International's Widney Brown stated that Carr's public suggestion that the Court owed Libya an apology for illegally detaining ICC staff was short-sighted and would 'undermine the independence of the International Criminal Court and create a precedent where governments think well, if we just lock somebody up then we'll get them to back off' (see Flitton and Lester 2012; see also Heller 2012a). Richard Goldstone (2012) wrote that any '[t]alk of securing a "deal" for the release of the four risks compromising the global authority of the court, which is backed by the full authority of the UN and the international community'.

Carr's declaration that the Court should apologize to Libya put the ICC in an immensely difficult position: either the Court apologized and risked undermining its authority and legitimacy or it refused to apologize and risked being blamed for prolonging Taylor's detention. Consequently, on 22 June 2012, the Court released a statement which declared that:

> The ICC deeply regrets any events that may have given rise to concerns on the part of the Libyan authorities. In carrying out its functions, the Court has no intention of doing anything that would undermine the national security of Libya (ICC 2012i).

The statement furthermore promised that any wrongdoing on the part of the ICC staff would be investigated,[9] and noted that the Court was 'extremely grateful to the Libyan authorities for their commitment to take all necessary action for the release of the Court's staff members' (ICC 2012i).

On 3 July, ICC President Song arrived in Zintan, where he, again, publicly expressed regret on behalf of the Court, declaring that he wished 'to apologise for the difficulties which arose due to this series of events' (see Simons 2012). All of the four staff were then flown in a plane organized by the Italian government to Rome and subsequently transferred to The Hague.

A game with no winners

The arrest of the ICC staff should be understood within the context of a fragile state protective of its sovereign prerogatives. As Barak Barfi and Jason Pack (2012) argue, '[i]n arresting Taylor and her colleagues, the NTC has sought to hamstring the ICC's investigation while sending the court a message Libya will not tolerate an infringement of its sovereignty'. Libya's Deputy Foreign Minister, Abdel Aziz, responded to the international outcry by defending the country's ability to govern itself: 'I would say the international community should be fair to Libya. You cannot continue to always push Libya to do this, to do that. There is the other side of the coin that has to be addressed too' (see Gumuchian and Shuaib 2012). Still, the arrest and detention of the ICC staff is likely to hinder the aims and interests of both the ICC and the new Libyan state.

The Court's apology is likely to undermine its authority. The Court effectively apologized to Libya for arresting staff members who enjoy immunity from arrest and prosecution and thanked them for their cooperation in the process.

Moreover, the ICC's response to Libya may undermine the capacity for defence lawyers to work in fragile political contexts. It may also now prove impossible for any staff from the ICC to effectively represent Saif in proceedings before the Court. Not long after the release of the ICC staff, the Libyan government cast doubt on 'the OPCD's ability to properly and genuinely represent Mr Gaddafi's views' and stated that 'communications between the Libyan Government and the OPCD appear to have irretrievably broken down' (ICC 2012j: paras 8 and 10).

A thorough report filed by the OPCD in August 2012 is indicative of the extent to which the relationship between Saif's defence counsel and the Libyan government has been tarnished. The OPCD noted that their point-man in Libya 'informed both the Counsel for Mr. Gaddafi and the ICC interpreter on independent occasions that the actions of the Libyan authorities were "retaliation" for the allegations, which had been set out in the OPCD report of 7 March 2012' (ICC 2012l: para 265). Earlier, Nick Kaufman similarly suggested that the animosity within the ICC filings put Taylor and her delegation at risk, stating that she had 'fallen victim of this hostility which is because of the intensity of the litigation', and that '[t]here is no doubt that these filings contributed to cementing the, shall we say, anger of the local authorities holding Saif, against Melinda and her superior [Keïta]' (see Callinan 2012). The bad blood appears to have spread into the OTP as well. In learning about the arrest of Taylor and her colleagues, Moreno-Ocampo refused to defend the OPCD staff members, blaming them instead for their predicament: 'It's not what we would expect of the court, of the defence' (see Gumuchian 2012). His statement was in stark contrast to other respected international lawyers.

The debacle over the arrest of the ICC staff likely tarnished Libya's international reputation and its case to prosecute Saif and Senussi in Libya. In the wake of the arrest of the ICC staff, high profile legal figures publicly voiced concern over Libya's commitment to international justice and human rights standards. Numerous international legal scholars demonstrated that *regardless* of what occurred during the meeting between the OPCD delegation and Saif, the staff members were entitled to diplomatic immunity (see Akande 2012; Heller 2012d; Cronin-Furman and Taub 2012). By refusing to release the delegation, Libya flouted its international legal obligations and may have made it less likely that the Court would be inclined to accept the government's admissibility challenge, once described as 'a brilliant piece of work [which] stands a good chance of success' (Heller 2012b). While ICC judges did not touch on the detention of the ICC staff in their judgment on Libya's admissibility challenge regarding Saif, siding with Libya would have risked reaffirming numerous contraventions of international law and the illegal treatment of ICC staff. In this context, Richard Goldstone (2012) wrote that '[w]hat is effectively an act of kidnapping also regrettably demonstrates that there is as yet no rule of law in Libya domestically. Ultimately, what has happened has justified the insistence by the ICC that Saif should be tried in The Hague'.

The ICC and post-Gaddafi Libya: implications and questions for transitional justice

A number of tentative conclusions regarding the implications of post-Gaddafi justice on the wider field and pursuit of international criminal and transitional justice can be drawn. This section considers three implications of the ICC's intervention on post-conflict justice in Libya and the field of tranitional justice more broadly: the ever-present risk of post-conflict victor's justice; the politics of complementarity; and the capacity of the ICC to function in fragile contexts.

Victor's justice

The pursuit of post-Gaddafi justice in Libya has played directly into perceptions that post-conflict accountability inevitably devolves into victor's justice. Not only have prosecutions almost exclusively targeted Gaddafi regime officials, but a blanket amnesty has been granted for any 'military, security or civil actions dictated by the February 17 Revolution that were performed by revolutionaries with the goal of promoting or protecting the revolution' (HRW 2012). With regards to the ICC, only Saif and Senussi remain indicted by the Court and, while other senior Gaddafi-era officials have been put on trial in Libya, there is little-to-no indication that serious violations by pro-revolution militias will be held to account.[10] Importantly, the OTP has contributed to the perception of one-sided justice and accountability. The public appearance of Moreno-Ocampo with leaders of the NTC and with rebels in Misrata, for example, has reaffirmed the OTP's positions of siding with the NTC and the rebels as well as its apparent lack of interest in investigating allegations of crimes by the rebels.

For the field of transitional justice, there is a need to conduct more research into the relationship between how conflicts end and subsequent approaches to achieving justice and accountability. Libya's approach to transitional justice is a direct result of the manner in which the conflict ended; the victor's peace of the rebels over the Gaddafi regime has largely translated into post-conflict victor's justice.

The politics of complementarity in post-conflict settings

Libya demonstrates that questions pertaining to where prosecutions should and can take place will remain a subject ridden with controversy. The country's experience with post-conflict accountability poses difficult questions for the field of transitional justice. Two, in particular, are worth highlighting. First, how are we to comprehend shifting interpretations of complementarity? The Libyan situation exposes the reality that the principle and practice of 'complementarity' is not understood in the same way across cases. Second, and relatedly, are the expectations of a state's capacity to prosecute perpetrators of international crimes following a significant period of atrocity and autocracy fair and feasible? Put another way, how long should a state transitioning out of a period of conflict have in order to prove that it is able and willing to prosecute members of a former regime? The experience of Libya would seem to indicate that *no* state that emerges from decades of autocratic rule, where an independent judiciary is non-existent, can be judged able and willing to prosecute key figures itself. In such contexts, the state will be expected simply to 'flip' individuals indicted by the ICC to The Hague at the earliest possible opportunity. If it does not, it risks being judged in contravention of its obligations under international law and castigated by the international human rights community. This may be deeply problematic and will surely be unacceptable to states emerging from periods of heightened political violence seeking to reassert their sovereign capacity and status. Indeed, such states face a difficult quandary: on the one hand, they view prosecuting their own citizens as a matter of upholding or rescuing their status as legitimate and sovereign members of the international community; on the other, their international reputation may be undermined by their insistence that they can prosecute ICC indictees themselves. These issues make exploring alternative, justice-sharing solutions between states and the ICC all the more relevant and pressing. Many of the tensions that emerge in the fight over where to try ICC indictees can be avoided by exploring and pursuing middle-ground options (for example an *in situ* trial or the sequencing of trials) where the interests of all parties can be met. However, as the case of Libya has demonstrated, such middle-ground options are too often neglected.

The ICC in fragile settings

It is entirely possible that the ICC's intervention in Libya will ultimately have greater effects on the Court itself than on Libya. This finding is of significance as it contradicts a generally held assumption that whenever the ICC intervenes in ongoing and or recently concluded conflicts, it will have a significant impact on the decision-making of state actors. In Libya, however, this does not appear to be the case.

The ICC's decision-making in Libya may have palpable ramifications on its future capacity to function effectively in fragile conflict and post-conflict contexts. First, the Court's apology to Libya may affect the capacity of ICC staff to operate in such situations in the future (see Cronin-Furman and Taub 2012). The apology appeared to send the message that the illegal arrest and detention of ICC staff was, at least in part, the fault of the Court. The danger is that this will set a precedent and encourage states to abuse the rights of ICC staff in the future. As Geoff Taylor has stated: if the ICC 'can't protect their own people when they go into these dangerous places, how will it work? Unless they can protect their staff, these courts can't function' (see Kyriacou 2012). Second, the OTP's leniency towards Libya and its currying favour with the NTC is something that must be more critically addressed as it has diminished the Court's ability to appear impartial and independent. Third, the bitter divisions that have emerged within the Court need to be addressed. In order, ultimately, to be a successful, independent and impartial Court, the ICC must have a well-functioning OTP *and* OPCD. Together, these developments and issues will have long-term implications on the capacity of the ICC to contribute to the pursuit of transitional justice in post-conflict settings.

Conclusion

Post-Gaddafi Libya has been a battleground for legitimacy and effect. The ICC has striven to demonstrate that it is a viable international institution which can positively affect the pursuit of post-conflict justice. Libya has sought to demonstrate that it is a functioning sovereign state able and willing to execute justice. In the end, however, both the Court and the Libyan state may be left disappointed.

This chapter has sought to provide a critical overview of events pertaining to the ICC's role and impact in post-Gaddafi Libya. In doing so, a precarious narrative emerges, one where Libya is viewed as a lawless country, uninterested in justice, versus a Court trying to maintain relevance and desperately seeking to have a positive effect on post-accountability justice in Libya. Critically, this narrative is an extension not simply of ongoing events, but deep-seated mistrust, prevalent animosity and poor lines of communication between Libya and the ICC. None of this was inevitable and, in numerous instances, aggravations of this tenuous relationship could have been avoided. Despite this, much can be, and remains to be, learned from the ICC's experience in Libya. The Court's intervention and its impact on the pursuit of post-conflict justice and accountability pose many important questions for the Court's role in fragile post-conflict contexts and for the field of transitional justice more broadly. How these questions are answered is likely to have profound effects on the future functioning of the ICC.

Notes

1 My deepest gratitude goes to Kevin Jon Heller, Elke Schwarz and Mohammad Shouman who generously took the time to read drafts of this chapter and offer their invaluable insights. Many thanks as well to Kirsten Fisher who kindly invited me to submit this chapter. It goes without saying that I bear all responsibility for any inaccuracies in the chapter.
2 Shorter versions of this article can be found at Kersten 2012a and 2012b
3 Henceforth referred to as Saif, although he is not to be mistaken with his brother, Saif al-Arab Gaddafi.
4 This phrase was authored by David Bosco in his 2012 article 'The Senussi Sweepstakes: Who gets Libya's former intelligence chief?'.
5 It should be noted that, in response to Libya's admissibility challenge, the OTP has expressed some concern about the fact that Saif is not in the custody of Libya. See ICC 2012e.
6 Libya has since appealed the Pre-Trial Chamber's decision.
7 The possibility of holding *in situ* ICC trials was explored for both the Democratic Republic of Congo and Kenyan cases.

8 In referring the situation in Libya to the ICC in Resolution 1970, the UN Security Council restricted the Court's temporal jurisdiction to 15 February 2011.
9 At the time of writing there is no indication that an investigation has been conducted.
10 See Ch 11.

Bibliography

ABC (2012) 'Libya set to free Melinda Taylor if ICC apologises: Carr', available online at www.abc.net.au/am/content/2012/s3528077.htm.

Akande, D. (2012) 'The Immunity of the ICC Lawyers and Staff Detained in Libya, EJIL: Talk!', available online at www.ejiltalk.org/the-immunity-of-the-icc-lawyers-and-staff-detained-in-libya/.

Al Arabiya (2012a) 'Aussie lawyer free if she reveals Libyan outlaw: report', available online at http://english.alarabiya.net/articles/2012/06/12/220148.html.

Al Arabiya (2012b) 'NATO chief urges ICC team release in Libya', available online at http://english.alarabiya.net/articles/2012/06/14/220592.html.

Al Jazeera (2011) 'Gaddafi's son in civil war warning', available online at www.aljazeera.com/news/africa/2011/02/201122023272596625 1.html.

Al Jazeera (2012) 'Libya rules out ICC trial for Saif al-Islam', available online at www.aljazeera.com/news/africa/2012/04/2012499216767703.html.

Al Shalchi, H. (2012) 'Libya snubs ICC, unveils courtroom ahead of Gaddafi son trial', Reuters, available online at http://af.reuters.com/article/topNews/idAFJOE83908N20120410.

Amnesty International (2011) 'Saif Gaddafi must be transferred safely to ICC', available online at www.amnesty.org/en/news/saif-gaddafi-must-be-transferred-safely-icc-2011-10-28.

Amnesty International (2012) 'Amnesty International Condemns Libyan Law Restricting Freedom of Speech as "Eerie Reminder" of Gaddafi Era', available online at www.amnestyusa.org/news/news-item/amnesty-international-condemns-libyan-law-restricting-freedom-of-speech-as-eerie-reminder-of-gaddafi.

Barber, B. (2011) 'The fate of Saif Gaddafi', *Guardian*, available online at www.guardian.co.uk/commentisfree/2011/dec/04/saif-gaddafi-no-fraud.

Barfi, B. and Pack, J. (2012) 'Libya wants ICC hamstrung via Aussie's capture', *The Australian*, available online at www.theaustralian.com.au/news/world/libya-wants-icc-hamstrung-via-aussies-capture/story-e6frg6ux-1226398005984.

BBC (2011) 'Libya: Gaddafi son Saif al-Islam in contact with ICC', available online at www.bbc.co.uk/news/world-africa-15496608.

BBC (2012a) '"No Libyan response" on Gaddafi son as deadline nears', available online at www.bbc.co.uk/news/world-africa-16479494.

BBC (2012b) 'Unreliable Evidence – Transitional Justice', Radio 4, available online at www.bbc.co.uk/programmes/b01gh8n2.

Bosco, D. (2011) 'Can Libya try the Qaddafis?', *Foreign Policy*, available online at http://bosco.foreignpolicy.com/posts/2011/08/22/can_libya_try_the_gaddafis.

Bosco, D. (2012) 'The Senussi Sweepstakes: Who gets Libya's former intelligence chief?', *Foreign Policy*, 17 March, available online at http://bosco.foreignpolicy.com/posts/2012/03/17/libyan_intelligence_chief_nabbed_in_mauritania.

Callinan, R. (2012) 'Lawyers warned of risks in Libya', *The Sydney Morning Herald*, available online at www.smh.com.au/world/lawyers-warned-of-risks-in-libya-20120614-20d63.html.

Chatham House (2011) 'Milestones for International Criminal Justice', Chatham House, 22 September.

Chatham House (2012a) 'Libya: Establishing the Rule of Law', Chatham House – MENA Programme: Libya Working Group Meeting Summary.

Chatham House (2012b) 'Libya: Re-establishing the State', Chatham House (transcript), available online at www.chathamhouse.org/sites/default/files/public/Meetings/Meeting%20Transcripts/250512elkeibQ&A.pdf.

Chatham House (2012c) 'Libya's Recovery: Prospects and Perils', Chatham House – MENA Programme: Libya Working Group Meeting Summary.

Chulov, M. (2011) 'Libya insists Saif al-Islam Gaddafi should be tried at home', *Guardian*, available online at www.guardian.co.uk/world/2011/oct/29/libya-saif-gaddafi-justice.

CNN (2012) 'Libya appeals ICC order to hand over Saif Gadhafi', available online at http://articles.cnn.com/2012-04-10/africa/world_africa_libya-saif-gadhafi-appeal_1_libyan-people-moammar-gadhafi-libyan-government?_s=PM:AFRICA.

Cronin-Furman, K. and Taub, A. (2012) 'Is the International Criminal Court Facing Its "Black Hawk Down" Moment?', *The Atlantic*, available online at www.theatlantic.com/international/archive/2012/06/is-the-international-criminal-court-facing-its-black-hawk-down-moment/258528/.

Flitton, D. and Lester, T. (2012) 'Amnesty cautions against "apology" to Libya', *National Times*, available online at www.theage.com.au/opinion/political-news/amnesty-cautions-against-apology-to-libya-20120619-20m5v.html.

Goldstone, R. (2012) 'ICC's Libyan crisis shows Saif Gaddafi should be tried in The Hague', *Guardian*, available online at www.guardian.co.uk/law/2012/jun/22/icc-libya-crisis-saif-gaddafi-hague.

Grant, G. (2012) 'Government struck financial deal with Mauritania over Senussi handover', *Libya Herald*, available online at www.libyaherald.com/2012/09/05/govt-struck-financial-deal-with-mauritania-over-senussi-handover/.

Gumuchian, M.-L. (2011) 'EXCLUSIVE – The capture of Gaddafi's son', *Reuters*, available online at http://af.reuters.com/article/energyOilNews/idAFL5E7MK01720111120?sp=true.

Gumuchian, M.-L. (2012) 'UPDATE 2 – ICC team visit detained colleagues in Libya', *Reuters*, available online at http://af.reuters.com/article/libyaNews/idAFL5E8HCI1C20120612?sp=true.

Gumuchian, M.-L. and Shuaib, A. (2012) 'Libya says it wants ICC's cooperation over detained staff', *Reuters*, at www.reuters.com/article/2012/06/16/us-libya-icc-idUSBRE85F0IW20120616.

Harding, L. and Black, I. (2012) 'Mauritania extradites Gaddafi spy chief Senussi to Libya', *Guardian*, available online at www.guardian.co.uk/world/2012/sep/05/mauritania-gaddafi-senussi-libya.

Heller, K.J. (2012a) 'Foreign Minister Bob Carr Goes Shopping in the Department of Bad Ideas', *Opinio Juris*, 20 June, available online at http://opiniojuris.org/2012/06/20/foreign-minister-bob-barr-goes-shopping-in-the-department-of-bad-ideas/.

Heller, K.J. (2012b) 'Libya Challenges the Admissibility of the Cases Against Gaddafi and

Al-Senussi', *Opinio Juris*, 2 May, available online at http://opiniojuris.org/2012/05/02/libya-challenges-the-admissibility-of-the-cases-against-gaddafi-and-al-senussi/.

Heller, K.J. (2012c) 'Libya's Dorda Prosecution – and My Modified Due Process Thesis', *Opinio Juris*, 18 September, available online at http://opiniojuris.org/2012/09/17/libyas-prosecution-of-buzeid-dorda-and-my-modified-due-process-thesis/.

Heller, K.J. (2012d) 'Why I Think the Detained ICC Personnel Are Entitled to Diplomatic Immunity', *Opinio Juris*, 15 June, available online at http://opiniojuris.org/2012/06/15/why-are-the-detained-icc-personnel-entitled-to-diplomatic-immunity/.

Hilsum, L. (2012a) 'Abdullah al-Senussi, Gaddafi's "black box"', *FT Magazine*, available online at www.ft.com/cms/s/2/a55d465e-aab1-11e1-9331-00144feabdc0.html#axzz20nZOCQNj.

Hilsum, L. (2012b) *Sandstorm – Libya in the Time of Revolution* (Faber and Faber).

Hirsch, A. (2012) 'Mauritania likely to extradite Libyan spy chief to France', *Guardian*, available online at www.guardian.co.uk/world/2012/mar/20/mauritania-likely-extradite-libyan-france.

HRC *Report of the International Commission of Inquiry on Libya*, A/HRC/19/68, 2 March 2012.

HRW (2012) 'Libya: Amend New Special Procedures Law', available online at www.hrw.org/news/2012/05/11/libya-amend-new-special-procedures-law.

ICC (2011a) *Warrant of Arrest for Saif Al-Islam Gaddafi*, ICC-01/11-14 (27 June).

ICC (2011b) *Prosecutor's Submissions on the Prosecutor's recent trip to Libya*, ICC-01/11-01/11 (25 November).

ICC (2011c) *OPCD Request for Authorisation to Present Observations in Proceedings concerning Mr Saif Gaddafi*, ICC-01/11-01/11 (28 November).

ICC (2012a) *Public Redacted Version Urgent Report Concerning the Visit to Libya*, ICC-01/11-01/11-69 (2 March).

ICC (2012b) *Application on behalf of the Government of Libya pursuant to Article 19 of the ICC Statute*, ICC-01/11-01/11 (1 May).

ICC (2012c) *Request to Disqualify the Prosecutor from Participating in the Case Against Mr. Saif Al Islam Gaddafi*, ICC-01/11-01/11 (3 May).

ICC (2012d) *Press Conference by Prosecutor of International Criminal Court on Libyan Situation* (16 May), at www.un.org/News/briefings/docs/2012/120516_ICC.doc.htm.

ICC (2012e) *Prosecution response to Application on behalf of the Government of Libya pursuant to Article 19 of the ICC Statute*, ICC-01/11-01/11 (5 June).

ICC (2012f) *Lawyers for Justice in Libya and Redress Trust's Observations Pursuant to Rule 103 of the Rules of Procedure and Evidence*, ICC-01/11-01/11 (8 June).

ICC (2012g) *Four ICC staff members detained in Libya; Immediate release requested*, ICC-CPI-20120609-PR805 (9 June), available online at www.icc-cpi.int/NR/exeres/82F7D00E-500E-46FE-BE04-906B269DCDB2.htm.

ICC (2012h) *Decision on the Request for Disqualification of the Prosecutor*, ICC-01/11-01/11 OA 3 (12 June).

ICC (2012i) *Statement on the detention of four ICC staff members*, ICC-CPI-20120622-PR815 (22 June).

ICC (2012j) *Libyan Government Requests for Status Conference and Extension of Time to file a Reply to the Response to its Article 19 Admissibility Challenge*, ICC-01/11-01/11 (30 July).

ICC (2012k) *Situations and Cases: Libya*, available online at www.icc-cpi.int/menus/icc/situations%20and%20cases/situations/icc0111/situation%20index?lan=en-GB.

ICC (2012l) *Public Redacted Version of the Corrigendum to the 'Defence Response to the "Application on behalf of the Government of Libya pursuant to Article 19 of the ICC Statute"'*, ICC-01/11-01/11 (31 July).

Jillions, A. (2011) 'Trying the Tripoli Three: Justice at Home or Away?', *Justice in Conflict*, available online at http://justiceinconflict.org/2011/08/24/trying-the-tripoli-three-justice-at-home-or-away/.

Kaye, D. (2011) 'What to Do With Qaddafi', *New York Times*, 31 August, available online at www.nytimes.com/2011/09/01/opinion/what-to-do-with-qaddafi.html?_r=2.

Kersten, M. (2011a) 'Having Cake and Eating it Too: An ICC Trial in Libya?', *Justice in Conflict*, available online at http://justiceinconflict.org/2011/08/26/having-cake-and-eating-it-too-an-icc-trial-in-libya/.

Kersten, M. (2012a) 'Libya vs. The ICC: Stalemate over Saif and Senussi', *Think Africa Press*, available online at http://thinkafricapress.com/libya/icc-game-no-winners-rome-statute-saif-gaddafi-senussi-ntc-zintan.

Kersten, M. (2012b) 'No winners in ICC-Libya standoff', *Foreign Policy – Middle East Channel*, available online at http://mideast.foreignpolicy.com/posts/2012/10/08/no_winners_in_icc_libya_standoff.

Kersten, M. (forthcoming) 'Between Justice and Politics: The International Criminal Court's Intervention in Libya', in C. Stahn, C. De Vos and S. Kendall (eds), *International criminal justice and 'local ownership': Assessing the impact of justice interventions* (Cambridge University Press).

Kyriacou, K. (2012) 'Husband of Brisbane lawyer Melinda Taylor says arrest in Libya puts all ICC workers at risk', *Herald Sun*, available online at www.heraldsun.com.au/news/victoria/husband-says-all-icc-workers-at-risk/story-e6frf7lf-1226396128427.

Lawyers for Justice Libya (2012a) 'LFJL Applauds the Supreme Court of Libya's Decision on Law 37', available online at www.libyanjustice.org/news/news/post/28-lfjl-applauds-the-supreme-court-of-libya%E2%80%99s-decision-on-law-37.

Lawyers for Justice Libya (2012b) 'LFJL strongly condemns new laws breaching human rights and undermining the rule of law', available online at www.libyanjustice.org/news/news/post/23-lfjl-strongly-condemns-new-laws-breaching-human-rights-and-undermining-the-rule-of-law.

Lynch, C. (2011) 'Rice says Libyan people can decide whether to try Qaddafi; ICC says not so fast', *Foreign Policy*, available online at http://turtlebay.foreignpolicy.com/posts/2011/08/23/rice_says_libyan_people_can_decide_whether_to_try_qaddafi_icc_says_not_so_fast.

Mark, M. (2012) 'Abdullah al-Senussi central figure in three-way custody battle', *Guardian*, available online at www.guardian.co.uk/world/2012/may/25/abdullah-al-senussi-custody-battle.

McGreal, C. (2012) 'US backs Libya in dispute over trial location for Saif al-Islam Gaddafi', *Guardian*, available online at www.guardian.co.uk/world/2012/jun/06/us-libya-saif-al-islam-gaddafi-trial.

Murphy, F. (2011) 'Libya vows it, not ICC, will try Saif, Senussi', *Reuters*, available online at www.reuters.com/article/2011/11/21/us-libya-icc-idUSTRE7AK08K20111112.

Olsen, T.D., Payne, L.A. and Reiter, A.G. (2010) *Transitional Justice in Balance – Comparing Processes, Weighing Efficacy* (United States Institute of Peace).

Papenfuss, T. (2012) 'Interview with Luis Moreno-Ocampo, Chief Prosecutor of the International Criminal Court, Global Observatory', available online at www.theglobal

observatory.org/interviews/197-interview-with-luis-moreno-ocampo-chief-prosecutor-of-the-international-criminal-court.html.

Pargeter, A. (2012) *Libya – The Rise and Fall of Qaddafi* (Yale University Press).

Parliamentarians for Global Action (2011) 'Parliamentarians for Global Action (PGA) calls for the prompt surrender of Saif Al Islam Gaddafi and Abdallah Al Senussi to the International Criminal Court (ICC)', available online at www.pgaction.org/uploaded-files/PGA%20PR%20ICC%20Libya%20arrest%20nov%202011%20ENG.pdf.

Prieur, L. and Al Shachi, H. (2012) 'Mauritania agrees to Senussi extradition, Libya says', *Reuters*, available online at www.reuters.com/article/2012/03/20/us-libya-senussi-idUSBRE82J0X120120320.

RIA Novosti (2012) 'Lavrov Pushes for UN Feedback on ICC staff detentions in Libya', available online at http://en.ria.ru/world/20120613/174009325.html.

Robertson, G. (2011a) 'Ending Impunity: the struggle for global justice', remarks given at The School of Oriental and African Studies, London, 21 November.

Robertson, G. (2011b) 'Why Libya Must Send Saif Gaddafi to The Hague', *The Daily Beast*, available online at www.thedailybeast.com/articles/2011/11/21/why-libya-must-send-saif-gaddafi-to-the-hague.html.

Security Council (2012a) 'International Criminal Court Chief Tells Security Council Libya Wants Domestic Courts to Handle Proceedings against Son of Former Libyan Leader Gaddafi', SC/10651, 16 May, available online at www.un.org/News/Press/docs/2012/sc10651.doc.htm.

Security Council (2012b) 'Security Council Press Statement on International Criminal Court Staff Detained in Libya', SC/10674 (15 June).

Sherlock, R. (2011) 'Libya: "the executioners" Abdullah al-Senussi captured', *Telegraph*, available online at www.telegraph.co.uk/news/worldnews/africaandindianocean/libya/8902861/Libya-the-executioner-Abdullah-al-Senussi-captured.html.

Shuaib, A. and Al Shalchi, H. (2012) 'ICC lawyer meeting Gaddafi son detained in Libya', *Reuters*, available online at www.reuters.com/article/2012/06/09/us-libya-icc-idUSBRE8580FH20120609.

Simons, Marlise (2012) 'Libya Frees Four From International Court's Team', *The New York Times*, available online at www.nytimes.com/2012/07/03/world/africa/libya-frees-four-from-international-criminal-court.html?_r=0.

Simpson, G. (2007) *Law, War and Crime – War Crimes Trials and the Reinvention of International Law* (Polity Press).

Smith, D. (2011) 'Gaddafi's son claims Nato wants deal with Libya', *Guardian*, available online at www.guardian.co.uk/world/2011/jul/01/gaddafi-son-nato-libya-deal.

Stahn, C. (2012) 'Libya, the International Criminal Court and Complementarity – A Test for "Shared Responsibility"', 10(2) *Journal of International Criminal Justice* 325.

Stephen, C. (2012a) 'Saif Gaddafi sets Libya's new rulers a test of commitment to human rights', *Guardian*, available online at www.guardian.co.uk/world/2012/jan/07/saif-gaddafi-libya-human-rights.

Stephen, C. (2012b) 'The secrets of Saif Gaddafi's jail: chef, satellite TV and a basketball court for just one', *Guardian*, available online at www.guardian.co.uk/world/2012/mar/18/said-gaddafi-libya-international-criminal-court.

Sydow, C. (2012) 'Libyens Ex-Geheimdienstchef Sanussi – Der Mann, der zu viel weiß', 7 September, available online at www.spiegel.de/politik/ausland/abdullah-al-sanussi-koennte-ueber-libyens-kooperation-mit-cia-berichten-a-854366.html.

Telegraph (2012) 'Australian lawyer held in Libya "could be freed with apology"', available online at www.telegraph.co.uk/news/worldnews/africaandindianocean/libya/9340696/Australian-lawyer-held-in-Libya-could-be-freed-with-apology.html.

Waters, T.W. (2011) 'Let Tripoli Try Saif al-Islam – Why the Qaddafi Trial is the Wrong Case for the ICC', *Foreign Affairs*, available online at www.foreignaffairs.com/articles/136726/timothy-william-waters/let-tripoli-try-saif-al-islam.

Chapter 11

Selectivity, legitimacy and the pursuit of post-Arab Spring international criminal justice

Kirsten J. Fisher[1]

The international pursuit of post-Arab Spring justice presents an interesting case study to examine questions of legitimacy in *jus post bellum* and international criminal law (ICL), specifically its principal institution – the International Criminal Court (ICC). Legitimacy refers to both the normative claim that the moral and legal foundation of the system is just and the perceived legitimacy of the system – the popular acceptance of a governing system. Biasness and selectivity reflected in the operations of the ICC affect both the real and perceived legitimacy of ICL. Arguably, the Court is viewed by some as simply another expression of a profoundly undemocratic international order (Morris 2002; Fichtelberg 2006). Its lack of capacity to independently decide to investigate all crimes that might fall within its subject matter jurisdiction globally and when it seemingly indicts suspected perpetrators from only one side of a conflict to the exclusion of indicting suspected perpetrators from the other side, the ICC opens itself to charges of subjectivity and partiality. Yet, for law to have legitimate moral standing it must be an impartial arbiter of behaviour; and for it to have moral and practical authority and influence, it must be perceived to be the objective application of promulgated rules. The current application of international and national law in transitional Middle Eastern and North African countries may risk further entrenchment of conceptions of international criminal law as partial, as victor's justice and as the instrument of the world's powerful actors.

Since questions of post-atrocity accountability began to surface in regards to the Arab Spring, there has been interest in the pursuit of international-led justice in countries that have experienced Arab Spring uprisings, such as Bahrain, Libya, Syria and Yemen for example (Polgreen 2012). There were calls for the involvement of the ICC in both Libya and Syria (Blomfield 2011; Human Rights Watch 2013). The ICC's involvement and lack of involvement in Libya and Syria, respectively, positioned it to face similar criticisms that international tribunals of the past have historically faced regarding their legitimacy. Historically, criticisms are typically based on two sets of questions. The first concerns authority and deals with the legal and moral basis for the judicial institution's existence and to prosecute those it deems in violation of promulgated criminal law. The second set is comprised of questions regarding the objectivity and justness of the legal structure as a legitimate system of law.

Legitimacy, in the context of this chapter, is not based only on the legal system's accordance with particular just foundations and principles but also on the perception of legitimacy by both the international and the local populations. Perceived legitimacy is not 'whether or not a particular criminal justice approach can be justified as legitimate on a theoretical level [but] . . . whether or not various local and international communities are likely, as a practical matter, to "buy in" to the approach and treat the activities of the institutions involved as legitimate' (Dickinson 2003: 301). That a criminal justice system is deemed legitimate by those under its jurisdiction is imperative to its purposes of being expressively significant (Fisher 2012: 121–44).[2] It must be seen to exist as a legitimate authority over those in its jurisdiction and to administer the law objectively, fairly applying the law to all subjects within its jurisdiction. ICL has, over its short existence, faced numerous challenges to its legitimate existence and its ability to pursue 'justice' in a just and objective manner, and challenges that were once touted as a result of growing pains could shortly hamper the enterprise of ICL in being regarded as anything more than a political tool.

Despite ICL having received growing recognition as a system of law that exists under legitimate authority, it is the subject of many debates: questioning its compatibility with pursuits of peace in situations of ongoing conflict and its ability to complement national pursuits of justice (Baines 2005; Hovil and Lomo 2005; Allen 2006: 86); and the limits of objectivity due to political considerations. The Arab Spring, and the perception that ICL responses to crimes committed before or during the popular uprisings might be politically biased, threatens to inflame this last debate to a point that could jeopardize the reputation of the ICC and the enterprise of ICL. The ICC has already faced criticism for selectivity and, in its steady development as the decisive international criminal response, with all of the influence that that entails, caution must be heeded that the Court and its operations avoid real or perceived partiality in regards to the situations it examines, the investigations it conducts and the indictments it issues.

Morally, a just legal system must be impartial; practically, the ICC might have difficulty recovering from global divisions if widespread distrust were to take root, especially if they were geographically concentrated in the Middle East or Africa. As decisions are made about how Arab Spring-related human rights violations (committed by the pre-transition authoritarian regime and the transitional rebel protesters) ought to be addressed, there is potential for post-Arab Spring criminal trials to advance the conception of ICL as a legitimate, objective and effective system of post-conflict justice or, conversely, to bolster a conception that it lacks objectivity, thereby undermining the legitimacy of ICL as a rightful international arbiter of just behaviour.

This chapter distinguishes three levels of selectivity perceivably at work in regards to the ICC and its involvement or lack of involvement in post-Arab Spring transitional justice: selectivity at the international level (international actors, including the UN Security Council); selectivity at the institutional level (the ICC); and selectivity at the national level (by the post-conflict government). There is also a distinction to be drawn between reasonable selectivity built into the structure of the ICC that limits indictments to the most grievous crimes and negative selectivity that results from politically biased decision-making regarding the cases and the sides of conflicts that the ICC will investigate and prosecute.

This chapter first outlines historical criticism partiality levelled against ICL. Then, using some historical cases to demonstrate problems of partiality, it explores the application of ICL to the Arab Spring transitions, many of which are very much in early stages. The Libyan situation is most demonstrative as the one case in which the ICC is involved at the time of writing; the situation demonstrates that both the limitations of the ICC that make it dependent on the potentially politically biased and self-interested referral of UN Security Council (UNSC) members and the ICC's own choices in regards to indictments help to further entrench perceptions of partiality and biasness. This chapter argues that neglect of objectivity and the appearance of objectivity in the enterprise of ICL is a dangerous oversight that can seriously affect the perception of legitimacy and, therefore, the effectiveness of ICL as an arbiter of actions on the international stage. With a better understanding of the challenges to and the failures of the ICC to project legal objectivity, better assessment can be made regarding the ICC's structure and its referral processes to work towards just impartiality before irreparable damage is done to the reputation of the ICC. Arab Spring transitional justice is a significant episode in the history of ICL and one that could potentially influence its future trajectory.

Legitimacy and international criminal law

This section briefly covers the history of the criticism of partiality with which ICL has had to contend. Certain growing pains can be expected of any new enterprise or institution, but ICL has come under significant and persistent attack for privileging one side of a conflict over another. International tribunals and internationalized domestic courts that apply international law have been criticized for equating *jus ad bellum* (the right reasons to engage in war), or even simply victory, with *jus in bello* (appropriate wartime conduct). Despite the fact that in particularly horrific conflicts it is often the case that both sides commit war crimes and crimes against humanity, perpetrators who fought for the losing or 'bad guys' side are historically more likely to be the only ones to be prosecuted.[3] This historic politicization of ICL diminishes its genuine and perceived legitimacy as an objective purveyor of legal justice.

The post-Second World War tribunals, which were set up to prosecute the worst perpetrators of atrocities committed during the war, were the objects of hope for ushering in a new era of preventing impunity, while at the same time being subject to great criticism. Problems of authority as well as selectivity hampered the legitimacy of these original tribunals. Before the tribunals had opened their first indictments, the moral standing of the courts as legitimate legal instruments was impaired. Preceding the establishment of the United Nations, these tribunals were established by the Allied victors and were designed to be presided over by citizens of Allied countries. Both the Nuremberg and Tokyo tribunals were criticized because the judges were appointed by the victor nations and, therefore, it was argued, could not be impartial. Furthermore, the fact that the trials were restricted to punishing only European Axis war criminals set the Nuremberg trials up for criticism. The London Charter actually restricted the trial to 'punishment of the major war criminals of the European Axis countries' (London Charter, Article 1), naturally fuelling concerns of legitimacy that arise when trials are established specifically with particular agendas. From the onset, the political biases of victorious parties negatively affected by the conflict and powerful actors in the international community influenced the decision-making of the courts to exclude possible 'bad' acts committed by actors other than those these parties wished to punish.

For example, the Tokyo panel of judges consisted of 11 judges, all from the victorious Allied states: Australia, Britain, Canada, China, France, India, the Netherlands, New Zealand, the Philippines, the Soviet Union and the United States. Justice Radhabinod Pal, the dissenting Indian judge, was the only one of his colleagues to question the legitimacy of the Tokyo Tribunal itself. He doubted the right of the victors to pass judgment on the vanquished, especially when the victors were likely guilty of crimes themselves. He wrote:

> It does not correspond to any idea of justice. Such a trial may justly create the feeling that the setting up of a tribunal like the present is much more a political than a legal affair, an essentially political objective having thus been cloaked by a juridical appearance. Formalized vengeance can bring only an ephemeral satisfaction, with every probability of ultimate regret; but vindication of law through genuine legal process alone may contribute substantially to the re-establishment of order and decency in international relations. (Pal nd)

Naturally, Pal's words speak not only to the post-Second World War era tribunals, but to all subsequent pursuits of post-atrocity justice, and traces of the same biasness for the victorious and powerful can be found in modern incarnations of international courts.

Almost half a century later, the International Criminal Tribunals for the former Yugoslavia and Rwanda (ICTY and ICTR, respectively) were established not by victorious parties to the specific conflicts they were to preside over, but by the UNSC. Both tribunals, then, as bodies of the UN, possess international authority. However, since the UNSC has the limited mandate to maintain or restore international peace and security and its composition includes five permanent members, each of which bears considerable global power and particular interests, its decisions can conceivably be seen to reflect the strategic interests and political motivations of the global elite. This is an issue that takes on a different nature in regards to the Arab Spring transitional justice, when 20 years later the issue is not whether the UNSC has the authority to become involved in post-atrocity accountability but whether its involvement should better reflect neutrality and objectivity.

When the ICTY and ICTR were established in the early 1990s, the UNSC was criticized for overstepping its Chapter VII authority in order to create them. It was seen at the time that the Council 'came to demonstrate an extraordinarily broad interpretation of its responsibility to maintain international peace and security' by establishing these courts (Chesterman 2001: 121). The tribunals faced charges of politicization which insinuated that they lacked grounding in genuine international authority.

Also, in creating the tribunals the UNSC was criticized for selectivity in regards to siding with particular parties to the conflict and applying ICL to coincide with its conception of right. The operations of the tribunals seemed to reflect similar partiality. The mandate of the ICTY does not explicitly direct the Tribunal to prosecute or exclude any particular actors – Article 1 of the Statute of the International Tribunal for the former Yugoslavia, adopted May 1993, expresses that the 'International Tribunal shall have the power to prosecute persons responsible for serious violations of international humanitarian law committed in the territory of the former Yugoslavia since 1991 in accordance with the provisions of the present Statute'; arguably, the temporal limitations of the Tribunal's jurisdiction helped to limit the scope of criminal investigations.

Fueling claims of politicization and selective prosecution, the Chief Prosecutor decided only to prosecute certain participants in the conflict, even though, arguably, other serious violations were committed within the temporal jurisdiction. Some argue that certain North Atlantic Treaty Organization (NATO) leaders should also be investigated for violations of international law (Benvenuti 2001). Although there was an inquiry into the NATO bombing campaign, the final report of the Chief Prosecutor determined that 'if one accepts the figures in this compilation of approximately 495 civilians killed and 820 civilians wounded in documented instances, there is simply no evidence of the necessary crime base for charges of genocide or crimes against humanity' (ICTY 2000: V. Recommendations). Whether or not the analysis was conducted adequately and the right decision was reached, justice is not seen to be done by many because the Tribunal is financially supported primarily by NATO members. Issues concerning NATO have arisen again in relation to the investigations and indictments in the Libyan situation.

Perceptions of illegitimacy and political agendas, therefore, arise from limitations of the courts, which demonstrate, to some, a lack of political support and will necessary to truly adjudicate all major crimes committed as part of the conflict, and because the creation of these tribunals followed a lack of international interest in ending the atrocities as the conflicts ensued but were created and controlled by the same international actors who would not or could not mobilize to protect the victims they then aimed to represent. Another concern for these courts, similar to that currently experienced by the ICC in regards to Libya, is that there was a threat that their proceedings would hold little legitimacy for the population against whom the atrocities were committed since there was no community ownership of the processes.

Besides concerns about the establishment and structure of the tribunals and their constitutions, there are concerns that international trials can be indisputably political as well as judicial, adding to doubts concerning the legitimacy of the trials as legal proceedings. In post-atrocity criminal procedures, there is often a desire to show the wrongness of the regime as a whole as well as the illegality of the particular actions of the accused. At a political trial, evidence that may be irrelevant to individual culpability, as well as inflammatory and prejudicial, may be admitted in an attempt to demonstrate negative qualities of the regime. Even the judgments can fall prey to political testimonials concerning the wrongdoing of the previous regime, as arguably occurred in the first case tried by the ICTY, that of Dusko Tadic (May 2005: 133).

One of the justifications for ICL is that international applications of law can be more objective in situations where it would be difficult for local administers of law to be objective (Roth 2003; O'Donohue and Rigney 2012). Therefore, objectivity and the perception of objectivity should be a high priority for ICL institutions. As the application, or lack of application, of ICL in Arab Spring transitions is being appraised and condemned, the ICC is the primary object of criticism. However, it is unfair to level all of the disapproval at its doorstep. As the next section demonstrates, partiality at different levels pair with structural limitations of the Court to challenge the objective application of ICL to the detriment of the system as a whole.

Selectivity and the Arab Spring

The ICC, a fundamentally different court from the ICTY or ICTR, faces the same criticism of politics in an unjust global system. The Arab Spring highlights problems with the enterprise of ICL that aims to protect and prosecute individuals but relies on states as principal actors. The ICC, unlike the tribunals, is a court independent of the UN, although its special relationship with the UNSC is becoming increasingly utilized to initiate investigations that could not otherwise be opened. The ICC is treaty-based, and it acts according to a principle of complementarity. The concept of complementarity, unique to the ICC because of a political compromise based on the Court's treaty foundation, applies to any situation under consideration by the Court, including those referred by the UNSC, and is the topic of great debate both in theory and, as Mark Kersten's chapter suggests, regarding practical application.

The ICC can establish jurisdiction in one of three ways: a member state can refer a situation; the Security Council acting under Chapter VII of the Charter of the United Nations can refer a situation; or the ICC Prosecutor can initiate an investigation in accordance with Article 15 of the Rome Statute. The first and third options can set in motion only investigations concerning member states. If the Security Council refers a situation to the ICC for investigation, however, the membership status of the state is extraneous. Such a case, then, is theoretically open to the same authority of or criticisms aimed at the international tribunals.

Also, the UNSC is then in the position of affecting the work and reputation of the Court by generating a condition in which its caseload is shaped by the concerns and self-interests of permanent members of the UNSC. These factors, alongside its own acts of partiality or acts that may only seem to be partial, hamper the Court's standing.

Selectivity at the international level

Because of the ICC's unique referral system, the cases that make it before the Court reflect not necessarily the worst or most deserving of all situations globally in which international crimes have occurred; rather, the Court's caseload reflects the membership of the Court and the judgment of the international community expressed through UNSC votes. This unique constitution brings some remarkable conflicting challenges, such as aims to grow a robust international court that respects local ownership of judicial processes and requiring the UNSC to refer some cases not otherwise under the jurisdiction of the Court while recognizing that UNSC votes can themselves reflect biasness.

Because none of the Arab Spring countries (except Tunisia) is a member state of the ICC, the only way in which investigation into these cases by the ICC can be initiated is by means of UNSC referral.[4] With the exception of Libya, which received the UNSC's unanimous vote to be referred to the ICC for investigation of its government led by Muammar Gaddafi, no other Arab Spring country has received attention from the Court (UNSC Resolution 1970). On 14 January 2013, a letter sent by Switzerland to the UNSC on behalf of 57 states – including the United Kingdom, Germany, Botswana, Tunisia, Japan and Costa Rica – called for a referral of the situation in Syria to the ICC to fill the accountability gap (Human Rights Watch 2013). Until that time, there had been global criticism regarding the imbalanced application of ICL by the UNSC but no indication that action to rectify the imbalance would be taken. At the time of writing, the UNSC has not addressed the letter. The lack of UNSC attention to Syria and other Arab spring countries aside from Libya is arguably partly because of the ties between these countries and permanent members of the UNSC that possess veto power and can protect their allies from investigation by blocking any attempts to refer a case to the ICC. Bahrain and Yemen have close ties with the United States, and Syria has ties with both China and Russia. To some critics, this state of affairs reeks of politics in the absence of objective justice (Chulov 2011; Jose 2012; Proudman 2013).

Since its entry into force in 2002, the ICC has made great strides forward in its pursuit of accountability for international crimes. One of the unique features of the Court, however, is creating for itself some distinctive challenges. In relation to Uganda and Libya, despite different referral sources, the principle of complementarity has led to certain amounts of animosity and/or resentment of the ICC by the state whose criminals it was invited to investigate. This challenge is dealt with in more detail below and in Chapter 10.

A significant feature of the first years of ICC operations, and one that also affects its perceived legitimacy, is that all of the cases before the Court involved issues in one geographical location: the African Continent. On its fifth anniversary, Judge Philippe Kirsch, President of the ICC, issued a statement about the prospects and promise of the Court and its initial successes (Kirsch 2007). In his statement Kirsch alludes to the trend of African cases without expressly referring to it, and while he was right to be optimistic about the Court's initial steps, one should question the repercussions to ICL and the Court of a caseload that was (and still is to an extent) exclusively focused on cases from particular geographic areas. This is especially appropriate when the Court is situated so far – physically, economically, perhaps culturally – from the contexts in which the crimes took place and in which the victims still reside. Gerry Simpson writes, 'the choice of potential defendants raises suspicions that the Court has been vested with the task of applying international justice to international society's outsiders' (Simpson 2007: 17). As the ICC becomes involved in the Middle East, similar criticisms are warranted as Middle Eastern countries, like those in Africa, can clearly be regarded as international society's outsiders.

The ICC's legitimacy, which was positively supported by African cases, is also negatively affected as scepticism grows: the African Union (AU) led a call for deferral of ICC proceedings in the al-Bashir case (Oette 2010); negative local attitudes towards the Court in Kenya may have been instrumental in the popular vote that brought to power ICC indictees Uhuru Kenyatta and his deputy William Ruto in the 2013 presidential elections (Wamai 2013); and African states even considered a mass withdrawal from the ICC (Menya 2013). Similar negative sentiments orbit the debate regarding where and how Gaddafi's son and his associates should be prosecuted. Where there is concern about community ownership and Western imperialism returning in a different form, similar concerns are surfacing in relation to the first attempts at international involvement in post-atrocity Middle East judicial processes.

The Western imperialism critique, which originated from Western involvement and lack of local ownership of processes that are internationally driven, was arguably weakened by America's strong initial opposition to the Court. The hostile opposition of the United States for reasons of domestic politics and concerns, especially when the opposition took the form of the bilateral Article 98 agreements, aimed to undermine the ICC and, to some extent, the United States accomplished its goal by weakening the ICC's legitimacy as a truly international court. However, as a permanent member of the UNSC, the United States is in a position to guide and determine ICC involvement in situations at the same time as the UNSC has begun to make referrals to the Court for investigation. This contradictory stance is arguably more detrimental to the legitimacy of ICL than its previous antagonistic position. The Obama administration has ostensibly sought a more cooperative relationship with the Court, different than that pursued by the more antagonistic Bush administration which preceded it, but the United States has yet to fully support the ICC as a state party under its jurisdiction (Koh 2010: Sections II and III(1)).

As the UNSC now refers situations and the United States is more supportive of the Court, the Western imperialism critique is arguably stronger because some countries can work to influence the cases investigated and prosecuted by the Court, but at the same time shield themselves from the Court's jurisdiction. What might be the solution to this problem is unclear. A condition of the Court's constitution as a treaty-based institution is that it only has jurisdiction over member countries unless there is a Security Council referral.[5] To those most interested in denying impunity for grave human rights violations, UNSC referrals seem to be a good thing. Perhaps the only answer is international pressure on the UNSC to exercise more neutrality in its referral practices (as was occurring at the time of writing in regards to Syria) and/or a policy where UNSC states abstain from votes in situations of law where it is likely that international crimes occurred and self-interest would negatively affect objectivity.

In relation to Libya, specifically, there are multiple examples of bias. On 25 February 2011, preceding the UNSC referral of the Libyan situation to the ICC, a Special Session of the Human Rights Council (HRC) created an independent international commission of inquiry to investigate violence against civilians in Libya (UN Human Rights Council 2011). Arguably, despite the fact that the mandate of the Commission was to 'investigate all alleged violations of international human rights law in the Libyan Arab Jamahiriya, to establish the facts and circumstances of such violations and of the crimes perpetrated and, where possible, to identify those responsible' (A/HRC-S/15/1, paragraph 11), there was a prejudice against one side of the conflict, namely Gaddafi's forces, in that the resolution establishing the commission speaks of 'the gross and systematic violations of human rights by the Libyan authorities' (A/HRC-S/15/1, paragraph 14). Kevin Jon Heller argues that 'There is little question that the HRC created the Libya Commission not to "impartially determine" whether the Gaddafi government was responsible for human-rights abuses involving civilians, but to confirm its belief that such abuses had already occurred' (Heller 2012: 9). He goes on to argue that the language used by the HRC in describing the atrocities allegedly committed by Gaddafi's forces 'might have been justified by the facts then available, but it also left little doubt that the Commission's mandate – at least in the eyes of the HRC – was to document Gaddafi government abuses, not to determine objectively whether reports of those abuses were true' (Heller 2012: 9). In addition, the HRC resolution made no mention of possible abuses committed by parties other than Gaddafi forces in their attempt to overthrow the government despite the fact that by the time the resolution was adopted most of eastern Libya was under *thuwar*[6] control and reports suggested that *thuwar* were engaged in illegal tactics. 'The absence of reference to the *thuwar* in Res. S-15/1 thus reinforces the idea that the HRC intended for the Libya Commission to focus its investigation on the Gaddafi government to the exclusion of other parties to the conflict' (Heller 2012: 9). Heller explains, however, that although there was no justification for the HRC's failure to mention possible human rights abuse by the *thuwar*, the Libya Commission generally corrected the biases inherent in the resolution when it interpreted its mandate (Heller 2012: 10). The international community, in this case represented by the HRC, revealed a bias that, although corrected in the exercise of the task, would continue to colour the analysis and conclusions of the Commission.

Despite the Commission redefining its mandate to focus on alleged violations committed by all parties, including 'abuses by those who rose up against the Gaddafi government' (UN Human Rights Council 2012: paragraph 11), its report nevertheless established 'a problematic tendency to rationalize *thuwar* human-rights abuses as regrettable but understandable reactions to the repressiveness of the Gaddafi government' (Heller 2012: 10). In doing so, it seemed to reinforce a bias that condones atrocities committed in furtherance of the 'right side' of the conflict or as an emotional reaction to previous crimes at the same time as it condemns both sides of the conflict as perpetrators of grave abuses.

The influence of the UNSC and other powerful global actors is also evident in the manner in which non-Libyan actors in the Libyan situation are treated. The International Commission of Inquiry on Libya investigated allegations of the commission of international crimes in Libya, including investigating allegations that NATO was responsible for violations of international humanitarian law (IHL). However, any crimes judged to have been committed by NATO personnel would almost certainly not be addressed by the ICC. The UNSC resolution referring the Libyan situation to the ICC specifically excludes from the Court's jurisdiction the nationals of any state other than Libya that is not party to the Rome Statute of the ICC (S/RES/1970 (2011) paragraph 6).

Selectivity at the institutional level

The ICC can be selective in who it chooses to prosecute from the situations it investigates. Selectivity in this case can be reasonable or negative, depending on whether the selection is a product of structural limitations created to prevent over-reach and delineate the boundaries of the Court's jurisdiction or a product of politicization. In terms of selectiveness of prosecutions, the number of situations investigated and cases prosecuted are necessarily restricted due to limited resources. The Office of the Prosecutor has a certain amount of latitude in determining which cases he or she will pursue, but is subject to various checks and balances. However, when the Prosecutor investigates and/or prosecutes only one side of a conflict, concerns of selectiveness and partiality arise. This was highlighted by the Ugandan situation when the decision was made that only Lord's Resistance Army (LRA) activity would be investigated and warrants issued for top LRA leaders, but not members of the government army, the Uganda People's Defence Force (UPDF), which reportedly committed its own share of atrocities. Such issues also arose when the Court issued arrest warrants for Muammar Gaddafi (since killed), his son Saif al-Islam Gaddafi and Abdullah al-Senussi, Gaddafi's former military intelligence chief, for crimes against humanity against Libyan civilians, when there were credible claims that anti-regime rebels, including those who killed Gaddafi, were also guilty of international crimes, specifically war crimes and possibly genocide.

In Uganda, Chief Prosecutor Moreno-Ocampo made explicit the objective intentions of the Court to Ugandan President Yoweri Museveni when the Court was invited to investigate the rebel LRA. Despite his insistence that the Court investigates all sides equally, the decision of the Court was that any crimes committed by the Ugandan army did not warrant ICC indictments (Moreno-Ocampo 2005). This decision was criticized both in Uganda and internationally (Branch 2007). In the Libyan situation, despite the concern raised by Moreno-Ocampo that 'the way in which Mr. Gaddafi was killed creates suspicions of … war crimes', no serious investigation of any side but the deposed Libyan government was initiated (BBC 2011b). This phenomenon can further entrench the perception that international criminal law is not law but a political instrument wielded by the more powerful global actors.

The Court must be objective and be seen to be objective. Selectiveness in prosecution refers to the choice by the court's agents to prosecute some perpetrators and not others. Real or perceived selectivity can hamper the legitimacy and/or perceived legitimacy of a legal institution or system. Good reason grounded the investigation of Colonel Gaddafi and those considered most responsible for crimes against the population of Libya by its government. There may also be good reason to investigate other parties in the Arab revolutions, including the Libyan rebel fighters who captured Muammar Gaddafi alive and in whose custody he was killed, along with Gaddafi's son, Mutassim. By not investigating all sides to a conflict, the Court leaves itself open to the criticism that international law (at least its application through the ICC) is politically biased and lacking objectivity. Failure to investigate objectively and to prosecute crimes committed by all sides could be seen as a blatant biased approach to justice, thereby jeopardizing the real administration of the international rule of law and the perception of international objectivity.

Simply investigating all sides and prosecuting when appropriate is not, however, the end of the story. Legitimacy and perceived legitimacy is also affected by real and recognized even-handed treatment of all perpetrators, regardless of which side they fought on. Atrocity crimes cannot be excused merely because they were committed by fighters on the side of the conflict deemed more just. An interesting example of partiality reflected not in the indictments but in the judgments is that rendered by the Special Court for Sierra Leone (SCSL).

The SCSL, in an attempt to deal with all sides of the conflict, indicted Charles Taylor and members of the rebel militia groups the Revolutionary United Front (RUF), the Armed Forces Revolutionary Council (AFRC) and the Civil Defense Force (CDF), the last of which was seen as a band of heroes attempting to reinstate democratically elected leaders. Of the three judges, the only Sierra Leonean judge wanted to acquit the CDF defendants on the basis that they were fighting a just war. The ultimate judgment concluded that the CDF defendants were guilty of murder, cruel treatment, pillage and collective punishments and one defendant was also found guilty of 'enlisting children under the age of 15 years into armed forces or groups or using them to participate actively in hostilities' (*Prosecutor v M F and A K* 2007). Nevertheless, although the CDF defendants were convicted of the aforementioned crimes, both defendants received what were considered very light sentences for their crimes. To justify their leniency, the judges cited mitigating factors: remorse, lack of prior convictions, lack of formal education or training, subsequent conduct and, finally, in concert with the dissenting opinion of the Sierra Leonean judge, 'the establishment of the much desired and awaited peace in Sierra Leone', that is, that they were fighting a just war (*Prosecutor v M F and A K 2007*, para 3.5.91). Therefore, this reflected a political bias despite the prosecution of all parties to the conflict suspected of committing illegal actions. In this case, political selectivity seeped into the court's procedures despite the efforts made by the establishing international bodies to assure its objectivity.

As mentioned above and in Chapter 10, the situation in Libya was referred to the ICC for investigation. The ICC subsequently issued arrest warrants for Muammar Gaddafi, Saif al-Islam Gaddafi and Abdullah al-Senussi for crimes against humanity (murder and persecution) allegedly committed in Libya in February 2011 through their control of the state apparatus and security forces (ICC 2011a). Even before Muammar Gaddafi's death there were some allegations of abuses by anti-government rebels (BBC 2011a). The case against Muammar Gaddafi was formally terminated following his death in October 2011 (ICC 2011b). Shortly afterwards, claims surfaced that anti-government rebels were responsible for wrongdoing in his death as well as for other crimes against civilians in the period of conflict that led to the overthrow of Gaddafi and his regime.

The report of the International Commission of Inquiry on Libya concluded that there was evidence of international crimes committed by both pro-government and anti-government forces in Libya (Section III). Specifically, the report concluded that crimes against humanity and war crimes had been committed by Gaddafi forces and that the *thuwar* (anti-Gaddafi forces) committed serious violations, including war crimes and breaches of international human rights law, the latter continuing at the time the report was presented (UNHRC 2012: paras 808-10). Notwithstanding the conclusions of this report, actors on only one side of the conflict were indicted by the ICC.

Then-Chief Prosecutor of the ICC, Moreno-Ocampo, claimed that if Gaddafi was killed in custody, there was the possibility that it was a war crime. He also claimed that Libya's interim rulers, the National Transitional Council (NTC), were asked about their plans to investigate alleged war crimes by all parties, including the rebels (Al Jazeera 2011). Under international pressure, the NTC promised to investigate how Gaddafi and his son Mutassim were killed. Seemingly, then, there were initial attempts to present the picture of even-handed objective investigation of war crimes committed by all parties to the violence. Moreno-Ocampo asserted that the ICC would step in under complementarity measures if the Libyan authorities were unable or unwilling to take action.

However, since then, little movement has been made beyond reiterations by the current ICC Chief Prosecutor, Fatou Bensouda, that even-handed justice must be a priority. Bensouda addressed the UNSC and called on Libya's authorities to ensure that justice is served in relation to any crimes committed during the overthrow of the regime of former leader Muammar Gaddafi (UN News Centre 2012). The lack of action may stem from a number of factors: the international community's bias against Gaddafi's regime and its desire to condemn pro-government forces; the ICC Prosecutor's own biases; the ICC's fear of becoming further engaged in the Libyan situation given the current condition of the Court's involvement in the country; or a genuine lack of belief that there is reason to support additional indictments in the Libyan situation. Nevertheless, perceived partiality may be a threat to the Court's legitimacy.

Selectivity at the national level

One of the purposes of ICL is that it can step in with objectivity when a domestic system cannot. Domestic courts, while regarded by international law and the traditional Westphalian doctrine as the option of first discharge, are probably the most poorly equipped to respond to widespread atrocity within their own territory because of biases for or against one of the sides to the conflict. A domestic legal system established in a new regime and wishing to distinguish itself from the old regime may be biased in convicting offenders of the old regime and imposing severe sentences. Such bias is evident in the domestic judicial system in Libya. Despite the tendency of the report of the International Commission of Inquiry on Libya to rationalize *thuwar* human rights abuses, it criticizes their lack of accountability.

In asserting that there is no evidence of '*thuwar* arrested or detained for such attacks or for other criminal acts' (p 776) and that '*Thuwar* are also evading accountability through the use of force' (p 777), the Commission concludes that the failure to hold *thuwar* accountable for infractions is symptomatic of a lack of equal implementation of the law' (p 778). In its summary, the report claims that 'The Commission is nevertheless concerned by the failure to hold accountable *thuwar* committing serious violations' and recommends that 'Libyan authorities can break with the Gaddafi legacy by enforcing the law equally, investigating all abused – irrespective of the perpetrator – and ensuring that amnesty processes comport with Libya's obligations under international law'.

Despite the fact that the report accuses *thuwar* of atrocity crimes and criticizes the domestic legal system for *thuwar*'s impunity, Heller argues that 'there is reason to suspect that the Commission intentionally downplayed the *thuwar*'s responsibility for crimes against humanity in its final report' (Heller 2012: 20). In addition, despite allegations of misconduct, the report was unable to reach a conclusion regarding the lawfulness of the deaths of Muammar and Mutassim Gaddafi and recommends further investigation of those deaths (p 811).

Domestic selectivity is only a consideration for the ICC in so far as it affects the conclusions drawn on complementarity and whether a state is able and willing to prosecute its most serious offenders. Lack of prosecutions is one thing, but when a country puts into place laws to legalize amnesty for certain actors it is a powerful statement of partiality. By mid-2012, the NTC in Libya had passed a number of laws, including Law 38 'On Some Procedures for the Transitional Period', which grants a blanket amnesty for any 'military, security or civil actions dictated by the February 17 Revolution that were performed by revolutionaries with the goal of promoting or protecting the revolution' (Human Rights Watch 2012a). Some particularly grave crimes, such as torture and rape, are excluded from the amnesty, but others, such as murder and forced displacement, are not explicitly excluded (Human Rights Watch 2012b).

Law 38, which protects from prosecution persons who committed crimes in the aim of promoting the revolution against Muammar Gaddafi, is problematic in that it promises amnesty for very serious crimes and contradicts the principle of legal objectivity. Joe Stark, deputy Middle East and North Africa director at Human Rights Watch, laments that this law, which 'allows people who committed serious crimes to walk free based on politics . . . propagates a culture of selective justice that Libyans fought so hard to overcome' (Human Rights Watch 2012a). The political biasness of Law 38 would seem to violate Libya's Constituent Covenant for the Transitional Period, which states that all Libyans are equal before the law and enjoy equal civil and political rights without any distinctions based on political beliefs (Human Rights Watch 2012a). A blanket amnesty that is politically biased also violates Libya's obligations under international law to investigate and prosecute serious violations of international human rights and humanitarian law and codifies a form of 'victor's justice' (Human Rights Watch 2012b).

This situation creates a predicament for the ICC's potential decision to allow Libya to try Saif al-Islam Gaddafi and Abdullah al-Senussi. If the Court agrees that they should be tried domestically, it could and probably would be criticized for tolerating and condoning an obviously political and selective judicial system. The ICC cannot be seen to excuse selectivity in the domestic systems of countries it has been asked to investigate.

Conclusion

War is political; as such, criminal cases that prosecute international crimes have a particular tendency to be political. Although the law does not recognise the attendant circumstances in terms of just and unjust conflicts, those applying the law do, and therefore there is a risk that ICL might inevitably be biased and political in its approach. Kersten argues that the ICC has striven to show that it is an entity that matters and that can have positive effects on post-conflict transitional justice (Kersten 188). For the ICC to be a legitimate arbiter of criminal law and to be perceived as such, special caution must be taken to ensure its objectivity and avoidance of politically based partiality. International and domestic politics can easily seep into the operations of the ICC, tainting what should be the bright light for ending impunity for grave violations of human rights with politicization and weakening the ICC's claims of objective legitimacy.

Current events in the Middle East and North Africa may have the effect of negatively shaping immediate actions and therefore further entrenching criticisms of ICL as inevitably partial, as victor's justice and as an instrument of the world's most powerful. Alternatively, the UNSC and ICC can right themselves to project a more impartial application of international law. Arguably, the Court's current complementarity challenges in Libya may be acting as an obstacle against progress in other cases regarding Libya, and also Syria. To push ahead with further indictments in Libya and the region may seem bullheaded in the light of Libyan opposition, but not doing so may send a message of un-even-handedness.

The avoidance of certain situations and cases also speaks volumes about their relative importance.[7] The challenge is to ensure that attention is warranted based on considerations of law and not political interests (unless they are 'in the interest of justice') (Rome Statute: Article 53). The satisfactory investigation of alleged crimes on both sides of any conflict and the even-handed prosecutions of those most responsible would help to promote the perception of objective ICL to operate impartially and without prejudice. This may also help to instil faith in the legal system and even better promote the deterrent abilities of ICL.

The ICC has received criticism for its lack of involvement in Arab Spring contexts other than Libya. Proper attribution of blame and recognition of the limitations of the ICC would better enable calls for reform that would actually strengthen the enterprise of ICL. Most Arab Spring countries are beyond the jurisdiction of the Court, but the UNSC has the power to refer any case. The motivations of the UNSC are not entirely clear, but there is little reason to conclude that decisions are inspired by only an attempt to apply a careful reading of international law. The UNSC, perhaps hindered by strategic interests of permanent members or immobilized by the turmoil that grew from the ICC's involvement in Libya, has chosen not to refer subsequent conflicts.

It is important to draw distinctions between selectivity originated by the international community, selectivity prompted by the state and selectivity brought about by the legal institution itself. Serious problems arise when such distinctions are not drawn, including heaping all of the blame of selectivity and bias on the institution to the detriment of a critical examination and possible constructive solution of the problems of legitimacy based on selectivity. Strengthening objectivity on all levels (international, state, institution) in regards to prosecuting atrocity crimes could help to fortify ICL as an arbiter of right behaviour.

Selectivity is problematic both morally and practically. Morally, the victims of wrongdoing deserve justice regardless of which side of the conflict the perpetrators of their crimes were fighting. In practice, obvious selectivity jeopardizes the enterprise of ICL by attracting criticisms of unjust politicization. The manner in which ICL is applied in the Arab Spring contexts is important not only because of the important implications for the countries concerned, but also because of the larger ramifications of perceptions of the ICC and international criminal law more generally, especially in light of the significant global attention being paid to events in the region.

Notes

1 The author would like to thank Mark Kersten and Laszlo Sarkany for comments on earlier drafts of this chapter.
2 An expressive justification for criminal law posits that the components of the system are social goods as instruments of social communication. The prosecution, conviction and infliction of punishment have symbolic significance and aim to communicate to the perpetrator and the broader community a particular message of condemnation for specific behaviour prohibited by that society and promulgated as law.
3 A great effort was made by the Special Court of Sierra Leone (SCSL) to investigate and prosecute suspected perpetrators on all sides of the conflict. The results of this effort are discussed later in this chapter.
4 Bahrain, Egypt, Syria and Yemen are all signatory states, each having signed the Rome Statute in 2000, but none has ratified the Statute and are therefore not full members or under the jurisdiction of the Court.
5 It is also possible for a country to accept jurisdiction but not be a member state. Côte d'Ivoire is an example of this.
6 *Thuwar* roughly translates to mean 'revolutionaries' or 'rebels'.
7 It may also speak to prosecutorial pragmatism, according to which cases that can be successfully prosecuted are paid the most attention; however, this may also be seen as unwarranted selectivity, thereby hampering perceived legitimacy.

Bibliography

Al Jazeera (2011) 'ICC prosecutor: Concerns over Gaddafi's death', 16 December, available online at www.aljazeera.com/news/africa/2011/12/20111216539115O3123.html.

Baines, Erin K. (2005) *Roco Wat I Acholi/Restoring Relationships in Acholiland: Traditional Approaches to Justice and Reconciliation* (September) (Liu Institute for Global Issues, University of British Columbia).

BBC (2011a) 'Libyan Rebels Abused Civilians: Human Rights Watch', 13 July, available online at www.bbc.co.uk/news/world-africa-14135530.

BBC (2011b) 'ICC says Muammar Gaddafi Killing May be War Crime', 16 December, available online at www.bbc.co.uk/news/world-africa-16212133.

Benvenuti, Paolo (2001) 'The ICTY Prosecutor and the Review of the NATO Bombing Campaign against the Federal Republic of Yugoslavia', 12(3) *European Journal of International Law* 503.

Blomfield, Adrian (2011) 'Syria: President Bashar al-Assad Faces Indictment by the International Criminal Court', *Telegraph*, 24 April.

Branch, Adam (2007) 'Uganda's Civil War and the Politics of ICC Intervention', 21(2) *Ethics and International Affairs* 179.

Chulov, Martin (2011) 'Libyan Government asks why ICC isn't also Seeking to Prosecute Syria', *Guardian*, 16 May, available online at www.guardian.co.uk/world/2011/may/16/libya-icc-arrest-warrants-reaction.

Dickinson, Laura (2003) 'The Promise of Hybrid Courts', 97 *American Journal of International Law* 295.

Fichtelberg, Aaron (2006) 'Democratic Legitimacy and the International Criminal Court: A Liberal Defence', 4(4) *Journal of International Criminal Justice* 765.

Fisher, Kirsten J. (2012) *Moral Accountability and International Criminal Law* (Routledge).

Heller, Kevin Jon (2012) 'The International Commission of Inquiry on Libya: A Critical Analysis', in Jens Meierhenrich (ed), *International Commissions: The Role of Commissions of Inquiry in the Investigation of International Crimes* (2013, forthcoming), at http://ssrn.com/abstract=2123782.

Hovil, Lucy and Lomo, Zachary (2005) 'Whose Justice: Perceptions of Uganda's Amnesty Act 2000: The Potential for Conflict Resolution and Long-Term Reconciliation', Working Paper Series No 15, Kampala: Refugee Law Project.

Human Rights Watch (2013) 'UN Security Council: Heed Call for Justice in Syria', 14 January, available online at www.hrw.org/news/2013/01/14/un-security-council-heed-call-justice-syria.

Human Rights Watch (2012a) 'Libya: Amend New Special Procedures Law', 11 May, available online at www.hrw.org/news/2012/05/11/libya-amend-new-special-procedures-law.

Human Rights Watch (2012b) 'Libya: Letter to the ICC Prosecutor on Libyan Amnesty Laws', 25 May, available online at www.hrw.org/news/2012/05/25/libya-letter-icc-prosecutor-libyan-amnesty-laws.

ICC (2011a) 'Pre-Trial Chamber I issues three warrants of arrest for Muammar Gaddafi, Saif Al-Islam Gaddafi and Abdualla Al-Senussi', Press Release, 27 June, available online at www.icc-cpi.int/en_menus/icc/press%20and%20media/press%20releases/press%20releases%20%282011%29/Pages/pre_trial%20chamber%20i%20issues%20three%20warrants%20of%20arrest%20for%20muammar%20gaddafi_%20saif%20al.aspx.

ICC (2011b) 'Pre-Trial Chamber I Orders the Termination of the Case Against Muammar Gaddafi', Press Release, 22 November, available online at www.icc-cpi.int/en_menus/icc/press%20and%20media/press%20releases/press%20releases%20%282011%29/Pages/pre_trial%20chamber%20i%20orders%20the%20termination%20of%20the%20case%20against%20muammar%20gaddafi.aspx.

Kersten, Mark (2014) 'Justice after the war: The International Criminal Court and post-Gaddafi Libya', *Transitional Justice and the Arab Spring* (Routledge) 188–207

Kirsch, Philippe (2007) 'ICC Marks 5 Years since Entry into Force of Rome Statute', in *International Criminal Court*, 5 July, available online at www.icc-cpi.int/NR/rdonlyres/C307EC9D-B735-47D6-BA5C-508D0A5D8C71/143884/PK_20070627_en.pdf.

Koh, Harold Hongju (2010) 'The Obama Administration and International Law', Speech by the Legal Adviser, US Department of State to the Annual Meeting of the American Society of International Law, 25 March, Washington, DC, available online at www.americanbar.org/content/dam/aba/administrative/litigation/materials/sac_2012/50-3_nat_sec_obama_admin.authcheckdam.pdf.

May, Larry (2005) *Crimes Against Humanity: A Normative Account* (Cambridge University Press).

Menya, Walter (2013) 'Africa: AU Summit Considers Draft Resolution on Withdrawal from ICC', *The Star* (Nairobi), 24 May, available online at http://allafrica.com/stories/201305250124.html.

Moreno-Ocampo, Luis (2005) 'Statement by the Chief Prosecutor on the Uganda Arrest Warrants', 14 October, available online at www.icc-cpi.int/NR/rdonlyres/3255817D-FD00-4072-9F58-FDB869F9B7CF/143834/LMO_20051014_English1.pdf.

Morris, Madeline (2002) 'The Democratic Dilemma of the International Criminal Court', 5 *Buffalo Criminal Law Review* 591.

O'Donohue, Jonathan and Rigney, Sophie (2012) 'The ICC Must Consider Fair Trial Concerns in Determining Libya's Application to Prosecute Saif Al-Islam Gaddafi Nationally', *EJIL: Talk!*, 8 June, available online at www.ejiltalk.org/the-icc-must-consider-fair-trial-concerns-in-determining-libyas-application-to-prosecute-saif-al-islam-gaddafi-nationally/.

Oette, Lutz (2010) 'Peace and Justice, or Neither?', 8 *Journal of International Criminal Justice* 345.

Polgreen, Lydia (2012) 'Arab Uprisings Point Up Flaws in Global Court', *New York* Times, 7 July, available online at www.nytimes.com/2012/07/08/world/middleeast/arab-spring-reveals-international-court-flaws.html?pagewanted=all&_r=0.

Prosecutor v Moinina Fofana and Allieu Kondewa, SCSL, Trial Chamber, Judgement on the Sentence, Case No SCSL-04-14-T96, 9 October 2007.

Proudman, Charlotte Rachel (2012) 'Syria Immune from being held Accountable by ICC for Atrocities', *New* Statesman, 30 October, available online at www.newstatesman.com/politics/2012/10/syria-immune-being-held-accountable-icc-atrocities.

Roth, Kenneth (2003) 'Try Saddam in an International Court', *Human Rights Watch*, 14 December, available online at www.commondreams.org/views03/1215-10.htm.

Simpson, Gerry (2007) *Law, War and Crime* (Polity Press).

UN Human Rights Council (2012) *Report of the International Commission of Inquiry on Libya*, A/HRC/19/68, Advance Unedited Version (2 March).

UN Human Rights Council (2011) *Situation of Human Rights in the Libyan Arab Jamahiriya*, A/HRC-S/15/1 (25 February).

UN News Centre (2012) 'International Criminal Court Prosecutor calls on Libyan Authorities to Ensure no Impunity', 7 November, available online at www.un.org/apps/news/story.asp?NewsID=43435#.UK4uNIY7qR8.

UN Security Council Resolution 1970 (2011) Adopted by the Security Council at its 6491st meeting (26 February).

Wamai, Njoki (2013) 'The International Criminal Court and the Kenyan Election', *Huffington Post*, 3 May, available online at www.huffingtonpost.co.uk/gates-cambridge-scholars/kenya-election_b_3206562.html.

Chapter 12

Transitions in the Middle East and North Africa: new trajectories and challenges for transitional justice?

Hugo van der Merwe

Transitional justice has emerged as a body of study and practice in response to the practical challenges faced in promoting various goals during a political transition. It is, this concluding chapter argues, a contested field to which activists, social movements and political actors seek to lay claim in order to promote particular agendas. We thus have another set of competing scholars and practitioners – domestic and international – from human rights, international law, conflict resolution, peace building, public health, etc seeking to establish particular goals as priorities to be pursued in a context of rapid political flux. On the one hand, this is a disagreement about norms – what goals and values should prevail in a particular context. On the other hand, it is a debate about what is feasible – what can realistically be achieved during this window of opportunity.

In order to assess the contribution of the Middle East and North African uprisings to the trajectory of the transitional justice field, this chapter first sketches out the key developments of the field up until 2011, and attempts to explain how the field has grown out of particular transitional challenges. The continuities and shifts presented by the Middle East and North African contexts are then assessed in order to gain some understanding of how they are impacting on the meaning of transition and transitional justice.

Evolution of the field of transitional justice

The term 'transitional justice' was first coined in response to debates among scholars and human rights advocates in relation to the set of challenges faced by transitions from dictatorship to democracy in the Southern Cone of America.[1] The starkest challenge presented in these contexts was how to promote human rights in a democratising context that was still so fragile – where military authority had been replaced by democratic rulers, but where these autocratic forces still posed a threat to new democracies. The position of conventional human rights advocacy was to pursue criminal accountability; but doing so in this political context was seen as a threat to consolidating democracy. The policy debate therefore focused upon how to balance the promotion of human rights with the need to consolidate a new democracy (Arthur 2009).

The initial focus of transitional justice was thus the theory and practice of balancing prosecutions and democracy. How much prosecution is feasible – or at what stage should it be pursued? What kind of amnesties would offer the least threat to consolidating democracy? What other forms of accountability can assist in promoting human rights? A key policy alternative that emerged in the Latin American context was that of truth commissions.[2] The argument presented was that truth could serve some of the same goals as prosecutions, particularly in terms of establishing certain facts, holding perpetrators accountable in the public eye and establishing new norms. Activists, scholars and policy makers were confronted both by moral dilemmas (how much should justice and democracy be compromised?) and by practical challenges (how far can justice be pushed before there is a backlash?).

After the focus on Latin America, the transitions in Eastern Europe in the early 1990s were also drawn into the ambit of transitional justice, and the scope of mechanisms used took on additional intervention alternatives and permutations. In the context of many of these transitions the key challenge was the need to deal with deeply politicised and authoritarian institutions which dominated many aspects of public life. Transitional justice here took on a range of new permutations. Vetting, for example, emerged as a critical tool in the transitional justice toolbox to pursue accountability of a broader set of perpetrators and promote institutional transformation.

The South African Truth and Reconciliation Commission took the transitional justice debate into a new realm. While drawing on the Latin American and Eastern European experience, South African policy makers set themselves a new agenda – promoting reconciliation while balancing human rights and consolidating democracy. Recognising that the South African context of racial oppression demanded different solutions, the model used in South Africa reformulated the transitional justice challenges as something that could be packaged into a theologically inspired amnesty–truth–forgiveness–reconciliation model, which supposedly trumped the need for justice (or at least justice understood as focusing on prosecutions).

As enthusiasm for transitional justice has grown, we find it being increasingly applied in various countries emerging from violent civil war, where transitional justice has to broaden its scope even more to incorporate a larger peace-building agenda that seeks to transform society, not just reform an autocratic state. The scale of the problems is much greater, including challenges related to dealing with hundreds of thousands of victims, devastated economies, failed states and displaced populations. Transitional justice interventions now also have to take into account a new set of challenges: historical division between ethnic groups, refugee resettlement, demobilisation and reintegration of conventional armies and rebel groups, and building democratic institutions where there is little pre-existing institutional capacity or democratic tradition.

The agenda for what was to be achieved in the transition phase had thus grown to include not just human rights and democracy, but also healing, reconciliation, social reconstruction and nation building. In turn, the toolset that had emerged in a range of contexts to address an array of transitional challenges had gradually taken on the more hegemonic form of a defining framework for transitional justice practice. Instead of being a field that sought to address a set of transitional challenges, transitional justice was increasingly understood as the application of a set of predefined instruments to a context vaguely defined as transitional. Rather than asking what the goals or needs of transition are in a particular context, the question being asked had become: how does one apply prosecutions, truth commissions, vetting reparations and memorialisation mechanisms? This is still true today – thus instead of asking what Egyptians want from their transition and how that can be best secured, scholars are asking 'Does Egypt need a truth commission', or even 'What form of truth commission does Egypt need?' The debate, as a result, becomes constrained by the already-existing set of tools established in other (possibly unrelated) transitional contexts.

Another element of transitional justice that has become increasingly dominant over the last 20 years is the role of international law and, alongside this, the increasing role of the international community in promoting and facilitating particular transitional justice mechanisms. The focus on the legal framework and mechanisms guiding transitional justice is particularly illustrated by the establishment of the International Criminal Court (ICC). A more worrying aspect of this shift is the increasing use and abuse of international norms and multilateral institutions by global actors to promote regime change under the guise of protecting human rights.

Since the turn of this century, the United Nations has increasingly endorsed and promoted transitional justice and adopted many of its mechanisms. The United Nations defines transitional justice as 'the full range of processes and mechanisms associated with a society's attempts to come to terms with a legacy of large-scale past abuses, in order to ensure accountability, serve justice and achieve reconciliation' (UNSC 2004). The United Nations Development Programme (UNDP) has also developed guidelines on a range of transitional justice mechanisms, or what it calls its 'Rule of Law Toolkit' (see UNHCHR 2006).

Transitional justice was also taken up by regional bodies, such as the African Union (AU), which took on an increasing role in supporting national efforts to deal with issues of accountability and peace-building. While wary of the international justice agenda, the AU played a supporting role in transitional justice initiatives in various countries.[3]

Inevitably it became obvious that all the hype about the 'magic' of transitional justice sounded too good to be true. Could all of these goals really be achieved through the right combination and sequencing of transitional intervention tools? Scholars and practitioners have cautioned against the search for quick-fix solutions to complex challenges such as mass trauma (Weinstein 2011; Mendeloff 2009) and reconciliation (Chapman 2009). Much of the assumed knowledge of the transitional justice field (the link between truth and reconciliation, the therapeutic value of testimony, the restorative potential of public hearings, etc) has been challenged as simplistic and not transferable to other political or cultural contexts. Even assumed 'best practice' models have been increasingly questioned, such as the effectiveness of truth commissions and other transitional justice interventions in preventing the recurrence of torture (McGregor 2013).

The enthusiasm of its promoters, however, has often meant that caution is thrown to the wind. Transitional justice has in many respects become a bandwagon (Editorial Note 2013) and is being promoted by a host of international technical experts and a transitional justice industry that stands accused of prioritising its own growth rather than the delivery of benefits for affected societies (Madlingozi 2010). In Chapter 3, Habib Nassar also cautions about the danger of international actors being rapidly deployed to devise transitional justice intervention at the expense of thorough local consultations with key stakeholders. The point here is that while international resources and expertise can be very valuable, the danger of marginalising local knowledge and broad local participation as well as local priorities in the rush to secure immediate policy gains is deeply problematic.

A second, deeper set of questions that has emerged asks: What are the ultimate goals of these transitions and what should be seen as appropriate priorities in a context of political flux? Viewing transitions as contested spaces where the trajectories of change are subject to violent conflict involving a range of stakeholders means that transitional justice needs to be understood in relation to its role in furthering or mediating between particular agendas. While transitional justice potentially presents a space for fair and peaceful engagement with a contested past, it may also open up new contestations over the values that will guide a future social order.

By 2009, the field of transitional justice was clearly showing signs of dissension and fundamental strains about its legitimacy. Is it still a coherent field of study and practice (Bell 2009)? And who defines its goals and boundaries? Critical questions emerged about its links to neo-liberal agendas (Nagy 2008), whether it was in fact responsive to local victim needs (Robins 2012; Madlingozi 2010) and whether it does in fact contribute to longer-term social justice concerns (including gender justice and social inequality[4]).

Established scripts for transition – the dominant one being a liberal peace with its focus on early elections, rule of law and market reforms – are often presented as uncontested or incontestable. Transitional justice had seemingly been co-opted by a liberal agenda that prioritised market regulation, international integration and political stability. It was thus a set of tools that was often seen as more closely associated with the transfer of power between elite groups rather than transforming structures of exclusion, inequality and oppression (Gready et al. 2010).

By reflecting on the historical roots of transitional justice, some scholars pointed out its emergence in the 1980s as linked to a global context of the retreat of the Left (Arthur 2009), the Washington consensus around neo-liberal economic models and a narrow global engagement with civil-political rights rather than socio-economic concerns. As Klaus Bachmann, Robert Stewart and Kirsten Fisher point out in their contribution to this volume, the transitions in Central and Eastern European countries occurred in a particular global environment that provided an implicit framework for understanding transition goals. While the starting point for the transition trajectory is different in various contexts, there is still a very clear assumed common end-point for transitions wherever they occur.

Alongside the growth (and conflict around) the economic model consensus that underlies much of the transition debates, we have also seen the emergence of international criminal law as the dominant framework for viewing how human rights abuses should be handled. This model for framing rights and wrongs and establishing responsibility for prevention and punishment introduced complex challenges regarding how powerful countries can and should interfere in local conflicts. It also raises deeper questions about how conflict and the re-establishment of peace and justice are to be achieved. Using the law (both international and national) as a defining framework for norms and values is a potentially powerful force for correcting historical imbalances and addressing recent injustices. It is also, however, a very blunt tool that often undermines more restorative processes, overwrites traditional understandings of community cohesion and shifts power in sometimes unexpected ways. Much recent debate has thus focused on the need for transitional justice to be guided by local knowledge and priorities rather than allowing international templates to dictate practice.

Transitional justice in the Middle East and North Africa

This brings us to the Arab Spring in the Middle East and North Africa (MENA). While the situations in these countries as analysed in this volume show some similarity with other transitional contexts, they also show interesting and instructive contrasts in how transitions and transitional justice is being conceptualised.

The MENA transitional contexts reflect many of the same challenges experienced by other recent transitions, and their transitional justice debates have spawned similar policy alternatives that have also become contentious. The specific character of these transitions does, however, crystallise certain debates that will help shape and define the future boundaries and fault lines of transitional justice.

Before the Arab Spring, transitional justice in the MENA was marked by two extremes – Morocco and Sudan.[5] These cases provide interesting contrasts in the taxonomy of transitional justice. Morocco presented the first example of a truth commission in an Arab country (generally praised as a positive contribution but within a very circumscribed transitional process), and Sudan is hailed as an example of a new frontier (or a dismal failure) of international justice. Neither is a useful template for engaging with policy options to address the transitions in Libya, Tunisia and Egypt, and perhaps Syria at some point in the future.

Other transitional justice contexts may offer more parallels, but that does not mean that their transitional justice models provide obvious examples to inform policy. As argued above, transitional justice interventions should not be guided just by the nature of past abuses, but more fundamentally depend upon the transformation goals being sought. Debates about the future of MENA societies appear to be subject to more fundamental questions about the nature of a future social order. As Salloukh suggests in Chapter 1, the rules of the game of being a free people are at stake. It is indeed a 'struggle over alternative visions of the politics, moral and social orders' which calls into question the form of government and law. This is particularly relevant given the push-pull of competing visions presently playing out between advocates of political Islam and those who support liberal democracy, a point that is emphasised very strongly by Khatib in Chapter 7.

The level of contestation over the future of the new society in these countries was for many years masked by an oppressive government which presented a facade of consensus that stifled public debate. Transitional justice debates thus occur against a backdrop of deeply divided visions of where the transitions are supposed to lead. In contrast to many transitional societies where transitional justice seeks a return to democracy or is guided by a consensus or imposition of a clear political and economic framework, the MENA transitions remain subject to passionate debate and violent confrontations over the fundamental shared basis of the society.

Transitional justice processes do not enter the picture as neutral tools to achieve clearly framed objectives. As Manea aptly points out in Chapter 8, one way to make sense of transitional justice is to look at it as 'justice with an instrumental purpose' (quoting Bell and O'Rourke 2007: 24). In Chapter 9, Hanna also cautions that notions of transitional justice have informed discourses of transition (rather than vice versa). Given that transitional justice is conceived as a tool of liberal peace-building (approvingly by some authors and with scepticism by others in this volume), it is understandable that it becomes a terrain of struggle which pits different ideological approaches against each other.

Salloukh and others in this volume have also warned about the continuities that limit the scope of transition being pursued. Rather than a process of fundamental transformation of the social order, there are elements of the old order that have managed to survive and redefine themselves. In Chapter 6, Bachmann, Stewart and Fisher note that the survival of certain elites is not an uncommon phenomenon. Transitions create new opportunities and some, due to their previously privileged positions, are well placed to avoid sanction and reinvent themselves in this new environment. Just as certain groups and individuals may shed their *ancien regime* skins effectively, institutions can also survive largely unscathed. As Salloukh indicates, new political groups can take over institutions and simply replicate the previous regime's hegemonic practices (an accusation that was made against Egypt's President Morsi during his one year of rule). Institutional cultures of abuse and exclusion all too easily survive in an environment where they are subject to new, narrow political agendas. Without a clear vision for a new society, it is also not surprising that some states have retreated to the old regime's abusive practices, including the neo-liberal economic policies that many blame for the social inequalities that gave rise to mass protests in the first place.

International concepts and policy recommendations are clearly not being taken at face value by local actors. The goals, appropriate intermediaries or relevant expertise and best practices that have guided much international transitional justice is treated with more than the usual amount of scepticism by local stakeholders in these countries. It is also a context where the role of the international community is more controversial and not necessarily viewed as benign (as a result of colonial legacies in particular). The historical role and responsibility of international actors for human rights abuses and their interests in promoting particular transitional outcomes are important considerations for national transitional justice debates.

How to conceptualise and address the role of international actors in human rights abuses committed in a country dealing with transition is a critical transitional justice question that has not been effectively unpacked in other contexts. Rather than treat countries as insulated and autonomous, transitional justice needs to engage with the reality of international involvement in internal conflicts and foreign interests in how transitions are managed.

This point emerges in the Lebanese case explored by Szekely in Chapter 5, who points out the danger of being caught up in regional agendas. It is not just the historical roles of outside actors that raise concerns about foreign intervention in transitional justice policy developments, but also the future regional and international interests in the transitional outcomes. As so clearly illustrated by Szekely's analysis of Lebanon's struggle with its violent legacy, regional engagement comes with powerful strings attached and presents a double-edged sword. Alignments between local stakeholders and foreign sponsors only make this relationship much more complex and dangerous. Moreover, the intervention of the UN through the Lebanon Criminal Tribunal seems to present a continuation of this trend rather than a break with the past. In Chapter 10, Kersten's examination of the Libyan context highlights the thirst for transitional justice to bolster a sense of sovereignty that is particularly resonant against the backdrop of centuries of colonialism. Where human rights abuses committed by colonial powers were never subjected to accountability mechanisms, the transitional justice policy recommendations now presented by these ex-colonialists is understandably treated with scepticism.

The challenge of building legitimacy for international actors, particularly the UN organs, is one that is likely to face particular challenges in the MENA context. As Fisher, in Chapter 11, spells out, the legitimacy of international bodies such as the ICC and frameworks of international criminal law more generally require a better track record of intervention to prove that these constitute a fair and responsive system that can be drawn on and constructively engaged with in these contexts. Given the AU's challenge to the legitimacy of the ICC in other African contexts and the appointment of an African head prosecutor in the ICC, North Africa will provide an important testing ground for the credibility of these interventions.

Truth commissions, prosecutions and reparations programmes have increasingly sought to engage actors beyond the narrow national boundaries that conventionally shaped their jurisdiction. Given the internationalised nature of human rights abuses and exploitative economies, the artificiality of national transitional justice boundaries has been increasingly questioned (Sriram and Ross 2007). The ability of human rights abusers to secure international financial support and to hide their illegal gains outside their borders directly challenges the conventional conceptions of accountability for abuses and responsibility for reparations.

The accountability of other countries for their role in human rights abuses committed by the MENA authoritarian regimes, or in the conflict to rid the countries of these regimes, has been raised by several authors in this volume. Nassar, for instance, questions whether and how international financial institutions can be held responsible for their role in financing the exploitative policies that abused social and economic rights of citizens. The transitional justice field is yet to confront the question of foreign profits generated by investment in or through exploitative and oppressive regimes. Nassar suggests the possibility of treating loans to such regimes as 'odious debt' for which new democracies do not have a legal responsibility to repay. This presents a new boundary that governments in other contexts have been fearful of crossing when pursuing transitional justice.[6]

Foreign direct involvement in conflict (such as collaboration with state security through intelligence and extraditions, and the killing of civilians in NATO bombings in Libya, as mentioned by Fisher) are also more central to or more overtly highlighted in transitional justice debates in MENA than in previous transitional contexts. Difficult questions are being asked about how international actors can be held accountable for their actions and what type of actions should be included in such accountability. This speaks very directly to questions of accountability of more powerful international actors. Whether transitional justice is to remain a process that mainly targets the defeated side will again be tested. While transitional justice policies have sought to present themselves as impartial and inclusive, global powers have up to now generally managed to avoid scrutiny (as Reiter, in Chapter 4, shows was the case with the US role in Latin America).

Western cultural assumptions underlying certain interventions and policy recommendations are also a matter of huge concern. A fear of this cultural imperialism is legitimate in a field where international transitional justice norms have framed the problems and solutions to present a very Western and sometimes Christian ethos of individual morality, social order and understanding of the meaning of citizenship and nationhood. However, to reject transitional justice ideas as un-African or un-Islamic because of this tainted association is not intellectually feasible or productive. These challenges need to be confronted sooner or later, preferably through more locally grounded conceptualisations of the problems and solutions. As pointed out by Reiter, Bachmann, Stewart and Fisher, as well as Szekely in other regional contexts, these challenges cannot be avoided by a withdrawal into amnesia about abuses or a denial of the damage that has been done.

Many of the conventional historical transitional justice mechanisms do seem to have some relevance in the MENA context. Processes to address accountability and punishment of perpetrators of mass human rights abuses, healing and reparations for victims, reconciliation initiatives among historically divided sections of society, and institutional transformation (particularly judicial and security sector reform) are clearly applicable in these contexts. The obvious similarities make simple transfers of lessons from other contexts tempting, but the nuanced and sometimes important differences in terms of how each context shapes these processes require serious reconsideration (and even reconceptualisation) of 'best practice' models. The meaning of healing, reconciliation and even the role of public institutions can be conceptualised in very different ways depending on historical, political and cultural contexts.

These are the issues that have been prioritised in many recent transitions and which have become the conventional defining features of transitional justice or even of transition. Prioritising these concerns over others or seeing them as indicators of successful transitions, however, is highly problematic. Ultimate goals and immediate priorities need to be locally determined, particularly in contexts where other immediate safety and survival needs may be paramount (Robins 2011; Vinck and Pham 2008). The prioritisation of certain abuses over others is directly reflected in the time frame used by transitional justice mechanisms. Focusing on more recent events (as pointed out by Massagee in Chapter 2) prioritises correcting only a small sample of abuses and avoids a more systematic review of the past.

While there may be important similarities between the case studies in this volume and previous transitional justice contexts, in other respects they present important contrasts. The temptation to look at transferring lessons learned elsewhere thus needs to be treated with serious caution. Transitional justice mechanisms developed in other contexts have not provided clear answers for key concerns raised by the MENA region, such as how to deal with socio-economic rights or broader issues of social justice and systematic economic inequalities. While this has been increasingly recognised as a challenge, those who have advocated an expansion of transitional justice to include such concerns have not provided clear answers for how they can be incorporated, and transitional justice mechanisms have been slow in expanding their mandates. While he calls for an expanded mandate for transitional justice in the MENA context, Nassar questions the availability of appropriate practical models for providing such accountability and relief. The civil-political rights focus of conventional transitional justice mechanisms do not seem to lend itself to an easy expansion to incorporate this broader mandate. Processes for engaging with corruption, land redistribution and social equality have thus generally been treated as parallel concerns rather than incorporated as part of more formal transitional justice mechanisms (Powell 2010).

While some transitional justice processes have expanded their human rights agendas to include issues of corruption and land allocation,[7] the conventional approach of most transitioning states has been to view such broader justice agendas as a second stage of transition after civil-political rights are secured, treating political rights as a foundation for promoting socio-economic rights. Given the closely intertwined nature of abuses, such as corruption, with civil and political rights abuses, some have strongly argued that they need to be addressed in a more integrated manner (Carranza 2008). However, there is a growing recognition of the need to treat social inequalities and economic exploitation as systematic abuses that qualify as central transitional justice priorities in international law. Former UN High Commissioner for Human Rights, Louise Arbour (2006: 2), has argued that transitional justice:

> must reach to, but also beyond the crimes and abuses committed during the conflict which led to the transition, into the human rights violations that pre-existed the conflict and caused, or contributed to it. When making that search, it is likely that one would expose a great number of violations of economic, social and cultural rights and discriminatory practices.

The protests that ushered in the transitions in the MENA highlighted the illegitimacy of economic systems that have entrenched a wealthy elite and have left large sections of the population destitute. The centrality of these concerns challenges transitional justice to speak to this broader agenda in a more immediate manner. Ongoing popular protests that highlight the lack of progress on these issues will be difficult for transitional justice policy makers to set aside as beyond their mandate (Abou-El-Fadl 2012).

Another challenge to conventional conceptions of transitional justice is that of gender justice. Gender-based and sexual violations that occurred in the context of conflict are now firmly established as a critical component of transitional justice. How to develop mechanisms that are appropriately structured, staffed and skilled to address these violations, however, is a constant challenge that has to be faced anew in each context, and it is difficult to transfer lessons from other contexts and apply them in a situation where the patterns of abuses and the local processes of recovery and empowerment are very different. In a context where women do not have a strong voice, where systematic and structural vulnerability to future abuses are not addressed and where services for victims are driven by a patriarchal structure, these challenges are likely to require serious prioritisation and advocacy efforts.

Yet the more fundamental gender justice concerns are not clearly spelled out in conventional transitional justice approaches. If transitional justice is narrowly conceived as a process to deal only with the overt political violence of the past, it will not address the issue of structural inequalities and social norms which oppress women. In order to include a broader gender justice agenda, transitional justice would need to be conceptualised as a process that seeks to address the root causes of violence in transitioning societies.

As Manea points out, conflicts and transitions present a rupture in traditional roles for women. It presents new opportunities for political engagement that disrupt old patterns and provide a glimpse of a different future. The challenge for transitional justice is to provide spaces to consolidate change, not just a mechanism to return society to some false ideal of the past.

A related set of questions with which transitional justice has increasingly grappled relates to the challenge of deepening democracy. Rather than just expanding democracy to include the participation of women, democratic institutions and processes are themselves being questioned as insufficiently open and engaging.

While democracy is a unanimous goal, the failure of representational governance through regular elections means that such a system is increasingly challenged as an adequate space for citizens' agency in the political life of their communities. The spontaneous nature of the uprisings in many countries, and the continued upsurge of this public involvement in voicing concerns, raises questions about whether democratic elections are a sufficient arena for the public to hold representatives accountable. Particularly in a context where political parties and public institutions have been discredited, simply creating space for new parties and ensuring the fairness of elections does not appear to address the gap between the state and its citizens. Transitional justice is itself presented as a foundation of this transformation by Manea, who proposes societal trust and inclusive participation as essential elements of these processes.

The challenge is thus not only to develop transitional justice policies in a more consultative manner, but to develop policies that affirm and create arenas for citizen engagement, dialogue and empowerment beyond the traditional political spaces that have compartmentalised and sterilised political life.

Conclusion

The Arab Spring in the MENA region is clearly pushing the boundaries of transitional justice and sharpening debate about its motives, its control and its feasibility. In many ways these tensions in the transitional justice debate echo developments in other regions, but it also seems to take the debate back to its roots. Are we still looking at promoting the twin goals of democracy and human rights? While these are still held up by the various stakeholders and over-arching goals in the Arab context, the meaning given to these concepts has become more contested. Which rights are seen as absolute or priorities, and what does democracy mean in practice?

Have we come full circle? Are we returning to a point where the basic legitimacy of transitions are themselves being questioned, and where a new consensus on the meaning of economic justice and political democracy needs to be forged for transitional justice to be viewed as an appropriate intervention by all sides? Transitional justice initially emerged at a time of international political shifts, when the Cold War was cooling down and the focus had shifted to strengthening individual human rights. Has the discourse of rights and globalisation of systems of abuse shifted to the extent that this narrow focus on civil and political rights and electoral democracy has lost its ability to frame transitional aspirations? Or are we entering a new stage where transitional justice, in each of its new manifestations, takes on more ambitious transformative goals that push existing boundaries? What seems clear is that the debates in the MENA present opportunities for developing transformative justice processes which prioritise local agency, resources and participatory policy processes and challenges unequal power relations and structures of exclusion. Whether these opportunities will be acted upon remains to be seen.

Notes

1 Some scholars trace the development of transitional justice to the Nuremburg trials or even ancient times. These analyses, however, look at post-conflict justice in broader terms (usually more focused on crimes of aggression, treason and war crimes), rather than through a specific human rights lens. See, eg Huyse 2012.
2 The emergence of truth commissions set (some of) the Latin American examples apart from the European countries that also struggled with democratic transitions in the 1970s (Spain, Portugal and Greece), where similar challenges of balancing democratisation and justice produced similar debates but different solutions.
3 While initially inconsistent in its stance, the AU has also gradually developed its own principles and framework for engaging with transitional justice intervention, which promises a more coherent and engaged approach. See 'African Leadership and Ownership in Transitional Justice' 2012.
4 The lack of transformation evidenced by the continued inequality and persistence of high levels of violence in South Africa has raised serious questions about the supposed success of the truth commission in that country. See, eg Editorial Note 2013.
5 In Ch 3, Habib Nassar focuses on Morocco as well as Iraq and Algeria as important regional precedents.
6 Even after the transition to democracy in South Africa, the new government chose to honour the debts incurred by the Apartheid government.
7 For example, the Kenyan Truth, Justice and Reconciliation Commission (Truth Justice and Reconciliation Commission Act No 6 of 2008).

Bibliography

Abou-El-Fadl, Reem (2012) 'Beyond Conventional Transitional Justice: Egypt's 2011 Revolution and the Absence of Political Will', 6(2) *International Journal of Transitional Justice* 318.

'African Leadership and Ownership in Transitional Justice' (2012) 3(1 and 2) *African Governance Newsletter* 4.

Arbour, Louise (2006) 'Economic and Social Justice for Societies in Transition', 40(1) *International Law and Politics* 1.

Arthur, P. (2009) 'How Transitions Reshaped Human Rights: A Conceptual History of Transitional Justice', 31(2) *Human Rights Quarterly* 321.

Bell, C. (2009) 'Transitional Justice, Interdisciplinarity and the State of the "Field" or "Non-Field"', 3(1) *International Journal of Transitional Justice* 5.

Carranza, R. (2008) 'Plunder and Pain: Should Transitional Justice Engage with Corruption and Economic Crimes?' 2(3) *International Journal of Transitional Justice* 310.

Chapman, Audrey (2009) 'Approaches to Studying Reconciliation', in Hugo van der Merwe, Victoria Baxter and Audrey Chapman (eds), *Assessing the Impact of Transitional Justice: Challenges for Empirical Research* (USIP Press).

Editorial Note (2013) 7(1) *International Journal of Transitional Justice* 1.

Gready, P., Boesten, J., Crawford, G and Wilding, P. (2010) 'Transformative Justice

– A Concept Note', October, at http://www.wun.ac.uk/sites/default/files/transformative_justice_-_concept_note_web_version.pdf.

Huyse, L. (2012) *Transitional justice after war and dictatorship: Learning from European experiences (1945–2000)*, Centre for Historical Research and Documentation on War and Contemporary Society, CEGES-SOMA, Brussels.

McGregor, Lorna (2013) 'Transitional Justice and Torture', 7(1) *International Journal of Transitional Justice* 29.

Madlingozi, Tshepo (2010) 'On Transitional Justice Entrepreneurs and the Production of Victims', 2(2) *Journal of Human Rights Practice* 208.

Mendeloff, D. (2009) 'Trauma and Vengeance: Assessing the Psychological and Emotional Effects of Post-Conflict Justice', 31(3) *Human Rights Quarterly* 592.

Nagy, Rosemary (2008) 'Transitional Justice as Global Project: critical reflections', 29(2) *Third World Quarterly* 275.

Powell, P. (2010) 'The Role of Constitution Making and Institution Building in Furthering Peace, Justice and Development: South Africa's Democratic Transition', 4(2) *International Journal of Transitional Justice* 230.

Robins, Simon (2011) 'Towards Victim-Centred Transitional Justice: Understanding the Needs of Families of the Disappeared in Postconflict Nepal', 5(1) *International Journal of Transitional Justice* 75.

Robins, Simon (2012) 'Challenging the Therapeutic Ethic: A Victim-Centred Evaluation of Transitional Justice Process in Timor-Leste', 5(1) *International Journal of Transitional Justice* 75.

Sriram, C.L. and Ross, Amy (2007) 'Geographies of crime and justice: contemporary transitional justice and the creation of "zones of impunity"', 1(1) *International Journal of Transitional Justice* 45.

UN Security Council (2004) *The rule of law and transitional justice in conflict and post-conflict societies: Report of the Secretary-General*, 23 August,

UNSCR (2006) 'Rule-of-Law Tools for Post-Conflict States: Truth Commissions', at http://www.ohchr.org/Documents/Publications/RuleoflawTruthCommissionsen.pdf.

Vinck, P. and Pham, P. (2008) 'Ownership and Participation in Transitional Justice Mechanisms: A Sustainable Human Development Perspective from Eastern DRC', 2(3) *International Journal of Transitional Justice*, 398.

Weinstein, Harvey M. (2011) 'Editorial Note: The Myth of Closure, the Illusion of Reconciliation: Final Thoughts on Five Years as Co-Editor-in-Chief' 5(1) *International Journal of Transitional Justice* 1.

Index

Note: Page numbers followed by an 'n' indicate footnotes